A SLICE OF CANADA

Watson Kirkconnell is one of the most familiar figures in the world of Canadian letters. Educated at Queen's and Oxford, he has published several volumes of poetry and poetry translations, was the founding father and first chairman of the Humanities Research Council, a charter member and national president (1942-44, 1956-58) of the Canadian Authors Association, and has shared in university life for 45 years.

He has been active in many other areas of public life; as one of the founders of the Prisoners' Aid Society (now the John Howard Society of Manitoba), a joint organizer of the Citizenship Branch, Ottawa, a founder and first president of the Canadian-Polish Society, as well as the Baptist Federation of Canada of which he was national president (1953-56). In widespread recognition of his work in these many fields Dr. Kirkconnell has received twelve honorary doctorates from universities in Canada, the United States, Hungary, and Germany, knighthoods from Poland and Iceland, and numerous awards from other countries.

The chronicle of such a full and active career offers a valuable look at many aspects of Canadian life: in his memoirs Dr. Kirkconnell has avoided a merely chronological arrangement of his autobiography but sought rather to take various phases of the Canadian tradition and to analyse his experience of each down through the years. This Slice of Canada demonstrates the author's discerning faculty of observation and his close involvement, not only with the arts, but with education, religion, politics and other areas of Canadian life.

WATSON KIRKCONNELL

from the portrait by Brenda Bury, of London, England

A Slice of Canada

MEMOIRS

by Watson Kirkconnell

Published for Acadia University by
University of Toronto Press

Reprinted in paperback 2016
ISBN 978-1-4875-9270-7 (paper)

TO MY FIVE CHILDREN

AND

MY TEN GRANDCHILDREN

WITH AFFECTION

Preface

A MICROTOMIC SLICE of tissue may be quantitatively insignificant, but placed under a microscope it can add its minute quota of fact regarding the major organism from which it came.

That is the metaphor underlying this book of memoirs. Properly speaking, it is not an autobiography, leading in a chronological sequence of chapters from childhood to old age. It is rather, for the most part, a series of aspects of life in Canada in 1895–1967, each sliced in terms of my own infinitesimal experience of it. Frequently the narrative is more concerned with national trends than with my own personal share in the movement or activity.

In some cases my role has been central, as with the Writers' War Committee of Canada (Chapter 23), the Humanities Research Council of Canada (Chapter 18), and the Baptist Federation of Canada (Chapter 16), where I was in each case one of the organizers and the national chairman. In the case of the Nationalities Branch (Chapter 20), I was again one of the organizers but refused an invitation to become its first director. My career has been largely identified with Canadian universities—as student, professor, and president—and these have their due place in the record (Chapters 2, 4, 12, and 13). War, peace, and religion have been major interests (Chapters 9, 10, and 15). There has been an active participation in music (Chapter 8), social service (Chapter 11), and Freemasonry (Chapter 19). An unquenched boyhood enthusiasm for nature study has provided background music for a predominantly literary and administrative career (Chapters 3 and 26). Scholarly research has led my feet to the major libraries of North America and Europe (Chapter 17). My master passion has been the interpreting of foreign literatures in thousands of pages of my own verse translation (Chapters 6 and 7), and this has become not unimportant in the blending of many traditions in the Canadian nation. With this has gone personal friendship with many of our European Canadian communities and travel in almost all of the countries of Europe, from Iceland and Ireland to Finland and Greece.

Yet I make bold to think of myself as primarily and essentially a particle of my native Canada, one twenty-millionth part of this young nation in an ancient land. For better or worse, this book is a slice of Canada.

I wish to record my gratitude to Acadia University for sponsoring the volume and to the Managing Editor of the University of Toronto Press for her invaluable advice in my final revision of the manuscript for publication. Thanks are also rendered to Messrs. Eyre & Spottiswoode and to the Executors of the late Major-General J. F. C. Fuller for permission to quote in Chapter 9 ("Of Things Military") four brief extracts from his volume, *The Second World War 1939–1945*.

W. K.

Wolfville,
Nova Scotia.

Contents

A section of photographs will be found between pages 166 and 167

A SLICE OF CANADA

1

Roots of the Family Tree

AT THE SOUTHEAST corner of the Stewartry of Kirkcudbright, Scotland, rises the bald, soaring crest of Criffell, easternmost and boldest of the mountain moors of Galloway. Fronting the morning sun from its grassy summit, one looks across a brief alluvial plain and the turbid waters of the Solway to the fields of Annan and the fells of Cumberland. To the left, a patchwork procession of meadows, wheatfields, and groves, hemmed in on the east by the narrow tidal estuary of the Nith, marches northward nine miles to Maxwelltown and Dumfries.

This is the Kirkconnell country. Here, about A.D. 600, Saint Connell, an Irish bishop and missionary disciple of Saint Columba of Iona, founded a church (to be known as "Kirkconnell," i.e., the church of Connell) near the site of a former Roman camp, two miles north of Criffell, and near pre-Roman crannogs that were vastly older still. Here, too, in 1235, a grateful Alexander II, after putting down a bloody revolt by the native Celtic gentry, vested the whole thirty square miles between Criffell and Dumfries in the hands of "William Fitz-Michael de Kirkconnell," apparently an Anglo-Norman retainer of John de Balliol, overlord of the entire Stewartry. It was, in fact, Devorguila de Balliol, widow of John Balliol, who founded on the Kirkconnell tract in 1273 the so-called "Sweetheart Abbey" and its abbey church, known also as "the New Abbey," to replace the "old abbey" foundation of Kirkconnell that had given its name to the ancient Celtic estate. In 1371, by a decree of King Robert the Bruce, the house of Douglas replaced the Balliols as Galloway overlords of the Kirkconnells, and the Douglas tartan is still, by tradition, wearable by the Kirkconnells today.

A farm and a hill six miles north of Kirkcudbright, a little mining town on the Upper Nith, and a ruined church beside the River Kirtle also carry the Kirkconnell name (the latter two with only one "l") and bear further witness to the missionary work of the old Irish saint, but, according to George F. Black's *Surnames of Scotland* and all documents and parish records of every sort, the surname is derived from, and associated only with, the estate of 1235 in the vicinity of Criffell and New Abbey.

Mediaeval charters enable one to trace a sequence of Kirkconnell lairds—William, Michael, Andrew, Thomas, Simon, Robert, and Andrew—from 1235 down to the death of the second Andrew and his sons at Verneuil, in Normandy, in 1424, when an army of English and Burgundians wiped out the ten thousand Galloway troops that had been taken to France by the Earl of Douglas to help the Dauphin. Andrew left only a daughter, Janet Kirkconnell of that ilk, with whose marriage in 1430 to Aymer de Maxwell, the younger son of Lord Maxwell of Caerlaverock Castle, just across the Nith, the Kirkconnell estate passed into the hands of the Maxwell family. By rigorous entail, it is still so held today.

Let us again climb Criffell, this time in 1618. Two miles to the north, the hamlet of New Abbey clusters about the shattered walls of Sweetheart Abbey, sacked and burned by Reformation mobs from Dumfries (following a mandate of the Scottish Privy Council in 1567 calling for its demolition), while a mile farther north is "Kirkconnell House," a manor house in a mixture of styles, built by Andrew Kirkconnell in 1410, partly destroyed by an English army in 1570, extended by Bernard Maxwell in 1600, and later, in 1760, destined to receive still further additions by James Maxwell, personal secretary to the Young Pretender. The 1410 wing, a four storey tower of stone, is described by J. M. Sloan's *Galloway* (1908) as "probably the oldest [house] still inhabited in Scotland." At the very foot of Criffell, however, in 1618 as in 1965, was a substantial stone farmhouse, "Airdwall," with another William Kirkconnell as its seventeenth century proprietor and with descendants bearing the old family names of William, Thomas, and Andrew for eleven generations to come (thirty-one Williams, twenty-three Thomases, and eight Andrews). Because of the almost universal holocaust of Scottish archives during the Reformation, no records survive to link this family with a cadet branch of the Kirkconnell lairds two centuries earlier, but their subsequent emergence in this same area, with the same Christian names and a tradition of the Douglas tartan (rather than the Maxwell), makes the continuity a reasonable extrapolation.

It was from this farm and family, some two hundred years still later (in 1819) that my great-grandfather, Walter Kirkconnell (1795–1860), migrated to Canada. The intervening generations (1618–1819) are all a matter of family record[1] but are too copious for reproduction here. One may merely cite the direct male line—William, Thomas, Walter, William, John, Walter, and Walter—all solid farmers, happy without

[1]Summarized in my volume, *The Kirkconnell Pedigree* (Wolfville, 1953), 54 pp.

history. Walter the First is described in a legal document of 1684 as "ane descreet man," and his grandson John, elected in 1740 to an eldership in the New Abbey kirk, according to the same parish's records, stoutly refused the office. No other traces of character remain from the unstoried past. As Walter the Third was his father's seventh child, without much prospect of any inheritance in Scotland, he came out by immigrant ship to Canada and settled as a pioneer in dense primeval forest on Lot 8, Range X, Chatham township, Argenteuil county, about five miles north of the Ottawa River and fifty miles west-northwest of Montreal. His coming was an almost imperceptible little ripple in the vast tide of Scottish immigration that flowed into Canada during the first half of the nineteenth century.

No Kirkconnells survive today in Scotland. A search made for me in 1953 by the Scottish Council was unable to locate anyone by that name. When I visited "Airdwall" in 1955, I found it, after nearly four centuries of existence, still firm and cheerful, but with a David Purdie as its present proprietor. Its fertile fields, flanked by a brawling brook from the braeside of Criffell, slope smiling down to the clear waters of a little tarn, Loch Kinder. The sense of the past is strong.

All Kirkconnells, living and dead, belong to this single family. I have secured records of them all for the past three centuries and they are all close cousins. Those in England derive from John, a brother of Walter the First. Those in Canada and the northern United States are descendants of Walter the Third or of his brothers John and Thomas. Those in the Caribbean area (Jamaica, Cayman Brac, and the Bay Islands of Honduras) are descendants of his nephew William (son of his brother James), who was shipwrecked on Grand Cayman about 1840, settled in the area, and had sixteen children. In spite of widespread enquiries, I can find no evidence that anyone named Kirkconnell has ever lived in Ireland, South Africa, New Zealand, or Australia.

In Chatham township, my great-grandfather found himself in the thick of a pioneer settlement of Perthshire Highlanders from Glen Lyon, west of Aberfeldy and Fortingall. Through propinquity and natural attraction, he presently married Mary McCallum, the sister of a John McCallum, from a Glen Lyon farm called "Carnban." I sought out the old McCallum home in the Highlands in 1955 and found only crumbling stone foundations in a field. Like the habitations of hundreds of other humble cotters in the eighteenth and early nineteenth centuries, the very dwelling of that earlier generation had passed forever. Only a few random families survive from the once teeming population of the glen. Mary's father and mother had been John McCallum and Janet McDiarmid, of Carnban, and her grandparents John McCallum and Kathrin Lumsden, of Craigianie. As remembered by my father, she was a little woman, had a bubbling sense of humour, knew all the Psalms by heart in the Gaelic, and was blind in her old age. She and Walter Kirkconnell had five children—John and Janet (twins, 1824), Kate (1826), Mary (1828), and Christena (1830). They moved in 1850 to a farm in East Hawkesbury township, Prescott county, Ontario.

When John Kirkconnell (1824–98) married Agnes Allison in 1855, he added an incalculable strain of ability to his descendants. Her father, Andrew Allison, was an engineer from Dalkeith, Scotland, who had helped to build the Rideau Canal in the early 1830's and then became a pioneer farmer in Prescott County. A remarkable flair for mathematics has characterized all of his descendants and has cropped out again and again wherever the slightest opportunity for advanced training has offered itself. It was apparently the stirrings of that intellectual bequest that drove my father, Thomas Kirkconnell (1862–1934),[2] to leave the farm in the face of heavy parental opposition and become in due time an honours graduate of Queen's in mathematics and science and the headmaster of high schools in Port Hope (1894–1908) and Lindsay (1908–1932). Mathematics was my own best subject at high school and my brother Walter (1893–1918), when he cared to work at it, was a better mathematician than I. My brother John became a graduate engineer and assistant to the Deputy Minister in the Federal Department of Mines and Technical Surveys. Among our Allison cousins there are numerous mathematicians.

A letter from my cousin, Albert McLaurin, who, as a farmer among farmers, had known all of the related families in East Hawkesbury, explains still another aspect of their several traditions: "A McCallum knows his horse as a scholar knows his book. The Kirkconnells worked methodically toward a goal. The Allisons used the proper word in the proper place and liked and were capable of directing an organization." This administrative bent has likewise been marked in most of Andrew Allison's descendants, including my father.

My mother was Bertha Watson (1867–1957), seventh child of Thomas Watson (1826–1912), a master from 1851 to 1886 in the old Common School in Port Hope. His father, Christopher Watson, came to Canada in 1819 from Alston, in Cumberland, where there are still Watsons by the hundred, and began life in the New World as a schoolmaster in York (now Toronto). Thomas, his youngest son by a Cumberland wife, Margaret Archer, also took to schoolteaching and taught successively at Allanburg, Beachwood, Lundy's Lane, Stamford and Port Hope. In 1851 he married Margaret Elma Green, of Lundy's Lane, whose grandfather, a United Empire Loyalist of Welsh extraction,

[2]His biography is given in my volume *A Canadian Headmaster* (Toronto, 1935).

had married a girl from Saxony, and whose father, an officer in Wellington's Peninsular army, had married a brunette beauty from a Spanish convent-school. From this highly diversified ancestry, my mother inherited the small stature and long narrow head of her Spanish grandmother and the intellectual interests of her father and grandfather. Physically I am very much my mother's son. Thus, for example, my father's cephalic index was 85, my mother's was 70, and mine is also 70. She was a precocious student and had secured her Second Class Certificate, with honours in French and Mathematics, at the age of fifteen. For three months, at the age of sixteen, she taught in the Port Hope High School. A permanent appointment came in the summer of 1887—permanent, that is, until my father married her two years later.[3]

There were marked differences of temperament between my parents. My father had an underlying mood of gentleness and a dislike for public utterance and public occasions that stemmed from his Kirkconnell ancestry, a spring of humour from his McCallum grandmother, an Arctic reserve from the Allisons, and an explosive temper from black-browed Agnes Menzies, the great Olympian wife of Andrew Allison. In my mother, on the other hand, there was a certain intrepidity of tongue that may have gone back to Wellington's officer and his Spanish wife. If I have ever showed any devout pugnacity in thumping big bad dragons on the snout, the hereditary source is in my high-mettled little mother.

In spite of strict genealogical researches going back through seven centuries, I have found no skeletons in any ancestral Kirkconnell cupboards. I can have nothing but gratitude for the long line of farmer forbears whose flesh and blood I mostly am. They seem, almost without exception, to have been honest and diligent tillers of the earth, devoted to man's most fundamental occupation without the slightest desire to stray from it into professional employment. I am not altogether sure that my father and all of his children chose the part of genealogical wisdom in turning from a life close to the soil into the hereditary hazards of a sedentary town career. Brief intellectual excitement for three or four generations may have been fatally bought at the price of rugged physical fitness. I sometimes think that, for the sake of the race, my generation ought to have returned to the land. The wish is now an idle one, since a town-bred man in his seventies has neither the strength nor the pliability for so radical a change and in any case his five children have all found their place in town or urban life. *Les jeux sont faits.*

[3]There were five children from this union: Helen (1890), who became a teacher and married W. H. Houser, later vice-principal of the Hamilton Technical School; Walter (1893–1918), a law student, killed in action at the Battle of Amiens; Watson (1895); Herbert (1900), an optometrist in Toronto; and John (1900), Department of Mines and Technical Services, Ottawa.

2

Student Days

MY FORMAL EDUCATION was somewhat late in beginning. As my health was none too good, I was seven years of age before I was permitted to follow my sister Helen and my brother Walter to the Port Hope Public School. Perhaps the fact that for the two preceding years, with twin babies in the house, I had been left a good deal to my own devices, will explain why from a very early age I tended to move in a solitary orbit and to work things out on my own initiative. For years, up to the age of thirteen, my favourite pastime was the single-handed building of hundreds of yards of neatly graded paths, about two feet wide, up and down the pine-clad slopes of the acre of land that was our home base and thence out into a wooded wilderness along the meanderings of a little brook. And my favourite resort, out in that sylvan realm, was a seat that I had built forty feet up in the crotch of a white birch, reached by steps that I had nailed up the slope of its shining trunk. Thither I would climb to a seventh heaven of solitude, with a book to read and unnumbered apples to munch. All of my construction work was done without the stimulus of any similar project by other boys in the neighbourhood. The only hint for the birch-tree eyrie was a chapter in *The Swiss Family Robinson.* The miniature highway enterprise "just grew."

A similar lone-wolf propensity to study without any external propulsion and to work things out, if necessary, by myself, was to characterize all of my years at school and college. There was the same compelling drive to build myself paths through the forest of an unfamiliar subject so that I might arrive at the thrill of organized and orderly comprehension. For better or worse, I never had to be urged to study. On the contrary, my parents felt constrained on occasion to push me out for sunlight and exercise.

I suspect that my teachers in the elementary school were traditional but thorough. Clarity of expression and inexorable drill were certainly the order of the day. "Grannie Shepherd," in the old Part Second (modern Grade III) used to demonstrate the annual and diurnal movements of the earth by carrying a globe in a wide ellipse around the classroom table, whirling it vigorously as she went. She also wrote endless series of columns of numbers on the blackboard, and had us incessantly adding them both vertically and horizontally. She seemed to sense that all of our subsequent mathematics would be founded on the corner-stone of her basic arithmetic, and she was determined that the superstructure should not fail through any fault of hers.

"Acceleration" was then still an unknown term in the jargon of pedagogy, but the principle was happily recognized in my case—permitting me to gallop through the last four grades of public school in two brief years. My first awareness of small-town journalism came when the *Port Hope Guide* reported, following my second Christmas-time promotion, that a local lawyer (whose bright son had not been so treated) had protested loudly at a school board meeting that I had been "shoved" simply because I was the son of the high school's headmaster. That summer there was quiet jubilation in the Kirkconnell home when the same *Guide* published the results of the provincial "Entrance Examinations," on which my aggregate was nearly fifty marks higher than that of any one else in town or county.

That same summer my father accepted the principalship of the Lindsay Collegiate Institute, some forty-five miles to the northwest of Port Hope, and my next five years of education were received in the classrooms of this excellent school. Latin and French began immediately (in Grade IX), and I have always felt that this was several years too late. There was no "acceleration" in my high school course, but there was a good deal of what more recent jargon calls "enrichment." Thus it was presently made possible for me to add Greek and German to my roster of foreign languages. As for mathematics, not only did I cover advanced algebra, plane and analytical geometry, and dynamics, but I was enabled, in my father's library, to go on to sample spherical trigonometry, conic sections, and the calculus, beginning this last with a riotous little book by Sylvanus P. Thomson. Physics, chemistry, and biology were all on my curriculum and my chief hobby was tramping the woods and swamps as a field naturalist. In July 1913, I wrote seventeen Senior Matriculation papers, in four foreign languages, English, history, mathematics, and the sciences. Such manual arts as woodworking were still unknown on the Ontario curriculum, but our fathers all had tools at home and in later years I was to build myself a score of bookcases and a sleeping cabin in the Haliburton woods and to supply my five children with bed-tables, swings, sandboxes, teeter-totters and toboggans.

Plugging side by side with me on scholarship subjects in the spring of 1913 had been George Hardy, later to be professor of classics in the University of Alberta. He won an Edward Blake scholarship at Toronto, while I went to Queen's. Another contemporary was Harold Scott, later Minister of Lands and Forests in the Ontario Government. In acknowledging a copy I had sent him of one of my books, he once wrote to me: "It lies on our drawing-room table; and when I show it to my friends, I throw out my chest to its full thirty-two inches and tell them that I used to copy my homework off you. But of course I never tell them about the time when you made a mistake and as a result the whole class was wrong."

Or I might recall Gardiner Eyres, now a Toronto business man, with whom I read aloud most of the plays of Shakespeare, taking turns on the speeches, in the wonderful summer of 1911. Slightly older contemporaries in the school at that time were Harry Balfour, ultimately chief inspector of secondary schools for the province of Alberta, R. A. ("Bert") MacKay, later to be Canada's minister to the United Nations and Ambassador to Norway, and Leigh Cruess, who became a top-flight actuary in New York City. Or I could mention John Carew's daughters, Gertrude and Robie, who were destined respectively to become the wives of the Frost brothers, Leslie and Cecil, who had been reared in Orillia but set up their law practice in Lindsay in 1921.

The most dynamic classics teacher of my high school experience was R. A. Croskery, who was with us for only the fall term of 1909 and then became registrar of the provincial Department of Education. "To the boards!" he would roar as he entered the classroom, and he had us all on the run for the entire period. Very effective likewise was Everton Miller, who succeeded him. Miller did not keep us under the same relentless and exciting pressure, but he knew his Latin and taught with systematic thoroughness. In utter contrast was Charlie Owens, with whom I took my Upper School Greek. Owens had not the slightest idea of discipline. The cadet corps under his misdirection marched enthusiastically through hedges and over fences as he forgot to halt them. And yet somehow his zeal for Homer and Xenophon was contagious for his tiny group of Grecians and we gained through sheer interest much of what we lost in slipshod teaching.

The science master in 1908 was Howard Rosevear, a tall, dark, handsome, and splendidly proportioned man, with a hair-trigger temper. He did not suffer fools gladly and was known to knock down the huskiest cadet on parade if there was the slightest hint of nonsense. On the other hand, he had taken postgraduate work in biology at Cornell University and warmed at once to any student who showed any sign of becoming a field naturalist. A few years later, his able successor was Thomas Firth, a tall, fair-haired teacher whose mental chemistry was acidulous rather than explosive.

English and history were taught by Edwin William Jennings, later to become public school inspector for West Victoria. Jennings believed in settling Hoti's business, in making sure that we used dictionaries to hunt up every new word, that spelling and pronunciation and grammar were faultless. If at times all this seemed fussy and tedious, we realized in later years that it was an invaluable discipline for mentally untidy youngsters. In history, moreover, he taught us to master a book, paragraph by paragraph and chapter by chapter. "Just to look over a book," he would moralize, "is to overlook it," and we were called on to summarize and digest until the volume was our intellectual possession. The one ingredient that he lacked—namely, inspiration—was supplied by his young assistant, Gordon Manning, who lit a fire for us in Shakespeare and Browning and roused an unquenchable desire for wide poetic horizons. His zest for scholarship and imaginative literature proved indeed one of the factors that persuaded me, when I later went to university, to turn my back on mathematics, in which I had twice led the Province, and devote myself to languages and literature.

The choice was not easily made, however, for my mathematics teacher was my own father, and he was the greatest of them all. In the pages of *A Canadian Headmaster*, published in 1935, the year after his death, I analysed the qualities that made him a supreme teacher. I have seen no reason to revise the estimate. Yet even my affectionate admiration for him and my own sheer enjoyment of his subject could not weigh against my sense that the vast structure of abstract thinking erected by mathematics did not come as close to the realities of human experience as did language (as an instrument of thought and emotion) and imaginative literature (as the projection of man's thoughts and passions in the drama of life). On the seventeen papers of my Upper School scholarship examinations, I led the field in mathematics, history and English, secured five other firsts but dropped to second class honours in Greek prose composition. Without hesitation, I decided to major in Greek and Latin as a preliminary to graduate work in English or comparative literature.

My father was a graduate of Queen's University. Not unnaturally he had suggested that I compete in 1913 for a Senior Matriculation scholarship there, and I enrolled "on the Old Ontario Strand" on the first of October.

In my chosen field of honour classics Thomas Callander was Professor of Greek and Alfred Codd was Professor of Latin. The former was a tall, slow-spoken Scot, a graduate with first class honours from both Aberdeen and Oxford, who could not conceal in our courses in Thucydides, Plato, and Aristotle that his political convictions were devoutly conservative. Codd, on the other hand, was a short, slight Welshman, impeccable in scholarship, who first taught me the affinity between Vergil and Wordsworth, and deepened my appreciation of both literatures. He died untimely, of tuberculosis, shortly after my graduation. A sense of the impending end was still earlier upon him, for when the admiring girls of our final honours Latin class presented him with a Roman toga that they had made, he grimly asked them if it were a shroud.

Nathan Dupuis, mathematician and astronomer, a silent survivor of an earlier generation, still stalked gauntly about the campus, but there were many senior lions who were still actively roaring—such as John Watson in philosophy, and James Cappon in English. Adam Shortt, bearded and formidable, occasionally came down from Ottawa, but O. D. Skelton was now the honoured head of the Economics Department. The most vivid member of the Faculty was J. L. Morison, ultra-Liberal and anti-feminist, who strode about the highways with a military cape flying out behind him. I still have a little handbook of Italian grammar that he gave me, along with a couple of Italian novels, to start me on a study of that language. He had been on walking tours of Italy and Greece, and assured me that the frogs of that region still actually said "Bre-ke-ke-kex, Ko-ax, Ko-ax!" as in the days of Aristophanes. I also owed much to L. F. Rushbrook Williams, lecturer in history, who fed me in his rooms and gave me a glimpse of Arabic and Persian. He left us in 1914 to become professor of Modern Indian History in the University of Allahabad and in 1925 the foreign minister of Patiala State. A rendezvous for many of us on Sunday evenings was the home of J. F. Macdonald, where a dozen students of both sexes would gather around the fireside after church and chat with "Reddy" and his wife.

Still other remembered personalities were those of W. E. McNeill, with his chiselled incisiveness of phrase and an unanticipated gift of humour, P. G. C. Campbell, a France-born Scot, who became the honorary president of our class ("Arts Sixteen"), "Freddie" Millett in English, a vision of sartorial magnificence, complete with flowing bow-tie, "Gunpowder" Marischal, a diminutive, atom-bomb Frenchman through whose classroom door students once pitched a fire-axe and a pail, just to see him explode, and a notable theological trio in Jordan, Scott, and Morgan.

Strange and unexpected things sometimes happened. Thus there was the occasion in a Kingston drawing-room when J. L. Morison subdued bashful Professor Taylor of the English department with a half-nelson and publicly took off his shoes, to the great embarrassment of their hostess. When professors were late for class, the men might start a chorus of "Ninety-nine blue-bottles a-hanging on the wall." The blue-bottles lessened one at a time, and when there were none left, the class felt free to disband. And there was the very dubious sequel to Hebrew studies when some of the theological students christened their landlady's noisy tomcat, "Yahweh."

When men of our Queen's generation get together, we tend to remember a day of epic warfare when the cohorts of Science attempted to storm the New Arts building. Fire hoses were freely employed on both sides, but notable feats of arms were performed by the Arts wrestling team (led by George Wilson and Don MacKenzie), who successfully held the first floor stairway and tossed assailant after assailant down the steps upon the heads of the attackers. The battle was at its height when a young lecturer in Economics, Swanson by name, sought egress from the building and remonstrated with one of the defending heroes. "Oh, go to hell!" was the impatient reply, and Swanson retreated in high dudgeon to the Economics office at the west end of the corridor. Here he voiced his indignation to his chief, Dr. O. D. Skelton: "He told me to go to hell!" he sputtered. "What shall I do about it?" Skelton's classic reply was mild and reassuring: "Don't go," he said.

During the spring term of my sophomore year, I wrote my diary in Attic Greek. This at least had the merit of keeping the record reasonably private. As a high school student, I had been writing undivulged Greek love poetry to female classmates who had no Greek and did not even dream that the shy boy in the back seat was turning out red-hot lyrics in their honour. At college I was more concerned with cultivating prose fluency in the language of Plato and needed no asbestos pages for my lucubrations.

I served on the *Queen's Journal* staff under two notable editors—in 1914–15 under John McNab, in 1915–16 under W. T. ("Wattie" or "Satan") McCree, both destined to be Moderators of the Presbyterian Church in Canada. I was circulation manager for the former and Arts editor for the latter. It was to the indulgence of McCree that I owed the publication of my singable but otherwise unmeritorious rhymed Latin version of "Mary had a little lamb" and of an even graver misdemeanour in an article on a Latin palimpsest that I had allegedly discovered, dating from the time of the Continental Wars of the fourth century A.D. It began cryptically: "Padi rota litar tu is aeris molli O," and, after several such lines, swung out into an obvious chorus:

ID SAL UNGUETO TIBUR RARI,
ID SAL UNGUE TEGO,
ID SAL UNGUETO TIBUR RARI
TUTE SUI TESTE GARRULAE NO.
GIBBAE PICI DELE,
FUR VELIS TERS' QUA,
ID SAL UNGUETO TIBUR RARI
PUTA MAEOTIS RAEDA.

McCree wrote me forty years later that there had been a wail of aesthetic anguish from another campus poet, Charlie Girdler, who proceeded to pen him a lengthy ode in the style of Browning's *Sordello*, "and did it so successfully that we cut his poem in two and published it as two separate pieces. Nor did it thereby gain or lose any of its obscure meaning."

More than forty years too late, I wish to apologize to some of my classmates for journalistic misdeeds of a graver sort. With a view to adding to the gaiety of the campus, I ran anonymously a series of purely imaginary "Impertinent Interviews" with a number of my friends and included an even more scurrilous one on myself in order to confuse the trail of authorship. Worse still, as editor of the *Year Book*, I dealt summarily with a number of cases where the write-ups had not come in to meet the printer's deadline by myself dashing off satiric thumbnail sketches in verse paragraphed as prose. In other cases, where the traditional quotation was missing at the end of the biography, I added a humorous but unflattering quotation from Shakespeare. It was only when one indignant victim, a friend from my home town, refused to accept his copy of the *Year Book*, that the full measure of my offence came home to me. I can only plead that a lad of twenty can be intoxicated with the ingenuity of his own risibilities. Like Gratiano, I was too prone to defy all seemly decorum for the sake of "a tricksy word." In later years, in Winnipeg, I was frequently saved from similar indiscretions by the cautionary scrutiny of my manuscripts by my office partner, Arthur L. Phelps, and his expostulation: "Kirk, you *can't* print *that*!"

The life president of my graduating class is "Fred" Paynter, a successful Montreal business executive. Education and the church claimed the majority of my classmates. In the former category I might mention W. A. ("Bill") Mackintosh, the principal of Queen's University in 1952–62, the late H. H. Sheldon ("H_2S"), professor of Physics in Roosevelt University, in Chicago, and a score of high school teachers. Among the year's clergymen, the late James Bertram Skene became Moderator of the Presbyterian Church in Canada in 1953–54. James Mortimer Clark became a missionary in China. Lorne Rae Cumming is Deputy Minister of Municipal Affairs for the Province of Ontario.

Only one member of the year was destined to enter politics—the late Dr. Harry Fleming, Liberal member for Humboldt, Saskatchewan. Another good friend and medical doctor was "Fred" Baugh, for many years the director of a mental hospital at Guelph, Ontario. Among contemporaries not of my year were George E. Wilson, later Dean of Arts and Science at Dalhousie University, and Charlotte ("Lottie") Whitton, destined to become Mayor of Ottawa.

In the Michaelmas term of 1921, I matriculated at Oxford University and registered as a graduate student. My college was Lincoln, a small establishment back-to-back with Brasenose and cheek-by-jowl with Exeter. Much of its revenue came from its ownership, since mediaeval times, of the nearby Mitre Inn and the vast wine-cellars beneath it. Almost a quarter of my contemporaries were British veterans of World War I and another quarter consisted of Americans. The phenomenally high percentage of the latter was credited to their alleged belief that "Abe" had founded the place.

The Rector in my day was J. A. R. Munro, a slight, bearded scholar with a high reputation in Ancient History. "Noght o word spak he moore than was neede." No such verbal reticence marked the Senior Tutor, Rev. Dr. A. J. Carlyle, whose field of omniscience was the history of ideas. Other academic notables were "the Marcher" (E. C. Marchant), editor of Thucydides and the Oxford Xenophon, and "the Sidger" (Alfred Sidgwick, F.R.S., D.Sc., a medallist of the Royal Society, who had taken a First in Natural Science in 1895 and a First in Literae Humaniores in 1897). My own graduate supervisor was D. H. Macgregor, of All Souls.

With my Queen's background of an M.A. in Latin and Greek, I should normally have gone on for "Greats" at Oxford (with an ultimate college career in view), but the loss of five years of my life through war service and subsequent ill health had frustrated me into deciding on journalism as a *pis aller* and on an Oxford B.Litt. in Economics as the best preparation for that humbler profession. As a result, I have had no direct experience of the Oxford undergraduate system and am not well qualified to compare it with that of Canada. I was given no tutorial assignments, no lectures, and no guided reading. I was, in fact, left entirely to my own resources and know the general Oxford routine only by hearsay.

As for social life, a punctual weekly letter to a fiancée at McMaster kept me bound to the mast and steeled against the sirens of Oxford, whether lay or academic. I cannot, indeed, remember meeting a young woman of either category during my entire year at the University. My social activities were wholly in the masculine context of my own college.

There were two student societies at Lincoln, the Fleming Society, named after Richard Fleming, Bishop of Lincoln, who had founded the college in 1429, and the Davenant Society, named after Sir William Davenant, an alleged natural son of William Shakespeare by the daughter of the landlord of the adjacent "Mitre." Davenant had been educated at Lincoln, became poet laureate to Charles I in 1638, was knighted in 1643, and wrote a long series of dramas, some one of which it became a tradition of the Davenant Society to stage in the college hall each year.

The play chosen in 1921–22 was *The Bloody Brother*, a horrendous tragedy in the vein of *Titus Andronicus*. There was also vigorous life in the Debating Society, which staged hilarious argument every Sunday evening in the Junior Common Room. The occasional J.C.R. "smokers" enjoyed programmes of Aristophanic humour, far too earthy to be included in any printed record.

During the first three months of my stay at Oxford, I kept a diary of some dimensions, extracts from which will throw a little light on my experiences there. Later on, I became much too busy to persist in the record, but the early days are set down in considerable detail. Take, for example, the preliminary entry on October 12, 1921:

> Went to Lincoln College and found out from the porter that I had been allotted rooms in residence, viz., Suite Nine, Set One. . . . Went up to see my rooms, guided by my "scout" Rawlings. We ascended a flight of stairs and entered a small lobby. From this, one door opened on my bedroom and one on my sitting-room. The bedroom was 18 feet by 10 feet by 14 feet, with a huge window, five feet by ten, in the long north wall. Its furniture consisted of a wash-stand, a chest of drawers, a towel-rack, a chair and a small iron bed. The sitting-room was about 30 by 18 by 14. Its furniture consisted of four straight chairs, four arm-chairs, a sofa, four bookcases and a side-board. The chairs and sofa, plus a window-seat, will probably accommodate fourteen or fifteen people. . . . Spent the afternoon buying tablecloths, serviettes, knives, forks, spoons and the like. . . .

I was given to understand that every student was expected to spend every afternoon in exercise of some sort. My solution was to buy a "Premier" bicycle for ten guineas and to undertake a systematic visitation of every village, church, archaeological remnant or historic site within a fifteen-mile radius of Oxford. Excellent handbooks of Oxfordshire and Berkshire were in all the shops and a remarkably open season favoured my project. The following diary extract covers a typical afternoon, in which I visited a district presently to be made famous by John Buchan in his romances, *Midwinter* (1923) and *The Blanket of the Dark* (1931).

OCTOBER 18, 1921

> Starting at 2.55, went on a bicycle trip to the northeast. Passed through Marston . . . Elsfield . . . and Beckley. Below the village, to the north, lies a great sedgy plain, known as Otmoor. Across this once ran a Roman road that came north from Dorchester through Beckley to Alchester. Throughout the Middle Ages, however, Otmoor became an almost impassable waste of marsh. About 1830 it was drained and enclosed, but even yet it is exceedingly mushy. There are no roads across it, merely two miry trails, one running north from Beckley and another east from a village called Oddington. The Beckley trail, which is almost indistinguishable, follows the line of the old Roman road. I coasted down a lane north of Beckley and then north across

the fields where the trail was supposed to lie. I very soon had to walk and push my bicycle. The dry season had so baked the wet clay that great cracks, six inches wide, gaped everywhere through the grass. Then there were gates to open, and suspicious cattle to mollify, and soon all trace of a trail died out. I kept steadily on, however, by dead reckoning, and after half an hour of grievous trudging reached a hay-stack where the trail became plain again and was met by the cross-trail from Oddington. Near this "cross-roads" I found the chief object of my search, an old Roman remnant (mile-stone or altar), known to the countryside as "Joseph's stone." Unfortunately, it was now broken in two and so badly crumbled on the outside that no inscription could have survived. I turned west along the Oddington trail and finally arrived, still on foot, at the outskirts of the village. Here, at a little bridge over the Ray River (at present completely dried up), I met an old grandam, who, when she learned of my itinerary, said that it had been thirty years since she had last been able to get over to Joseph's stone. Oddington once had a Cistercian abbey, but the site was so damp that the monks moved away to avoid permanent mould. . . . Rode back to Oxford by Islip, Gosford and Kidlington, having covered about twenty miles in all.

The next two items are among many that touch on the social aspects of the College:

OCTOBER 21, 1921

This was the evening when the Rector and Mrs. Munro were to be formally "At Home" and so I dropped across the street from 8.15 to 9.00 P.M. The only other caller was a student named Bowdley. Coffee and chat. . . . The sky is quite lurid tonight from the burning of a big malting establishment down by the station. The Rector says that its demolition will be a hard blow for the University!

OCTOBER 26, 1921

Attended a Barnet House lecture at 5.00, given by Dr. Arthur Shadwell on "The evolution of the modern industrial system." Had to sit on the fender in front of a blazing fire and was nearly roasted alive. . . . In the evening went to a meeting of the Davenant Society. Dr. A. J. Carlyle spoke on "The Unity of European Literature." It was a somewhat prolix utterance, but highly erudite and not a little stimulating.

At a subsequent meeting of this Society, I undertook to advance the theory, as against this formidable 60-year-old savant, that ideas may absorb a national flavour, and that while certain ground-swells of art and thought may have spread through all West European countries, they nevertheless were differentiated in various national fashions. My ammunition for this foray came from John Theodore Merz's four-volume *History of European Thought in the Nineteenth Century*, which I had bought and digested while at Kapuskasing and with which I now refreshed my familiarity in the Radcliffe Camera. I cannot claim to have matched the earlier exposition, but the "old Damoetas" of our college circle was himself prompt to give me generous credit for the attempt.

OCTOBER 27, 1921

In the evening went over to the Union and listened to the debate for about an hour and a half. The debating style adopted was quite new to me. Pungent epigrams and grandiloquence of phrase were sought after, rather than logic or facts. Indeed, some of the reasoning was very muddy. The debate, however, was quite diverting. The subject was "Resolved that in the opinion of this House the growth of modern urban industrialism at the expense of the country is ruining the nation."

OCTOBER 30, 1921

In the evening, went to the Debating Society meeting in the Junior Common Room. I myself had the task of introducing the motion, which was "That this House supports the Government's present unemployment policy." The leader of the Opposition was an American from Seattle, S. S. Smith (known as "Bolshevik Smith" or "Steamship Smith"). He displayed a phenomenal knowledge of international politics, all of which he brought in in relation to the Government's policies as affecting unemployment. On the final division, the motion was supported by a majority of eight votes (18 to 10). Lingered for much further private argument with Smith.

NOVEMBER 9, 1921

In the evening went to a meeting of the Davenant Society in R. T. Paine's rooms. Paine read a paper on "The Prose Works of Shelley." The after-discussion degenerated into a gabble of cross-questions and crooked contradictions. I think that the Society would benefit greatly from a rule such as has been adopted by the Twenty Club whereby each member would speak once and only once and would not be subjected to interruptions (and perhaps thrown off the track entirely) by garrulous fellows with a host of undigested second-hand ideas. With one chap named Macdonald I find it hard to remain polite, for he makes it a point of honour to belittle Shakespeare ("a mere hack who wrote for the stage in some stinking tavern-garret") and to abuse every scene which is traditionally given high praise by the critics. His attitude is the purest cant, for it is the present fashion among Oxford undergraduates to cavil at all that has been honoured by the past.

NOVEMBER 12, 1921

At 7.40 P.M. most of the college, arrayed in dinner-jacket suits, gathered in the Hall for the Junior Gaudy (or "Gaude"), a species of convivial debauch by which to initiate the freshers into the mysteries of college life. I presided at the end of the most easterly of three long tables, there being still another "high table" running across the Hall at the far end. The menu was as follows: Potage St. Germain; Filets de Merlans Frits, Sauce Anchois; Kromesquis à la Russe; Poulet au Riz, Choux de Bruxelles; Pommes purées; Pêches Cardinales; Laitance sur canapes; Dessert; Café. With the soup went "Amontillado" (reminiscent of Edgar Allan Poe); with the fritters and meat, "Château Monton d'Armilhacq, 1911"; and with the dessert, "Port." Those of us who so desired were permitted to set ourselves down as non-alcoholic, and there were at least a dozen of us who did so. After the coffee and the toast to the King, we adjourned for a short time and changed into old clothes; then met in the front quad. One of the Seniors wanted to know whether I was Scotch or American; for it seems that the Scotch students had been claiming me as Scotch and the Americans as American. . . . After an hilarious interval, the college fell in on the front quad along with an impromptu band consisting of one big drum and a score of kazoos, whistles, horns and squawkers. There was an orderly–disorderly parade round and round the quad and finally through into the Grove, where all formed a square around a plot of grass and Bullocke, as President of the J.C.R., planted an acorn in the centre. Then the crowd indulged in a grotesque war-dance, singing unholy goliard songs, while Mitchell, in a kilt, did the Highland fling on top of the acorn, and two knights, riding pickaback on human steeds, rode each other down in the hollow square and gave the mystic rite the sanction of their downfall. We then came back to the Hall and the toast-list proper began. As part of the toast to the College came the "Lincoln Litany," a vocal versification of the Alphabet, one stanza per letter, sung by Hockliffe, with the rest joining in on the refrain: "Jolly old Ox, jolly old Ox, jolly old Lincoln." "A" stood for the Acorn, "B" for Bullocke, etc. When they reached the letter "K", I heard the following:

> "K's for Kirkconnell, a jolly old chap.
> Can he speak Anglo-Saxon? The answer is Yep!"

Then came toasts to all the different athletic clubs in the College, some seven in all, and in each case a special club-song was sung. By 11.00 P.M. there was virtual pandemonium in the Hall. At least a dozen were downright drunk and a score of others were woozily happy. Half the *gaudentes* were on top of the tables and the other half were having wrestling matches and convivial discourse in the centre of the room. . . . Braithwaite, the college's worst stutterer, was standing on a table, pouring the contents of a bowl of hot punch into his empurpled face and shouting forth intermittent bursts of stutterless eloquence. The piano and the toast-songs tinkled on unnoticed. . . . I managed to slip out and away to bed at 11.30.

NOVEMBER 16, 1921

In the evening, went to the League of Nations (Oxford) Assembly, held in the Union hall. Parkes, of Pembroke, gave a lucid introductory address; and Professor Gilbert Murray, who acted as President for the evening, showed himself a charming speaker but a most inefficient chairman. Delegates were present from about twenty-two countries. The United States, Newfoundland, Korea, Syria, Palestine, Irak and Egypt were all admitted to membership by vote of the Assembly, and an application from Cyprus was referred to Committee. The American delegates were somewhat inclined to play the hedgehog when called on to state their point of view.

Nearly ten weeks later, on February 23, 1922, I was destined to speak in the Union before the Fourth Session of this same Assembly. A committee report on Northern Epirus was to be presented (in favour of Greece) by Count L. J. Mercati (Greece) and I was to be the straw man, or devil's advocate, who would submit weakly dissenting arguments on behalf of Albania, the other claimant to the territory. There was no Albanian student at Oxford that year and I was the only enrolled student who had even seen the country. The sequel may best be given in excerpts from the *Oxford Magazine* for March 16, 1922:

> Mr. Kirkconnell, Lincoln, spoke next as Albanian expert; with infinite ability he contested the accuracy of previous deductions, produced new factors, and although his fervour in expressing Albanian aspirations added a paradoxical element to his statements, he conscripted considerable sympathy for a cause which a few minutes before had seemed practically indefensible; it certainly would have remained so in the hands of a less subtle debater. . . . The committee report in favour of Greece was then voted on and rejected.

That year's Vice-Chancellor, L. R. Farnell, who lived next door in Exeter College, gained deep unpopularity with all the ardent Left-Wingers through his attempts to prevent Communists from coming, on student invitation, to address University clubs. One morning, while he and Mrs. Farnell were sitting at breakfast with a distinguished guest, Frederick Soddy, Lee's Professor of Chemistry and a Nobel Prize winner in 1921, the postman delivered a parcel addressed to Mrs. Farnell. It proved to be an anonymous box of chocolates, and a somewhat mystified breakfast-table examination discovered that the interior of several of the chocolates had been filled with a strange white powder. Soddy hazarded the opinion that it might be "a subtle Oriental poison" and the Nobel Prize winner in Chemistry was so reported in all the evening papers. Next day the criminal mystery collapsed with a thud. The white powder was merely Epsom salts!

Of the students who were my contemporaries at Lincoln, I have lost track of all but a few. Our two top academics were probably H. G. Hanbury, who became Vinerian Professor of English Law in the University, and S. R. K. Glanville, who became Professor of Egyptology at Cambridge. Bullocke, president of the J.C.R., ended up on the staff of the Royal Naval College at Greenwich. C. Lewis became Professor of German at Trinity College, Toronto, and "Joe" Brandt served for a spell as President of the University of Oklahoma. Several of the men I knew best—Soden, Wood, and Vallance—became ordained clergymen. Corvin Edwards, with whom I spent an Easter "Vac" in Germany, is with the Bureau of Industrial Economics at Washington. Roy Vollum, a fellow-Canadian, from British Columbia, became lecturer in Pathology at Oxford. A fair-haired little New Zealander named Ryburn is Chancellor of the University of Otago. To a far-off "Colonial," the rest are now scarcely shadows of names. My only unfailing contact through the years has been with the Munros (Mrs. Munro since the Rector's death). With Canon V. J. K. Brook, our adored dean of residence, there has been more intermittent correspondence. It was a matter of pride that when I visited the College in 1955, after thirty-three years' absence, I was at once recognized by George Pratley, in the porter's lodge, and assigned by him to my proper staircase. Porters and elephants never forget.

It is hard to compare the relative merits of Queen's and Oxford. In the Queen's of my day, there were no residences for men and only one very small residence ("the Hen-Coop") for women. I was the only student in my rooming-house on Frontenac Street and could be sure of long, uninterrupted hours of study, six nights a week if need be, neatly divided according to a curricular time-table. The only daily routine of intercourse with other students, apart from lectures, was at the Misses Nicols' boarding-house, where two dozen of us lined the sides of a long dinner table. As a result, there was far too little of the endless discussions that made life at Oxford so stimulating an experience. An Oxford college, with perhaps two hundred students "living in," made for far more vocal interchange. Perhaps the fact that I was older than most of the Lincoln undergraduates made me feel that some of them would rather talk than think and that many of them were parroting poseurs, mouthing pretentious nonsense. It became obvious, however, that some of the more serious senior students had made allowance for this flux of talk by working on their courses during the vacations. In this way, they came up to Oxford bursting with academic health and quite able to undergo a haemorrhage of conversation without serious consequences.

At a later stage, during the quinquennium 1925–30, I was to room on the top floor of the men's residence at United College, Winnipeg. Although I was a member of the professorial staff, I had no administrative responsibilities and simply lived along with some sixty students in a sort of uneasy symbiosis. The uneasiness sprang from the fact that I was working under terrific pressure and published six books during that five-year period, while work of any sort seemed the last thing in the world desired by some of these healthy young animals. As my nerves rebelled more and more at their uproar, I invented, for college journalism, a creature called the "Tywhoopus" and published a list of Ten Commandments for him, based on actual daily experience, for example: (2) When you wish to speak to a fellow tywhoopus, never go to his burrow and look for him. Just stand in the corridor and howl his name. (6) Soak your socks in the wash-bowls overnight. The flavour lingers. (9) Telephone annunciations should always make the windows rattle. If you can't do it alone, let ten men help. Later came a full-length "Monograph on the Tywhoopidae," in which some eighteen species were identified and described in detail, ranging from *Asellus sibilans* (the Whistling Tywhoopus) to *Asinus noctambulans* (the Night-prowling Tywhoopus), *Asinus Cacchinans* (the Laughing Jackass), and *Asinus pipiens* (the Hooting Tywhoopus or Yelping Yahoo).

It was during this period that intimacy with college and university journalism made me the faculty representative on the *Manitoban*. The editor, an intrepid and candid youth named Leonard L. Knott (now an eminent public relations counsel in Montreal), ventured to criticize his employers, the Students' Council, and was warned to "lay off." Enraptured by this rebuff, he doubled the dose, and was sacked, along with his staff. Nothing daunted, he launched a paper of his own, *The Manitoba Student*, to whose support I even devoted a crisp dollar bill of my own. Then there was surreptitiously printed, by still another group, one issue of a truly scandalous sheet called *The Red Herring* ("It smells but it sells"), Case I, Tin 1, Feb. 9, 1927. It was a four-page edition in black ink on red paper, and almost every article was good for a libel suit. For a wonder, President McLean was awake, struck immediately, seized the edition, and burned it—but not before a few advance copies had reached United College. One of them still perfumes my files. The alleged editor was Herr Ring and the business manager, Jack Fish. A feature column was entitled "The Stewed Aunt." A big boxed advertisement declared that "The Red Herring Is All Backbone—Has 100 Eyes, Is Read All Over, And Swishes A Mean Tale." *The Calgary Eye-Opener* was kindergarten stuff compared to *The Red Herring*.

I recall this episode as one of the things that reassured me as to the brilliance and potential industry of our Western students. One of the chief Herring-trailers (later a distinguished theological professor at Yale) tried eloquently but unsuccessfully three times to bluff his way through my examination on the English Novel and flunked each time through a dare-devil failure to read any of the prescribed fiction. One of a University's problems—whether at Queen's, Oxford, or Manitoba—is how to mobilize such gifts for academic service.

3

In the Margins of Science

THE FIERCE OLD FELLOW who sat unconcernedly at our supper table and was actually to sleep that night in the big oak bed in our spare room had the beard of a Hebrew prophet and the forehead and eyes of a Roman proconsul. Five young Kirkconnells, ranging in age from six to sixteen, had learned beforehand, open-mouthed, that the prospective guest was one of Canada's greatest geologists and a world authority on glaciers. His name was Coleman[1] and he was professor of geology in the University of Toronto. What we heard from this incomparable old man that night transformed our thinking for a lifetime. One hundred thousand years ago (he said) a stupendous glacier had been sitting right on top of what was now Port Hope and had brought down from the North the masses of sand and clay that now formed the hills of the town and the wave-washed bluffs along the Lake Ontario shore. More recently, only twenty thousand years ago, a still mightier lake than Ontario, known to geologists as "Lake Iroquois," had covered Port Hope and the whole countryside for five miles north of the town, and there its cliffs and beaches could still be plainly traced. A familiar hill near Quay's had once been an island in that lake. Most staggering of all, the Ganaraska River, now flowing through the middle of Port Hope, had washed away the glacial drift right down to flat beds of Ordovician limestone and there we could chip out the fossils of trilobites (a kind of giant sowbug) that had crawled hereabouts in the mud of palaeozoic seas some millions of years before.

The challenge was irresistible. With supervision from our own father, a Queen's graduate in science and mathematics, we explored the Ganaraska rock-flats in the days that followed and found not only trilobites but enough other denizens of the primordial ooze to have

[1]Arthur Philemon Coleman (1852–1939), Ph.D., LL.D., D.Sc., F.R.S., F.R.S.C., author of *Ice Ages, Recent and Ancient.* His treatise on "Lake Iroquois" was published by the Ontario Bureau of Mines in 1936.

started a small museum. Walking and cycling through the countryside now took on a new meaning. Drumlins were common to the northeast, vast inverted half-grapefruits formed by glacial rivers. Long eskar-ridges beyond Monkey Mountain had been built up by streams underneath the glacier. We cycled to the ancient north shore of Lake Iroquois and traced it for miles to east and west, several hundred feet higher above sea-level than the shore of its shrunken successor, Lake Ontario. The old man's incredible story was true.

Thus began a life-long habit of noticing the geology of every area or country visited, and especially to watch for evidences of glacial action. When presently, in 1908, the family moved to Lindsay, forty-five miles northwest and on the other side of Central Ontario's great range of morainic sand-hills, we found ourselves still in old glacial territory. Lindsay's notorious mud was the bottom of the pleistocene "Lake Schomberg," while "Lake Algonquin," a glacial lake that combined and expanded the areas of Superior, Michigan, and Huron, then had its outlet not by a Niagara River but down the Trent Valley into Lake Iroquois and thence (since the St. Lawrence Valley was blocked by an ice-barrier) past Rome, N.Y., into the Hudson. In Victoria County, south of Balsam Lake and elsewhere, I industriously traced out the raised beaches of Lake Algonquin and found where its mighty river-outlet, near Fenelon Falls and Bobcaygeon, had left clear-swept limestone floors, covered today, after twenty millennia, with only clumps of grass and stunted juniper. Still later I was to spend two years (1917–19) at Kapuskasing, in the former bed of the pleistocene "Lake Ojibway," and eighteen years (1922–40) at Winnipeg, in the dried-out bed of "Lake Agassiz." The chief characteristic of the former site was a heavy blanket of glacial clay that smothered the drainage system of the whole area, while in the Red River Valley the silt of the prairie streams was rendered almost chocolate-coloured by the ancient lake's deep deposits of organic matter. Still later, on a plane-trip across Finland (1938), I was impressed with the resemblance of that country's innumerable lakes throughout a granitic countryside to the vaster version of the same profile in Canada's glaciated and moraine-strewn pre-Cambrian Shield as seen on a visit by plane to the Red Lake gold-mining area. An air trip from Winnipeg to Resolute revealed a still starker version of the North.

Another formation that was to lure me into exploring was the "cuesta," an escarpment formed where part of an area of soft sedimentary rocks has been capped by a very hard rock layer, protecting that part of the region from rapid erosion and resulting in a cliff-front along the line of the obstinate cover. The "Hamilton Mountain" or "Niagara

Escarpment," marking the edge of the Silurian sedimentaries, is one of the most celebrated cuestas in the world, and for eight years (1940–48) its precipitous rock-front, only three hundred yards from my back door, drew me out into many exploratory rambles. Twenty years earlier, in 1920–21, and in Victoria County, I had run across a smaller cuesta where the northern edge of the Trenton formation (of the Middle Ordovician series) ran roughly east and west across the county. Its most southerly angle was only four miles from my home. Consultation with friendly authorities in the Geological Survey of Canada revealed that it had never been mapped as a cuesta, and so, with a large-scale topographical survey map on which to plot my countours, I traced out about forty miles of the cuesta (travelling on foot and by bicycle in July 1920) and published a report on "the Trenton Cuesta," complete with an India ink map, in the *Canadian Mining Journal.* Still another cuesta was more roughly traced on my sketch some twenty miles farther north, where the Lower Ordovician limestones abutted on the crystalline limestones of the Grenville series. Fossils were a matter of interest in the Ordovician rocks of Victoria County, but as the formations were earlier than those in Port Hope, trilobites were rare and brachiopods small but very abundant. In Devonian outcrops in the Kapuskasing area, I again chipped out fossils, and in cases of uncertainty (for example, branching corals) sent the specimens, packed in boxes of sawdust, to my good friend Professor Manly Baker at Queen's University. One by-product of my studies in the field was a technical article, "The Paleogeography of Ontario" (*The School,* Toronto, October 1925).

Since coming to Nova Scotia in 1948, I have undertaken a rather systematic exploration of its highways, with an eye open for geological novelty. The Triassic traps of the North Mountain, the morainic hills of Annapolis County, the wealth of plant fossils in the seaside cliffs at Joggins, the huge gypsum beds in Hants County, the Carboniferous seashore in the Sydney area, and the heavily glaciated gold-bearing Maguma tracts of the Eastern Shore have all stirred my imagination.

Only the casual impressions of a traveller linger with me from widespread contact with the geology of Europe, North Africa, and Western Asia. Volcanic Iceland might be *sui generis,* but Norway recalled the British Columbia coast; the Alps, the Carpathians and the Taurus suggested our own Rockies but with an added plenitude of human associations, while the historical atmosphere became overpowering (to an old Classics man) in the mountains and valleys of Italy, Greece, Crete, Cyprus, Western Asia Minor, Syria, Palestine, and Egypt. During the six agonizing years of World War II, the armies of many nations marched and counter-marched in my consciousness across nearly all of the lands that I had known from the Atlantic eastward to the Tallin–Riga–Lemberg–Bucharest line and southward to the Aegean and the Nile. Yet even for these, geology played its part in providing the scene for the human drama and the problems for human logistics. I think that my boyhood training helped me somewhat to understand it.

It was my maternal grandfather, Thomas Watson (1826–1912), who first introduced me to astronomy. The full-bearded old Methodist saint had been headmaster of the Union School in Port Hope from 1851 until his retirement through poor health in 1886, but he remained active, both physically and mentally, until his death at eighty-six from falling out of an apple tree. Even as a small boy, I learned from him to recite the signs of the zodiac and to recognize all the major constellations at their rising. On one notable occasion he took me to see a lantern lecture on the moon, where high-power magnification transformed the "orbèd maiden" into a new world of wonder. Later on, I discovered books on astronomy in my father's mathematical library and learned to apply my newly acquired trigonometry to astronomical problems. At Queen's University, where, instead of majoring in mathematics, I turned my path into honours Latin and Greek, Daniel Buchanan, a burly, black-haired giant in the Mathematics Department, nevertheless made me at home in the University observatory, where I watched the moons of Jupiter and Saturn's shining ring, and saw vast shadows creep across the craters of the waning moon. For amateur work I acquired three small telescopes—first a second-hand ship's glass, then a collapsible cardboard instrument that perished in a thunderstorm, and finally a large Bauer and Richter refracting telescope, complete with tripod.

Still later, in the Cavendish Laboratories of Cambridge University in 1953, I was introduced to the radio astronomy that Martin Ryle and his associates had developed there, with their twin-aerial, interferometer system. Here was a new and vastly larger window opening on the cosmos, the addition of an extra sense that could detect a ghost universe of hitherto invisible stellar masses co-existing with the visible universe and manifesting incredible potencies of radiation—like "Cass" and the Cygnus galaxies. The eternal calm of the Psalmist's firmament became an infinite jousting-ground where galactic knights-errant, in the explosive shock of head-on collision, wrote large the universal clash of atom on atom in the realm of the infinitesimal.

Not all small boys are lucky enough to have an amateur entomologist as an uncle. My mother's youngest brother, Dr. Adam Watson, was a dental surgeon by profession but spent all his spare hours perambulating the countryside to east, west, and north of Port Hope in search of beetles, and amassed a collection of over 10,000 specimens (about 2,000 species). From him we learned to sally forth with sandwiches in one jacket-pocket and a cyanide killing-bottle in the other, ready for a full day in the field. From him we learned to canvass a wide range of plants for the beetles peculiar to each, to search under boards, leaves and stones, to break open rotting mushrooms and bracket-fungi, to rake the pools with a water net and the meadows with a sweep-net, to spot a tiger-beetle on a sandy summer roadside or to smear sugar mixtures on trunks and fence-rails for night collecting. Pine, oak, hickory, basswood, and all the other patient "monarchs of the forest" were shown to be lousy with their own particular brands of coleopterous parasite. All of the non-beetle insects were objects for general knowledge, but were understood to be too numerous for collecting in the spare hours of a single lifetime. Beetles, however, of which there were only some fifteen thousand named species in North America, were a neat, manageable sector of the insect front. For the same reason that I finally limited my postage-stamp collection to a fairly complete set of the issues of Hungary, rich in surcharges and occupation issues, I restricted my entomological taxonomy, as Uncle Adam had largely done, to the beetle tribes. Even here great gaps always remained. For example, although I bought Blatchley and Leng's monumental handbook on the *Rhyncophora or Weevils of North-Eastern America*, I confess myself baffled to this day by the intricacies and obscurities of this exasperating suborder.

Mention should be made, in passing, of another abbettor of such youthful field work. Lawson Caesar, a graduate in Classics of Toronto and Oxford, had taught Latin on my father's staff from 1901 to 1906. Thereupon a passion for entomology possessed him and he transferred to the Ontario Agricultural College—first as a student, then as a lecturer on insects, and finally as director of all provincial research in economic entomology. I recall one instance about 1910 when he was our house-guest in Lindsay, Ontario, and scandalized my mother by estimating at the dinner-table the astronomically numerous descendants of one plant-louse in a single favourable summer if food supplies were unlimited and enemies were absent.

Other zoological interests were not lacking. On the banks of the Scugog, near our swimming-hole by a beached hulk, "the old Kenosha," we watched female snapping-turtles bury their clutch of white, leathery eggs in the warm sawdust. In swampy woodlands by Maclaren's Creek, vernal snakes slowly sloughed off their old skins. Later in life I spent a summer month on snails, storing my specimens in wood alcohol for later classification.

In field work in botany, I had my first training from my father. As teacher of science for a time, he had himself ransacked the immediate neighbourhood of Port Hope for specimens, armed with a small, black, tin vasculum and a leather-bound pocket-edition of Spotton's key to the flora of Ontario. When after our removal to Lindsay I became a serious botanist, he gave me Gray's *Manual* as a more adequate guide and had a much larger vasculum made for me by a local tinsmith. For drying the plant specimens that I brought home over a period of five years, I bought some hundreds of sheets of coarse blotting-paper from a local printing office. For mosses, I later acquired Grout's volumes, as well as hand-lenses and a low-power microscope. For fungi, my father's library was adequate. For lichens, I have only a little handbook by Kershaw and Alvin.

But the chief stimulus to botanizing came from Frank Morris, a friend of my father. Morris was an Englishman, a Double First at Balliol College, Oxford, who came out to Canada to teach in Trinity College School, Port Hope. Here he became intimate with my father and was treated as a sort of "honorary uncle" by the young Kirkconnells. He was a heavily built, clean-shaven man, with thick glasses and an Old Country accent, but to our youthful minds it seemed that, like the dying Falstaff, "a' babbled o' green fields." He ultimately became English master in the Peterborough Collegiate Institute, but his ruling passion was botany, especially a field study of orchids and ferns. His book, *Our Wild Orchids* (New York, 1929), wedded as it is to the magnificent photographs of his bog-trotting associate, Edward A. Eames, is without doubt the best existing book on the orchids of North America east of the Mississippi and north of Tennessee and North Carolina. When I was a lad in my teens a field trip with him was a tramp through the Seventh Heaven. I can recall the early July day in 1911 when he introduced me to the "Old Ramsay Swamp" near Newtonville, Ontario. There in a single spot near the centre of the tract we found jewel-like stands of *Arethusa*, *Calopogon* (the grass pink), *Calypso*, the rose pogonia and the white fringed orchis. In a shadier corner, under evergreens, we found three varieties of twayblade and some healthy specimens of the stemless lady's slipper, and in a still deeper retreat a whole patch of a real rarity, *Botrychium simplex*, a minute moonwort, less than two inches in height and vastly more thrilling than the neck-high jungle of flowering fern that flanked the road by which we had entered the swamp.

The greatest excitement that I ever witnessed in Frank Morris was many years later when I met him at Port Arthur just after he and his wife had located an unbelievable stand of bog adder's mouth in open sphagnum bog at Thunder Cape. Only the year before, a single specimen —the first ever reported in Canada—had been announced from there by

Professor H. C. Cowles of the University of Chicago. The Morrises travelled eight hundred miles to the region, and after two days of tireless search discovered fifty-five specimens, along with stands of four very rare ferns. When we met, he was still lyric with enthusiasm.

It would be tedious to trace my own wanderings in search of gems of the bog and the woodland. My best station for the ram's head lady's slipper was in the Byrnell Swamp, about five miles walk from Lindsay; a wonderful stand of striped coral root was to be found in the pine woods near the "Old Fort" on Balsam Lake; and in 1918 I found the *Calypso borealis* in great profusion near the east bank of the Kapuskasing River, about three miles down stream from that town; and so I might go on for hours.

The chief by-product of my taxonomy was a slim volume, *Botanical Survey of South Victoria* (Lindsay, 1926), in which I summed up the ecological factors of the region and gave a checklist of all the plants, including fungi and mosses, that I had identified there. Articles of mine —"The Flora of Kapuskasing and Vicinity" and "Bryophyta of Boskung"—had already appeared in the *Canadian Field-Naturalist* (May 1919 and November 1921).

Other friends whom my botanical enthusiasms won for me were Reginald Buller, the fungi expert at the University of Manitoba, W. T. Macoun, the Dominion Botanist, J. H. Craigie, of the Dominion Rust Research Laboratory, Winnipeg, to whom the Royal Society awarded the Flavelle Medal in Science in 1942, the same year that it gave me the Lorne Pierce Medal in Literature, and Frère Marie-Victorin of the University of Montreal.

Ornithology followed in the wake of a bird-guide tactfully given to me on my twelfth Christmas. Dated bird-records began the following spring and by June I was busy trying to differentiate amongst the various species of warbler, vireo, and sparrow in the Port Hope area. My chief friend in this field was P. A. Taverner, of the National Museum in Ottawa. In the spring of 1919 I had mentioned in the *Canadian Field-Naturalist* some of the birds that I had noted (for example, a huge white Arctic owl) in the vicinity of the Kapuskasing Internment Camp, and that very June the friendly, bearded ornithologist came to call on me at the officers' mess, copied my checklist of the birds I had observed in the district, and spent two weeks in the neighbourhood, collecting bird skins for the Museum. He pitched his tent on the east bank of the river just a little below the railway bridge, and there we fellowshipped together in the lore of flying things.

At Kapuskasing, where I also kept daily records of temperature, wind, and air pressure for nearly two years and shared the results by mail with the Dominion Meteorologist, Sir Frederick Stupart, living things struggled against rigours unmatched even in the Polar regions. February temperatures sometimes reached the sixties below zero Fahrenheit. Little then remained active in the frost-racked spruce forest but whisky-jacks, Arctic owls, rabbits, and occasional wolves. Over a hundred prisoners of war and several of the troops succumbed to mental illness, chiefly melancholia, during the long, inexorable winter months. In 1917, the ice finally went out of the river on the 23rd of May, working parties (digging drains) found permanent frost six feet down in the clay soil in mid-August, and in September the snow came again to stay. But in the brief sunlit season between snow and snow, there was a stupendous surge of natural vitality in moss and tree and fern and jewelled flower. Birds swept in on the tides of summer and flies and mosquitoes were almost a living mist on the air. Every man felt a strange exhilaration as part of that intense, spontaneous animation of a world unchained from ice and death.

In 1919, I almost became an anthropologist. Wide reading in the field had aroused my interest and with the prospect of imminent release from the armed forces I had resolved to register at Columbia for a doctorate in the somatological aspects of the science. On the personal advice of Edward Sapir, however, I made a special trip to New York in April 1919 and sought the advice of the head of the Department, Dr. Franz Boas. Boas was a lean, belligerent-looking little man, whose face had been rendered more grim by sabre scars from duels in his youth at Heidelberg. In a candid burst of pessimism, he urged me to stay out of professional anthropology. Such a department was regarded as a frill by North American universities and was the first to get the axe whenever times grew hard. It would be folly to proceed, for I should run a great risk of starving. I took his warning and went no further. Today, Toronto is the only Canadian university with a formal Department of Anthropology, while six others have one non-somatological anthropologist apiece assigned to some other department. Boas cannot have been very far wrong.

This science, like all the rest, therefore, remained only a hobby for me. Cephalic indices became a matter for research, using a physician's pelvimeter that I had bought for convenience in taking measurements. As a sequel to an article of mine on "Mendelism and Cephalic Index" (*American Journal of Physical Anthropology*, Oct.-Dec. 1925) came a fellowship in the Royal Anthropological Institute and life-long anthropological correspondence with Dr. R. Ruggles Gates, formerly at the University of London and later at Harvard, who warmly supported my assignment of the distribution of cephalic indices to Mendelian inheritance as opposed to Franz Boas's theory that environmental influences in North America were moulding the indices of successive generations towards a common type. Certainly my own data could be interpreted only in Mendelian terms. Another long-distance friend through the years was Rev. Wilhelm Schmidt, S.V.D. (1868–1954), of Vienna, whose huge synthetic survey of all the world's languages, *Die Sprachfamilien und Sprachenkreise der Erde* (Heidelberg, 1926), came early to my shelves and whose three-volume *Rassen und Volker in Vorgeschichte und Geschichte des Abendlandes* (Lucerne, 1946–49 edition), which he sent me in instalments on publication, is an erudite survey of Occidental history based on such data as anthropometrical indices and evidences of cultural dispersion. Father Schmidt's books were on the Nazis' *Index Expurgatorius*, for he had a scientist's scorn for the racial dogmatism of the Third Reich.

In 1920, in the town of Lindsay, I became intimate with a letter-carrier, Johnson Paudash, a chief of the band of Mississauga Indians whose reserve is near the debouchure of the Otonabee River into Rice Lake. Chief Paudash had been a deadly sniper in the Canadian forces in Europe in World War I but was now peacefully delivering mail on a postal route in my home town. From him I learned much about the arrival of the Mississaugas in Central Ontario in 1740 and their sternly punitive campaign against the Iroquois that cleared Victoria County for Mississauga settlement. With the help of Chief Paudash and Colonel George Laidlaw of the "Old Fort," Balsam Lake, I was able to map in the county some fifty-five village sites from the pre-Mississauga period and some fifteen Mississauga villages. The antiquity of some sites near Lindsay was shown by the stumps of huge trees that had subsequently grown above them. It was nearly forty years later that geological and carbon-14 dating began to give me chronological perspective in Ontario's Amerindian prehistory. The Rice Lake Serpent Mound, with its shadowy witness to a dead religion, then became contemporary with Alexander the Great. The Old Copper Culture man, whose cache of weapons and utensils was exhumed at Farquhar Lake, a few miles from my Haliburton County summer cabin, was as old as the Exodus. The upper layers of the Sheguiandah quartzite quarry site on Manitoulin Island were dated 7000 to 10,000 B.C. and its lower, interglacial beds of artefacts had geological datings of from 20,000 to 30,000 B.C. and were coëval with the Cro-Magnon culture. The "New World" is no longer new when we find it already occupied by skilled human artisans for thousands of years before Egypt and Babylon were born. For me, indeed, the forests of Ontario are filled with the ghosts of ancient civilizations. The sense of history that floods over one in Europe, Africa, or Asia is at last our heritage in Canada as well. We can now see our white civilization here as a palimpsest, written on parchment from which the ancient earlier texts had all but vanished.

I have no claim to be an authority in any of the disciplines touched on in this chapter. As a matter of fact, the serious work of my life has lain entirely in other fields, and neither a careful study of books like J. T. Merz's *European Thought in the Nineteenth Century* nor friendly discourse with such an historian of science as the late George Sarton of Harvard has done more than co-ordinate the odds and ends of my scientific knowledge.

The effect of it all on my thinking has changed with the years. In the beginning, no doubt, there was little more than the young magpie's instinct to accumulate shining facts and gloat over them, to add species to species and formation to formation. Taxonomy can easily remain a sort of open-air philately unless it is somehow related to the enduring issues of life.

At twenty-one, I underwent a period of utter pessimism. In comparison with the length of the Pleistocene, the span of a few millennia of human civilization shrank into insignificance; in the perspective of the Palaeozoic, man was scarcely a flicker of the terrestrial eyelash. Astronomy moved in on me to show even our earth as the fifth-rate satellite of a stellar nonentity in space so absolute that the numberless galaxies were almost numberless light-years from one another and constituted an endless infinity of infinities. There is danger to the human spirit in letting the imagination stray too far and too long in the endless abysses of the night. A few thousand generations of human caddis-flies flutter their meaningless wings in the margins of eternal darkness. Existentialism of the more fatal sort whispers a denial of all sense, all purpose, and all ambition.

From that pit of despair I found my way out again, partly by religious faith, partly through metaphysics and imaginative literature, and partly by the sheer indwelling vitality of a life force that refused to deny its own validity. Turning back to biology, I could glory in the power and range of living things, cramming land and air and sea with myriad forms, adapted with infinite ingenuity to the demands of ten thousand habitats and thereafter controlled by an information store, coded in the genes. Plants and animals were no longer mere varieties to be catalogued or vermin for wanton destruction but created personalities in the great Pattern of Being, creatures to be confronted with reverence and good will. Man himself, with all his imperfections, was still the culmination of that pulsating empire and had a spiritual destiny, in living by the light of natural and revealed religion. I knew myself the member of a race, of a nation, of a family. I had a life to live and a duty to fulfil. And so I came home to a world that had not even been aware of my philosophical absence.

The rocks and the stars measure out time by a chronology too vast for the human heart to endure. They stand in the background of consciousness with an infinite austerity that rebukes our pride and our pettiness. With their rhythms in our blood we may strive to live, as Kant would urge, so that every act may be the expression of a universal law. On a stage so immense, we must play our brief parts in honesty and humility. But we must not forget our lines as men, lest stage fright at the silent infinities round about us choke us and we fall.

4

The Sinews of Speech

THE LABOURS of my lifetime have been more in the field of language study than in any other. Some thirty of my books, totalling several thousand pages, consist of my verse translations from the poetries of many lands, and my treatise on Magyar grammar, published serially in 1934–37, merely betrays another aspect of the same ruling passion.

Up to my thirteenth birthday, no such major interest could have been predicted. English was the sole language of our home. My father was a mathematician, who could speak a little German and less Gaelic; he and my mother and my older brother and sister had a reading knowledge of Latin and French, but none of these partially mastered languages had thus far fallen on my youthful ears, so far as I can recall. My only semi-linguistic exploit, following the reading of Edgar Allan Poe's "Gold Bug," had been the invention of a cipher of my own, and in this a number of documents were carefully transcribed and buried in a tin box, ten paces due west of a wild apple tree on Monkey Mountain.

My study of Latin and French began in the First Form (now Grade IX) in the Lindsay Collegiate Institute. German and Greek were added two years later. Four years of French and Latin and two of German and Greek were thus my language ration in the secondary school. My teachers were excellent. I am convinced, however, that my language studies should have been started at least seven or eight years earlier, when my mind, at five or six years of age, could have picked up vocabulary and idiom much more promptly and completely. Starting as I did in my fourteenth year, I have never felt fully at home in speaking foreign languages, except in an occasional dream when speech in some other tongue has flowed uninhibited from the subconscious mind. Had I begun earlier, I might have become a linguist. As it is, I reckon myself little more than a hardworking man of letters, who has devoted far more time to literature than to either lexicology or linguistics.

The philological impulse came from reading in the Lindsay school library. Here some earlier teacher had placed volumes by Max Müller of Oxford and William Dwight Whitney of Yale, both former students of Franz Bopp in Berlin, where their grasp of comparative philology had been firmly based on a mastery of Sanskrit. Both were princes of exposition. As a lad of seventeen, I found Max Müller's verbal fireworks vastly more exciting than the quieter style of Whitney, but both co-operated in setting my own enthusiasm on fire. Later I acquired August Schleicher's *Vergleichende Grammatik* and *Chrestomathie* of the Indo-Germanic language and Monier William's *Grammar of Sanskrit*, and thus helped to build for myself the structure so thrillingly blueprinted by Müller and Whitney, but the drive towards philology began with these masters. Up until this time, mathematics and science had claimed my major allegiance and had seemed my most natural field of specialization. But when the time came for me to go to Queen's University in the fall of 1913, an obstinate young Canadian had decided to major in languages.

The course that I had mapped out for the next five years was in many respects blundering and wrong-headed. At eighteen, I had still no idea as to the exacting requirements of modern scholarship. The concentration required for the mastery of even one academic field was only a matter of vague undergraduate rumour, and the impossibility of successfully combining several fields had never even occurred to me. A crazy young beaver at the edge of the woods fancied that he could quite easily chew the whole forest down, and without asking any older beaver's advice, he started in to gnaw the tree trunks with great enthusiasm. The programme was certainly ambitious: by cramming more than the normal number of classes into each year, I planned first to take an M.A. in Latin and Greek by the spring of 1916. In the next two years, still at Queen's, I would add similar honours courses in Romance languages, Germanic languages, and English, and so be ready, at the age of twenty-two, to go on for a soundly based doctorate in comparative philology or comparative literature. I had no doubt that I would end up teaching in some university but I had only the haziest idea as to the nature of my ultimate post. What I wanted at the moment was to achieve a comprehensive knowledge of languages and literatures worthy of the vision that had descended upon me.

For the next two and a half years, the pattern scarcely changed at all. In general, I stuck faithfully to my Latin and Greek, even to the extent of slogging through Greek dramatists and philosophers in the summer vacations. I am not sure, however, that I did much real thinking at this period. I was too much in love with language for its own sake, and worked prodigiously on the authors of the prescribed curriculum for the joy of the linguistic activity and the stimulus of great literature.

My design for an all-round philological career seemed splendid and easily attainable.

World War I wrecked most of this boyhood scheme. In April 1916, at the age of twenty, I had indeed secured my Classics M.A., with the University medals in Greek and Latin, but my older brother, Walter, had already been overseas since 1914 and I too now volunteered for service, first in Intelligence (where there were no openings in an almost non-existent department) and then as a combatant officer in the 253rd Battalion (Queen's University Highlanders). Six years later, in September 1922, I found myself by sheer accident back in a university setting and began to pick up the lost threads of my old philological dream. A prospective eight months of teaching in Wesley College, Winnipeg, stretched out to eighteen years, and a new pattern, at first largely linguistic, presently worked itself out.

Of the original blueprint, not too much remained. The years that the locust had eaten could never be restored. My age was twenty-seven and I had neither the funds nor the time to go on into doctoral work in philology or comparative literature. All further education had to be hewn out by myself in the margin of a busy life as a teacher, a husband, and a father. In all this, I could not complain. My brother Walter and sixty-two thousand other young Canadians lay in war graves overseas, and who was I, alive and well, to remonstrate because my education had been first confused and then cut short? Self-education was still an enduring possibility, and even here the omens were now propitious. Arthur Phelps and I taught the full undergraduate Arts course in English between us. As he had no interest whatever in language study, all that side of the curriculum fell to my lot—including Old English, Middle English, and the history of the English language. The background out of which I treated these courses could be as broad as I wished, and while classroom instruction had to be kept within the range of undergraduate comprehension, I could carry myself back into Gothic, Sanskrit, and Indo-European comparative grammar. As a running-mate in the University, I had a first-class mediaevalist in the person of Aaron J. Perry, editor of John Trevisa for the Early English Text Society. At the same time, Rev. Dr. John Maclean, a veteran missionary among the Plains Indians, who was spending his old age as librarian at Wesley College, was introducing me to the infinite complexities of the Blackfoot language, so copious that the paradigms of a single verb would fill the entire wall of a room. In 1933 I was offered the headship of the Classics Department in United (formerly Wesley) College and welcomed the opportunity to concentrate again on those earlier studies and to cross-fertilize them with English. In the summer of 1940, I entered on an eight-year period as head of the English Department at McMaster University, and the cross-fertilization continued.

As I shall explain more fully in another chapter, I had expanded my library in 1925–1930 to include all of the languages of Europe and a few more remote tongues such as Hebrew, Egyptian, Persian, Arabic, Turkish, and Chinese. One whole bookcase housed over eighty big dictionaries in sixty languages. In another were an almost equal number of grammars. Sets of phonograph records (Linguaphone and American Army) in a dozen languages, ranging from Icelandic and Magyar to Russian and Hebrew, gave phonetic actuality to my studies. Through friendship with Edward Sapir and Roland G. Kent, I became a member of the Linguistic Society of America and gained a sharpened perspective of linguistics as a world-wide science. For several years running, the most interesting contributions to the Society's journal, *Language*, were the continual instalments of E. H. Sturtevant's decipherment of ancient Hittite, a by-product of one of the twentieth century's most dramatic discoveries of linguistic archaeology which had demonstrated in the cuneiform archives of the Hittite kings at Boghazkeui the existence of four extinct languages—the Indo-European Hittite and Luish and the non–Indo-European Khattish and Khurrish. Only the Ventris decipherment of Cretan Linear-B could compare with it in importance. Two life-long friends and correspondents of mine, in the linguistic field were A. R. Nykl of Harvard and Father Wilhelm Schmidt, of Vienna, both now dead. Nykl was a prodigiously erudite Czech scholar who had a speaking and writing knowledge of seventeen languages, ranging from Japanese to Arabic. His most fundamental work dealt with the influence of Arabic prosody on the rise of troubadour poetry in Spain and southern France. From Father Schmidt's monumental *Sprachfamilien und Sprachenkreise der Erde* I first learned, about 1925, that there were some 1,500 distinct languages in the world, shredded out into at least 30,000 dialects, and that modification of a word's meaning may be effected not only by suffixes (as in Latin) but also by prefixes (as in Khattish), by a wilderness of compositional elements (prefixes, suffixes, and infixes) in agglutinative languages such as Basque, and even by syntax without any inflectional change, as in modern Chinese. In this setting, the comparative grammar of August Schleicher began to appear as a paltry treatment of only one among many possible aspects of human language throughout the world.

My lifetime has seen scholars fantastically active in various sciences of language—structural, semantic, and basically philosophical. As these several disciplines have sharpened their techniques and built up their pyramids of erudition, I have been steadily alienated in sympathy by the sheer dehumanization of their subject matter.

It was probably Otto Jespersen who first taught me to recoil from the ponderous lumber room of Sanskrit inflection, where shades of meaning rendered elsewhere by a mere particle or a modal verb were crystallized out in huge, intricate paradigms of strange moods (benedictive, precative, potential), or in causal, desiderative, and frequentative verbal forms. The vast machinery of early Indo-European accidence and phonology was seen to be like Blackfoot, hopelessly redundant in morphology as compared with supple analytical languages like modern English, where parts of speech are determined by the human use of words and not by the fiat of the dictionary-maker. The monumental skeleton of *Tyrannosaurus Rex* was rejected in favour of the lithe little lizards of a later age.

Professor R. A. Wilson, of the University of Saskatchewan, who had sat like me at the feet of John Watson of Queen's, produced in his time an interesting thesis (based on Plato and Kant) that human language bears stamped upon it the signatures of space and time and the various Kantian (or Aristotelian) categories of comprehension. In more recent days, Benjamin Whorf, lyric over Amerindian linguistics, has declared that "the Hopi language and culture conceal a metaphysics such as our so-called naive view of space and time does, or the relativity theory does, yet a different metaphysics from either." When some of his contemporaries go on to explain that "metalinguistically considered the several episemes of the episeme me of the morpheme 'democracy' give insights into as many different philosophies of politics in modern thought," one begins to wonder if a comparatively simple idea is being blown up by jargon into a gas-balloon of system. At any rate, this is one of the most active battle fronts and the end is not yet. Whorf may be right in assuming that "we dissect nature along lines laid down by our native languages," but whether the differences are substantial and each one experimentally profitable in a cultural pluralism of equal values is something else again.

I may have found structural philology increasingly dreary as a formal discipline, an intricate and laborious pseudo-mathematics. The case has been even drearier with the semanticists and the logicians. I ploughed through Ferdinand de Saussure's *Course in General Linguistics*, Ludwig Wittgenstein's *Philosophical Investigations*, and N. L. White's *The Concept of Language*. I found scope symbols borrowed from Whitehead and Russell's *Principia Mathematica.* I trudged ever deeper into an arid wilderness of pragmatics and semantics. Wittgenstein might talk brightly about exploring "the sinews of language"—and at such a metaphor a lover of literature might dream of organic phrases poised for imaginative action, only to find the sinew-analysts going beyond histology to microscopic anatomy and cytology. They murder to dissect. It may betray a lack of scientific rigour in my poor brain, but I have turned aside again and again from the dusty deserts of pure linguistics in order to revel in the lush flora of natural languages.

Quite apart from pure literature, one recurring enthusiasm has had me botanizing for immigrant etymologies in the fat dictionaries on my shelves —Meyer-Lübke, Boisacq, Walde, Blöndal, Kluge, Gesenius, Liddell and Scott, *et hoc genus omne*. Simmering on the back burner for over thirty years has been a formidable research project in this discipline. I planned it as a very large volume, to be entitled *History in Human Vocabulary*, in which the borrowings of a number of languages throughout their recorded history would be used to reveal the cultural significance of their international contacts. Thus I dredged my way through Greek lexicons of the Ancient, Byzantine, and Modern periods, sorting out upon thousands of slips the sources of all non-Hellenic words. A by-product of this labour was a lengthy paper on "History in Greek Vocabulary" that I read before Section II of the Royal Society and published in the *Transactions* for 1948. Of peculiar interest were the borrowings from pre-Greek Mediterranean tongues (*wine, olive, hyacinth, cypress, narcissus*, etc.), from Egyptian (*pyramid, acacia, ebony*, etc.), from Semitic tongues (*balsam, nard, crocus*, etc.), from Latin after the Roman capital was moved to Byzantium (*augur, centurion, dormitory*, etc.), and from Turkish after the Moslem conquest (*vizier, pasha, fez*, etc.). I had already published a briefer glimpse at Latin's borrowings, set forth in the *Manitoba Arts Review*, and a detailed study of Icelandic etymology in the *Icelandic Canadian*. I had gathered the raw materials for similar essays on Magyar and Rumanian. As a sort of grab bag, I issued in 1952 a monograph on *English Loan-words in East European Languages*. Rather more specialized is my *Toponymy and Cultural Stratification in Canada* (Winnipeg, 1954).

Wittgenstein may have affirmed in his *Tractatus* that "the frontiers of my language mark the frontiers of my world." To the school of semantic analysts this may imply that these frontiers should be rigorously defined and belligerently defended; in other words, that meanings should be sharpened as nearly as possible to the exactness of the syllogism and the mathematical sign. For a mere man of letters a very different sermon could be preached on the same text, stressing the importance of pushing out one's frontiers to a maximum depth, so as to deepen one's imagination and one's taste. Spread wide in the literature of the Western world is a record of the triumphs of great writers and thinkers in their conquest of the inadequacies of their native tongue in expressing difficult or unfamiliar ideas. Aristotle in the history of logic and science and Shakespeare in his great coinages in poetic diction (for example, "the multitudinous seas incarnadine") are among those who have thus extended the boundaries of human expression. By going beyond a single language, moreover, one becomes aware of strictly untransferable resources—as in the Greek participle or in the delicately varied array of diminutives in Ukrainian and Russian.

Anyone cognizant of the brevity of life and the intense and kaleidoscopic range of artistic experience available in many great literatures may perhaps be pardoned for at last turning his back on linguistic science and seeking to enjoy and to share with others the poetry of the West, or, to alter the figure, for abandoning the semantic spit and polish boys on their barracks square and joining in the jungle warfare of living literature.

> Grau, treuer Freund, ist alle Theorie,
> Und grün des Lebens goldner Baum.

I am sometimes asked for an explanation of my working familiarity with so wide a range of tongues. That languages usually come in families—Slavonic, Germanic, Romance, and the like—means that the mastery of one or two trunk languages in each family gives one an easier entry into several sibling variants. It is comparable to the modulations of a standard game in draughts—Ayrshire Lassie, Bristol Cross, and their sisters. In working up, or refreshing, my grasp of a language, I have also made heavy use of foreign language records in order to immerse myself in a tide of sound and syntax. Apart from this, my self-scrutiny can recall no pedagogical gimmick or any freak psychological gift from Pentacost. I have been fortunate, of course, in having an acute visual memory, intense powers of concentration, and intellectual enthusiasms that never seem to abate. The rest has been hard work and a rigid rationing of my time for the past sixty years. When each unforgiving minute is filled with a ruling passion, the hours and the years add up to a surprising total.

5

Original Verse

MY ORIGINAL VERSE runs to nearly 1000 pages, the more important moiety of which appeared in 1965 as *Centennial Tales and Selected Poems.* As to when the poetic sap first began to run, I cannot say that "I lisped in numbers, for the numbers came"; yet the enthusiasm for verse arrived very early indeed. When I was still a small boy, my grey-bearded maternal grandfather, a pillar of the local Methodist church, paid me a cent a stanza for memorizing Isaac Watts's *Divine and Moral Songs.* Every Sunday after morning church, under his venerable supervision, I laboriously copied out on foolscap in pen and ink the pages that I had mastered during the previous week. Then the stanzas were counted and the little workman, "with shining morning face," received his wages. From an entire volume thus committed to memory, I gained considerable cash, indelible recollections of many edifying verses, and an incorrigible love of prosody. Neither of us dreamt that back of several of Watt's poems lay the fine Latin hymns of the Polish Jesuit, Kazimierz Sarbiewski (1595–1640).

My first remembered poem, a highly moral lyric on "Evening," came fully formed into my brain as I lay in bed one Sunday morning. Somewhat to my regret, I can still quote it. It stirred my ten-year-old heart but was completely without value. During high school days, I scribbled verse industriously but achieved nothing worth printing except possibly a nature sonnet that made the *Queen's Quarterly.* Light verse for family occasions was then, and always has been, a welcome occupation—its product easier to write than prose, for rhyme has heuristic value in luring the sense along into endless and unpredictable paths. The following lines open a birthday tribute on the twelfth anniversary of my sister's twins:

On August the thirteenth, Nineteen-twenty,
The Houser household sure got plenty:
A double ration of squeaky yowling,
Fat twin babies, red and howling.

Mother beamed like a cow in clover;
Father laughed as he looked them over.
"This little wart," they said, "is worth a
Name and a home. We'll call her Bertha.
This little squealer with nothing on
Looks like his uncle. We'll call him John."
So Father and Mother, nothing loath,
Looked them over, and kept them both. . . .

Another such tribute was written for the eighty-ninth birthday of one of my mother's sisters, Miss Ella Watson, of Port Hope:

I'm a terribly strict Sabbatarian;
My rules for the Day do not vary an
  'Arf inch. But avaunt!
  I'll write verse to an aunt
Who is awfully octogenarian.

Perhaps you object to my "awfully,"
And yet I employ the term lawfully
  When its mood is restricted
  To nephews addicted
To octogenarianophily.

My first published volume of original verse was *The Tide of Life*, written about 1928 and published by the Ariston Press in 1930. Horace's counsel, *nonum prematur in annum*, ought certainly to have been applied to it, with the complete suppression of most of it after that long delay. The trouble was that the greater part of the volume was experimental in the application of exotic metres to the English language: Roman and Greek stanza forms, Sanskrit, Old Icelandic, and Old Irish were drawn upon, often for measures never used before or since by an English poet. As with a cross-word puzzle in the London *Times*, one could feel pride in having arrived at any solution at all. What I only dimly realized at the time was that I had proved nothing except the intractability of English in these alien forms. Ezra Pound and T. S. Eliot might also be dragging far-fetched erudition into their verse, but they were getting away with it by keeping closer in form to the traditional measures of Western Europe and even using no form at all to bother the allusion chasers.

A very minor by-product of this same period was a chap-book entitled *Canada to Iceland* (1930), in which I paid tribute to that year's millennium of the Althing, or Icelandic parliament. In this I superimposed Icelandic rules of alliteration on poems in ancient Greek and Modern European metres, and even included two poems in Old Icelandic court measures, painfully aware that only an Icelander would realize what I was doing. Thus a poem to "Thingvellir," where the Icelanders of

A.D. 930 met at the "law-mountain" to dispense justice and legislation, began:

Silent Sinai of Iceland,
Set amidst these unforgetting
Majesties of lake and mountain,
Motionless and old as ocean,
Thronging nations thrill to see thee,
Thread today thy clefts and ledges;
Countless lips with kindling fervour
Con thy thousand years of honour!

In the biennium 1930–32, all of my literary energies were poured into a book-length original poem, *The Eternal Quest.* The bankruptcy of my publisher, Louis Carrier, had given a sudden halt to my prospective series of twenty-four 200-page volumes of my own translations from the whole range of European poetry, and the emotional river, dammed up in that channel, spilled over into a long lateral valley of original expression.

For at least three years, I had already been pondering such a work and had made most of the major aesthetic decisions. I had made a practice, moreover, of jotting down relevant ideas and possible phrases upon many hundreds of research cards for ultimate use about 1940 when I was due to gain my freedom from the great twelve-year programme of interpretation. Now it became suddenly possible to throw all this scrap iron into the furnace of poetic composition and pour out the white-hot metal into the mould of a long philosophical poem. This proposed to set forth, in more or less allegorical narratives, a search for vital human experience in keeping with twelve human types: the scholar, the scientist, the artist, the warrior, the gambler, the athlete, the capitalist, the jurist, the inventor, the lover, the physician, and the worshipper. Its ultimate length was 4455 lines, or slightly beyond the dimensions of Robert Bridges' *Testament of Beauty.*

The decision to go back to Spenserian stanzas at a time when free verse was in the ascendant was made deliberately. I disagreed with modernist friends who felt that no twentieth-century poet was worth his salt unless he pitched traditional prosody overboard and steered by the wandering stars of Mallarmé and Valéry. With some personal knowledge of most of the literatures of Europe in their original languages, I could appreciate the evocative allusions and echoes in Eliot and Pound and could build my bridges as well as the next man across the crevasses in their thought, but avant-garde techniques were useless in a long narrative poem. I therefore assayed the various metres that had served English narrative well and chose the one that was closest to my present purpose.

The poem owes to Edmund Spenser both its twelvefold structure and its stanza form. In my use of the latter, I made an intimate study of Spenser's own technique and made free—as a friendly A. E. Housman immediately noted—to shift the caesura about in the Alexandrine instead of keeping it monotonously after the sixth syllable as Shelley and Byron had decreed. I also made an earnest effort, in some of my revisions, to base my tone-colour on the vowels much more than on the consonants.

The first of the twelve divisions of the book (subtitled "The Way of a Scholar"), was published in July 1932 in the *Dalhousie Review* as "Ta Grammata," a phrase that I borrowed from Gilbert Murray's *Religio Grammatici.* Its fundamental teaching went back to Plato, although in actual design the Hall of Mirrors stemmed also from Kant's *Prolegomena.* Part II, with its exaltation of the beauty of the earth as a high good, but not the highest, contains obvious debts to Arnold, Wordsworth, and Ruskin. In Part III there is a carefully elaborated picture of the pain and evil of life, from the lowest bacterial parasites up through insects, reptiles, birds, and mammals to the agonies of a Lear or a Christ. In a Part IV that owes much to Ossian, Homer's "Nekuia," and the Gilgamish epic, the Scholar finally learns his lesson: Literature is no facile or superficial thing but an arduous task, calling for man's starkest toil. Only by his life-blood can he fully enter into the heritage of the great minds of the past. Only by toil can he perpetuate his own spirit.

A detailed commentary on all the influences behind *The Eternal Quest* could easily run to two or three hundred pages. At times the structure collapses under the weight of the erudition, and as a disclaimer of more than sporadic excellence in a book-length poem I had set a couplet from Martial on my title-page:

> Sunt bona, sunt quaedam mediocria, sunt mala plura
> quae legis hic: aliter non fit, Avite, liber.

I was heartened by enthusiastic personal letters from Laurence Binyon, John Drinkwater, Walter de la Mare, J. W. Mackail, John Buchan, George Gordon, and Louis Cazamian.

One midsummer explosion should be mentioned in passing. Having been suckled on Edward Lear's *Nonsense Rhymes*, I have always been interested in limericks. One weekend in 1932, I took a gazeteer of Manitoba and turned out one hundred limericks on Manitoba place-names. On Monday I sold them to John W. Dafoe for fifty dollars and for several weeks they appeared as a daily feature in the *Winnipeg Free Press*, the ostensible work of one "Harry Homer." As a supplement, I presently dashed off fifty more, on Saskatchewan place-names and sold them to the *Regina Leader-Post*. One or two specimens will help to explain why a pseudonym was used:

A young boxer out in Swan River
Tried courting his girl in a flivver;
    But she broke up a clinch
    That he thought was a cinch
With a wicked left hook to the liver.

A crabby old dame from Regina
Once asked for some fruit in the diner;
    When they told her that Bennett
    Had tariffs agen it,
Ten constables couldn't confine her.

A grocer in Winnipegosis
Had a son with pronounced halitosis;
    He remarked with a sigh
    As he mixed up some lye,
"Well I'm glad that I know what the dose is."

It was about that same time that I wrote two uninhibited pieces of political satire, "The Lay of Elijah" (by "Jerry Meyer") dealing with R. B. Bennett, and "The Ayrshire Muse" (by "Tam Rabson"), on the Canadian political scene in general. Both were published in the *Canadian Forum*. The former, in the style of *Hudibras*, ran to about three hundred lines. Its "Canter One: Compute the Prophet" began:

Of all the prophets raising hell
Throughout the coasts of Israel,
The loudest noise, the biggest shot,
The joker of the poker-pot
And readiest of all to guide ye
Was the great man of God, Elijah.
He was a seer of portly build
With Bashan's beef and fatlings filled,
So crammed with vitamins and victuals
That life seemed always beer and skittles.
Hard times but made his heart more staunch
And bravely amplified his paunch. . . .

"The Ayrshire Muse," on the other hand, was written in the Doric and in one of Robert Burns's favourite stanzas, and was first tried out on the brethren in one of Winnipeg's Masonic lodges. Two sample stanzas run as follows:

Auld Cloots o' Calgary ye ken
Is farst amang the sons o' men
For bleezin hot wi' tongue an' pen
    An' blastin-powder,
An' when elections come again
    He whoops still louder. . . .

But wae is me for Wullie King,
Wha's too weel fed to wark or sing;
The Fat Lad winna do a thing
    But sit on's bum
An' trust that wi' anither spring
    His turn will come.

Fifteen years later I was to fall back on the same dialect and stanza in "Holy Joe," a long satire on certain clerical "liberals":

Warst of all fools beneath the ban
O' folly is a clergyman
Wi' pinkish maggots in his pan,
    The sort we know
Fulfillin Satan's sootie plan
    As "Holy Joe".

What deil has blastit altogether
This brain o' bran, this saul o' leather?
Just name in any kind o' weather
    The Red slave-nation,
An' lak a sheep he'll start to blether
    In adoration.

Two university occasions also called for utterance in the mid-thirties. The bimillennium of the birth of the Roman poet Horace came in 1935, and I provided the University of Manitoba, on request, with a lecture for the occasion that concluded with an elaborate tribute in verse:

All, all are gone: those comrades who with laughter
Joined in your jesting and convivial mirth—
Silent their voices, and their lips thereafter
Ashes in silent earth. . . .

You only, Horace, of those friends consorted,
Passing like us to join the shadowy dead,
Still linger on in spirit where they sported,
Though centuries have fled. . . .

Two years later the University celebrated its sixtieth anniversary with a large book of essays by some nineteen of its professors. Mine, which opened the volume, took the form of a poem, "Manitoba Symphony," in four movements: Andante, Allegro, Scherzo, and Adagio. The last of these used the heroic stanza and began:

The Red Man passes like the lordly bison
That once he slaughtered with exultant cry;
Nothing endures except the dim horizon,
The vast, green steppe-lands and the high blue sky.

Assiniboine and Sioux are vanished faces,
And now the Celt and Saxon likewise wane,
Passing away and leaving other races
To rule the ancient marches of the Plain.

The pioneers depart; they yield to nations
Whose loins have not forgotten to forget;
Until our fading names and generations
Are one with Bohun and Plantagenet. . . .

The seed from which my next substantial volume, *The Flying Bull*, was to grow was a suggestion to me by the English poet, John Drinkwater, with regard to *The Eternal Quest*. "You have shown that you can write first class poetry," he said, in effect, "but there is more of Plato than of Manitoba in this volume. Why don't you make poetry out of your own back yard?" I re-read the letter and gazed out of the kitchen window at the black, soggy, rain-soaked earth, a fine Winnipeg sample of the "gumbo" of the Prairie. How in the world could one make poetry out of "gumbo?" The only conceivable rhyme was "mumbo-jumbo," and what connection had that with Western Canada? A couplet suddenly crystallized out of nothing:

And there, by heck, stood Mumbo-Jumbo,
Up to his belly in the gumbo!

But who, or what, was this strange creature with a name from the Dark Continent? And what was he doing in the prairie mud? Then was another click of unseen machinery in the depths of the subconscious, and I had all the answers. "Mumbo-Jumbo" must be a huge, black Aberdeen Angus bull, big brother to one that Sidney Smith, Walter Crawford, and I had met the previous autumn on the farm of Bert MacDonald, near Neepawa, on our way home by car from addressing teachers' conventions at Swan River and Dauphin. And a tornado had, of course, carried him from a farm near Neepawa to a slough full of gumbo near Plum Coulee. The next step was to jot down a detailed sketch of the monster, keeping in mind the half-hour lecture on the fine points of the breed that had been given us by Bert MacDonald:

His ribs were like a Roman arch;
His back was level as the prairie.

After that the poem flowed from subconscious springs as fast as I could scribble it down, and appeared in 1940 as the first in a collection of seventeen such yarns, a volume to which it gave its name. Actually twenty tales were written, but the good judgment of my publisher, W. H. Clarke, persuaded me to drop three of them as too feeble for the series.

The other sixteen tales did not emerge with quite the same suddenness, yet for the most part they were written, one each week during a period of four months. My college programme from Monday to Friday was so heavy that there was only an occasional half-hour in which I could jot down ideas, phrases, and thumbnail sketches for one of the narrative poems, things like:

Borne by a piercing autumn wind,
Grey clouds in drifting ribbons thinn'd
Across tall crags of naked stone
That shone as cold as polished bone,
And colder still behind them rose
Fantastic summits white with snows. . . .

Or of a highway in the Dust Bowl:

Like ashes on the floor of Hell,
Grey dust kept sifting ceaselessly
Across the half-hid parallel
Of buried fence and ditch, as we. . . .

Or of a frog in the Netley Marshes:

Thus waiting for the tune to hatch,
He sat there like a lifeless hummock,
And only stirred at times to scratch
A few mosquitoes off his stomach. . . .

On Saturday, however, I shut myself up in my study and wrestled with the Muse, emerging at supper time, weary but triumphant, with a completed tale to read to the family for its criticism or commendation. First I called the yarns "Manitou Tales," and then "Manitoba Tales." The present title was finally chosen by Bill Clarke from a list of seven or eight others that I excogitated at his request.

A geographical pattern is discernible, as I tried deliberately to cover most of the most typical scenery in Manitoba: the Red and Assiniboine rivers, the Netley Marshes, the pre-Cambrian Shield, the open prairie, the Drought Area, the Riding Mountains and their Slavic settlements, and the Hudson Bay coast. A second problem was to devise a plot in keeping with each geographical setting. A third was to map that plot in episodic form, so that its exposition would have clarity, rapidity, and, if possible, a definite quality of suspense. Rhyming octosyllabic verse was chosen as the vehicle throughout, and a general prologue was inserted, introducing the group of Westerners who told the stories. E. K. Brown scolded me for neglecting my opportunity to present this cross-section of Western life in similar detail to that used in Chaucer's General Prologue and to use a wide range of metres appropriate to the several characters. I can only plead that while I had thought of these possibilities I considered my whole series as too slight to bear so elaborate a structure. It seemed more important, moreover, to unify them by means of a common metre than to diversify them by seeking out a miscellaneous assortment of metres, some of them questionably effective for narrative purposes.

Some of my plots are derived from literary sources. "The Drifting Corpse" comes from a poem by Pushkin on a peasant who was similarly visited by a floating corpse to which he had refused burial. I had translated the poem from the Russian the year before and now applied it to a fratricide on the banks of the Assiniboine. "The Red River Tragedy" is the old Scottish ballad, "Helen of Kirkconnel," transposed to a Red River problem of atavism in the French-Indian cross. Readers of "The Manitoba Stonehenge" will recognize my indebtedness, in some slight degree, to the story of the three rioters in "The Pardoner's Tale" by Geoffrey Chaucer. On the other hand, the plot of "The Abandoned Farmhouse" was entirely original, apart from a suggestion by W. P. Ker that the most tragic situation was murderous conflict between close kinfolk, as father against son or brother against brother. I therefore chose *twin* brothers and set their enmity in the grim atmosphere of the Dust Bowl.

Wherever possible, I drew on my own experience. For eight months at Fort Henry, I had been "the nosey adjutant" of "The Butcher's Tale" and had myself probed the old fortress in every corner and recess in a vain search for the legendary tunnel. For two winters at Kapuskasing, I had endured the subarctic winter and had watched the morning spires of smoke from the settlement's chimneys, each one

> A slender column, pale and wan,
> Athwart the sundogs of the dawn.

A replica of a "Manitoba Stonehenge" in the Winnipeg Museum blended with my visit by air to the Red Lake gold mine to produce the setting for another tale. Five years as secretary of a visiting committee at Headingly Gaol instigated the tale of "The Jobless Gaolbird" and a glimpse of a fifteen-foot Hudson Bay whale in a store window on Portage Avenue begot the story of "The Captain's Cat." A summer in Budapest and a visit to Kolozsvár, in Transylvania, gave me the background for "The Magyar Violinist," and a description of mosquitoes in the Danubian marshes near Komarom, published in a Hungarian monthly, provided the formidable insect chorus in "Usquedunk, the Frog King." Two stories, "The Jobless Gaolbird" and "The Dynamo King," grew out of moral indignation and are therefore among the least successful in the volume. In the former, I pilloried our penal system and in the latter the cowardly juries that fail to convict the drunken young punks who murder innocent citizens by furious driving. The cursing from the altar in "The Men Who Vanished" grew out of an episode in the Catholic church in Lindsay, Ontario, in the 1840's, which I had unearthed in writing my *Victoria County Centennial History* (1921). During the decade 1930–40, we had had two girls in our home, one Ukrainian in name and the other Polish, but each with one parent from each of these two national groups, and this Canadian solution to the political enmity between their communities appears in "The Courtship of Olga Karg." Familiarity with the Icelander's pride in genealogy blended with knowledge of actual ice-floe tragedies on Lake Winnipeg to produce "The Gimli Prodigal."

A high compliment paid to the *Flying Bull* volume was the translation of the title-poem into German by P. J. Klassen and the rendering of "The Gimli Prodigal" into Icelandic by Sigurdur Julius Johannesson. But the chief recognition of *The Eternal Quest* and *The Flying Bull and Other Tales* was to come from the Royal Society of Canada. Soon after the publication of the former, Ned Pratt, Sir Charles Roberts and Duncan Campbell Scott, *facile principes* among the poets and men of letters of Section II, became so enthusiastic that they nominated me for membership. When the Nominating Committee for 1935–36 refused to include me in the year's quota because many much senior men were on the waiting list, my three poetic sponsors defiantly joined forces with Pelham Edgar and W. D. Lighthall in a personal canvass of all the other Fellows of Section II and succeeded in getting them to elect me as a "write-in" candidate, displacing one of the official nominees. I had not sought the honour and was deeply touched by their good will. When *The Flying Bull* appeared four years later, Ned Pratt, *sua sponte*, nominated me for the Society's Lorne Pierce Gold Medal in Literature, awarded "propter operam summam ad litteras patrias augendas." A hasty letter to me, dated May 6, 1942, reads in part: "When I was in Ottawa last month, I put up your name and it was accepted. Now the President has asked me to read your *Citation* and present you, which I am delighted to do." He drafted the citation himself, and it is to be found in the *Proceedings* for 1942. Stressing particularly the *Quest* and the *Bull*, he concludes: "This poetry is the effective focussing of a very full and vigorous life and is the main ground of the present award."

Up to this date, Roberts, Scott, Carman, and Pratt had been the only poets to be thus recognized by the Pierce Medal. The CBC also showed keen interest in my poetry and a dozen of my Chaucerian tales were presently read and directed by Tommy Tweed and Ben Lepkin in a long series of nation-wide broadcasts, each with appropriate background noises.

In my Western yarns, I had bidden a complete farewell to my earlier attempts—imperfectly in *The Tide of Life* and more successfully in *The Eternal Quest*—to make poetry out of erudition. As a form of recantation, I even wrote a parody on T. S. Eliot and his learnèd appendices, in which almost my entire poem was a patchwork, from my own library shelves, of some four-score high-sounding phrases from all literatures and all periods, including Chinese, Japanese, Ancient Egyptian, Hebrew, Hindi, Hungarian, Basque, Polish, Breton, and Arabic, each with its appropriate footnote. E. K. Brown, to whom I showed it, warned me, with a grin, to keep my unholy hands off the Ark. One of the less scholastic passages ran:

> But kneeling in an empty wayside Shantih,
> Poor Sweeney has gone Sadhu—Model "A"—
> His flippant scherzo soften'd to andante
> And mute the strident strings of yesterday.
> There in secluded thought encyclopedic,
> Cleistogamous with Essences of Light,
> He listens to the thunder gargling Vedic
> Up in the noisy bathroom of the night:
> Lhude sing da-DA, a learnèd note,
> And Adolf and Benito win the pot.
> But no! . . .

It was only years later that I encountered Eliot's own apology for the accident by which his erudite apparatus was included at all.

Public life, administrative duties, Milton research, and massive translation from Polish and Ukrainian left no leisure in 1940–63 for a full-length volume of further original verse. There had been two or three more narrative poems in the Flying Bull tradition: "A Western Idyll," "The Crow and the Nighthawk," and "A Rime of Glooscap," this last based on a study of all the Micmac folklore regarding the legendary god-man. There were political ballads over the suicide of Count Paul Teleki and the murder of Mihailovitch by Tito's régime. There had been more than a score of annual Christmas poems, sent out to friends. There had also been a number of lyrics for music, including the whole score of a light opera, dealt with in another chapter.

In 1963, public occasions evoked from me two blank-verse plays, *The Primordial Church of Horton*, with its setting in a pioneer Valley community in 1763, and *Let My People Go*, a tragedy in strict Greek form with its *mise en scène* before the palace of Pharaoh on the night before the Exodus. The action may take place in the fifteenth century B.C., but the conflict of human issues is equally applicable to the world of our time. Pharaoh echoes Khrushchov in his indictment of the avant-garde, while Moses is a spiritual brother of Madariaga in his insistence on liberty.

Special circumstances unleashed an unusual spurt of creative energy in 1964. On the evening of February 1, at the height of a very busy and difficult academic year, six months before my scheduled retirement at 69, I was struck down by a severe coronary thrombosis, rushed to the Wolfville hospital, doped with morphine, and placed under an oxygen tent for the night. For the next three weeks I was not permitted to feed myself, to wash my own face and hands, to toss around in bed, to read, to receive visitors, to listen to the radio, or even to raise my arms to the pillow above my head. To a man whose brain was still running at top speed, this lowering of the boom was apocalyptic in its completeness. There was danger in racing my mental engine, but how could I use it at all without hazard? The solution came in repeating to myself thousands of lines of poetry, chiefly English but also French, German, Italian, Latin, and Greek, that I had memorized in my far-off youth. Dante, Catullus, Vergil, Sophocles, Goethe, and Verlaine came back without effort, but Shakespeare led all the rest, with whole scenes from the great tragedies chanted on the radio of my mind's ear. At the end of three weeks, my consciousness was a saturated solution of "something rich and strange," and original verses of my own began to crystallize out of the succulent flux. I therefore asked the heart specialist if I might have a scratch-pad and a soft pencil to scribble down this new poetry before it slipped away into oblivion. As I was soon to be eased out into a further ten weeks of convalescence at home, the permission was cheerfully granted.

The first product of this imaginative precipitation was a series of ten light poems dealing with my hospital experiences and later published as "The Coronary Muse." More important was the blue-printing of some thirty poems, chiefly narrative, presenting episodes in Canadian history from the earliest Amerindian beginnings down to the present day, with the general title of *Centennial Tales*. For narrative purposes, I again deliberately avoided the elliptical free verse and cryptic phraseology of the contemporary "lyric" and turned to the metrical forms that had proved their capacity for sustained narration—heroic couplets, octosyllabic couplets, classical hexameters, blank verse, terza rima, ottava rima, and even ballad measure in the Macaulay style. Remembering E. K. Brown's strictures on the lack of prosodic diversity in *The Flying Bull*, I sought to use a variety of forms, each adapted to its theme. For instance, "The Quebec Conference, 1864," with its sketches of the Fathers of Confederation, found a natural prototype in Oliver Goldsmith's "Retaliation." Nothing more apt than Byron's version of the ottava rima in his "Vision of Judgement" could serve for my criticism of international folly in "All We Like Sheep." Ovid's elegiac couplet, with the melancholy finality of a weighted pentameter following each hexameter, seemed absolutely right for "The Vimy Memorial," "The Italian Campaign," and "The Canadians in Cyprus." While "The Twa Muses" owed its architecture to Burns's "The Twa Dogs," heroic couplets seemed better than octosyllabics for the critical subject matter. Similar reasoning lay behind all other choices of metre.

While only one tale ("The Man Who Wrestled the Grizzly Bear") came home with me from hospital in its final form on March 7, nearly all of the others were represented by jotted fragments of verse that were to grow into complete poems before the year was out, especially during the weeks following my official retirement in August. During May, June, and July, I had again been completely immersed in university administration.

It may be thought by some that in my devotion to narrative poetry and traditional prosody I have been an ignorant and naïve survivor of an obsolete generation. Be that as it may, my choice of matter and form has been deliberate. After a preliminary phase of Spenser study in technique (but not in content), my chief models have been Chaucer, Shakespeare, Dryden and the later Byron. All the poetries of Europe are on my shelves; I have translated into English verse some 5000 pages from a dozen languages, and my awareness of the whole contemporary field has left me unrepentent in the orthodoxy of my original poetry. I have enjoyed the verse of many of my Canadian contemporaries, from my old friend Ned Pratt to Abraham Klein, the early Birney, and the intensely personal lyrics of Raymond Souster. My decision, however, has been to follow my own bent and write narrative poetry and occasional satire. Damned if I would kowtow to the high priests of avant-garde dogma, who deny any merit to poets who will not fit their bed of Procrustes! I was writing in terms of myself and not to cater to *Poetry* and *New Directions*. The result might be present oblivion but some future archaeologist would dig me up.

There are three main streams of thought in modern European literature: Marxist, existentialist, and the analysis of personality. The socialist realism of the first has been vitiated by Party pressures and has achieved its greatest triumphs when a brief relaxation of gag-law has permitted an up-surge of inspiration—as with Maxim Rilsky and Volodimir Sosiura during World War II. An existentialist like Jean-Paul Sartre attains his most significant artistic utterance in a play like *Les Mouches*, pressured into protesting power by Nazi occupation, although a notable body of philosophical writing, as in *L'Etre et le Néant*, had already provided him with a massive metaphysic. Others find their satisfaction in "research in depth" into the human psyche, with Freud or Jung or some other mystagogue to lead them. In contemporary verse this has produced not only a free-verse shredding of subconscious moods into vivid slices but also a flood of pseudopsychological gobbets patterned after the authentic researchers. According to that wise old patriarch, Carl Gustav Jung, we are living in a time that calls for "a metamorphosis of the gods," i.e., of the fundamental principles and symbols of religion. It is questionable, however, whether the infinitesimal insights of avant-garde verse will supply the spiritual metamorphosis that Jung calls for. Some great poets may presently rise up to achieve that liberating task, but their central quality will be originality of insight and not some novel gimmicks of technique.

In the meantime, my poetry is content to find human significance in tales of action and, more occasionally, to shoot Folly as it flies. As this present book will intimate, I have touched life, both active and cultural, at a score of points; I have swum in many literatures, ancient and modern; I have even done my homework on dialectical materialism and have studied Soviet legislation in twenty years of *Pravda*; and out of the experience of a full life I am persuaded to reaffirm my adherence to positive ethics, a deep individual faith, and the great tradition in literature.

6

Verse Translation

TRANSLATION from foreign poetries into English verse has been one of the major activities of my life. Thus far I have published some twenty volumes of my translated verse (chiefly from Magyar, Ukrainian, Polish, Icelandic, Dutch, Latin, and Italian), totalling nearly 4000 pages, and another 1000 pages are sleeping in my files. The prosodic product has varied greatly in quality. For better or worse, however, it has brought me a dozen honorary degrees, chiefly in letters, from universities in Canada, the United States, Hungary, and Germany, knighthoods in Poland and Iceland, a dozen medal awards in several countries, and seventeen of my thirty-six memberships or honorary memberships in learned societies across the world (cf. Curriculum Vitae, pp. 369–371).

I drifted into this performance almost by accident. For a time, I had been interested in translation in the opposite direction and in my first year at Queen's had purchased a *Gradus ad Parnassum* to help in turning Tennyson's "Morte d'Arthur" into Latin hexameters, purely as a pastime. Early in the following year there was a sign given me, if I had only understood it. In a small class in Latin unseens, Professor Codd handed us a passage from the *De Rerum Natura* of Lucretius to turn into English prose. In fifteen minutes, I had completed the assignment and sat there, idly wondering how I might fill in the remainder of the period. How about trying blank verse, I thought, and to my pleased surprise the metre flowed from the nib of my fountain-pen almost as freely as prose. Both versions were turned in, neat and complete, but somehow I never thought of this as a special gift and eleven years were to pass before I turned again to verse translation.

The occasion which then prompted this activity was a sudden and overwhelming bereavement. Since the night of that disaster was shared with W. H. ("Bill") Clarke, later to be the publisher of several of my books, the storm and stress of our joint experience demands telling here.

On the night of July 15/16, 1925, Bill and I lay, anxious and fully dressed, on cots on each side of the entrance hallway of the Ross Memorial Hospital, Lindsay, Ontario. In an alcove down the first corridor, my young wife, having given birth at noon to twin sons, was fighting a life-and-death struggle with albuminuria and convulsions. Dr. W. H. Clarke, Bill's father, was the physician in charge, and Bill, aged twenty-two, had acted that night as his father's chauffeur. As the black, rainy night wore on, the chauffeur and the husband were given a cot apiece to lie on, although we could not sleep. At about 4.00 A.M., there came so loud and imperious a knocking at the main door, about ten feet from us, that we both rushed to open it. To our horror, there was no one there. No one, and nothing. Nothing but utter darkness and torrential rain. As we looked at each other in a wild surmise, hurried footsteps came down the corridor and a nurse summoned me to the bedside of my unconscious wife. The vain struggle was over and she died quietly a few minutes later. On such a night, perhaps, Admetus lost Alcestis and left a myth for dramatists yet unborn to fashion, but alas, there was no one to wrestle on my behalf with the dark, invisible Visitor.

A few weeks later, I returned to teach my college classes in Winnipeg, leaving my baby sons with their maternal grandparents. Our household belongings in Winnipeg were stored in the college garret. I myself took a room on the top floor of the men's residence, eighty-five steps up. In the agony of the long, lonely months that followed, I somehow turned to the translation into English of elegiac poems from other languages. It proved to be far more than an anodyne, not merely

> A sad, mechanic exercise,
> Like dull narcotics, numbing pain,

but a sublimation of emotion into English verse that in each case caught something of the artistic feeling of the original. As these versions accumulated, an audacious design took shape. I would draw on the elegiac resources of all Europe, ancient and modern, and would marshal these poems, in my own translation, as a memorial to my lost wife. Books were secured from all over Europe, and through winter nights that might otherwise have seemed interminable, I poured my grief and my linguistic zeal into the task.

Some of the hurdles to be cleared were formidable. Take a language like Basque, where "every word is spelled Solomon and pronounced Nebuchadnezzar." On closer acquaintance, it turned out to be not a formal language at all but a bundle of dialects, at least eight of them, and all completely unrelated to any other language in Europe. The only bilingual dictionaries and grammars were Basque-Spanish. I bought two dictionaries, a grammar, and three volumes of poetry; but the dictionaries were both of the Guipuzcoan dialect, the grammar was of the

Biscayan dialect, and the poetry came from Navarre. Frequently there were no lexicographical resources in English. For Slovak, Albanian, Rumanian, Lithuanian, Estonian, Serb, Romansch, and Old Irish, I had to depend on dictionaries and grammars prepared by German scholars, although for Serb I presently acquired Vuk Karadshits' big triglot *Lexicon Serbico–Germanico–Latinum.* The only available grammar of Albanian was in Italian. The best dictionary of Icelandic gave its definitions in Danish. Catalan had to be approached through its sister, Castilian Spanish. My only dictionary of Latvian was Latvian-Russian. Ukrainian I had to decipher in those days through Hrinchenko's Ukrainian-Russian dictionary; for only later came the Ukrainian-German lexicon of Kuzela and Rudnyckyj (1943) and finally, in 1955, a bulky 1173-page Ukrainian-English dictionary by Constantine Andrusyshen. The only Frisian dictionary was Frisian-Dutch. A fair knowledge of the trunk languages of Europe alone made possible what might otherwise have been an impossible task. My library today includes sixteen feet of dictionaries, most of them acquired before 1926. They are my well-worn tools.

By April 1926, completion of the volume was in sight and I wrote to Messrs. George Allen & Unwin, London, England:

Dear Sirs,—

Under the terms of our Agreement regarding my *International Aspects of Unemployment*, you were to have the first offer of my next book.

I have now in preparation the manuscript of a book that will be ready by next August; but it is of so unusual a character that I am writing in advance to learn your probable attitude towards it.

Entitled *A European Book of Elegy*, it is to be a collection of one hundred poems, predominantly elegiac in tone, chosen and translated by myself from some forty different languages, past and present. . . . The projected order of the poems in the volume is neither alphabetical nor chronological, but in accordance with a plan of emotional development, similar to that in Tennyson's *In Memoriam* yet more in harmony with the *Weltanschauung* of the twentieth century. . . .

I should be grateful if you would, in stating your attitude towards such a volume, give me at the same time your candid advice on one point. Would you think it desirable to print throughout, on opposite pages to the translations, the originals in the forty languages? . . .

Such a letter from a man known to them only as the author, on their lists, of a successful volume in economics, apparently gave Allen & Unwin justifiable doubts as to my sanity. At any rate, their answer was curt:

As you ask for our "candid advice", we will say quite frankly that we think you have undertaken too big a task. We do not believe that there is any living man so intimately acquainted with forty different European languages, past and present, as to be able to translate poems from those languages.

In the face of such incredulity, I realized that publication would be impossible until my versions had been certified by responsible authorities in the various linguistic fields. As soon as I had finished my hundred poems (now from fifty languages, if one includes the Old and Middle stages of a number of modern tongues), I sent the originals and my translations to the following scholars: Professor Nevill Forbes of Oxford University (Slavonic group), Professor Raymond Weeks of Columbia University (Romance group), Professor John Edward Lloyd and Professor Ifor Williams of Bangor (Celtic group), Professor J. G. Robertson of the University of London and Professor W. H. Howard of Harvard University (Germanic group), and Dr. W. H. D. Rouse of Cambridge (Romaic). There was a universal chorus of approval. A sample comment is that of Dr. Raymond Weeks, professor of Romance languages at Columbia and general editor of the Oxford Romance Texts:

> I am your debtor for the pleasure with which I have read this collection of brilliant translations from the Latin and Romance languages. You showed that you understood sufficiently the meaning of the originals . . . but I wonder if you, the translator, realize that these versions are genuine poems, just as you give them.

For a time, I found it hard to locate a guarantor for my Finno-Ugric group (Estonian, Finnish, Lappish, and Magyar). When I sent them to Dr. Bloomfield, professor of comparative philology in Johns Hopkins University, he replied: "I am entirely unable to help, as I have no first-hand knowledge of any of the Finno-Ugric languages. Furthermore, I know of no scholar who has." I then sent the group to Mr. Joel V. Lehtonen, president of the Finnish Authors' Society, Helsinki, who replied:

> These interesting renderings of yours have been shown to several members of the Society and other persons. There can be no question of your complete competence in matters concerning these translations. . . . Several renderings seem to be more expressive and living than the primitive text.

I could now face Allen & Unwin, or any other publisher, with equanimity, but had a heavy task of correspondence in tracking down all of the authors of copyrighted poems in a score of countries and securing permisison to publish my translations of their work. University professors and the officials of authors' associations were of the greatest assistance in this tedious though necessary task, but it was 1928 before *European Elegies* was issued by Graphic Publishers, Ottawa, without the original languages but supplemented with an essay on translation and with biographical notes on the original poets.

The response in friendly correspondence from authors and scholars in many lands fills a large file, and it would be fatuous to quote their comments in any detail. Among these correspondents were Sir Andrew Macphail, Sir Robert Falconer, Gilbert Murray, John Galsworthy, J. W. Mackail, John Drinkwater, Douglas Hyde ("An Craoibhin"), and Guido Mazzoni, secretary of the Royal Academy, Florence. Robert Bridges, penning his note in characteristically beautiful script, wrote:

I thank you very much for your kindness in sending me a copy of your marvellous book. I have read your account of poetics in the preface and was delighted to find it fully accordant with my own convictions. It is clearly put, but I do not suppose that anyone will trouble to understand it.

An open postcard from George Gordon, president of Magdalen College, Oxford, and later the University's Professor of Poetry, read: "I have been reading your book of *Elegies* for a week now, and am greatly moved by it. This postcard is the poor medium of my gratitude, sympathy and admiration."

A hand-written note from Per Hallström, secretary of the Swedish Academy's Nobel Prize Committee on Literature, added its comment:

I have to thank you for a most remarkable book, unique, I think, in its mastery of so many languages, and perhaps unique too—at least in our days—in its widespread and intense feeling for the emotional utterance of mankind. I have translated poetry myself, and have thus got some insight into the scope and problems of that art, enough at least to appreciate such a vast and difficult labour as yours.

Of the book reviews from many lands, one may cite *Die Literatur* of Berlin, Germany ("It is a memorial humanly gripping and wholly unique in character, and at the same time a work of art of rare charm.") and *Lögrjetta*, Reykjavik, Iceland ("One thing is certain. Since Tennyson achieved IN MEMORIAM, this is the most glorious wreath that any man has laid on the grave of the beloved dead.").

European Elegies had been a shock-absorber during a very painful year. It had also opened doors for me into new worlds of imaginative experience. As I put it in my preface:

In the years before, I had believed in an academic way in the common humanity of mankind. My studies in history, economics and anthropology had helped towards a fuller intellectual realization of that truth. But I remained emotionally blind to the reality until my heart, made sensitive by grief, had felt through the lyric and elegiac poetry of fifty literatures man's common perception of the sacredness of grief and the beauty of life even in its tragedy.

The keys to these new doors had been the many scores of dictionaries and grammars that I had accumulated, and the treasuries that were being opened were the library shelves of European poetry that I had begun to build up. The next question was, in what further way could I share with the English-speaking world my new experience of man's common humanity? This would-be project passed through two or three metamorphoses before it assumed its final form.

The first proposal was a colossal volume of *Occidental Poetry*, tracing its development from the Graeco-Roman, Germanic, and Celtic traditions down through the Middle Ages, the Renaissance, the Augustan period, and the Romantic movement, and illustrating it at every stage with my translations from the originals. My friend Edgar Tarr slipped me a three-hundred-dollar cheque to help in securing grist for my mill, and I recall that one of my most rewarding purchases was a huge four-volume *Antologia de Poetas Hispano-Americanos*, published in 1928 by the Royal Spanish Academy in Madrid. Academic counsel came from Dr. A. R. Nykl, of Harvard, who helped me to bridge the gap between Arabic poetry and the troubadour movements of southwestern Europe.

Much work had been done on *Occidental Poetry* when I began to think of shifting from its chronological plan to a linguistic and regional one. As a trial run on this new scheme, I published a series of six long articles ("An Outline of European Poetry") in the *Western Home Monthly*, tracing, with illustrative translations, the development of poetry in the Scandinavian, South Germanic, Romance, Northern Slavonic Celtic-cum-Finno-Ugric, and Balkan groups. In May 1929, as a by-product of the larger work, I gave a paper before the Slavonic section of the Modern Language Association entitled "The Genius of Slavonic Poetry: A Comparative Study," and this was published the following January in the *Dalhousie Review*. Another by-product was a lengthy paper on "Spanish-American Poetry," published long afterwards in the *Proceedings* of the Shevchenko Society of Sciences.

But somehow the sheer mass of my material overflowed all conceivable boundaries of a single volume or a series of articles, and I sold to a young Montreal publisher, Louis Carrier, my plan for a series of twenty-four volumes of my verse translations. Each volume would run to some two hundred pages and I was to supply two complete book-manuscripts a year for twelve years. It must be remembered, of course, that for eight months of the year I was a full-time professor, giving full measure of work to my students and translating only in the evenings, but for the fourth months of the academic vacation, I could work ten hours a day on my literary enterprises. For the whole series, a contract was duly signed on a straight ten per cent royalty basis. A "North American Book of Icelandic Verse" was to lead off the procession, because 1930 was the millennial year for the Icelandic parliament or "Althing." By May 1930, this volume was being set up in New York, for simultaneous American and Canadian editions, and a "North American Book of Magyar Verse" was completed in manuscript. The third, or Polish, volume was on the stocks.

Then came disaster. Carrier went bankrupt, one of the early casualties of the great depression. I had planned to go to Iceland along with my book, but the latter would simply not appear at all unless I paid the New York bills for printing and binding, a straight outlay of one thousand dollars. I therefore cancelled a trip that I could no longer afford, said good-bye to my Icelandic-Canadian friends on the wharf in Montreal, and shipped most of the edition on a consignment basis to Mr. Snaebjörn Jónsson, a bookseller in Reykjavik. In ten years, the edition sold in driblets at a fraction of cost, and it was obvious that the portentous twenty-four volume series was as dead as a doornail.

This Icelandic volume was to have been a model for the whole series. It began with an essay on the whole range of Icelandic verse and then gave 208 pages of translations, ranging from the pre-Christian "Hávamál" down to a lyric by Kristmann Guðmundsson (born 1902). Biographical and critical notes were prefixed to each contribution. Not least satisfying in the whole enterprise were the friendly letters that I received from most of the major Icelandic poets then alive, as I wrote to them for permission to publish my versions of their work.

I was not the only author to suffer in the Carrier crash. In July 1930, I had a letter from Sir Andrew Macphail, penned at Orwell, his Prince Edward Island retreat, saying in part: "I spent a summer day over your Icelandic poems, with pleasure and profit and with admiration of your skill, courage and industry. I observe the imprint and remind myself that "Carrier & Co." became bankrupt in May for ten thousand dollars. I have lost all my royalties."

Probably I ought to be grateful that the great translation project crashed. I may have had favourable reviews from Archibald MacMechan in the *Standard* and Kemp Malone in the *Saturday Review*, not to mention the Icelandic press in Winnipeg and Reykjavik; I may have had friendly epistles from Norse specialists like Sir William Craigie; I may even have been elected an honorary member of the Bókmentafjelag ("Society of Letters") in Reykjavik and of the Icelandic National League in Canada (and ultimately a Knight Commander of the Order of the Icelandic Falcon); but I was all too conscious that haste and an imperfect knowledge of the foreign tongues made each volume considerably inferior to even my own possible product if I could have given it the spare hours of three or four years instead of the spare hours of six months! My self-imposed programme was really preposterous and the seeming disaster of 1930 saved me from wrecking my health by adhering to a fantastic time-table.

But what was I to do with the completed manuscript of my Magyar anthology? By way of sharing its contents with the Hungarian-Canadian community, I gave my excellent friend, Béla Bácskai Payerle, permission to print most of it in instalments in his weekly paper, *Kanadai Magyar Ujság*, and in a new English monthly the *Young Magyar-American.* A small anthology, "A Magyar Miscellany," was also published in the learnèd London quarterly, the *Slavonic and East European Review*, in March 1931. A Hungarian learnèd society, the Petőfi Tarsáság, elected me to honorary membership and in November 1932 my inaugural address, *in absentia* but in Magyar, was delivered before a session in the great hall of the Academy of Sciences in Budapest. It was Lord Rothermere, a devoted friend of Hungary, who finally made publication possible. When he visited Winnipeg in 1932, I had lunch with him at the Royal Alexandra Hotel and explained my predicament. He replied with a prompt cheque for two hundred dollars to buy the paper on which to print one thousand copies of the 228-page book. Béla Payerle did all of the linotype and press work gratis, out of sheer devotion to the task. The Hungarian government itself placed orders for five hundred volumes in order to present a copy to every high school in Hungary. With these encouragements, the book, now entitled *The Magyar Muse*, came off the press in January 1933. A foreword had been contributed by Francis Herczeg of the Hungarian Academy. The scope of the volume ranged from A.D. 1400 down to A.D. 1932. Thanks to the greater time within which the manscript had been allowed to ripen before publication, its poetic quality was distinctly superior to that of its Icelandic forerunner. The verdict of the *Hungarian Quarterly*, Budapest, was reassuring:

> It is amazing with what verbal and atmospheric sensitiveness this Canadian scholar and poet has succeeded in reproducing the expressions of ancient and modern Hungarian poets. When confronted with technical, psychological, or purely linguistic problems, his translations rarely show stiltedness or lack of poetic unity.

For the next eight years, I devoted a great deal of time to Hungarian literature and to further translations from its poetry. For one thing, I worked diligently on the expansion of the *Magyar Muse* for a projected 500-page, two-volume American edition. The manuscript was completed but the publisher died untimely. More successful in appearing in print was a carefully edited translation of one of Hungary's chief epics, *The Death of King Buda*, by János Arany, published in 1936 by the Benjamin Franklin Bibliophile Society, Cleveland. Every academic precaution was taken. Béla Payerle and his wife Lulu collaborated with me on the preliminary prose draft; Joseph Szentkirályi, of the Department of English in the University of Budapest, checked my final verse draft with the original, line for line; Géza Voinovich, secretary- general of the Hungarian Academy, wrote a foreword; and Professor Árpád Berczik, of the University of Budapest, supplied copious notes. The result was a definitive English edition. Dr. Elemer Császar, professor of Hungarian literature in the University of Budapest, writing in the official journal, *Irodalomtörténeti Közlemenyek*, of the Hungarian Academy of Sciences, declared that the work was an authentic success: "The translator achieves his object with magnificent feeling. In vivid, appropriate, expressive, stirring, colorful and graphic language, classical in its perfection, he adapts himself to the style of Arany and the inner dynamic of his form of expression."

Other sparks from the Hungarian anvil were a book-length *Primer of Hungarian*, an introduction to Magyar grammar, published serially in the *Young Magyar-American*, two lengthy articles, "The Poetry of Ady" and "Quintessence of Hungary," published in the *Hungarian Quarterly*, Budapest, and a continuing series of "Magyar Miscellanies," issued from time to time in the *Slavonic and East European Review*, London. Further recognition presently came from Hungary: I was elected a corresponding member of the Kisfaludy Society (another literary academy), awarded a medal of honour by the PEN Club, invited to lecture on Hungarian poetry at the 1938 summer session of the University of Debrecen, and finally awarded the honorary degree of Doctor of Philosophy by that same university. The story of my visit to Hungary in 1938 is told elsewhere.

During this decade, following my happy second marriage in 1930, still further children had arrived to gladden my heart and cramp my opportunities for literary work. By Christmas 1936, I could refer to our children as a "vocal quartet" (a fifth child was born in 1945) and note in a Christmas poem:

Loud uproar from the cellar crashes
  In mimic warfare, wild and bloody;
A small, blue-eyed Valkyrie dashes
  Undaunted into Daddy's study;

Even wee Janet in her carriage
  At three months old is far from quiet;
It seems the chief result of marriage
  Is to beget a living riot. . . .

Dr. Ernest Fewster of Vancouver had a word of sympathy for my wife in a letter of January 7, 1937:

Poor Mrs. K.! I am glad that "Hope" is her name, with four ragamuffins pulling at her skirts twenty-four hours at a stretch and sentenced for life. I imagine that "hope" is about all she can call her own. However, please give her my warmest regards for a very happy New Year and tell her I wish her better luck in her next incarnation.

An admirable Ukrainian girl, "Domia," helped marvellously and was succeeded by an equally admirable Polish maid, "Julia," but I also took my full share in the rearing of the small Kirkconnells.

Any further activity in the Hungarian field has been sporadic. In 1947, the American Hungarian Federation, in Washington, D.C., published a *Little Treasury of Hungarian Verse*, a collection of some of my better renderings. In the summer of 1950, I turned into English about a hundred pages of the religious poetry of László Mécs, at the request of the Premonstratensian Order, of which he was a canon regular. This was duly published by the Saint Norbert Abbey Press, DePere, Wisconsin, in 1964. In 1957 my spontaneous translation of a striking poem by "Tibor Tollas" led to my meeting the man himself and to my translation of most of the "freedom fighter" anthology that he and his fellow revolutionaries of 1956 had issued as *Füveskert*. In September 1959, I was touched to receive from the Lido di Rimini, Italy, a many-signatured letter of good will from Hungarian writers who had gathered there in conference from eighteen European cities. Dr. Béla Déri, of Brussels, Belgium, headed the list. Still another enterprise, well begun but long left unfinished, was a verse translation of the epic *Toldi*, by János Arany, which I began in collaboration with Tivadar Edl, of Budapest, who presently perished in World War II. This epic I finally completed in the spring of 1967 as the opening major item in a 750-page anthology of my renderings from Magyar verse, now ready for the linotype and scheduled for publication in 1968. Three further Hungarian medals have also been bestowed on my work—a Gold Medal of Freedom from the Freedom-Fighters (New York), the George Washington Medallion of the American Hungarian Studies Foundation, and a Canadian medal from the Hungarians of Toronto.

Meanwhile, the third or Polish volume in the European series was slowly taking form—slowly because there was no great hope of publication. Fortunately I thus had ample time to receive advice from Professor Waclaw Borowy of London on the selection of fine lyrics in the modern field and assistance from Dr. Noyes of Berkeley and Dr. Dyboski of Cracow in my preparation of biographical and bibliographical notes. Dr. Borowy's superb new collection of Polish lyrics, *Od Kochanowskiego do Staffa*, was a particularly rich meadow from which to gather flowers. A "Polish Miscellany" was skimmed off for the *Slavonic and East Euro-*

pean Review in July 1935, and the quality of the work was so clearly an advance on that in the *Magyar Muse* that the Polish Government, on the recommendation of its consul in Winnipeg, offered to contribute the price of five hundred copies if an edition of one thousand were printed. Thus there appeared in 1936 *A Golden Treasury of Polish Lyrics*, half the length of the Icelandic and Magyar volumes but greatly superior in technical skill. Dr. Roman Dyboski, professor of English literature in the University of Cracow, contributed a preface and a subsequent review in which he declared: "I have not seen any translations of Polish poetry into English that approach his felicity in rendering the rhythmical and melodious effect of the original in a profoundly different language without any violence done to the natural cadences and accustomed verse-forms of the language itself." The *Warsaw Weekly*, in another review, spoke of its "rare surprise and pleasure to find poems shining with polished brilliance, from the exquisite passages done from Kochanowski and Morsztyn, through the pregnant and unexpected figures of Norwid, to Tuwim's intense longing." Polish national appreciation expressed itself in two awards—the Silver Laurel of the Polish Academy of Letters and a Knighthood in the Order of Polonia Restituta. Election to membership in the Polish Institute of Arts and Sciences in New York, in the Kosciuszko Foundation, and in the Polish Institute in Brussels, Belgium, were to come later, along with honorary membership in the University of London's School of Slavonic Studies.

Since that time, I have twice returned to work on Polish literature. In the summer of 1936, George Rapall Noyes, of the University of California, had struck a log jam in his preparation of a large volume of translations by several hands from the work of Poland's chief poet, Adam Mickiewicz (1798–1855). Some forty pages were still untranslated from *Dziady*, "Forefathers' Eve," Part III, and he besought me to come to the rescue. A month at a summer cottage in Ontario was devoted to this assignment; the English verse was duly mailed to Berkeley; and the 486-page volume, comprising all of Mickiewicz's non-epic poetry, ultimately appeared in New York with the imprint of the Polish Institute of Arts and Sciences in America. In 1951 a further challenge was offered to me. The year 1955 was to be the centennial of the death of Mickiewicz. His poem *Pan Tadeusz* (published in 1834) is the greatest national epic of modern Europe. Noyes had himself prepared a prose version forty years ago but a new verse translation, using the heroic couplets of the original, would be a glorious tribute to the poet's centenary. The new rendering was to be made by Noyes and Kirkconnell. But alas, the epic ran to 9843 lines or something more than the length of *Paradise Lost*. As a university president, I had no time available for such a task except the one summer month (July) that was supposed to be my "vacation." For three such Julys, I toiled at my task—even to working ten hours a day on board ship in crossing and recrossing the Atlantic in July 1953. The best that I could do was three books out of twelve, or one-quarter of the total. If I had not given the winter nights of three years to the single-handed preparation and editing of an *Acadia Record of Graduates (1838–1953)*, containing the potted biographies of some eight thousand former students of the University, I might conceivably have finished the epic on schedule. A line of verse takes much less time to write than the life history of an alumnus.

There was destined to be a sequel, however. In 1958, I had been goaded almost to the point of apoplexy by what I felt to be venomous and unfair personal attacks on me over the CBC and in the columns of two Toronto newspapers. This exasperation now supplied the emotional drive to push me into a desperate resumption of my abandoned *Pan Tadeusz* project. Noyes was dead; I was now on my own, but a sort of frenzy drove me on in every spare moment for the next three years. New auspices, moreover, had made publication realistic. The impending millennium of the founding of the Polish state made it seem fitting to the Canadian Polish Congress and the Polish Institute of Arts and Sciences in America to underwrite the publication of my book as a tribute to their motherland's millennial year. Mr. G. H. Southam, Canadian Ambassador to Poland, contributed a generous personal cheque towards the cost of the Canadian edition. Dr. William J. Rose of the University of British Columbia agreed to supply a historical introduction and Dr. H. B. Segel of Columbia a revised set of notes. My Acadia colleagues, Dr. Konstanty Rayski-Kietlicz and Dr. Adam Gillon read through my entire manuscript and made valuable suggestions. A six-man fly-speck reading panel, supplied by the Polish Institute, also made a line-by-line check of my translation with the original Polish. In the background, President and Mrs. Arthur P. Coleman, of Alliance College, kept making enthusiastic noises. The big volume, Englished as some 12,572 lines in heroic couplets, was finally published simultaneously in New York and Toronto in 1962. Its finest reception was in the *Times Literary Supplement*, of London. In due course, I was made an honorary life member of the Canadian Branch of the Polish Institute and was brought to New York for a one-man programme in honour of my translation.

There have been many minor enterprises. In 1936, I furnished the English for eight songs in a songbook published by the Church of All Nations in Toronto. In 1937, there were several translations from Romansh in a paper on "Rhaetoromanic Literature" that I contributed to the *Transactions* of the Royal Society of Canada. In 1947, I collaborated with Paul Crath in turning the Old Slavic epic, *Prince Ihor's Raid against the Polovtsi* into English—a version that Dr. Clarence Manning, then chairman of the Slavonic Department at Columbia, rashly said deserved "to be ranked with Fitzgerald's 'Omar Khayyam' . . . and included in any anthology of great translations into English."

One of my major projects in verse translation lies in the field of Milton studies and will be given a chapter to itself (Chapter XVII). Instalments of the work already published are *The Celestial Cycle* (1952, 728 pp.) and *That Invincible Samson* (1964, 218 pp.), both issued by the University of Toronto Press with financial assistance from the Humanities Research Council of Canada. The former (dealing with 329 analogues of *Paradise Lost*) includes my translations of a Latin play, two Italian plays and two Dutch plays, and portions of four epics in Latin, Old English, and Italian; the latter (dealing with 107 analogues of *Samson Agonistes*) involves my translations from three plays in Latin, one in Italian, and one in Dutch. Analogues of *Comus, Lycidas*, and *Paradise Regained* are still on the anvil.

The most redoubtable enterprise of all lies in the field of Ukrainian studies. It may be most succinctly introduced by setting down some paragraphs from an address that I delivered in Winnipeg on September 5, 1964, following a dinner at which I received a large bronze Shevchenko plaque prepared by the sculptor, Leo Mol:

> Permit me at the outset to thank the Ukrainian Canadian Committee for this marvellous banquet that they have given in honour of the Andrusyshens and the Kirkconnells. I am also grateful for the generosity with which they adopted and financed our large anthology of Ukrainian poetry in addition to the definitive edition of all of Shevchenko's Ukrainian verse.
>
> The full story of how we came to be involved in these colossal tasks has never been told, and Mr. Kochan has suggested that I tell it to you this evening. A sequence of dates is significant.
>
> On the 10th of March, 1961, I had given a public address in Edmonton on the centenary of the death of Taras Shevchenko. Flying back to Nova Scotia the next day, I stopped for a few minutes at the Saskatoon airport for a chat with my old friend and pupil, Professor C. H. Andrusyshen, and I learned that, while his big Ukrainian-English dictionary had been published in 1955, he was not at the moment engaged in any major literary project. On the 19th of March I therefore made bold to invite him to collaborate with me in preparing an anthology of Ukrainian poetry in English translation. On the 3rd of April, he accepted my invitation. On the 10th of May, the Ukrainian Canadian Committee rather took my breath away by asking me to prepare a translation of all the Ukrainian poetry of Shevchenko, this for publication by May 1964. I consulted at once with Dr. Andrusyshen, as to whether we might perhaps substitute this project for the Anthology. He wrote back that for the Ukrainians of North America the Anthology was even more important than a complete English *Kobzar*. He was willing, however, to undertake *both* volumes with me. I hesitated, for I was swimming in the galley-proofs of my English verse translation

of *Pan Tadeusz*, by Adam Mickiewicz, a large undertaking that I had only recently completed, and I would not be free to start on any Ukrainian manuscript before July 1961.

In a spirit of reckless idealism, however, I finally agreed with him to undertake the double task. Mentioning nothing about the Anthology, I wrote to the Ukrainan Canadian Committee on June 14th, consenting to translate the Shevchenko on two conditions: first, that Dr. Andrusyshen should be my collaborator, and second, that the Committee should type out the Ukrainian text of the entire *Kobzar* for us, triple-spaced, so that Dr. Andrusyshen might more readily supply me with an interlinear English version. Time-saving devices were of supreme importance.

On July 1st, 1961, at a summer cottage in Ontario, I began on the Anthology, starting with an excellent English version of the *Slovo* on which my partner had already been working. Fifteen months later, in September 1962, the monumental double task of translation was completed and we divulged to an astonished Committee that we had *two* large books for their consideration instead of one. The combined manuscripts totalled some 1500 pages, typed double-spaced, later printing as 1144 pages, or considerably more than the *Iliad* and the *Odyssey* combined. There remained a scholarly checking of both manuscripts by Mr. Sviatoslav Hordynsky and our meticulous revision of certain passages in the light of his suggestions, especially in the *Slovo*, and those of some of his consultants—Mrs. Hordynsky, Bohdan Boychuck, Yuri Tarnawsky, Patricia Kylyna, and Bohdan Rubchak.

I ought to emphasize the fact that I had more than a full-time job quite apart from this task of translation. I was the chief executive officer of a famous old university that trebled its enrolment and its budget during my sixteen years as president and added five large buildings to a previous thirty at a cost of three and a half million dollars. I also taught two advanced courses in English in the spring term of 1962. The only way in which I could render any literary service to the Ukrainian people was by working a 70-hour week. My vacation each year was limited to the month of July and during those thirty-one days of freedom from administrative duty I toiled on translation for ten hours a day. It is to be feared that the coronary thrombosis from which I am now convalescent was not unconnected with this terrific pressure of work. Alexander Pope, with no other employment and several collaborators, took twelve years to complete an English verse translation of Homer totalling less than one thousand pages. I hope that critics of the Andrusyshen–Kirkconnell volume will keep in mind the almost intolerable load that both translators have carried.

I say "both" since Dr. Andrusyshen also had a full burden of university work apart from the tasks of translation. For our two volumes, he provided not only the basic meaning of the texts but chose the authors and selections for the Anthology and wrote introductions and biographical and explanatory notes. In the later stages of composition, he suggested revisions for all of my work and I did the same for his notes and introductions. Writing to me as he finally laid down his pen, he said: "This work, done at top speed, has left me well-nigh exhausted. From now on I shall have to take it easy, in order to regain the energy I had before I began work on the anthology."

It is most fitting, moreover, that Mrs. Andrusyshen and Mrs. Kirkconnell should have been invited to tonight's banquet, for they lived a pretty lonely life while their husbands shut themselves away in their studies, evening after evening and month after month, toiling over Ukrainian poetry and finally stumbling to bed late in the night in a state of mental and physical exhaustion. These women have also been martyrs to the Great Enterprise and were, I feel sure, grateful to have their husbands restored to them when it came to an end.

The Ukrainian Poets is vastly superior to the one-man Ukrainian anthology that I had planned for my 24-volume series back about 1930. At last I had a collaborator who was a master of the original language and literature. In our partnership, each of us was invaluable to the other. Dr. Andrusyshen chose the selections, provided me with a close and exact interpretation of the basic texts, and furnished the book with notes and an Introduction. My contribution was a facility in versification developed over fifty years and a sufficient knowledge of Ukrainian to understand the prosodic challenge of each poem as it came. The 103 poets who were included were chosen with political impartiality, those who had served the Communist state standing side by side with that larger group who had been done to death by bullet or concentration camp. With this massive anthology of over 500 pages, Ukrainian literature, on the poetic side, may at last come of age for the English reader.

Much less diversity but comparable interest is to be found in the 614-page edition of all the Ukrainian poetry of Taras Shevchenko (1814–1861), generally acknowledged as the greatest poet of his nation. Born a serf but set free at the age of twenty-four, he became an artist (ultimately an academician) and a poet. His fulminations against the Tsar's enslavement of his people, individually and as a nation, earned him ten years of military penal servitude in the remote east. When he returned to St. Petersburg in 1857, he was a broken man, although flashes of the old poetic brilliance still appeared before his untimely death. More than any other Slavic poet, he has been acclaimed by all Ukrainians, nationalist or Communist, as the prophet of his people's freedom, an incomparable blend of Lincoln, Uncle Tom, and Harriet Beecher Stowe.

To have shared for fifteen months in the recreation of these two volumes in English verse was a deeply moving experience. To set forth the ruling passion that has dominated my whole metamorphic endeavour over the past four decades, I cannot do better than reprint a few declaratory sentences from the Preface to my *North American Book of Icelandic Verse* (1930):

On this North American continent I find folk of all the stocks and traditions of Europe; I find, too, that barriers of language make for grave misunderstanding and misjudgment on the part of all citizens, "old" and "new"; I disagree profoundly with those who would hack off completely all roots of European culture and then hew the mutilated trunk into conformity with some arbitrary nationalistic pattern; I believe rather that the perpetuation of the finest elements of Old World culture will incalculably enrich the life of the New World. This is the corner-stone of my venture. North Americans of Welsh or Scottish extraction are not worse but better citizens when they can still proudly drink from the springs of their ancestral literatures. Shall we not likewise seek to cherish the magnificent literatures that are the heritage of nearly every European stock?

A man, the sheer bulk of whose verse translations exceeds eight *Iliads* or fifteen *Aenids*, has presumably thought out some working principles in the course of his labours. I may therefore be forgiven if I briefly expound the rationale of my task as I see it.

Each age has its own fashions in translation. A fair statement of the old orthodoxy was the *Essay on the Principles of Translation* read in 1790 to the Royal Society of Edinburgh by Alexander Fraser Tytler, Judge-Advocate of Scotland. Its major postulates were that (*a*) the translator must not omit any part of the original, (*b*) the style and manner of the translation must reproduce those of the original, though not necessarily in an identical metre, and (*c*) the translation should have all the ease of original poetry. These requirements were important in this order, but all three should be sought after.

For the past fifty years, however, the avant-garde of the English-speaking world has preached a wholly different gospel of translation, based on the practice of Mr. Ezra Pound. As one of his disciples, Mr. Donald Davie, has recently phrased it: "We must understand 'translation' in its widest and loosest sense, as covering all the activities variously described as imitation, adaptation, sustained allusion, paraphrase." In this new school, Tytler's first two principles are tossed out of the window and the primary aim is to produce a substantially new poem, demonstrating the brilliance of the "translator" but not necessarily reproducing the meaning or the manner of the "original." Apart from Italian, Mr. Pound's knowledge of foreign languages, ancient and modern, seems to be rudimentary. Thus in his well-known chorus from *The Women of Trachis* he mauls Sophocles' text unmercifully. In the Greek, at dawn the dying Night gives birth to the Sun and lays the blazing Baby in his cradle. Pound, however, has the Sun "slay and lay flaked Night upon her blazing pyre." In such alleged translations, any resemblance to the actual words of the original is purely accidental. As proof that he cannot even quote correctly or intelligently, he gives Hadrian's famous "Animula vagula blandula" as "Blandula, tenulla (*sic!*), vagula." In spite of all this, in poem after poem his verse takes on a vitality, wholly his own, that has been one of the delights of our age. But one must modulate Richard Bentley and say: "A pretty poem, Mr. Pound, but you must not call it Sophocles—or Sappho—or Rihaku—or Ibycus."

As an introduction to my *European Elegies* (1928), I printed a lengthy essay on verse translation as I then understood it. The final paragraph summed up my theories:

> The translator must cope with a complex incantation of verbal cadences in another language; he must consider the meaning and the imaginative significance of the original; and above all he must seek to communicate the power of emotional experience. The deficiencies and idiosyncrasies of English render the adequate reproduction of the incantation almost impossible; a literal rendering of phrase and figure may result in dish-water insipidity; but if the translator is inspired with the emotion of the original, or better still reinforces it with analogous experience of his own, he can trust to the genuine sincerity of his emotion to produce work of value.

This was obviously close to Tytler's triad of rules and stressed the importance of conveying the prosodic pattern, the meaning, the style, and the emotional force of the original. With the exception of extracts from Latin, Greek, and Anglo-Saxon, I used the poet's metre and stanza form. By consulting half a dozen outstanding scholars, I made sure that the meaning was fully and accurately rendered. And by sharing, through my own bereavement, in the mood of the hundred elegies, I succeeded, to a fair measure, in passing along the emotional voltage of the original.

My next 500 pages of translation after the *Elegies* proved the least satisfactory of all my work and most of it remains unprinted. The impulse of kindred emotion was gone, and in any case I had come to realize that emotion was not enough. I was therefore, by incessant application, learning the technique of English prosody, especially through a study of Chaucer, Spenser, Shakespeare, Dryden, and Byron, but most of it was still journeyman work. Moreover, until I had acquired facility of this sort, I was the less likely to reproduce the essence of others' verse with any of "the ease of original poetry." I was discovering by the experience of the workshop that each language has its own texture, its own resources of accidence and syntax, its own genius. The technical difficulties presented by foreign poetry of all periods and all styles were a fascinating challenge, but until I had acquired considerable versatility in English prosody I could wrestle with them in only the clumsiest fashion. True to my primal practice, I still tried to reproduce the *ipsissima verba* of the original and regularly sought to have my versions checked for accuracy by first-class scholars in their several fields. I also tried to use the metres of the original poems or else some English metre of a similar character.

The nature of the problem is hinted at in my Preface to *The Poetical Works of Taras Shevchenko*, where, in the case of a poet almost entirely narrative but with intractable non-English folk-metres, I consider the rhythms and stanzas that have been most successful in English narrative verse:

Most of Shevchenko's poetry is in forms of ballad measure (the *kolomiyka* and the *koliadka*) that are virtually unknown in English and as uncongenial to it as quantitative hexameters. For that matter, even the simple Chevy-Chase metre has had small currency in English since the later Middle Ages and its use by poets like Coleridge and Southey is made tolerable only by inflated stanza-forms in "The Rime of the Ancient Mariner" or by sprung rhythm in "The Old Woman of Berkeley." The standard English narrative metres are octosyllabic couplets, heroic couplets and blank verse, with a lesser place assigned to such forms as *ottava rima*, the Spenserian stanza and the heroic stanza.

In the dramas and epics of my *Celestial Cycle* and *That Invincible Samson*, I faced a variety of problems. The *ottava rima* of Valvasone's *L'Angeleida* slipped naturally into my own, but the French-style heroic couplets of Vondel's *Lucifer*, *Samson*, and *Adam in Ballingschap* found greater freedom in blank verse in English. Since the important Latin play, *Adamus Exul*, by Grotius, was to be printed facing a line-for-line English version, I found that the only English metre that would exactly contain the full meaning of each iambic senarius was the "free Alexandrine," popularized by Robert Bridges in his *Testament of Beauty*. The dialogue in Latin plays by Zieglerus, Wunstius, and Rhodius and in Italian plays by Andreini and Salandra—unhampered by the line-for-line requirements—went freely into blank verse, permitting rhymed stanzas to be reserved for the choruses. Giattini's Italian oratorio, *Il Sansone*, however, was so involved in its rhyming incantation that I fell back on line-for-line free verse. In three Latin epics, by Avitus, Ramsey, and Masenius, respectively, I rejected their dactylic hexameter (never really acclimatized in English) in favour of blank verse. A footnote to my English version of the Old English "Caedmonian *Paradise Lost*" gives a revealing glimpse into the problems of the workshop:

In my translation, an attempt has been made to adapt the old alliterative line to the much less inflected character of Modern English and to the acquired habits of modern prosody. Thus, while preserving the strict rules of alliteration, the lines have been made more predominantly dactylic and anapaestic rather than trochaic and iambic, in order to accommodate the sense to a more analytic language. A much greater uniformity of rhythmic pattern is also maintained; inversions and archaisms have been avoided as much as possible, and the hemistitch-gap has been omitted in printing, as presenting the modern reader with a very real hindrance to free reading and appreciation, a sort of disconcerting visual hiccup in the centre of each line.

Yet another glimpse of the poet-translator facing the problems of prosody may be found in the Preface to my version of János Arany's Magyar epic, *The Death of King Buda*:

Here I did not feel free to choose any form at will, with a view only to absolute suitability to the narrative, for while the utmost liberty is conceded to the translator of Greek and Latin, he who renders modern European verse into English is commonly censured if he deviates widely from the verse-form of his original. Homer may be recast in blank verse, heroic couplets or Spenserian stanzas; but it would fare ill with the man who turned Goethe's *Faust* into free verse or Hugo's *Les Châtiments* into *ottava rima*. On the other hand, the original Magyar of *Buda halála* employs such quatrains as have in English little standing and less efficacy, viz., a mere sequence of two closed iambic couplets. In Hungarian the effect is dignified, simple and somewhat archaic, as befits an epic on a primitive theme. In English the form is adulterate and ambiguous—neither honest quatrains nor good continuous heroic verse in couplets. It would, of course, be possible, by printing Arany's cantos without stanzaic division, to produce a false semblance of continuous heroic couplets; but as Arany has clearly organized his thought in four-lined stanzas, my obvious solution was to preserve the stanzaic form but to alter the rhyming scheme to a-b-a-b instead of a-a-b-b. The result is the old "heroic stanza," to whose suitability for epic narrative John Dryden long ago paid tribute in his foreword to *Annus Mirabilis*: "I have chosen to write my poem in quatrains or stanzas of four in alternate rhyme, because I have ever judged them more noble and of greater dignity both for sound and number than any other verse in use among us." I have, however, permitted myself, contrary to Dryden's precept, the occasional use of feminine rhyme, especially in dialogue. The result, I trust, will be found not unpleasing.

An interesting encounter with the "Ezrapoundite" school of "adapters" came in connection with my translation of the volume of Magyar Freedom-Fighter poems, *Füveskert* ("Grassy Lawns"), first published in Vienna in 1957. My manuscript version, totalling about ninety typed pages, was passed along to Tibor Tollas, the spokesman of the group, in July 1958. Steps were taken by his friends and mine in the United States to raise funds to publish this English edition, and one of its chief sponsors in Washington, Mr. E. C. Rowan, wrote to thank me for my "singular service in bringing us this rich and moving verse." In 1959, there were hints that left-wing liberals were trying to move in on the deal. In April 1964, the picture came into focus. A covey of "Ezrapoundite" American adapters, to whom scholarly accuracy in translation was wholly reprehensible, were using my manuscript as raw material for their own free declamations. When the volume was finally published in April 1966 as *From the Hungarian Revolution*, I found that not one of my translations was included. On the contrary, the editor, a young college professor, had limited the book to a score of bright young avant-garde poets and their "adaptations," a crop of vivid little toadstools of improvisation, saprophytic on the buried timber of my faithful renderings of the original. It may be that only thus could the basic principles of avant-garde "translation" be faithfully carried out. I could not help feeling, however, that the volume was not so much a tribute to the Freedom Fighter poets and their verse as a monument to the eager virtuosity of disciples of Ezra Pound.

7

Canada's Unseen Literatures

ONCE UPON A TIME two groups of fishermen seined the waters along the coasts of Utopia. One group used a great trawl and caught an abundance of cod; the other group favoured a purse-seiner and got vast quantities of herring. Neither breed of fish was particularly large, but they were both caught in such numbers that men deemed them the only fish of the area. One day, however, a scuba-diver prowled the shallows of the continental shelf and found salmon, halibut, tuna, swordfish, redfish, flatfish, mackerel, and haddock. The waters off the shore were actually alive with the greatest variety of first-class food.

When I settled in Winnipeg in 1922, no one in Canada seemed to have heard of any literatures except those in English and French. Historians and critics of Canadian letters mentioned no others. These were the only annual catch. At Wesley College, however, I found Icelandic colleagues and students, and a section of the library given over to Icelandic literature, written both in Iceland and in Canada. Two Icelandic weeklies, both published in Winnipeg, were spangled with lyrics by Canadian Icelanders, and the *Tímarit* of the local Icelandic National League was rich in creative literature. Thus arose the odd circumstance that I came to know Icelandic poetry first in its North American incarnation. To climax all this, the little subarctic republic, seeking in 1930 to celebrate the millennium of the Icelandic Parliament, issued in Reykjavik a monumental 730-page anthology of Icelandic verse and prose (lyrics, plays, fiction, and essays) written "from the west over the sea" and hence entitled *Vestan um haf*. Closer acquaintance with Winnipeg's Magyars, Ukrainians, Poles, Swedes, Norwegians, Germans, Greeks, and Italians made me aware that still other linguistic communities among Canada's newcomers were creating considerable literatures, each in its own ancestral tongue. I therefore proceeded to build up a polyglot Canadian bookshelf, chiefly in poetry. Next, I sought out all of the poets themselves, personally or by questionnaire, and accumulated a file of biographical and bibliographical information.

Presently, in 1935, I published in Winnipeg at my own expense a volume of *Canadian Overtones*, "an anthology of Canadian poetry written originally in Icelandic, Swedish, Norwegian, Hungarian, Italian, Greek and Ukrainian, and now translated and edited with biographical, historical, critical and bibliographical notes." The book included the work of fifteen Icelanders, five Swedes, one Norwegian, three Hungarians, one Italian, one Greek, and seventeen Ukrainians, and covered a time-span from 1900 to 1935. My expressed hope was that "these new Canadian poetries, themselves the 'overtones' of our national literature, may assist in preserving the overtones of our national experience by awakening or preserving in our manifold racial strains an awareness of something sprung from their own blood that can be at once a glory to their fathers and an inspiration to their children's children."

This volume had a twofold sequel. One was my series of critical articles on individual Icelandic poets in the *University of Toronto Quarterly* and the *Transactions of the Royal Society of Canada*. The other was an invitation from the then editor of the *Quarterly*, Arthur Woodhouse, to contribute an annual review of "New-Canadian Letters" to the *Letters in Canada* survey of each year's books. Since my first such essay, in 1937, included the whole period 1935–37, so as to go back to the same *terminus a quo* as the comprehensive survey, I have now covered almost all Canadian publications in languages other than English and French for a period of thirty-one years. The one serious omission has been Yiddish, where my competence is too limited to be of much value. The customary annual chore now involves reading about 70 books—usually in Icelandic, German, Magyar, Czech, Polish, and Ukrainian—and my private library of such Canadian books has accumulated to a total of about 2000 volumes. In my will this collection, together with all my files, has been bequeathed to Acadia University.

As of 1966, some four million Canadians have European homelands other than France and the British Isles. With nearly all of these there has been a brief period in which those of the first generation among us have embodied their experiences, tragic and moving, in the form of literature. As long as fresh migration from the homeland continues, Canadian authors have continued to write in the tongues of Pentecost. The Icelandic chapter, after more than sixty years, is nearly at an end. The stream of Ukrainian, Czech, and Magyar authorship is still in full flood. Taken together, these minor literatures present an unrivalled picture of the human predicament, of lives uprooted from a far country and planted afresh with difficulty in Canadian soil. Perhaps the one thing for which I shall be remembered a century hence will be that single-handed I discovered, surveyed, and recorded in Canada's cultural

Registry of Deeds this diverse collectivity of literary achievement, revealing as it does a major factor in the life of the New World.

For economic reasons, the first medium of publication in each group has been the vernacular press. Pioneers are poor; there are no professional book publishers in Canada other than English and French; and therefore, although the literary activity of many of these newer communities has been prodigious in extent and often authentic in value, the vast bulk of it has appeared only in upwards of one hundred foreign-language weeklies and annuals. Sometimes such poems by a single author will be collected and issued in book form, poorly printed and flimsily bound, at the poet's expense, by the same printing shop that issued the newspaper. The very public for whom he writes will likewise be poor and exceedingly limited in number. The part of the iceberg projecting above the arctic waters will be very small and unimposing. For several years, before the editor of the *University of Toronto Quarterly* reduced me to books only, I was reporting annually on the foreign language press, as well as books, and checking through 52 weeklies, quarterlies, and annuals in 17 languages in search of literary contributions. This gave a more accurate picture of cultural activity but was an excessive invasion of my time and of space in the *Quarterly*.

What are the chief characteristics of these New Canadian literatures? At the outset, differences of language, tradition, and communal experience have produced books of widely varying character in the several communities. Today's Icelanders and Swedes have had little experience of war; both nations are highly educated and devoted to belles lettres and erudition. The Czechs, Poles, Magyars, and Ukrainians have passed through the crucible of war, death, and political subjugation and their Canadian literature is tense with the memories of national martyrdom. With the Mennonite Germans, group suffering is blended with pietistic devotion. It will therefore be wise to take some of these communities one at a time.

The Icelanders are among the most actively poetic people in the world, and even the humblest fisherman or farmer feels capable of turning out soundly fashioned alliterative verses. This tradition has been transplanted to Canada. In 1936–40 some ninety Icelandic-Canadian poets achieved publication. Stephan G. Stephansson (1853–1927), of Markerville, Alberta, was one of the major Icelandic poets of this century and was so recognized in the land of his ancestors. His collected poems fill five large volumes (some 1700 pages) and his essays and letters fill another four volumes. Nearly all of those who have written Icelandic verse in this country were born in Iceland and were saturated in its language in their youth. A notable exception is Guttormur J.

Guttormsson, born on a pioneer farm beside Lake Winnipeg in 1878.

Nearly all of their poetry is lyric in form, and imposes strict rules of alliteration on all other prosodic patterns. Suitable poems are almost invariably written for weddings, golden weddings, and the sixtieth and seventieth birthdays of their friends. The Icelanders are also very fond of brief, stabbing, four-line epigrams, of verse tribute to the dead, and of elaborate commemoratory odes for public holidays. In other words, original poetry, written for the occasion, is a natural and integral part of community life.

Two or three typical epigrams will demonstrate this genre. Thus Stephan G. Stephansson pillories the wartime profiteers (1916 model):

In Europe's reeking slaughter-pen
They mince the flesh of murdered men,
While swinish merchants, snout in trough,
Drink all the bloody profits off.

Or he has a post-1918 quatrain entitled "The Unknown Soldier speaks":

In Paris was my Burial Number One;
My second was in London; and now vexed
By vaunting hands I'm lugged to Washington.
Where next, O Lord? Where next?

Less caustic but equally pointed is Guttormur Guttormsson's epigram entitled (after St. Luke's narrative) "Carried by the Angels into Abraham's Bosom":

A widower read long in Holy Writ,
Then sent aloft a frantic prayer-o-gram:
"I'd rather that my wife in hell should sit
Than warm the bosom of old Abraham!"

Canada figures side by side with Iceland in their poetry. On great public occasions, odes are read in honour of the Old land and the New, and there is no protest against becoming Canadian. It is rather that, like the Highlanders of Nova Scotia, they feel that an affectionate knowledge of their ancestral past can enrich their contribution to the Canadian present. Thus Gísli Jónsson's "Toast to Canada," written originally in Icelandic, begins:

Land with forests like the ocean, shoreless prairies, giant hills—
Every prince of song has praised thee, high in verse that warms and thrills,
Therefore I, who lack their stature, thinking on their towering state,
Stammer and hesitate. . . .

The Canadian landscape has also become an integral part of their poetry. Thus Stephan G. Stephansson, in a long poem on prairie travel, writes

But the land itself lay like an infinite board,
Unslivered, unknotted and clean,
As if all of the stuff of Creation were smoothed
And stained an ineffable green.

Ukrainian poetry in Canada has had three distinct phases: first, a long period of folk poetry, in which the pregnant experiences of the first humble pioneers were recorded; second, the blending of second generation Canadian university graduates with a more highly educated contingent of post-1918 refugees, and finally a full tide of professional intelligentsia who had escaped from Eastern Europe and from the Communist-cum-Allies slave-catching net in post-1945 Western Europe. Teodosiy Osmachka, who lived briefly among us, was doubtless the greatest of these poets, even as his sufferings in the inferno of Stalinist martyrdom had been the keenest of all. His poetic description of life in a Soviet concentration camp has all the hopelessness of actuality. Among the scores of other fruitful poets one may mention Petro Karmansky, M. I. Mandryka, Stepan Semczuk, Honoré Ewach, and Yar Slavutych.

Most Ukrainian-Canadian fiction deals with the horrors of Communist Europe. Hardly had the first post-Revolutionary wave of immigration written itself out when an even greater and more articulate post-1945 wave of refugees came to our shores and sought to record their appalling experiences in the purges and hell-camps of Stalin. Thus Alexis Luhowy's *For the Freedom of Ukraine* and *In the Claws of the Two-headed Eagle* were succeeded by Teodosiy Osmachka's *Gallery of Assassins* and by Nicholas Prychodko's *One of the 15 Million* and *Along Distant Paths*. There were, however, novels with a setting in pioneer life in Canada. Such were Elias Kiriak's *Sons of the Soil*, Honoré Ewach's *Voice of the Soil*, and Alexander Luhowy's *Without Shelter: The Children of the Prairie*. Memoirs with the emotional force of fiction were O. Hay-Holowko's *Duel with the Devil* and Nicholas Prychodko's *At the Crossroads of Death*.

German poetry in Canada has until recently been largely confined to the Mennonite communities of the West. Their flood of hymnody has usually shown more piety than poetry, but there is sometimes a rough vigour about it, as in Isaac P. Friesen's protest against spiritual inertia, "With the Current," which begins:

It's easy with the current floating;
All things drift down in slothful dream;
Just trail your oars in idle boating—
Even a dead fish goes down stream. . . .

Since World War II, a number of individuals writing in the modern idiom have emerged in Montreal and Toronto, but they still lack the encouragement of an integrated German-language audience.

For German Mennonite fiction, the chief inspiration has been found in the horrors that their people endured in Russia during the Communist revolution. Thus Gerhard Toews has written three vivid novels entitled *Die Heimet in Flammen*, *Die Heimat in Trümmern*, and *Hinter der Roten Mauer*, all dealing with this engrossing theme, and a similar impulse lies behind Johann Peter Klassen's *Dunkle Tage* and D. Neufeld's *Tagebuch aus dem Reiche des Totentanzes*.

A field like drama differentiates the traditions of the several national groups. The people of Iceland, living for the most part in lonely farmsteads or tiny fishing hamlets, have lacked the milieu out of which practical drama might have developed. Only two Icelandic-Canadians, Johannes P. Pálsson and Guttormur Guttormsson, have seriously attempted to write plays, and these are literary rather than dramatic in character. Their tendency is both tragic and symbolic, as in Pálsson's *The Black Seat* and Guttormsson's *The Circle*. In strong contrast with the tradition of the Icelanders is that of the Ukrainians, whose experience has its warm focus in the village and the community hall. Here, simple drama and the ballet find a natural place. Here, too, with the passage of time, the Ukrainian-Canadians have begotten a number of practical playwrights, whose plays, though often lacking in literary finish, are thoroughly stageworthy and give satisfaction to crowded audiences. Hunkievich, Kowbel, Luhovy, and Toolivetro had already achieved a high reputation 25 years ago. One of the strongest of the recent plays is *The Black Vulture*, by Mykola Kowshun, of Hamilton, with its tragic setting in Ukraine during the Stalin-made famine of 1934 that cost five million lives. The Mennonite Germans also have community drama, but their commonest product is a brief one-act play, humorous or religious in character, suitable for performances at church socials. Totally different again is Márton Kerecsendi Kiss's Magyar "fairy-tale play," *Beyond the Seven Seas*. This full-length verse drama is an intriguing blend of traditions. There are hints of Hans Christian Andersen's "Snow Queen" and Maurice Maeterlinck's "Blue Bird"; the hero owes something to John Osborne's "angry young man"; and the setting is in harmony with Hungarian folk-tales. The mood, however, owes more to the tensions of our bomb-haunted world, and the picturesque fairy-tale theme, colourful as embroidery from Mezökövesd, is actually symbolic of man's contemporary search for meaning and happiness in his existence. Only the cinema could do justice to its complexity of light, scene, and costume.

When I moved to Nova Scotia in 1948, Dr. MacGregor Fraser introduced me to the Gaelic poetry of that province and especially to John

Maclean's agonizing masterpiece, "A' choille ghruamach," which he helped me to translate. The anguish of exile is similarly vivid in the Magyar poetry of Ferenc Fáy, of Toronto, and the Czech poetry of George Skvor ("Pavel Javor"), of Montreal. Both men have come to Canada during the past decade or so, and to both men the separation from a beloved country has been a traumatic experience. Fáy's torment of heart often shadows itself forth in grim symbolism:

BLOODPOISONING

Out of your soul all memories slowly dry
Because the deadly wound has formed a scab.
Though through the fevered night in fear you lie,
Your pulse grows ever stiller and more drab.

Still like a beaten dog your fears you nurse,
Crouch in a sweat beneath the stifling night,
Count up to thousands, gabble some old verse,
And with forged prayers pretend to heal your fright. . . .

Fáy's wife came with him to Canada, but George Skvor voices the anguish of separation from a loved one, pain that grows keener as he realizes how they will continue to drift apart with the years into the remoteness of unshared experience:

. . . You await me in the house alone;
Your dog still watches on the stair.
The gulf of distance makes me moan,
And longing that I cannot bear.
The same sun gives your mouth its kiss,
The same wind soothes your lips with dew,
The same moon peers at you with bliss
But I am now no longer I
And you, perhaps, no longer you. . . .

In the closing paragraph of my 1961 Royal Society Paper, "Homesickness in Several Minor Keys," I sum up the more torturous aspects of the poetry of transition:

All too few Canadians are aware of the vastness of the problem faced by our uprooted newcomers, whether among the lonely crowds of an automationist Megalopolis or in the crushing loneliness of a pioneer cabin. The old status, the old skills, the old language, the old friends may all be lost or useless. The immigrant may be bleeding inwardly from warfare, bereavement, indignity, or even physical torture. His past may be in ruins. In the sporadic poetry of a generation in transition we may, if we will, glimpse the inner world of its painful metamorphosis.

But the New Canadian literatures also happily record the cases of those who have surmounted Hill Difficulty (scroll in hand) and have outfaced Giant Despair. Sociologists who would study the forming of the Canadian nation will find many of their answers written out large and living in these books.

An adequate exposition of my 2000 New Canadian volumes would run to several hundred pages. In addition to poetry, fiction, and drama, they are rich in biography, autobiography, essays, current affairs, history, economics, theology, arts and crafts, and scholarship of all sorts, from literary criticism to bibliography and onomastics. The present brief chapter has only sought to hint at the experiences they have brought me during the past forty years.

When in 1966, because of an inoperable traumatic cataract in my left eye, I at last reluctantly signed off from the annual survey, Dr. David M. Hayne, editor of the *University of Toronto Quarterly*, wrote me a letter of thanks that reads in part:

> Your participation in "Letters in Canada" has been so unique, both in length of uninterrupted service and in the extrordinary variety of material treated, that it is impossible to express to you the editors' gratitude in the ordinary terms that come to mind on such occasions. The "Letters in Canada" issues could never have lived up to their title, nor could they have won the esteem they at present enjoy, if you had not taken upon yourself the burdensome responsibility of reviewing "Publications in Other Languages." As you now take your leave of us, it is certain that no other person in Canada will be so rash as to attempt to take your place. We shall be fortunate indeed if three or four reviewers can be found to do what you have done single-handedly for more than a generation.

8

Music from the Sidelines

AS WITH MANY other aspects of family experience, it was my maternal grandfather, Thomas Watson, who gave our household its initial push in the direction of music. It was he who had seen to it, in 1882–85, that my mother, who had secured her third-class certificate with honours at the age of fifteen and then had to wait three years until she was old enough to go to Normal School, concentrated in the meantime on piano studies of an advanced nature; it was he who gave her a piano as a wedding present in 1889; and it was he who repeatedly supplied the funds to pay for music lessons for her children, including myself.

All of us fell a thousand miles short of my mother in mastery of the piano, and throughout our childhood her old music books, with their wealth of Beethoven and Bach and Brahms, filled us with a sort of awed incredulity. In their treasures we shared scarcely at all, even at her hands. A schoolteacher's wife with five children and a minimum of household help had no time for anything but the kitchen and the nursery. Our chief joy in music in the home came rather from family song-fests with my sister Helen on the piano-stool. "The Kerry Dancing" and "Polly Wolly Doodle" were about our level, with "In the Gloaming" for our more sentimental moods.

The little towns of Port Hope and Lindsay were not musical centres in any real sense. Music, moreover, still had no place on the curriculum of the schools. The only academic training in singing that I can recall in Port Hope was a rehearsal of "The Maple Leaf," to be sung on the occasion of a visit by Earl Grey, the Governor General, in 1908. Practices were held in the town drill shed under the gunpowdery direction of Choirmaster Renwick of the Methodist Church. My own chief recollection is that of being led down by the ear from the bleachers and ejected from the hall like a naughty puppy because I had been talking to the girls in the row behind. Much more abiding in its influence was the fine organ music to which I was exposed for a couple of years as "blow-boy" or "pumper" of the pipe organ for week-day practices in Saint John's Anglican Church. Miss Freda Gaudrie, who lived in Port Hope but was an organist in Cobourg on Sundays, paid me ten cents an hour for pumping air into the great bellows, topped for pressure with ponderous slabs of limestone, and some of her heavy pedal work had me worked into a lather. Her repertory of voluntaries, however, was in a different world from the programme in the Baptist and Methodist churches, where I sat in a pew on Sundays, and I came to realize the glorious difference.

My liveliest early impression of the organ, moreover, was the mouse-eye view of the instrument from behind and beneath, with the imposing edifice of the sectional organs, spread out through all their diversified ranks of pipes, towering above my juvenile head and hungrily demanding the air by which they might chant through a thousand noble nostrils. Persons in the nave and the choir might be aware only of the console, the casework, the display pipes, and the gowned figure on the organ bench, by whose grace

> . . . through the long-drawn aisle and fretted vault
> The pealing anthem swelled the note of praise . . .

but in behind the organ the young slave of the machine, glued to the pump-handle by pecuniary hopes, was only too well aware of the infinite resources of the total treasury from which she drew her riches. Flute and flageolet delicacies on the choir organ meant an interlude in which one could take it easy, while a fanfare of double open diapasons on the pedal organ and the great organ stole the air from the bellows in great gasps that forced one to work like mad to maintain the supply in that huge leather lung.

Thirty years later, on a visit to Hungary, I was amazed to find in a museum on the site of Aquincum, an extinct Roman town near the modern Budapest, the remains of a Roman pipe organ. As the province of Pannonia was organized here during the boyhood of Christ, this organ may actually be older than Saint Cecilia. I should have remembered that the Romans were then already using large pipe organs and that descriptions of an hydraulic organ, to reinforce the pneumatic system, were published in times B.C. by Hero of Alexandria in Greek and by Vitruvius in Latin. I could not but gape in fascination, however, at this venerable ancestor of the monster whose breathing I had toiled to satisfy in my boyhood.

Port Hope, with its musical poverty at the turn of the century, was not typical of the larger centres of Canada, for we heard vaguely of large choral groups in Toronto (the Mendelssohn Choir, the Orpheus Society, and others) and still more faintly of opera in Montreal; but a little town of four thousand was an inevitable backwater. In Lindsay, with a population of eight thousand, I was given a fleeting glimpse of a wider musical world through the performance of Mendelssohn's *Elijah* by the choir of St. Andrew's Presbyterian Church, for which Ruthven MacDonald, a bull-necked soloist from Toronto, was imported to sing the part of the old prophet. I walked in a seventh heaven for weeks afterwards. There was still, however, no school training in music until close to the end of my high school course. Cecil Carl Forsyth, the Methodist organist, was then brought in to train a small chorus and a double quartet, of which I was an eager member. From this it was a natural step at Queen's University to a place in the bass section of the Glee Club and a spot in the back row of the choir at the First Baptist Church. Then came actual singing lessons from Mrs. Dobbs, the organist at Chalmers Presbyterian Church, who sometimes drafted me into her own choir and paved the way for occasional solos in other city churches.

Terpsichore, by the way, has played a much smaller part than Polyhymnia in my musical education. "Sir Roger de Coverley" was the only dance known at the sedate parties of my Port Hope childhood. In high school days, dancing was not permitted at the social functions of the Lindsay Collegiate Institute and a "conversazione" consisted of the prim conversational perambulation of the Assembly Hall, two by Noachic two. Even "class parties" at Queen's were commonly limited to games and talk. I was a Master of Arts and a Captain in the Armed Forces before my Baptist feet first joined in the gaiety of a formal university dance. Only the waltz and the two-step were learned in those days. Years later, in chaperoning endless class parties with my wife in Winnipeg, the fox-trot came to be added. To the more recent importations from Africa and Spanish America I am a total stranger. At a modern university dance, my attempts at a rapid and vigorous circumnavigation of the dance floor mark me out as hopelessly Palaeozoic to the modern youths who endlessly spin their female tops, each on one unchanging spot.

A brief spasm of concentrated music study came in the winter of 1919–20. I was just back in Lindsay after some weeks in a military hospital in London, England, and was being fattened up by a solicitous mother. Presently I learned that Francis Coombs, a voice teacher at the Toronto Conservatory of Music, now came to Lindsay one day a week to instruct local pupils. Soon after I had enrolled with him, he gave me such a sales talk on a musical future that I was persuaded to move to Toronto, where I could get two lessons a week and practice long hours every day in the sound-proof practice rooms at the Conservatory. He even inflated my ego by prophesying an operatic career in New York. Soon I was ensconced in a top-floor bedroom at 36 Russell Street, and was dividing my time between the Conservatory and the Toronto Public Library. Lieder and oratorio were mixed seductively in with scales and exercises and all went merry as a marriage bell. But it was too good to last. Spanish influenza, at the end of the great post-war epidemic, struck me down, and pleurisy followed. With my chest heavily buttered with Antiphlogistine, I listened to a medical verdict that I would have to go home and recuperate for a long time. Thereafter, a chronic ethmoid and antrum infection gave rise to annoying and unpredictable bouts of laryngitis. Any vocal career had clearly gone down the drain. The dream had been exhilarating while it lasted, but I was wide awake again.

During the next fifteen months, while I spent most of my time writing and recovering strength through my mother's cooking, I was engaged, without salary, as choirmaster of the Lindsay Baptist Church. There were virtually no trained voices in the group, and the anthems, based on cheap American choir magazines, had to be kept on a very elementary level. Meanwhile, I had bought my first gramophone and began to accumulate albums of records—at first chiefly opera and then, increasingly, chamber music.

Now began my first real awareness of form in music and my growing eagerness to analyse its structure, especially in relation to the prosodic forms that I had already encountered in Greek, French, Italian, and English poetry. Thus the binary form of the seventeenth-century sonata, or better still the contrasting themes and keys within, say, the first movement of a Beethoven sonata, reminded me of the Petrarchan sonnet, in which octave and sestet are in contrasted pattern, yet with the closing line of the sestet giving the impression of "being safe home in the original key." The sonnet, however, seemed only a miniature, a verbal cameo, beside the imposing mass of the sonata, the concerto, or the symphony, and for a more adequate poetic analogue I was driven back to the architecture of the Greek ode, in which strophe and antistrophe presented two distinct themes or subjects (*Hauptsatz* and *Seitensatz*) in contrasted keys, and the epode finally came as a sort of *coda*. The French *ballade* seemed at first to present a parallel to the ternary form in music, but it became obvious, on reflection, that the three main stanzas involved no necessary use of the contrast that is so basic in musical development.

I had to realize more and more that while similar principles of rhythm and pattern might underlie both music and poetry—and merge gloriously in the hymn and the oratorio—yet pure music had intricate laws of its own. Poetry and music did not coincide with the ease of congruent triangles, and much careful study lay ahead of me before I could properly grasp the principles of form, harmony, and counterpoint. As with my daughters years later, when they studied these subjects on the Acadia University curriculum, I had to sit down at the piano-bench with the music and pick my way, phrase by musical phrase and sentence by sentence. Later I was to try to carry some of this new lore back into poetry, as when, in 1937, I was to write a "Manitoba Symphony" (*Andante-Allegro-Scherzo-Adagio*) as a preface to a diamond jubilee volume of *Manitoba Essays* published by the University of Manitoba.

Another difficulty for a non-professional music-lover in the twentieth century has been the maelstrom of new styles and schools flooding past one's door. After coming to know a feast of intellect and emotions in the works of Bach, Beethoven, Mozart, and César Franck, for example, after even arriving at a more or less intelligent appreciation of what Debussy and Bartók are trying to do, what is a poor man to think when first introduced to Stravinsky's *Rites of Spring* or Schoenberg's *Pierrot Lunaire*? It takes considerable effort to realize that the dodecaphonist, for example, while leaving the main tradition of music as valid as ever, has yet opened up an authentic new field of expression, just as five- or six-dimensional geometry, while not rendering Euclid obsolete, is still intellectually valid. Such a truth can be recognized, after a struggle, but what of those who ape Schoenberg's style without any of his inspiration? As with many of our avant-garde poets, I have been ready to tear my thin thatch over young composers who have assumed that a new idiom in style absolves them from the necessity of saying anything. It has not dawned on them that novelty and originality are two completely different things, that a great writer (or composer) in a traditional style that is congenial to his genius can turn out great work but might be frustrated in some ultramodern fashion of composition that is alien to his nature. The style is relatively unimportant as compared with the thought, the imagination, and the energy behind the style. My quarrel with too many of our young Canadian composers is not that they try to write like Schoenberg or Boulez but that they have nothing to say. Modernity in itself is worthless unless it is fitted to the logic and emotion of the composer (or the poet) and enables him best to communicate significant creative energy. Whether the real novelty of the "musique concrète" of Pierre Schaeffer and his disciples will endure must be left for posterity to decide.

With still others my complaint has been, not that they say nothing but that they say evil things: their deity is not Fatuity but Belial. These are the "hep-cats," the "rock 'n' roll" (*"Felsen und Semmel"*) maniacs, who go back to the jungle for their inspiration and by the clamorous essence of sex and violence appeal to the bestial core of human personality. Sometimes a thin line of improvisation is tinkled out by a piano or bleated by a demented saxophone, or a whiskey-voiced alto may croon a few drooling remarks over a microphone, but in a more typical phase some slavering goon will try to tear the front teeth out of the piano, to the braying of raucous brass, "solid sound in the writhing room." Through some strange delusion, this type of uproar has been hailed by many as the true proletarian music of our time. If this were indeed the case, then the cultural decomposition of our huge urban population-clots would already be far advanced.

Oddly enough, the self-styled proletarian régime of Soviet Russia has condemned this "pseudoproletarian music" of the West as a proof that our bourgeois culture is hopelessly rotten. On February 10, 1948, the Central Committee of the All-Union Communist Party published in *Sovietskaia Múzyka* a denunciation of similar trends in recent Russian composition, particularly "enthusiasm for confused neuropathological combinations that transform music into cacophony . . . the rejection of polyphonic music . . . and an enthusiasm for monotonous unisonic music."

But let me revert chronologically to my return from Oxford. Miscellaneous musical experience came in Winnipeg from 1922 on. Just to keep my larynx unrusted, I took lessons for a couple of years from Professor W. H. Shinn. I also qualified as a "charter member" (bass section) of the Winnipeg Philharmonic Choir, a choral group just being formed by the initiative of Stanley Osborne and under the direction of Hugh Ross, a slender, impeccable Scot with an absolute sense of pitch. We practised in the Sunday School hall of the Broadway Methodist Church, and our annual concerts were given in the old Board of Trade Building, on Portage Avenue East. My chief recollection of them is not of our own repertory but of the superb contributions of such guest soloists as Anna Case and Vladimir Rosing. Hugh Ross left us about 1926 to head the Schola Cantorum in New York and has been its director ever since.

A more humble but more active role for me in 1923–24 was singing second bass in a Wesley College male quartet along with Lall Montgomery (first tenor), "Bob" Frayne (second tenor), and Max Peacock (first bass). These three undergraduates had lost their "anchor-man" from an earlier quartet and drafted me to fill out their number. We were much in demand about town that winter, but when we tried out for a variety turn on the stage of the Strand Theatre on Portage Avenue, the manager, after listening gloomily to us in an empty theatre at 11.30 P.M., rejected us as hopelessly old-fashioned. Our repertoire was strictly

1850 and not 1924. (Lall Montgomery is today a medical doctor in Gaston, Indiana, Bob Frayne died in 1953 while senior Protestant chaplain of the RCAF, and Max Peacock is a lawyer in Edmonton.)

Choir-work for the next thirty years was only intermittent, apart from eight years of steady service (1940–48) in the bass section of the MacNeill Memorial Baptist Church choir in Hamilton, Ontario.

My experience in listening to music has been spasmodic. The Gaiety Theatre in Kingston in my student days rarely gave us any musical programmes, although American road-companies occasionally performed such musical comedies as *The Bohemian Girl*, *Martha*, and *Sally*. In the spring of 1919, while on a short leave in New York, I finally had a taste of the real thing at the "Met." in a performance of Saint-Saëns' *Samson and Delilah*, with Enrico Caruso as Samson and Margarete Matzenauer as a voluptuous Delilah. That same year, in London, England, I enjoyed Oscar Ashe in *Chu Chin Chow* at His Majesty's Theatre and heard superb symphony concerts conducted by Sir Henry Wood at Queen's Hall.

A month in Dresden, Germany, in the spring of 1922, brought an unprecedented programme of musical delight. My days were being given to the writing of a book-length thesis in economics for the B.Litt. degree at Oxford, but on four or five evenings a week I attended the current season at the State Opera House. The operas were chiefly Italian (*Rigoletto*, *I Pagliacci*, *Aïda*, *Cavalleria Rusticana*, *Il Trovatore*) and German (*Der Freischütz*, *Die Meistersinger*, *Der Fliegende Holländer*, *Das Rheingold*, *Parsifal*, etc.), but all were sung in German. When Easter came, the house had been sold out for *Parsifal*, but an American Rhodes Scholar and I, thanks to the fantastic inflation of the time, rented the private box of the former King of Saxony for twenty-five cents apiece. The climax of the season, however, was not opera at all but Sebastian Bach's *St. Matthew Passion*, which I heard sung in the *Drei-Königs-Kirche*, in Dresden Neustadt.

German Lieder had first come over my horizon in high school days, when Miss Whyte, our German teacher, used to invite her German students to her boarding-house and gather them around the piano. Francis Coombs had put them on my Toronto Conservatory programme; but in Dresden the acquaintance was greatly expanded, for our landlady's daughter, Norah, was studying voice at the Dresden Conservatory, and we not only went to a recital in which "der Wirtin Töchterlein" took part but spent many musical evenings in family songfests where Schubert, Beethoven, and Schumann ruled supreme.

In Winnipeg, there was no native opera, oratorio, or symphony, but Mr. Fred Gee imported a series of community concerts that gave us such performers as Rachmaninoff and such conductors as Eugene Ormandy. To appreciate these visiting celebrities, however, we needed systematic day-to-day familiarity with great music, and that was slow in coming. It was so easy for the concert-goer to regard music merely as a fashionable amusement, or, if serious minded, as a sort of spiritual massage. School music, and the establishment of an annual music festival, however, began to lay the intelligent foundations of good music among a whole new generation. The programme, moreover, is continually growing, even to the inclusion of Burl Ives's incomparable folksongs for children—"Mr. Rabbit," "The Whale," and their like.

One chapter that is unforgettable is the gypsy music that I encountered in Budapest and other parts of Hungary in the summer of 1938. From the Opera House to the open-air cafés on the slopes of the Gellérthegy, these haunting strains seized me with a strange fascination. It probably reveals my lack of musical comprehension, but I found these fiddle-tunes of the *czigány* vastly more moving than the profound studies of folk-tunes for strings by Béla Bartók. The latter might speak to the intellect but the former struck straight for the emotions.

In 1927, Marius Barbeau opened windows for me into the folk music of the French-Canadian and of the aboriginal races of Canada. I had already come to know something of the linguistic complexity of the *Urkanadisch* population, with 176 distinct languages, from Micmac to Kwakiutl, for the old anthropologist–missionary, John Maclean, had shared some of his lore with me. Here, however, was Barbeau's evidence of a rapidly fading fabric of Amerindian and Eskimo musical civilization, with its own variegated and almost incredible range of scale-forms, rhythms, and sounds, unsuspected by the millions of white men who had swarmed into the half-empty continent since Cartier's day. Even among many of these white communities there were unknown treasuries of music. Thus Ukrainian scholars had shown me large printed collections of Ukrainian folk songs, running to many thousands of items in several volumes, and their choral work in Winnipeg was a rich delight.

As for formal composition, the change in Canada in my lifetime has been striking. Formal music is no novelty here, for music was composed in Canada before Handel and Bach were born, but the recent sweep of modernity and of influences other than British and French has been conspicuous. When in 1955 I purchased a new anthology of *Piano Pieces by Canadian Composers*, edited by John Weinzweig, I began to fear that I was suffering from aesthetic arteriosclerosis. The general impression was one of harsh defiance, as of some cross-eyed Moses marching out into a technical wilderness, with no Promised Land beyond. Two or three of the caravan were able to strike water from the rock: Weinzsweig's own "Waltzling" was a charming little piece and there was a flavour of *Gemütlichkeit* in Oskar Morawetz's "Scherzino" and Jean Papineau-Couture's "Deux Valses," but in many of their colleagues (Betts, Kasemets, *et al.*) I found only nonsense or ugliness or both. Alexander Brott's "Sacrilege" (the manhandling of a Bach two-part invention) showed more sadistic frenzy than genuine humour.

An experience in 1932–36 that gave me an awareness of the steady improvement in Protestant church music in Canada was my membership in a "Baptist Hymnary Committee of Canada," set up by the Baptists of all the provinces to bring in a more adequate hymnbook than the thoroughly unsatisfactory oddments that were then in use and ranged all the way from Old Country Baptist collections to Moody and Sankey gospel songbooks. The committee was given complete freedom to set up a new hymnbook or to approve, with revisions, any existing volume. Our almost unanimous choice was the *Hymnary of the United Church of Canada* that had been published in 1930 under the editorship of Rev. Dr. Alexander MacMillan, father of Sir Ernest, and the only question thereafter concerned what hymns we might wish to substitute for less acceptable items in this volume of 771 selections. In the end, there were exactly forty-eight of these substitutions, most of them based on denominational familiarity. The editor of our new version, *The Hymnary for Use in Baptist Churches*, was Rev. Dr. George P. Gilmour, later the president of McMaster University. So far as energy and initiative were concerned, he was both the engine and the driver of our car, and by the same analogy I fear that I was scarcely even an unused spare tire.

It was natural that many of the changeling hymns were by Baptist authors—Charles Haddon Spurgeon's "Amidst us our Beloved stands," Principal McGregor's "McMaster Hymn," two hymns by John Bunyan ("Who would true valour see" and "He that is down need fear no fall"), and a hymn by Krishnu Pal, William Carey's first convert in the foreign field. Popular demand brought in the lusty doggerel of "Yield not to temptation"; but we also added John Leland's "Lord keep us safe this night," to music by Beethoven, and the "Crusaders' Hymn" from the German of the seventeenth century. The largest groups of hymns extruded were those by Charles Wesley (eleven dropped, with thirty-two retained) and those from the Scottish Psalter.

The *Hymnary* that we now use so widely in our churches is a truly catholic anthology of hymns from all periods and branches of the Christian church, ranging from translations of Ambrose, Gregory, Bernard of Cluny, and John of Damascus and ancient canticles and liturgical sentences down to at least twenty tunes composed or arranged by Canada's own Healey Willan. Haydn, Handel, Beethoven, Mendelssohn, Mozart, and the Bachs are all represented, but there is an overdose of William Howard Doane, John Bacchus Dykes, W. J. Kirkpatrick, Lowell Mason, and Robert Lowry, and some of our churches gargle them incessantly. All in all, however, the improvement in Baptist church music—although not in the zeal of the singers—has been prodigious during the past fifty years.

Some study of the hymnody of the Christian church (particularly in Latin, German, and Icelandic) has helped me to realize how intensely difficult it has always been to write a good hymn—suitable for congregational or choral singing, devout without being mawkish, rich in tonal effect, fresh in imagery, and capable of communicating vital experience. Perhaps a hundred thousand Latin hymns have been written in the long history of the Catholic Church, but how few of them have proved viable! The German Reformation brought another hundred thousand hymns in German and hymns in the English language must total half a million, yet all but a few of them are dead today. Even the most fluent hymn writers have failed far more often than they have succeeded. Charles Wesley, for example, came up to bat some 6500 times and fanned out in all but a score of glorious instances. Few nations have had a sacred poet with so well sustained an inspiration as Hallgrímur Pétursson, whose "Hymns of the Passion" occupy 165 pages (in the original Icelandic) in my copy of the Sálmabók of the Evangelical Lutheran Icelandic Church. A really ecumenical hymnbook would include a far greater proportion of hymns in the various non-English traditions than we now have in the *Hymnary*, but the remarkable thing to a Baptist is how little Baptist hymnody is to be found in the book. Peronnet's "All hail the power of Jesu's name" and Fawcett's "Blest be the tie that binds" are perhaps the best known of our contribution in a collection where Catholic, Lutheran, Calvinist, Unitarian, Quaker, Methodist, and Baptist praise God together.

The chief enemy to be defeated is not denominational hymnody but bad hymnody. In our time we have had to cope with the popularity of some truly dreadful "sacred" music. Among the horrible examples of musical piety divorced from poetry, and even from common reverence, are the Western-ballad atrocity, "Life is like a railroad track," and the syrupy lyric in which a male quartet assure us that they will "cling to the old rugged Cross" of the Atonement, only to turn it in some day, in a modern car-dealer's technique, on new-model crowns for themselves. But the nadir of Canadian hymnody is probably a selection that I heard, in July 1912, on an excursion steamer plying between Toronto and

Niagara Falls. A little group on the upper deck had come prepared to make a joyful noise to the Lord. With tinny guitars, tinnier voices, and an even tinnier tune, they sang tirelessly an invariable theme:

> Ev'ry promise is a cheque upon the Bank of Heaven.
> Oh, the promises! The precious promises!
> What you ask in faith will unto you be given.
> Go cash the promises of God!

To pass from this to Beethoven's *Missa Solemnis* is to enter a different world.

My contact with the universities of French Canada, particularly as chairman of the Humanities Survey (cf. Chapter XVIII), also made me aware of a vigorous reform movement in Roman Catholic music, dating from the encyclical *Motu Proprio* in 1903. On the whole, it tends to be an austerely erudite return to the Gregorian chant and the concordant classical polyphony as the twin standards of good church music. Most modern music is repudiated as being suitable for the concert hall but not for the congregational worship of God.

A frequent avocation of mine, on the margin of music, has been the provision of words for others to sing. When Murray Gibbon arranged for a folk-song festival for European-Canadian groups in Winnipeg in 1928, I supplied English versions for most of their programme. In 1937, when the Budapest University Chorus came to the United States, I supplied English words for their entire Magyar repertory, running to some twenty-nine numbers. Churches came to me for hymns for special occasions, drafted out to the accompaniment of well-known hymn-tunes. For the fiftieth anniversary of Wesley College, Winnipeg, I wrote, on demand, a jubilee hymn to the tune of "Praise, My Soul."

My first venture into supplying words for a composer came when the late Charles Rice, of Montreal, who had written music for my English version of the Swedish poet Almqvist's lyric "My Galley," asked me for three more poems, all original, so that he might compose a *Sea Suite*. The result became not unfamiliar to Montreal audiences. Collaboration on a much more ample scale came after my removal to Wolfville in 1948. The dean of Acadia University's School of Music, Edwin A. Collins, was deeply versed in composition and some months before my first spring convocation asked me to write an elaborate "Graduation Anthem." For this he supplied music for choir and orchestra and launched the new number at the baccalaureate service on May 16, 1949. Next came a Nova Scotia suite of five songs for voice and piano—"Blow me down, Blomidon," "Grand Pré," "Annapolis Valley," "South Shore," and "Cape Breton." But all this was merely the prologue to a full-length light opera, *The Mod at Grand Pré*, which the Kirkconnell–Collins team wrote in 1955 and happily saw staged in March 1956. My libretto wrote itself in less than two weeks at Easter-time, often at the rate of four or five arias and choruses a day. The suggestion that I compose a light opera had been made to me by Professor Rex Lucas, the 1955 campus producer of Gilbert and Sullivan's *Patience*. Although I laughed off the idea at the time, it remained as a time-bomb, ticking away in my inner consciousness, and at last suddenly exploded. Two weeks later, to my own amazement, I handed him a copy of the complete libretto.

The plot was simple, although somewhat fantastic. A Louisiana "Cajun" widow, Madame Leblanc, arrives back at Grand Pré in the early summer of 1955. She and her eighteen daughters are celebrating the bicentennial of the expulsion of their Acadian French ancestors. They now meet a field party of eighteen Highland Scots engineering students, who have come out from nearby Acadia University under their bachelor instructor, Professor MacTavish. After many vicissitudes, the two groups pair off. In Act II, MacTavish relives in a dream the events of 1755 as they might have been if the British troops in the area had been Highlanders and not New England colonials.

I had some misgivings lest Dean Collins, with his musicological erudition and his taste for intellectualist modernity in style, might misread the text that I presently set before him. Happily he rose to the occasion, drawing particularly on French and Scottish types of musical theme for the contrasted racial groups. The musical hits of the show were the Acadiennes' chorus,

> Hail, genealogy!
> Blest fruit of ancient times
> Shining upon a tree
> That to the future climbs. . . ,

the young men's advice to the embarrassed professor,

> MacTavish,
> Be lavish
> With ardour to woo!
> Recapture
> The rapture
> Of twenty and two! . . . ,

the male chorus (MacTavish and Highlanders),

> Love at first sight with a dream of delight,
> What is surprising in that?
> Love was no felon when Paris met Helen
> And loved her in ten seconds flat.
> Time in our lives has been broken in two:
> Time before meeting, and after, with you. . . ,

the milkmaid's song, "Mimi, my Gaspereau cow,"

> I'm looking for Mimi this late afternoon,
> A cow quite unequalled my verses attune,
> Her breath is as sweet as an orchard in June—
> Mimi, my Gaspereau cow. . . ,

and the great double-chorus finale, "Glory, glory to the Valley"— to the tune of "John Brown's Body." My own favourite lyric, however, is one in which the French girl Marie tells of over three centuries of apple-blossoms in the Annapolis Valley:

> The Thirteenth Louis reigned in France
> And Charles was Scotland's king
> When fruit-trees to the Valley brought
> Their snowy blossoming.
>
> Pierre Martin brought out the slips
> In sixteen-thirty-three
> And gave them in the Valley's earth
> Fair immortality;
>
> For kings may come and kings may go,
> They linger but a breath
> And pass in silence to the still
> And dusty hands of death;
>
> But ever through the Valley sweep
> The blossom-tides of May,
> As fair as in that ancient time—
> That farthest yesterday.
>
> When we in turn at last grow old
> And to the graveyard pass,
> And when our children's children sleep
> Beneath the Valley's grass,
>
> These white, eternal tides of spring
> Through every farm will flow
> And spread across these deathless fields
> Their surf of living snow.

I can never be grateful enough to the Acadia Light Opera Society, which decided to stage our opera, to the student cast, which threw itself with joyful enthusiasm into practice and performance, and to Professor Rex Lucas, whose dramatic training and stage sense not only formed the opera as a living production but gave me invaluable hints for the recasting of episodes for greater dramatic effect.

9

Concerning Things Military

THE EARLIEST HINT of warfare in my young life was at the time of the South African War. The little town of Port Hope was proud of its militia record and the place of honour in front of the Town Hall was occupied by a big bronze statue of Colonel A. T. H. Williams, who had died of brain fever while serving with the town's contingent in the Northwest Rebellion of 1885. The local 14th Field Battery, under Lieutenant-Colonel William McLean (father of J. Stanley McLean, later head of Canada Packers), had repeatedly won the Gzowski Cup for its marksmanship, and the 46th Regiment, with its fine brass band, had enchanted our young eyes and ears as the redcoats marched down Walton Street to the intoxicating strains of "The Soldiers of the Queen." Eleven soldiers from Port Hope had gone to serve in South Africa, and our excitement reached its peak in the very early spring of 1900 when my six-year-old brother Walter dashed home from school and gasped out, rather incoherently: "Lady Smith has relieved!"

That evening there were great doings in the market-square behind the Town Hall. A pile of wood was reared in the open and above it, from an impromptu gibbet, dangled an effigy of the Boer leader, "Oom Paul" Kruger. Then, when a huge crowd had filled the square, the pyre was lit and we all—including a little codger, aged almost five, on the edge of the throng—sang over and over, in a sort of frenzied incantation, and to the tune of "John Brown's Body":

Hang Paul Kruger on a sour apple tree,
Hang Paul Kruger on a sour apple tree,
Hang Paul Kruger on a sour apple tree,
As we go marching by!

Such was our celebration of the Relief of Ladysmith. As a family extra, we children christened our bull-terrier pup "Buller," after the British general.

For several years thereafter, war, even as a vaguely comprehended piece of excitement, retreated from our consciousness. At the Lindsay Collegiate Institute, of which my father became headmaster in 1908, there was an active cadet corps, extended in 1909 to include every able-bodied boy in the school, organized as No. 44 Cadet Battalion. Zeal ran high, and the corps repeatedly won first place for efficiency in Military District No. 3.

In the spring of 1912, I learned that a six-week summer course at Stanley Barracks, Toronto, would qualify one as a cadet instructor, a physical instructor, and a militia lieutenant. With this training went sufficient allowances to enable one to take the course without financial sacrifice. For motives that at this distance are completely obscure, I registered for the course. Thanks to excellent training as a cadet for the three previous years, I found the Stanley Barracks regimen a comparatively easy one and acquired my certificates without trouble. That autumn the cadet battalion was to be placed in charge of our new classics teacher, Charles Owens, who, as a brand-new college graduate, had taken the instructor's course along with me during the summer. Unfortunately he proved immediately and hopelessly incapable of maintaining discipline, and companies drilling on the school grounds climbed the woodpile or went over the fence in joyful abandon. The only other qualified instructor at the school was the principal's seventeen-year-old son, a student in his Senior Matriculation year; and so—no doubt with some shaking of grey heads—the School Board put me in charge. Whether it was a result of fear of the Principal or of *esprit de corps* towards a fellow-student thus conscripted for duty, I cannot be sure, but the morale of the corps for the rest of that year was magnificent and discipline no problem whatever. For this I cannot be too grateful, for I was carrying a heavy academic programme and wrote seventeen Senior Matriculation papers the following June.

The summer of 1913, when I had just turned eighteen, brought still another course of training—this time as a Musketry instructor—under Lieutenant-Colonel R. A. Helmer at the Dominion Musketry School on the Rockcliffe Ranges at Ottawa. It was as blisteringly hot as the 1912 summer at Stanley Barracks had been cold, and for most of the time the heat mirage was so bad that there was little use in trying to shoot from anywhere beyond the 200-yard range. Standard equipment at that time was the "Ross rifle," although we were also introduced to the "Lee-Enfield." It was typical of the time that we learned nothing about machine-guns. It was still the day of the individual sharp-shooter.

On the night before the course broke up, a number of my fellow-officers, with the venal co-operation of three or four husky young sluts from the mess kitchen, held a grand fornication party behind blanketed windows in the back wing of our barracks. Naked sons of Priapus, noisily mobilizing business and collecting dollars throughout the dormitory, were indignant at my refusal to join in their promiscuous delights and proposed to pull me out of bed, frog-march me down the corridor, and throw me to the lionesses. In the nick of time, however, their ringleader, discovering a Greek Testament beside my pillow, announced that I must be headed for the priesthood and was entitled to a dispensation from the joys of the flesh.

On August 4, 1914, the First World War burst upon a startled world. On August 5, my brother Walter, who held the rank of militia lieutenant in the 45th Regiment at Lindsay, volunteered for active service, and fifteen days later left for Valcartier and overseas on his twenty-first birthday. His unit for almost four years was to be the 14th Battalion (Royal Montreal Regiment). In the muck of Salisbury Plains during the first winter, he shared in the epidemic of spinal meningitis, but somehow recovered without any permanent disability. In a letter to me dated January 27, 1918, he describes a small-arms refresher course that he had recently taken:

> I finished my revolver course about a week ago, and in the final test got 11 bulls out of 12 shots—at moving targets exposed for one second each! It almost sounds like a Wild West tale, doesn't it! But it's true—and the last six shots were fired from a trench full of gas—and me with a gas helmet on.

All this skill availed him little in the early hours of August 8, 1918, in the Battle of Amiens, when the platoon he was leading ran into a nest of machine-guns in a grain-field south of Villers-Bretonneux. I visited his grave on December 13, 1921, in the tiny "Toronto British" cemetery, twenty-two kilometres east of Amiens, on the broad grassy summit of a hill and two hundred yards north of a still obvious line of trenches. There, five thousand miles from our common home, I felt as never before the pathos of the verses of Catullus at his brother's grave in the far-off Troad:

> Multas per gentes et multa per aequora vectus
> advenio has miseras, frater, ad inferias. . .

I had long ago committed the entire poem to heart but now could not finish it for tears.

It was August 1916 before I myself volunteered for overseas service with the 253rd Battalion, CEF ("Queen's University Highlanders"). In the autumn of 1914, when a battalion of the Canadian Officers' Training Corps was formed at Queen's University, I was the only undergraduate with an officer's papers, was at once gazetted a lieutenant, and, after further training and examinations, received a certificate as captain dated June 29, 1915. During the next academic year, I commanded "B" Company of the Queen's Contingent and also lectured to the Battalion on map reading and field sketching. My only original contribution to the pedagogy of this subject was a new theory of contours. If Noah's flood were to subside at the rate of one hundred feet a day, the beach-lines at a given hour on successive days would be equivalent to one-hundred-foot contours on a map. In the summer of 1916, my training as a musketry officer was invoked during a three-month spell as Assistant Musketry Officer of Military District No. 3. We were all under canvas at Barriefield Camp under Major-General T. D. R. Hemming. My task was to supervise the musketry training of some seven battalions, first on the miniature range and then on the service range. At the end of August, when I had already been appointed to the staff of the Royal Military College, Kingston, one of my old professors, Major P. G. C. Campbell, the commandant at Fort Henry, invited me to go overseas with the 253rd Battalion, of which he had just been appointed the commanding officer. Without delay, I sought an interview with the somewhat surprised commandant at RMC and persuaded him to release me.

For an interval of two months, Major Campbell continued as head of Fort Henry, with myself as his adjutant. In November 1916, he at last quitted the Fort to organize the 253rd, and I was gazetted to the new unit along with him. Unfortunately all of this had been undertaken without consulting medical officers, and after three successive Medical Boards had declared me unfit for overseas service, I had to reconcile myself to duties in Canada. I was actually free to return to civilian life and could have turned to teaching or further postgraduate work, but my military experience and the needs of the country made this unthinkable.

I therefore served until late in 1919 with the Department of Internment Operations, for eight months as adjutant at Fort Henry and for over two years as paymaster at Kapuskasing Internment Camp in the "Clay Belt" of Northern Ontario. My commanding officer for this entire period was Major W. E. Date, a heavily built man from Montreal, one of Canada's few Staff Course graduates and one who combined intense efficiency with an explosive temper. Major Campbell, before his departure, had predicted a Rehoboam, whose little finger would be thicker than his own loins, and no comparison could have been more apt. He ruled Fort Henry and Kapuskasing with a rod of iron. The régime was vastly more efficient than before but personal feelings were trampled ruthlessly under foot. The prisoners staged a strike at Fort Henry for a few days in January 1917, and a second strike at Kapuskasing lasted for nearly three months, from August to October 1917. Some of his own guard officers plotted against him that same fall and intrigued with the Honourable George Howard Ferguson and the Honourable Charles Cochrane to have him quietly returned to civil life. Political cabals, however, made no headway with General Sir William Otter, the Director of Internment Operations, and the plotters themselves were promptly ordered back to Toronto. From all of his disciplinary problems, the "O.C." emerged grimly triumphant but never the object of affection from troops or prisoners. At the very outset, I, too, tended to resent the rigorous efficiency of the new broom, but I presently learned to appreciate it. Indeed, if I have ever shown any effectiveness in administration, I owe most of it to nearly three years of apprenticeship under a first-class administrator.

At one stage in the Kapuskasing strike there was an episode that might have had serious consequences for me. We learned by the grapevine that a mass break of our twelve hundred prisoners was timed for a certain morning at the moment when one contumelious prisoner, Otto Rennert, arrested for insurrection, would be brought back from the orderly room to the "Clink," facing the main gate. The plan was to crash the gate and take over the camp. As repeatedly happened in times of crisis, Major Date took me out of my paymaster's office and placed me in charge of the guard. I then marched my men down by the compound; there, in full sight of the prisoners, I had every rifle loaded with a full clip of live ammunition, and calmly faced the main gate and the cursing mob inside it. Seeing that I meant business, they lost their nerve and dispersed to their bunkhouses. It was easy to imagine, however, the outburst of indignation from some members of the House of Commons if I had found it necessary to shoot. I could well have been made the scapegoat of a very messy situation.

Generally speaking, I could feel little animus against our German prisoners. Guarding them was simply a job. It was their duty to try to get away and our duty to try to prevent it. The ingenuity that they displayed in their attempts at escape was being duplicated by our men in German captivity. There was nothing done in our Canadian camps like the deviltry later devised by Communists and Nazis for the torture and extermination of political opponents. Of "concentration camps" on the Bolshevik–Fascist model there was never any hint in Canada, where the terms of the Hague Convention of October 1907 were faithfully, though strictly, obeyed.

If I tell of three episodes where I had a share in thwarting such attempts, it is in no sense in order to exult over the unsuccessful, but rather to illustrate the efforts with which both sets of men, the captors and the captives, sought to carry out their duties.

At Fort Henry, on Sunday, February 4, 1917, Q.M.S. James Anderson asked to speak to me in private. It transpired that he had been given a tip that some sixty prisoners were planning to escape that night. He had been unable to learn anything more definite. We decided to keep the matter to ourselves and to undertake a tour of exploration. Soon we were down in the moat wading through snow-drifts and searching in every port-hole for signs of recent damage, but we could find nothing. There remained only the caponiere, a long, low bastion of stone which ran out into the moat from the centre of the north wall. This defensive work had formerly been connected with the ground floor of the Fort by a doorway just opposite the partition wall between two casemates known as 12B and 13B and was thus connected with both by a short, three-foot passage-way. In 1915 the Engineers had bricked up the doorway, cemented the floor, and put in a brick wall level with 12B, thus leaving a small cupboard in the corner of 13B. The portholes of the caponiere were below snow-level but we felt that this was our last hope and so dug away the snow from a port on the east side. To our delight we found that the stone had been chiselled away from the inner faces of the embrasure. In point of girth, Sergeant Anderson was close kin to Falstaff but, fortunately, I myself was built more like Justice Shallow, and so, stripping off my greatcoat, I squirmed down head first into the gloom of the caponiere. In summer its floor was flooded with water but all was now solid ice. I picked myself up and began my search by the light of a few matches. Stretched out on the ice were the component parts of an extension ladder which could have scaled the walls of the moat, and underneath the bricked-up doorway was a narrow hole stuffed with sacking. The way of escape was indeed complete. I had seen enough and was soon brushing myself off in the moat outside.

Deciding to act at once, I re-entered the Fort and started on my daily inspection of quarters. On reaching 13B I sought out the cupboard adjoining the old doorway to the caponiere. The corner was dark and murky so I had the room captain, a big, sulphurous German named Belitz, light matches while I examined the place. The cupboard was full of old clothes, and on the floor were several pairs of boots. These were cleared away under protest, and for a moment I was nonplussed, for the walls were untouched and the floor was of solid cement. But another match revealed a narrow crack along the edge of the floor. I set my fingers to it, pulled, and the whole cupboard floor lifted up in one piece. The original cement had been torn out, a board cover made, and new cement bound to this by chicken wire. Underneath, of course, lay the route to freedom. I ordered the occupants of the room to move, bag and baggage, to a vacant casemate farther down the square, and then went and reported the whole affair to the commandant.

The only attempt to tunnel out from Kapuskasing Camp came during the strike period, and its frustration helped much to break down resistance in the compound. Persistent rumours reached us of a tunnel leading from No. 1 Bunkhouse, the most westerly of the buildings in the second-class yard, and so on September 30, about 11.00 P.M., four of us officers started out to explore the situation. We first dug a small opening under the west wall of the suspected bunkhouse and found that fresh clay had been packed in tightly under the flooring. Adjourning to the interior of the building, we warned all prisoners that they must stay in their bunks or risk being fired on, and then examined the floor. We found it clear and inviolate except for a small seaman's chest under one bunk-section, and on moving this we discovered a neat trap-door. Two of us descended at once. Directly beneath was a moist pit, eight feet by four, drained by a sump and ventilated by long lateral air-shafts. From this pit led a subterranean passage-way, about four feet in height and three in width, carved out of the clay, floored with wood, and strongly underpinned. This tunnel ran due west for about fifty yards to the substrate beneath a building occupied by some first-class prisoners, who had a private trap-door entrance to it in the corner of a bedroom, and then headed northwest towards the Quartermaster's Stores which stood outside the fence sixty yards away. In the Stores lay all the spare rifles and ammunition of the camp, and the tunnelling, if successful, would have permitted a surprise attack by a hundred armed Germans.

One remaining attempt may be narrated here, not least because of the hardships endured by both pursuers and pursued. On the night of May 27, 1919, two prisoners, Adolf Rino and Frank Miller, who were undergoing treatment in the camp hospital, slipped out of the ward in their pyjamas and vanished into the darkness. For twelve days every effort to locate them was unavailing. Patrols sent east and west along the railway encountered nothing. Then, on Sunday, June 8, a local trapper reported his discovery of an old smudge twelve miles up the Kapuskasing River, and it was at last thought possible that the prisoners might have attempted to strike up stream and traverse the hundred miles of wilderness that lay between the camp and the CNR on the south. Although heavy rains were falling, immediate action was taken. Two canoes were borrowed—unfortunately old, waterlogged freighters, twenty feet in length. Rations were hastily served out, rifles, ammunition, axes, pails, and kettles got together, and at 4.10 P.M. a party of five—Privates Gauthier (French-Canadian), Marshall and Nelson (both Scottish-Indian half-breeds), Sergeant A. B. Bower, and myself in command—paddled upstream in the toughest of civilian clothes. What followed may perhaps be best described in an extract from my official report of June

15, 1919, based on pencilled notes made day by day beside the campfire:

We reached Kabahose Falls about 7.30 P.M. and, portaging over, camped for the night above the falls. Just below the falls and on the right-hand bank we found a rough raft made of two logs wired at one end and nailed together with a strip of wood at the other. It was held to the bank by a couple of stakes and had apparently been abandoned where made. In the woods a few yards away we found a smudge and some axe cuttings, both some days old. As troops off duty visited this locality daily, however, no importance could be attached to this evidence.

On Monday June 9th we portaged in the early morning over Sesebegagan Rapids and Camp Falls, and later, about noon, over Fingernail Rapids. Near the portage-trail here we found the print of a heavy boot, some days old, but here again a trapper or fire-ranger might have been responsible. After dinner here, we portaged over Kabatase Falls and an hour later over another rapids. Later in the afternoon, just below White Otter Falls, two thunderstorms sprang up from opposing quarters and collided directly overhead. The sequel was tragic, for our canoes were half full of water before we could reach the portage landing. We then camped for the night at White Otter Falls. This was the extreme limit of activity for fire-rangers and trappers, and we knew that in the wilderness beyond we could meet no white men except the fugitive Germans.

The morning of Tuesday June 10th was occupied in portaging over White Otter Falls, Old Woman Falls, and Twin Rapids, about ten, fifteen, and five chains in length respectively. At 3.05 P.M. we found, caught on the left bank of the river, a raft made of three cedar logs nailed together with small cross-pieces at each end. We were at once jubilant, though still half unconvinced. The cutting was the crude work of an unskilled axeman, which helped to clinch the evidence. From there on, one canoe took each bank, searching for the origin of the raft. At 3.35 P.M. we found fresh smudges at a deserted Indian camp on the right bank, also footprints in soft mud on the shore, one set corresponding with that seen at Fingernail Rapids and another of a finer, dress boot. At 4.00 P.M. we found where the raft had been made. On the right bank, about fifteen feet from the shore, we discovered the chopped ends of cedar logs corresponding with those in the raft; also a smudge several days old, and the same footprints as before. We were now confident that our men had crossed to the left bank, and that such a crossing was well premeditated was suggested by the existence of a wide tributary river on the right about a mile farther on. We spent the night at the deserted camp of an Indian trapper on the edge of a large marsh where we saw several moose. On crossing the river here to cut balsam boughs for our beds, we found, on a moose trail in the densest of woods, a small smudge about four days old and beside it a small piece torn from the corner of a Toronto newspaper. The mosquitoes through this marshy section of country, (about thirty miles in extent) were indescribably numerous and ferocious and the prisoners must have suffered terribly with them.

On Wednesday June 11th we paddled steadily all morning without seeing any trace of the prisoners, though we did see a great number of moose. At 2.30 P.M. we caught sight of a canoe cached in the woods on the left (east) bank. Landing we found some of the now familiar bootprints and a wide blaze on a tree across which someone had written in pencil "Lost in the Woods." From this we followed their trail for a few hundred yards by means of broken twigs, but as these and the blaze were at least two days old we returned to our canoes. About half a mile further on, the country suddenly became mountainous and we were confronted by a roaring rapid a good mile in length. This nameless and uncharted portage, now dubbed Steep Dog Portage by our party, is over a mile long, climbs straight up over a hilltop, and through disuse is badly bedevilled with second growth; so as both our canoes were twenty-foot freighters, waterlogged, we cached one of them and all five went ahead in the other. We picked up the trail again after scaling this portage, and after paddling against a stiff current for another two hours camped at 7.30 P.M. at the foot of "Long Dog Rapids," about 75 miles from Kapuskasing.

We spent most of Thursday morning, the 12th, in surmounting Long Dog Rapids. These rapids follow a winding course and roar down without a break for a distance of almost three miles, while the portage trail is two miles long, very hilly, and covered with deadfalls and second growth. We portaged the dunnage, each trip requiring an hour, and as it was a physical impossibility to carry our water-soaked freighter over, we dragged it up the edge of the rapids through water sometimes knee-deep, sometimes neck-deep. It was a fearful performance but we had to get through. Again, just above Long Dog, we had to pass two shorter rapids and as the portage trails were impassable, we dragged the canoe up as before. Just above this again we once more found footprints on the bank where the prisoners had stooped to drink. At 12.15 P.M. we smelt smoke, and landing immediately found a small camp-fire still smouldering and beside it a bed of balsam boughs and some rags off a pair of hospital pyjamas. This was quite evidently their camp of the night before, so we knew that we were very close. At 2.50 P.M. on turning a sudden bend, we found ourselves at the foot of another rapids, and saw at once on the left-hand bank a shirt hung out on an alder-bush to dry. Paddling up noiselessly, we could see on the shore a fire, a couple of small pails, and an axe stuck in a log. Fearing that our quarry might even now bolt into the forest and be lost, I took my Automatic and walked in from the shore. About thirty feet in I found the two men wrapped up in blankets and sound asleep. I spoke to them and they woke with a start. As I was in civilian clothes and wore a five days' beard they did not recognise me or any of my party, but thought us prospectors, claimed to be lost in the woods, and asked for a lift. I broke the news gently, and complied.

The prisoners had two small axes, the remains of two fifty-pound sacks of flour, of three pails of lard, and of two tins of baking powder, two suits of pyjamas, 2 pairs of boots, 2 pairs of pants, 2 blankets, 1 woollen coat, 1 sweatercoat, 3 cakes of soap, 1 toothbrush, 1 file, 1 razor, some candles, and $11.55 in cash. Most of these belongings were in a large packsack. Rino claimed that when they started out they had also had two tins of cocoa, one large ham, a small tent, a revolver and ammunition, a gold watch, and a compass, but had lost all this in escaping from quicksand in a moose marsh.

Miller, who was manifestly the weaker vessel, had nothing to say and seemed very much out of spirits. Rino, however, was quite talkative and gave a fairly full account of himself. He had, during April, made preparations for an escape via working parties, and had had all necessary supplies brought in from outside and cached for him by a friendly trapper. His admission to hospital with a sprained ankle was an unexpected windfall and he decamped as soon as his ankle began to improve, Miller, a sufferer from phlebitis, chancing it with him. They had slipped from the hospital ward on the night of May 27th shortly before midnight and had heard the alarm given not fifteen minutes later. Their plan had been to get a canoe over behind Married Quarters, then paddle down stream and up the Missinaibi, finally portaging over to Michipicoten, Lake Superior, and the States. The untimely arrival of two civilians kept them from getting a canoe, so they changed their minds and started up stream. Just below Kabahose Falls they tried to make a raft but it proved unserviceable so they left it moored to the bank, and trudged ahead on the same shore. The undergrowth was terribly dense and hostile; they had to make detours to avoid marshes; flies and mosquitoes left their bodies an ugly mass of scabs and swellings; their net progress was seldom more than five miles per day. A few miles above Twin Rapids they built a raft and paddling up stream for some distance landed on the east bank and turned their craft adrift, hoping that it would float down over the falls and be broken up. Soon after, in crossing the narrow river-entrance to a moose lake, Rino had been caught in quicksand and had had to throw off his load to escape. Only what Miller was carrying was saved. They now felt completely down and out, but a mile farther on they found an old Indian canoe. It had two holes in it but they patched it with birch bark and spruce gum and proceeded by water as far as Steep Dog Rapids where they failed to find the portage and abandoned the canoe. From there they went forward on foot until caught. They said that they had not expected anyone to follow them so far up, and further that they had thought it impossible for canoemen to get above Steep Dog and Long Dog Rapids and that beyond them they were safe. Indeed, that very morning they had paused for the first time to shave, wash their clothes, and rest up thoroughly before completing the last stages of their trip. Our arrival and identity proved, therefore, a great surprise.

Our return trip was uneventful but exceedingly trying. Our rations were running short and in our race with starvation we covered 45 miles on Friday, including three bad portages, and the remaining 25 miles and 7 portages on Saturday. Had it not been for the prisoners' supplies we should have been without food on Friday, and as it was, our larder gave out on Saturday at noon on a last lunch of cheese and hardtack. The two men gave us no trouble on the way back. From the point of capture to Steep Dog Rapids the following morning, we travelled seven to the canoe, plus dunnage, and so had had to be very careful. At night each of us spent two hours on guard over the prisoners, who did not sleep at all but kept stirring restlessly in the light of the campfire with one open eye fixed furtively on us. We reached Kapuskasing, ravenous and weary, at 4.00 P.M. on Saturday, June 14th, and returned our prisoners, unscolded, to the Compound.

A guest at our mess for a day or two in 1919 was the Governor-General, the ninth Duke of Devonshire, together with his young aide and son-in-law-elect, Mr. Harold Macmillan. The staff's post-mortem verdict on the visit was that His Excellency was a very dull dog indeed. What he thought of us is not recorded. In retrospect, one can doubtless see that he felt no compulsion to sparkle in conversation at our glum, hyperborean table and was content to be his naturally taciturn self among these oafs of the subarctic.

My return to civil life towards the end of July 1919 did not mean the end of my service with Internment Operations. A month later, I was invited to be transport officer in charge of 445 prisoners and an escort consisting of a medical officer, two NCO's, and 23 other ranks, on board the S.S. "Pretorian" sailing from Quebec on September 3, turning over the prisoners to Dutch guards at Rotterdam twelve days later. That they bore me no ill will for my performance at Fort Henry and Kapuskasing seemed clear when on the wharf my former prisoners called for "three cheers for Captain Kirkconnell," and gave them lustily.

During my lifetime, Canada's attitude towards war has changed profoundly. At the time of the South African War, enlistment in the armed services was not a duty but an exotic privilege embraced by the rare few. In the earlier phases of World War I, participation was still very much an individual option, but as the struggle on a world scale grew more and more grim, public insistence on "conscription" grew more and more clamorous. In World War II, there was from the outset an awareness of the principles of "total war" and a decision to mobilize all of the resources of the country in a struggle for survival. This is not the place to analyse that administrative performance in detail. I have already done so in the *Encyclopedia Americana*, first, year by year, in the "annuals" and then in consolidated form in the new edition of 1953.

It was typical of Canada's vast scale of national operations during the six years of World War II that my services could be relevant in certain non-combatant ways—lecture tours on war issues for the Association of Canadian Clubs in 1939–41, a share in unifying such communities as the Ukrainians into a single national committee behind the war effort, a share in organizing the federal Department of National War Services and in serving on the advisory committee of its Nationalities Branch, and, last but not least, in serving as the first and only chairman of the Writers' War Committee of Canada. These several activities are described in Chapters XIV, XVIII, XXIII, and XXIV.

One considerable section of my personal library of 7000 volumes had been built up around this appalling "World War II" and its even more appalling consequences. An invaluable commentary consisted of the five massive volumes of Francis Neilson's *The Tragedy of Europe*, supplemented by his *Makers of War*, *The Churchill Legend*, and *My Life in Two Worlds* and by a hoard of pamphlets that he mailed to me regularly. Or one may cite James J. Martin's invaluable two-volume work on *American Liberalism and World Politics, 1931–1941*. Equally relevant were Harry Elmer Barnes's symposium, *Perpetual War for Perpetual Peace*, George N. Crocker's *Roosevelt's Road to Russia*, Albert C. Wedemeyer's *Wedemeyer Reports*, Charles Callan Tansill's *Back Door to War*, Norman Angell's *The Steep Places*, Thomas Callander's *The Athenian Empire and the British*, Jacques Maritain's *Twilight of Civilization*, Tufton Beamish's *Must Night Fall?*, J. K. Zawodny's *Death in the Forest*, Captain Russell Grenfell's *Unconditional Hatred*, F. J. P. Veale's *Advance to Barbarism*, and *War Crimes Discreetly Veiled* and scores of similar volumes. The evil fate inflicted on a dozen once free countries with the concurrence of Roosevelt and the unwilling acquiescence of Churchill was expounded in magistral books by Reuben Markham, Stephen Kertesz, W. J. Sheridan, John H. Wuorinen, David J. Dallin, John Flournoy Montgomery, Sisley Huddleston, Adam B. Ulam, V. Raud, David Martin, Joseph M. Kirshbaum, Ants Oras, J. Hampden Jackson, Clarence A. Manning, Richard Hunter, and Wm. Henry Chamberlin.

When I went on to read books by masters of military strategy—notably General J. F. C. Fuller, Captain B. H. Liddell Hart, and Colonel F. O. Miksche—I was almost beside myself with grief and anger at the military crimes and follies that they described in such trenchant and unanswerable detail.

One of the most harrowing of British errors was the decision to bomb civilians. On February 15, 1940, the British Prime Minister assured the House of Commons that his country would adhere to international engagements and its own earlier declarations in the matter of the bombing of non-combatants: "Whatever be the length to which others might go, the Government will never resort to blackguardly attacks on women and other civilians for the purpose of mere terrorism" (*Hansard*, vol. 357, H. of C. Deb. 5s, col. 924). Alas, in General Fuller's *The Second World War* (p. 222) the responsibility for the mass bombing of civilians is placed squarely at the door of the Churchill administration in its bombing of the peaceful old university city of Freiburg on May 11, 1940. Thus he quotes Mr. J. M. Spaight, Principal Assistant Secretary of the Air Ministry: "We (the British) began to bomb objectives on the German mainland before the Germans began to bomb objectives on the British mainland. That is an historical fact which has been publicly admitted. . . . Yet, because we were doubtful about the psychological effect of propagandist distortion of the truth that it was we who started the strategic offensive, we have shrunk from giving our great decision of May, 1940, the publicity that it deserved" (*Bombing Vindicated*, by J. M. Spaight, 1944, pp. 68, 74). General Fuller then proceeds: "Thus, on Mr. Spaight's evidence, it was Mr. Churchill who lit the fuse which detonated a war of devastation and terrorization unrivalled since the invasions of the Seljuks." General Fuller then emphasizes that for three months, May to August, there was no retaliation from Hitler, and he concludes that there is little doubt that these three months of British air massacre in Freiburg and other German cities "pushed him into his assault on Britain." Yet as recently as August 1965 the CBC was blithely assuring Canadians that the bombing of civilians in World War II had been begun *by the Germans* and *in August 1940.*

Month by month and campaign by campaign, Fuller exposes the military stupidity of this mass bombing in contrast to the vastly more effective tactical bombing of oil, coal, shipping, and railways that finally won the war. The chief result of the sheer destructiveness in mass bombing was that the RAF and USAF blew the bottom out of the peace that was to come, for rubble heaps are no foundation on which to build a new order. (cf. Fuller, *op. cit.*, p. 317).

An equally disastrous decision was made by the West's two leaders in the matter of war aims, for they announced at the Casablanca Conference of January 1943 that the "unconditional surrender" of all enemies was their inexorable purpose. This insane slogan was thenceforward "to hang like a putrifying albatross around the necks of America and Britain," for it united the Germans in desperation behind the leaders that they had been ready to repudiate and it also made certain that all equilibrium in the European power system would be utterly smashed, leaving Russia as the only effective military power on the Continent. This guaranteed "the replacement of Nazi tyranny by an even more barbaric despotism" (Fuller, *op. cit.*, p. 259).

Finally, in *Advance to Barbarism*, published in 1953 by the English barrister, F. J. P. Veale, with a commendatory preface by Dean Inge, the author sums up a closely documented analysis of the Nürnberg trials: "The war-trials actually left in ruins the principles of justice which had been accepted without question by all civilized peoples for many centuries . . . and made mandatory the utilization of the most savage methods in warfare in order to avert defeat and judicial lynching" (*op. cit.*, p. 297). The war-trials chickens were coming home to roost in 1966 with the captured American pilots in North Vietnam.

The military analysts find Hitler likewise guilty of colossal errors. One of these was his obsession that Slavic peoples, such as the Ukrainians, were an inferior human species, fit only to be ploughed under by the Nordics. More than half the population of Soviet Russia was ready to welcome the Germans as deliverers from Communism, and honest collaboration with their hopes would have seen the Soviet Union fall apart. When Hitler, on the contrary, treated them as conquered people and turned their leaders over to his political police, he forced all nationalities into resolute resistance. His military strategy, in cases where Hitler himself intervened against his generals, was again defective. Thus, the "miracle" at Dunkirk was due simply to Hitler's personal refusal to let Field Marshal von Rundstedt annihilate the English with his five panzer divisions (cf. Fuller, *op. cit.*, p. 76). Hitler's also was the fatal decision in July 1942 to postpone the reduction of Malta until after the "conquest of Egypt" was completed (cf. Fuller, *op. cit.*, p. 167). The plan of a single campaign to seize the Caucasian oil fields without simultaneously occupying Moscow and Saratov and paralysing Russian rail transport was again Hitler's amateurish decision and one that cost him the Russian War. Fuller (*op. cit.*, p. 117) considers that this was because he imagined he could finish off Russia in a single blitz campaign before the Americans could mobilize for war.

General Fuller and Captain Liddell Hart have their own counsels for the international predicaments of today.

The former, for example, cites the UN forecast of 1,600,000,000 Chinese by A.D. 2000, and envisages this industrial colossus as sprawling over Asiatic Russia in its desire for living space. Under that pressure, the Soviet Union, he suggests, might reasonably agree to an alliance with the West on such terms as the liberation of Eastern Europe and the reunification of Germany. In the meantime, however, and as long as the Soviets remain committed to the overthrow of all non-Communist governments in the world, the Western powers should avoid all conferences with them as they would the plague. Whenever we consent to dicker with them, especially at "summit conferences," we betray our own front line, the captive peoples of Eastern Europe. Captain Liddell Hart, in his turn, advocates unlimited patience. "Settlements" in treaty form should be avoided; they are dangerous, because they are not adjustable to changing conditions. "War is not a way *out* from danger and strain. It is a way *down* into a pit—of unknown depth." Situations charged with the peril of war can change for the better if war can be avoided *without surrender*.

The gladiatorial states of Thomas Hobbes's international polity must keep the peace lest the whole amphitheatre become nothing but bloody sand and universal death. But for some of the gladiators to throw away their weapons as a matter of unilateral policy, would only mean their own extermination.

10

In the Cause of Peace

DURING MY TIME at Oxford University, enthusiasm for the League of Nations ran high and I was privileged to share in an "Oxford International Assembly" that duplicated at the Oxford Union some of the debates of the League Assembly. "Bliss was it in that dawn to be alive, But to be young was very heaven." Echoes of the new epoch followed me about Europe. In Prague, for example, I found a "Woodrow Wilson Railway Station," dedicated to the memory of the great idealist.

Zeal for peace came back with me to Canada, and in no time at all I leaped into a fight. *Saturday Night*, Toronto, then under the editorship of Hector Charlesworth, had been pontificating against the financial "waste" of Canada's participation in the League, and my first contribution (June 25, 1923) to that forum of opinion was a belligerent defence of our share in the world organization.

Needless to say, I was active almost from the beginning in the Manitoba branch of the League of Nations Society. One of its strong early leaders was the Rev. Dr. David Christie, of Westminster Presbyterian Church. Another was his gaunt, Savonarola-like successor, John Sutherland Bonnell, later the minister of the Fifth Avenue Presbyterian Church, New York. Still another was Lewis St. George Stubbs, then a senior county court judge and a doughty fighter in local politics.

Early in the 1930's, I was invited to head up a local "peace conference." The instigators were the local executive of the Womens' International League for Peace and Freedom. I had very little acquaintance with the organization, but some of the women were well and favourably known. There were to be study sessions in the old Law Courts building of the University, a youth session in Theatre "C," a peace luncheon at the Marlborough Hotel, and a final evening session in Theatre "A," to which it was hoped to attract a large section of the general public.

At first all went well. The study sessions were well attended and only once or twice was there a tense moment when the female watch-dogs of the WILPF bared their teeth at a hint of a statement that was something less than one hundred per cent pacific. At the luncheon, I myself was the speaker and dispensed a highly spiced postprandial mixture of my recent reading on international armament firms' intrigues and on Zoroastrian religion. The "merchants of death" obviously belonged to the demonic hosts of Ahriman and were giving the angelic hosts of Ormuzd a bad time of it. Interest quickened at the youth session when a Young Communist League delegation under Joe Zuken arrived and proceeded to monopolize the discussion. I had never been chairman at quite so refractory a meeting, nor at one in which the manifest victory of Communism throughout the world was so resolutely prophesied. But the real excitement came at the evening session. I had persuaded John W. Dafoe to be the speaker. His subject was Woodrow Wilson and the founding of the League of Nations. Dafoe was in great form that night and paid eloquent tribute to his hero: the United States had had three supremely great presidents—Washington, Lincoln, and Wilson—and Wilson was not the least of the three! A discussion period followed and some of the audience began to needle him with regard to Canada's participation in World War I. Finally the lion lost his temper, shook his great red mane, and roared: "In the late War, the Canadians who really wanted peace fought for it." Instantly, four score pacifists were on their hind legs screaming at him. Five seconds later, eight score veterans, wives of veterans, and widows of veterans were standing up and shouting at the pacifists. The meeting broke up in hopeless disorder.

Two weeks later, I myself fell from grace with the Women's International League. Colonel George H. Gillespie, chief cadet officer for Manitoba, had invited me to testify before the Winnipeg School Board as to the value of cadet training for character and citizenship, and I had gladly done so. From several years of participation in the movement, I knew that it faced the realities of our world and did well by the young people who took part. I also believed that for the free world to disarm, physically and morally, in a world of iniquity and aggression, was simply to invite our own destruction. A security system under a League of Nations implied a willingness to invoke sanctions and a strength to impose them. All this was consistent with a sincere desire for peace and gave it sanity. As the colonel and I came out of the meeting, we met in the corridor a group of grim-faced matrons "Who glared upon me and went surly by." It was a delegation from the WILPF, waiting to go in and assure the School Board that a cadet corps was an invention of the Devil. I was never again invited to manage a peace conference for them or for anyone else. At this very time, of course, with almost negligible exceptions, Canada had no soldiers, no modern arms, no tanks, no armoured cars, no medium or heavy artillery, no anti-aircraft guns, no uniforms, no coastal defence, and no armament industry. We were spending less on our defence budget than any other nation in the world. I was not surprised, years later, when the USSR was spending colossal peacetime sums on arms, to find some of the WILPF women running on a Communist ticket in Toronto. Some of those who had clamoured against toy drums and tin soldiers were no doubt honestly concerned over *bella matribus detestata*, but some were mainly concerned in keeping us weak in the interests of the World Revolution.

Actually it was very difficult to keep the general public even mildly interested in international affairs. When Dr. Bonnell went to New York City in 1935, I succeeded him in the presidency of the Winnipeg branch of the League of Nations Society and began to realize how public enthusiasm had ebbed. My invaluable secretary was first Mr. David Howard and later, a law student, Sam Freedman, now Mr. Justice Freedman. A good example of public apathy occurred at that time. The Japanese had opened their campaign of aggression on the Asiatic mainland—a campaign that was later to over-run all of Southeast Asia and to threaten India and Australia. I arranged for a meeting in Theatre "B," Broadway site, to be addressed by Dr. Edgar J. Tarr, our chief Canadian authority on the Pacific, who had only recently returned from the Far East. The meeting was well advertised in the Winnipeg dailies and over the radio. Yet the total audience that gathered to hear a vital talk on a vital topic consisted (in addition to the president and the secretary) of one forlorn woman.

My successors in the presidency were Rabbi Solomon Frank, now of the Sherith-Israel Spanish–Portuguese Synagogue in Montreal, a very tall, burly Ph.D., who easily made two of me physically, Mrs. Jessie Maclennan, an ardent Labour leader, and C. Rhodes Smith, later dean of the Manitoba Law School.

Several of the books that I wrote and published between 1927 and 1935 might also be regarded as contributions to the cause of peace. Such was *The European Heritage* (1930) of which *The Bookman* of London was kind enough to say: "If every newspaper in Europe would devote a column to this volume, baptising themselves in its grace . . . more would be done in the way of putting an end to war than is possible by the mouths of prelates and state orators." Making also for a deeper human understanding were the numerous volumes of translations, beginning with *European Elegies* and launching out into the great European series of which Icelandic, Magyar, and Polish were brought to completion.

Oddly enough, I was finally consigned to the doghouse insofar as the League of Nations Society was concerned. In the summer of 1938, I had visited most of the countries of Europe. That winter, a little United College student monthly, *Vox*, had asked me for an article on the boiling pot of European politics. In the course of that article, I had occasion to refer slightingly to what I considered an unrealistic statement by Senator Cairine Wilson regarding the functions of the League on behalf of Czechoslovakia. To my astonishment, I was promptly and loudly spanked in public on the editorial page of the *Winnipeg Free Press*. An assistant editor, who had never given a damn for the Society and had not attended a meeting within living memory, had come across my humble article and gleefully decided to make an example of me. Back of all this lay a hangover of resentment because I had criticized the *Free Press* a few months before for printing the Runciman Report on Czechoslovakia with all of its anti-Czech paragraphs neatly suppressed. Nor was this all. At the national office of the League of Nations Society in Ottawa, a young secretary, who had been in short pants when I was already a public champion of the League, proceeded to lift the *Free Press* denunciation and print it in a box in the national *Bulletin* of the Society. I scarcely knew whether to be angry or amused.

Senator Wilson herself did not seem to have taken offence. My original remark had been a difference of opinion and not a personal affront. In years thereafter we worked amicably together in the Refugee Organization. But to readers of the *Free Press* and the *League of Nations Society Bulletin*, I was now an ill-mannered enemy of the Society! Twenty years of faithful service had apparently been rubbed out overnight by the spleen of two bright young men.

Perhaps I ought not to have worried too greatly. Early in 1941, I was invited to address the Ottawa branch of the League of Nations Society on the problem of nationality in the modern world and was given a royal reception.

In the autumn of 1940, I had been approached by friends soliciting my support of the "Union Now" project, proposed by Clarence Streit. A letter from Bill Deacon of Toronto, dated October 28, 1940, stated in part:

DEAR KIRK:

Undoubtedly you must be familiar with the Union Now idea, the immediate program for which is merely the amalgamation of our Commonwealth and the United States. This may soon be an urgent military necessity. Large bodies belong to the English and American ends but there is no Canadian society as yet. So a few of us—Librarian Charles Sanderson in the chair—will meet Jean-Charles Harvey as temporary head for Canada at the Authors' club rooms, 99 Yonge St., this Friday evening at 8:30 to set up an organizing committee. . . . I am sorry I haven't time to explain very fully but come if you can. Further, if you have friends who are seriously interested bring them along, provided the name is not Tim Buck. . . . U.S.A. and Britain are anxious that Canada take the initiative, and I think the small, informal gathering on Friday may become historic. . . .

My reply on October 30 was a mixture of enthusiasm and caution:

MY DEAR BILL,—

If Friday's meeting looks towards a union of the Commonwealth and the U.S.A. with Canada as an honest broker between the two, then I am all for it and shall try to get over on Friday.

My only misgiving is over Jean-Charles Harvey. I have just been reading this week's issue of *Le Jour*, and find him strongly urging an immediate union of Canada and the U.S.A., without any hint of Britain, the Commonwealth, or the free democracies. I think the narrower version is political dynamite that would shatter any hope of the larger consummation and leave us stunned and begrimed amid the fragments. For God's sake, keep Britain in the picture!

In the sequel, nothing came of the movement. Over thirteen months were to pass before the United States became a belligerent and hence even eligible to consider organic union. In the meantime, most serious-minded people were concerned with concentrating every ounce of effort on a war of survival. Less creditable but far more potent was the drive, after June 23, 1941, to stampede the Commonwealth and the United States into the most intimate friendship with the Soviet Union—a drive exploited by Moscow for purposes of espionage and pro-Communist ballyhoo. In this thickening Red fog, the plant of Anglo-Saxon union quietly withered and died.

For the "United Nations" organization that succeeded the League of Nations in 1945, I found it hard to feel any enthusiasm. The participation of Soviet Russia made all our talk of freedom, peace, and humanity a hypocritical fraud. Soviet armies were murdering men and raping women by the million all over Eastern Europe. In ten once-free nations, a systematic extermination of whole strata of the population was under way. Yet, in the midst of this betrayal of human freedom, Western diplomats and journalists fawned on the Soviet representatives at San Francisco and uttered pious generalities about the new world of human rights and human freedom that they were inaugurating together. It was nauseating, and still is.

I tried at least to keep the Canadian record clear and published in the *Evening Telegram*, Toronto, a whole series of articles telling the grim truth that was being suppressed. "Of Soviet-Imperialism" and "Preface to San Francisco" were the main indictments, with special detailed supplements on Poland, the Baltic States, and Jugoslavia. It was impossible to see how stooge governments that held ten nations captive and were making war on their populations could be counted on to maintain international peace.

Underlying all of these activities of mine and giving them meaning has been a lifelong interest in historical reading on the subject of war and peace. Just when such reading began, I cannot be sure, but I can recall a significant episode at Queen's in 1915, when I was a youth of twenty and a captain in the COTC. For an interclass debate, our year (Arts '16) was to propose a subject and the freshman class was to have its choice of side. When appealed to in committee, I suggested "Resolved that the Triple Entente shares in responsibility for the outbreak of the War in 1914." The freshman promptly chose the negative and won by default, for the seniors found it impossible to field a team. Even that early in the campaign, it was deemed impossible to face the public emotions supporting the official version of the War. A good deal of material would have been available. Morgan Shuster's *The Strangling of Persia* (1912) had revealed the dark deeds of Britain and Russia in Iran, on behalf of predatory big business. E. D. Morel's *Morocco in Diplomacy* (1912) had proved that behind a public treaty guaranteeing the integrity of Morocco lay a secret Franco-British treaty approving of the partition of Morocco between France and Spain. The London *Times* of November 19, 1912, had said indignantly: "Who, then, makes war? The answer is to be found in the Chancelleries of Europe, among men who have too long played with human lives as pawns in a game of chess." Above all, Francis Neilson's *How Diplomats Make War* (1915) had indicted the secret diplomacy of Lansdowne, Grey, Asquith, Delcassé, Cambon, Sazonov, and Zvolsky, the belligerent activities of Fisher and Churchill, and the sinister meddling of Edward VII. But I had been childishly naïve to imagine that academic detachment could be preserved in such a wartime debate, even at a quiet Canadian university.

With the coming of peace, there emerged a whole series of volumes to confirm my callow intuitions as to a shared culpability. The former Lord Chancellor, Lord Loreburn, wrote *How the War Came* (1919), and made it clear that Grey and Asquith had lied to the House of Commons, in declaring that Britain had no military commitments abroad, while all the time they had been tied militarily to France since 1905 and to Russia since 1908. Lord Fisher's *Memories* (1919) boasted that he had invented the Dreadnought expressly to "Copenhagen the German fleet" and had abusively turned down Tirpitz's appeal for a limitation of armaments. In the *Intimate Papers of Colonel House*, we find a letter to President Wilson, dated May 29, 1914—a month before the Archduke was shot at Sarajevo—that affirms: "Whenever England consents, France and Russia will close in on Germany and Austria." This is amply confirmed in the pre-war despatches of the British ambassadors to Paris, St. Petersburg, and Vienna as published in 1926 in an honest interlude under Snowden and MacDonald. Criminally amputated versions had been published earlier to support government propaganda, and the French Yellow Book of 1914 included actual forgeries that sought to shift the blame for mobilization from Russia to Germany. Alfred Fabre-Luce's *Histoire de la révolution Européenne* gives the real time-table: "Now the order for Russian general mobilization was given at 4 P.M. on the 30th of July, twenty hours before the order for Austrian general mobilization and the German proclamation of a state of 'danger of war' and forty-eight hours before the German and French mobilizations." Churchill, with the consent of the Cabinet, had mobilized the British fleet for war on July 24, and Grey at once notified the Tsar. The fleet put out from Weymouth on July 25 "to bottle up the German navy." The best of all the research volumes was Sidney B. Fay's *Origins of the World War* (1928) a masterly recapitulation of the whole sorry business. In a full note (pp. 377–382) to Neilson's *How Diplomats Make War*, the so-called Belgian Treaty of 1839, whose alleged destruction by Germany was later given by the British cabinet as a pretext for fulfilling their secret agreement with France and Russia, turns out to have been a guarantee to the Netherlands, and it had been made clear as far back as Salisbury's day, in 1887, that there was no obligation of Britain alone to defend Belgium. Woodrow Wilson had lied the United States into the War in 1917 by citing as a *casus belli* the sinking of the *Sussex* with the loss of American lives—whereas the *Sussex* had not been sunk nor had any American lives been lost on it. Later he found, to his dismay, that his allies had concealed from him a whole nest of secret agreements for the division of the spoils. On his return from Paris in disgust in 1920, he declared that the whole bloody war had been fought by the Allies for trade advantages. This gave scant comfort to the survivors of twenty million dead and to the victims of astronomical taxes.

After an evil war came an evil peace. The Carthaginian treaties laid down, in complete breach of the Armistice terms, carried with them the explosive certainty of further disaster. John Maynard Keynes's *Economic Consequences of the Peace* (1920) not merely condemned the war as one for trade but also prophesied in careful detail that its economic terms were perilous and impossible. Their political terms were even more implacable and grim. And the League of Nations, although originally formed by an idealist and regarded as a potential device for modifying the injustices of war-fever treaties, became in practice a quagmire of talk and bureaucratic inertia, frustrating every attempt to redress the woes of the vanquished. A notable example was the outrages inflicted by the dominant Czech minority on an actual majority of non-

Czech population in their synthetic state. Some nineteen appeals in twenty years were made to the League by these minorities, and all were smothered in the Circumlocution Office. The same fate swallowed up appeals by Germans, Austrians, and Magyars. In Hungary, Count Paul Teleki, who always sought peaceful solutions, presented me with some thirty Magyar volumes on the Treaty of Trianon and its evil consequences. Yet I clung to the hope that a sincere use of the League could remove injustice and maintain a world at peace.

When I turn to my own *International Aspects of Unemployment*, I find that I was still deluded in 1922 by such bogus evidence as Cambon's mendacious letter to Pichon from Berlin in 1913, the false Morgenthau story of the "Potsdam Council," and the "Lerchenfeld documents" into assigning blame for the war to the wrong culprits, but my studies and travels in central Europe and the Near East left me in no doubt as to the appalling consequences of the Punic peace terms. In Central Europe, I had seen the *hybris* of the Czechs and the starvation of the Viennese, while in Asia Minor and Syria I had gazed at the fatal consequences of commercial greed on the part of France and Italy. Of the chaos of those times I wrote:

> Two other vials of calamity, however, have been poured out upon us. One is the evil influence of the various peace treaties by which the Allies have sought to solve Europe's problems on a basis of nationalism and retribution; the other is the virtual collapse, in many countries, of the money economy on which modern credit and trade have been based. . . .

I found France the chief villain of the piece:

> If Poincaré succeeds in dominating Europe, the crazy Continent will soon crash to the ground. . . . The sabre-rattling spirit of Louis XIV and Napoleon I dictates too often the present policies of France. . . . Her irresponsible nationalism may be regarded as the greatest single obstacle to European reconstruction. . . .

In my next political volume, *Canada, Europe and Hitler* (1939) I based my estimate of the Nazi régime on a careful reading of Hitler's *Mein Kampf* which I had bought in Berlin in July 1938, ploughing through nearly eight hundred pages of crabbed and belligerent German on my homeward voyage. What I read alarmed me, for he talked with complete frankness of his plans for conquest, especially in his section on "Ostpolitik." Francis Neilson has since argued with some acuity (*The Makers of War*, pp. 178–195) that a timely adjustment of the immoral terms of the peace treaties of 1919–21 might have blunted the edge of his ardour and contributed to a safe political balance in Europe. The Hitler who wrote *Mein Kampf* in 1925 might conceivably have been more than a blazing rebel against injustice. It was disquieting, however, to hear him lament the Germans' previous lack of monolithic unity, because otherwise they would now be masters of the world—*Dann würde das Deutsche Reich heute wohl Herrin des Erdballs sein.* Even a brief visit with friends in Germany had convinced me, moreover, of the reality of informers and the secret police.

I realize with regret, however, how little I foresaw in October 1939 the disastrous collapse of intelligence and morality that the war would bring, for I wrote in my innocence:

> The statesmen of Britain, in their wisdom, realize not merely that a war explicitly to destroy or cripple German nationhood would so unite that great people in a frenzy of resistance that we might well lose the war, but also that without the explicit ideal of ultimate peacetime collaboration with a liberated German nation, our wartime passions would issue in a vindictive peace settlement which would again sow dragon's teeth for our children.

What is the wartime duty of a citizen who deplores the diplomatic intrigues that have drawn his country into the cataract? When politicians and journalists are lashing the citizenry into a frenzy of patriotic fervour, shall he dare to court contumely and internment by pointing out some of the awkward facts of history? It is a difficult problem. A strong sense of loyalty binds him to his own nation in its peril. On the other hand, he sees the misguided whipping up of passions making impossible any sort of post-war settlement, except one that will shower redoubled calamity down upon the heads of his grandchildren. To speak out on the mingled truth and falsehood of pre-war policies may only serve to label the truth as "disloyal" and make it still more difficult for veracity to prevail. He may seem, albeit innocently, to be echoing the agents of intrigue from other countries, and may thus either aid their conspiracies or be fouled with their filth in the public mind. A Bertrand Russell may have the metaphysical poise to walk this tightrope with equanimity, but a man who has been more involved in communal life and has numerous young children to share in his personal disaster will think twice before taking up a belligerently unpopular position.

Loyalty in wartime is completely natural, but this ought not to include a readiness to utter conscious falsehoods for one's country. Hence it was that the Writers' War Committee of Canada, under my chairmanship, never tampered with the truth for propaganda purposes. In 1943, however, the Honourable Brendan Bracken, Great Britain's Minister of Information, assured an astonished House of Commons that the Soviet Union had never broken its word—although scores of instances were on the record. The British Broadcasting Corporation doctored wartime broadcasting to Jugoslavia in the interests of the Communist, Tito, and an honest English journalist, F. A. Voigt, who dared to point out this fact, was viciously slandered for it until he took his case to the courts and won back his reputation. When on the eve of the San Francisco

Conference, I made bold to publish several articles on Russia's record of butchery, rape, and looting, a Toronto newspaper proprietor tried to have me dismissed from my university post at McMaster. In a world of propaganda, to "tread upon the lion and adder" does not necessarily bring angelic intervention on behalf of the truth.

Hence it was that during World War II my chief effort went into the preserving of Canadian national unity. Many Anglo-Canadians in their folly would have abolished the entire foreign language press, but my *Canada, Europe and Hitler*, chiefly written before the outbreak of war, vouched for the patriotic worth of most of them and helped to prevent this reckless amputation. For the first two or three years of the war I was constantly in action, before Canadian Clubs and in conjunction with the Wartime Information Board and the CBC, in stressing the essential integrity of the Canadian people, regardless of origin. My anthology, *The Quebec Tradition*, chosen by Séraphin Marion and translated by myself, was a sympathetic presentation of the Canadian French to the Canadian English. All of these patriotic endeavours might have been jeopardized had I gone overboard for an unpalatable version of the origins of the war. One could only seek privately to sort out the current facts from the flux of press and radio and hope that sanity might return with peace. Rereading Thucydides, however, brought no assured optimism, for the old Athenian noted the complete demoralization of semantics during a prolonged struggle:

> Words had to change their ordinary meaning and take that which was now given them. Reckless audacity came to be considered the courage of a loyal ally; prudent hesitation, specious cowardice; moderation was held to be a cloak for unmanliness; ability to see all sides of a question, inaptness to act on any. Frantic violence became the attribute of manliness; cautious plotting, a justifiable means of self-defence. The advocate of extreme measures was always trustworthy; his opponent a man to be suspected.

Looking back over the years, I have seen a gradual emergence of truth after each wartime orgy of lying for victory, but we have always seemed to reconsolidate at a still lower moral level. After one more such period of manipulated historiography, we shall have sunk to the ineffable party history of *Nineteen-Eighty-Four* or the *Great Soviet Encyclopaedia*, incessantly doctored by the "court historians" in the interests of an entrenched bureaucracy. With the suppression of the "Tyler Kent documents," we are already far along the road. The orotund *Commentaries* of our new Caesars give us eloquent literary versions of martial events, but the concurrent maintenance of drawn blinds by the blackout squads of the national archives shows how far we have come: "Debilis nunc est veritas, et numquam fortasse prevalebit."

11

Social Service

LONG BEFORE THE SUN was up on wintry mornings in 1900, we children could hear the tramp of heavy feet on the wooden sidewalk in front of our Bedford Street home. Six days a week the straggling processional went past shortly before 7.00 A.M., and six days a week it returned in grimy weariness shortly after 6.00 P.M. It was the era of the sixty-hour week, and these were the workers at Craig's Tannery, the Nicholson File Factory, and the Brewery—all on Cavan Street, amid the humbler cottages of the recent Irish immigrants.

Of how they lived, we had little idea. Our own home, which had been built for himself long before by Mr. William Craig, owner of the Tannery, and had been purchased by my father on a long-term instalment basis, was an eight-room, red-brick box, originally heated by some seven fireplaces but more recently supplied with a hot-air furnace for the ground-floor rooms. We had outdoor privies, an outdoor soft-water cistern, and an outdoor hard-water well whose pump had to be thawed out and primed in cold weather. We knew nothing of electricity or telephones until we moved to Lindsay in 1908. In default of regular household help, all five children learned the arts of housework and shared in the chores. The four sons slept in a single bedroom. It may be surmised that there was no great gulf between the family of the high school headmaster (himself a farmer's son) and the factory-workers' children with whom we presently associated daily in the town school. In fact, one of my childhood heroes was "Dawe" Hills, the massively built son of a humble Cavan Street family, whose good temper and good judgement were exemplary.

Apart from housework, tending the chickens, and hoeing in the family garden, however, I knew little of manual labour until the age of seventeen, when I tried a summer job in a Lindsay concrete-tile factory, pushing a wheelbarrow full of wet sand. My back soon gave out and I ended up in bed. Commercial jobs in my high school days were clerking in Neills' shoe store during the Christmas holidays and hawking baskets of grapes on the sidewalk each year in front of Mortons' Confectionery during the three days of the fall fair. My record in industry and commerce was brief and humble.

Neither had I had much of a glimpse of the field of social service. Once or twice our Port Hope family had been taken for a seven-mile drive down the gravelled toll road towards Cobourg and had seen an "Old Folks' Home" on the outskirts of the latter town. In Lindsay our Baptist Young People's Society had occasionally put on a Sunday afternoon service for the elderly folk in the bleak "House of Refuge" out on the Little Britain road and sensed something of the drab hopelessness of the place. I had even gone with our minister, Rev. G. R. Welch, to the "Children's Shelter" where waifs from rural slums in the remoter parts of the county were held, pending adoption. The uncontrolled farm-settlement of hopelessly inferior tracts of Ontario wilderness, underlain by sterile sand, gravel and bed-rock, had resulted in demoralized, in-bred communities, too poor to sustain health and too exhausted to move to better territory. A devoted woman, known to my generation as "the Kidnapper," salvaged some of the hapless offspring of these backwoods homes on behalf of the Children's Aid Society. Only a wholesale resettlement of hundreds of families on arable land somewhere could have healed these suppurating abscesses of population, and at that time nobody had the vision or the force of character to attempt it. Welfare agencies could only touch the edge of the open sores with a little social peroxide. All of this was completely marginal to my experience and laid no hold on my boyhood emotions.

It was perhaps surprising therefore that in my graduate studies at Oxford University I chose a thesis on unemployment. I had arrived in England in the autumn of the general strike (1921), and the ensuing swamp of joblessness was the thing that impressed me most in those unhappy times. As I look back, however, over my resulting volume, *International Aspects of Unemployment*, I can see now that my very real sympathy with human distress was secondary to an intellectual interest in the analysis of a complex problem. My diagnosis of the malady was that of the medical school clinic and not that of a man whose family had known the disease.

The book was published in both London and New York and received a more enthusiastic reception than any other book that I have ever written. From the *Economist* and the *Spectator* to the *New York Times Book Review* there was a chorus of approval for style and content. Yet as my Preface warned, it was written "not as an addition to economic thought . . . but as a tract for present times." Only one-fifth of the book was devoted to a standard analysis of the multitudinous well-recognized causes of unemployment in a nation's economy, while the bulk of the thesis traced out the wastage of a great war, the paralysis of an uneconomic peace, and the hazards of monetary flux, all worsened by the mad nationalisms of our time. Surrounding all this was the perilous growth of the world's population through medical research and an increasingly complex system of finance. As a gloomy epilogue to the whole exposition came a final chapter entitled "Cerebral Decay," stressing the world's impending collapse because "one-quarter of each adult generation begets one-half of the succeeding generation and this more fertile one-quarter tends to coincide with the lowest qualitative one-quarter of the national population." The comment on this trend in the world's population was completely pessimistic:

> There can be only one end to this process, an end which finds its nearest analogue in human cytology. In the neurophagy of senile decay, the brain cells are outbred and absorbed by the individual's own phagocytes; the governors and philosophers of the body give place to the scavengers of the body. . . . Signs of that decline can be found throughout the whole of our international civilization. The possible collapse, through man's generic imbecilification, of the whole system of life is the most profound of the international aspects of unemployment.

Recent travel in the Middle East had heightened my mood of pessimism. In the Balkans I had seen incredible tatterdemalions obviously close to starvation. In Smyrna (soon to be destroyed by war), the hillside streets were full of garbage and feces, waiting for the rains to wash them away. In the Moghrebim quarter of Jerusalem, I had waded ankle-deep through human filth to visit the ancient Wailing Wall. I had seen hunger and disease rampant in Egypt's pullulating population and watched emaciated little girls gathering fresh cowdung off the roads in baskets and carrying it dripping home on their heads to a one-roomed hovel of dried mud. Meanwhile the *fellahin* were rejecting a clean water supply on the ground that Nile water allegedly increased male potency—a power already vastly in excess among their exploding millions. There was a temptation to echo a phrase from Goethe:

> Die Welt geht auseinander wie ein fauler Fisch,
> Wir wollen sie nicht balsamiren.

To face the colossal misery of the world and to realize, like Oxenstjern, *quam parva sapientia mundus regitur*, was almost to despair of the future of mankind.

I was a bachelor, aged twenty-seven, when my dark thoughts on unemployment and its implications were written and published. When I married two years later, I was convinced by what I knew of my ancestors that their stock was worth perpetuating. I have since begotten six children (three sons and three daughters), five of whom have survived to maturity.[1]

All in all, however, and considering that I felt that our civilization, with all its welfare agencies, was ultimately doomed by the race suicide of its abler families, it was not surprising that for almost a decade after the publication of my unemployment volume in 1923 I took no part in welfare work and concentrated all of my energies on teaching, study, and authorship in the field of the humanities. On September 1, 1932, however, I met with ten other citizens of Winnipeg in order to set up an organization that might assist discharged prisoners. Judge Frank A. E. Hamilton, of the Juvenile Court, had sent out the notices for the meeting. The other charter members of our "Prisoners' Aid Society" were Canon Carruthers, Howard A. Albright, W. E. Duperow, Rev. J. M. Shaver, Rev. Dr. J. H. Riddell, J. K. Sparling, Dr. H. M. Speechley, E. W. Watts, and Rev. Dr. G. A. Woodside. Of the eleven founding fathers, I am now the only survivor. In the interim, the group had become successively the Prisoners' Aid Association, the Welfare Association of Manitoba, and (since 1957) the John Howard and Elizabeth Fry Society of Manitoba. Since 1933 it has been affiliated with the Penal Association of Canada. Since 1965, J. Vecchione has been its executive director. During 1965, the Manitoba organization had 3124 interviews with 932 persons, a record that would have seemed incredible to us in the 1930's.

Back in those early years, we of the executive used to meet for lunch once a month at the YMCA, to discuss policy and hear reports from our relief committee, our employment committee, and our visiting committee. The one I knew best was the visiting committee, of which Dr. Riddell was chairman and I myself secretary. At least twice a month for five years we drove in his old car out to Headingly Gaol to interview prisoners who were soon to be released and for whom help of some sort was either needed or requested. Heavy clothing for transients imprisoned in the summertime but released in winter was one of the

[1]Tom, aged 42, is a professor of modern languages in West Virginia; his twin-brother Jim is vice-president of an advertising firm in Toronto; Helen, aged 33, after teaching school music in Digby for three years on a licentiate from Acadia University, married Gordon Campbell, now vice-principal of the Weymouth (N.S.) Regional High School; Janet, aged 30, after studying for nine years at Acadia, Toronto, Cologne, and Freiburg universities and teaching at Mount Allison and Victoria, is now completing her doctoral thesis on Jean-Paul Richter on a fellowship from the Canada Council; and Susan, aged 22, has Acadia's B.A. and B.Ed. and the Birks gold medal in education, and married Edward Colquhoun in June 1967. Tom has four children, Jim has two, and Helen has four, including our family's sixth set of twins in three generations. Tom's wife is the former Dorothy McGwynn, R.N., and Jim's wife the former Marjorie Smith, B.A.

commonest requirements, but a much more fundamental problem was the difficulty of getting employment in view of a prison record. Our whole undertaking was a depressing one. Most of the prisoners were very young and one rarely sensed any dawn of a new resolution. All too often those who sought our help were those most palpably ready to exploit our good will in cold blood. Yet the need for remedial action was so urgent in the delinquency of our time that we were ready to drudge on at the task in the hope of reclaiming even a few. The later reforms in Canada's penal system have been due to many causes, including eminent royal commissions, but I like to think that the insistent campaigning of penal associations such as ours was also a contributing factor to the bringing on of a new day.

One sample experience from these years was an unannounced inspection of Headingly Gaol on September 3, 1934. On August 10, 1934, serious charges against conditions in the gaol were made in writing to the Attorney-General of Manitoba by the Communist-front "Canadian Labour Defence League" and two weeks later similar accusations were published in a Toronto periodical. In view of these allegations, the Attorney-General wrote to the Chief Justice of Manitoba, requesting an independent investigation of conditions at Headingly. Chief Justice Macdonald then solicited such an investigation from the Prisoners' Aid, whose Executive appointed a committee consisting of Dr. Woodside, Cliff Brock, and myself "to investigate complaints and report on conditions in Headingly Gaol."

We made a surprise visit at the gaol on the morning of the third and stayed all day. Prisoners were interviewed privately without any prison official being present. A stenographic record was kept of all such conversations. The Committee not only cross-examined a large number of prisoners but ate prison rations for dinner and supper and inspected all parts of the gaol. Employed prisoners from the staffs of all departments were also privately questioned by the Committee. Such prisoners were not chosen by the gaol administration but were picked out arbitrarily and at random by the Committee. In the inspection of the gaol cells, every prisoner of the entire institution was offered an opportunity to make complaints or state opinions.

After seven hours of diligent investigation, we were unanimous in finding that the accusations of the "Canadian Labour Defence League" were a tissue of falsehood from start to finish. We learned from several prisoners of an occasion when a Communist prisoner, presumably the Labour Defence League's star informant, had caused a riot by sneaking soft soap into the day's soup supply, but this was scarcely a ground for condemning the administration. Our report was categorical in its denial of the charges:

> The Committee satisfied itself by specific personal inspection that every department, every ward, every cell, even every individual toilet was spotlessly clean. The food was found adequate in quantity and excellent in quality. The health of the prisoners was good and all reasonable precautions were being taken to safeguard them from infection through barber-shop and kitchen . . . a competent physician of twenty years experience visits the Gaol three times a week to examine newly committed men, to take blood-tests, to perform all major and minor operations and to care generally for the health of the inmates. . . . Smoking at Headingly . . . has since January 1934 been permitted for all prisoners at stated hours.

We had recommendations of our own to make, however, and spread them out at some length:

> We would urge that removing the dark paint from the windows of the "Discipline Cells" would eliminate the last excuse for calling this airy and capacious ward "the Black Hole.". . . Games are of well known value in helping the embittered and the ill-adjusted to take their place with others in society. At the present time the only physical recreation at Headingly is a monotonous march of the inmates around and around an inner quadrangle. We would earnestly recommend the consideration of games—such as ball or quoits—at any rate for the well-behaved inmates. It was argued by the administration that as the prisoners were all employed daily in physical work on the farm or the gaol staff, physical recreation was unnecessary; but the committee still feels that the physical game, involving such factors as team-play, would have a medicinal value for the mind. In making this recommendation, we wish to give due credit to the steps already taken to provide other forms of recreation. The Gaol has an excellent circulating library, the popularity of which is evidenced by the presence of books in most of the cells. Attempts have been made to teach illiterate prisoners to read and write, and some good results have been obtained. We found evidence of perhaps a score of checker games throughout the various wards. Something has been done, especially at Christmas and New Year's, towards providing entertainment and organizing a concert program among the prisoners themselves. . . .

We closed with the grim problem of rehabilitation:

> The chief defect of the present system, however, seems to be the lack of any effective method of reintegrating the prisoners with society at the time of release. When the sentence has been worked out, the man is simply turned loose, and, in these times of economic depression, is frequently taken up again for vagrancy or theft within a few days. . . . It might be that the provision of temporary employment at the Old Gaol Farm east of Winnipeg might tide many men over the critical period of transition. . . .

The 1936 report of our visiting committee, drafted, like the foregoing, by myself, will give some idea of the dimensions of our task:

> The needs of the situation are far beyond the powers of the Committee. At Headingly, for example, 1500 men pass through the institution in the course of an average year. Adequately to interview each individual before release

and to prepare a brief report on each case for the guidance of our field secretary, would require one hundred half-day visits per annum to the Gaol, in addition to three hundred hours at the typewriter for the Committee's secretary. For a voluntary committee, each member of which is already hag-ridden by excessive responsibilities in other directions, such a task is quite impossible. It is turning into a nightmare for private citizens a type of work more suitable for a permanent official—one who might combine the functions of a field secretary with those of a visitor and a follow-up probation officer. . . . Our recommendations with regard to recreation, which resulted two years ago in the installation of radios, have been further implemented by the authorities this past winter with the inauguration of games of Volley Ball, Basket Ball and Carpet Bowls. . . . The major problem of rehabilitation remains practically untouched. . . . At a time when thousands of the socially fit are unable to find work, and when thousands of wholesome and intelligent young people annually come out from our schools and colleges into a world that cannot employ them, the task of finding places for men with a criminal record is supremely baffling. . . .

Or one might consider part of the report on an unannounced visit on May 11, 1936, at the Vaughan Street Detention Home (Winnipeg):

The committee's only misgivings concern the recreation facilities for the boys. These latter sleep in a bright, airy dormitory on the first floor, but spend their days in a small basement recreation-room requiring artificial light at all times. They have books, magazines and checkers, but no chance for getting outside sunshine, air or exercise. The present staff is too short-handed to permit of the boys being taken outdoors under escort, and escape from the small backyard of the establishment would be easy, even under escort, unless the fence were remodelled. In present circumstances, however, the boys bleach in the basement, without sunshine or exercise. . . .

Still another excerpt covers a visit made without warning at the Manitoba School for Girls, in North Winnipeg:

We wish to pay admiring testimony to the thoroughly competent administration of the Home. Here girls aged twelve to eighteen are given thorough training in gardening, in cooking and general housework, and in sewing, knitting, crocheting, etc. Regular school instruction is also provided up to the end of Grade VII. As a very high percentage of these girls have venereal infection, the Home has a first-class clinic for their treatment. The average enrolment is thirty, drawn from all over Manitoba.

So far as actual administration goes, the committee has little to suggest. We are not convinced, however, that more might not be done to prevent moral relapse when the girls return to the communities from which they came. A woman who could be a sort of probation officer and who would at the same time, by part-time service in the Home, know the girls well before release, might do a great deal towards consolidating the results of reformative training. As it is now, those who know the girls best lose track of them completely after release. . . .

In January 1938, I finally withdrew from my impossible labours in the Prisoners' Aid. My letter of resignation makes the circumstances clear:

> It is with regret but with a sense of absolute necessity that I am herewith tendering my resignation as a member of the executive of the Branch, after being identified with its work for over five years. Certain primary responsibilities—the College, my home and my church—now make so emphatic and legitimate a claim upon my time and energy that it is quite impossible for me to carry out the duties that a member of your Executive naturally incurs. I have a full-time professorial job, a family of four small children to help my wife bring up, and major denominational responsibilities, not only local but also provincial and national. I also carry a considerable load of authorship, in an attempt to keep the family budget from utter shipwreck. Under the circumstances, duties in connection with the Prisoners' Aid are simply more than I can handle.

In the summer of 1938, I went to Europe as a visiting lecturer at the Stephen Tisza University in Debrecen, Hungary. With the aid of press articles that I syndicated to the whole Southam chain, I took my wife along as well, and together we visited not only Hungary, but Denmark, Norway, Sweden, Finland, Estonia, Latvia, Lithuania, Dantzig, Germany, Czechoslovakia, Austria, Jugoslavia, Italy, and Romania. In this range of travel, I had an incomparable opportunity to compare the economic and social systems of many different countries. Here was Warsaw, growing with the explosive vitality of Toronto in the 1950's and with an even wider range of social services. In Bucharest, Romania, on the contrary, we saw a similar breakneck expansion of modern industry, side by side with the most pitiful, tattered poverty in Europe outside of Soviet Russia. In Sweden, we found a model of civilized restraint, with nearly half the annual budget going to education and social services, but with race suicide threatening the survival of the nation. In Oslo, Norway, we made a tour of housing projects, where the whole of the capital's slum population had been transplanted into modern apartment blocks or into garden villages. Health insurance in the city was universal and medical services were free for all serious cases. By comparison with a Canada that was just crawling out of the Great Depression, the Scandinavian countries seemed almost like social Edens, apart from the rigidity of their Socialist doctrinaires.

One serpent in the Swedish paradise was the alcohol problem and I was interested in studying the flexible methods by which the country sought to deal with this ancient menace. Total abstinence from alcohol was deeply engrained in the Kirkconnell family tradition, at least as far back as the Scottish Baptist community with which my great-grandfather linked himself and his descendants. The pioneer pastor, Rev. William

Fraser, who was minister of the Breadalbane, Ontario, church in my grandfather's day, once declared, "I never heard an oath or saw a glass of liquor drunk in Breadalbane."[7] I can bear the same testimony as to my father, and have tried to live up to the same temperate standard myself. But none of us has had the axe-edged fanaticism that makes for an effective zealot. We recognized the drunken calamity that had ruined the lives of hundreds of men and women of our own acquaintance but we were not prepared to sit in moral judgement on these shipwrecks.

During the period 1942–48, while living in Hamilton, Ontario, I was chairman of the social service subcommittee of the Board of Social Service and Evangelism of the Baptist Convention of Ontario and Quebec. This experience overlapped on a nine-year stretch (1944–53) as chairman of the Social Service Committee of the Baptist Federation of Canada. The Baptists had no full-time social service officials like Canon W. W. Judd of the Church of England in Canada or the Rev. Dr. J. R. Mutchmor of the United Church of Canada. The chief function of our Baptist committees was to keep our conventions and churches informed on social issues, especially through carefully framed resolutions brought before annual meetings. In this we leaned heavily on the studies made by our more professional colleagues in the other Protestant bodies. The "activism" of North American Protestantism was not as vocal in Canada as in the United States, although the United Church was more ready than the rest of us to jump the gun on any exciting current issue and hit the headlines in the Toronto press. For over ten years, then, it was my duty as a social service chairman to make social service thinking explicit for the Baptists of Canada.

I was not just a saprophyte on the annual reports of Dr. Judd and Dr. Mutchmor. I had had over five years of specialized social service in Winnipeg. My contact with foreign language groups in the West had opened up other sociological problems. I had served on the Canadian Refugee Committee and was for many years a director of the Canadian Conference of Christians and Jews. My 1938 trip to Europe had shown me the issues of social welfare in many countries. Most important of all, I had undertaken fundamental studies of the Soviet system, based especially on Soviet legislation in the original Russian of *Pravda* and *Izvestia* and was able to keep the Baptists informed on issues where almost universal pro-Moscow propaganda in 1941–46 had muddied the thinking of some other denominations.

My efforts to keep the record straight did not go unchallenged. Each year as I brought to the Convention some resolution denouncing the brutality with which the Soviet Union dealt with its citizens and those of its captive nations, I could be sure that Rev. R. G. Quiggin, who had a Plymouth Brother slant towards the left, would rise up and smite me. One year he fooled me, for he assailed not my attack on the Communists but my criticism of post-war Britain for continuing to use the forced labour of prisoners of war whose repatriation was long overdue. Less than a month later, all the bishops of England repeated my accusation, but in the meantime Quiggin had had his day, had successfully appealed to the pro-British feeling of the Convention to defeat my resolution, and had seen the *Toronto Daily Star* feature the episode with headlines of triumph.

One phase of Canadian life of which only a blind man could remain unaware was the rise of the mass-entertainment industry. The "nickel shows" of my boyhood have risen like a genie out of a bottle and have been joined by two vast fellow-genies, radio and television. Fifty years ago, I watched clumsy but honest movie versions of Dante's *Inferno, The Fall of Troy*, and *Cabiria* (dealing with the Punic Wars). The mass-entertainment people have not gone on from there to develop more and more civilized entertainment. As purely commercial enterprises, they have aimed at the lowest common denominator of interest in the juvenile group, in order to make a maximum profit. They have usually been content to dish out sex and violence in shock doses of steadily increasing potency. Organized pressure groups make sure that no controversial issues are permitted. Responsibility to the community is undermined by catering to audience fantasy, the solution of frustrations by murder and robbery, and the reduction of mankind to "good guys" and "bad guys" among whom virtues and vices are so confused as to be indistinguishable. Brutality and sadism for their own sake are also purveyed in books by the Mickey Spillanes of our time, with whom moral standards simply disintegrate. Radio and television, with an entrée into the home, have been more circumspect than the movie theatre and the drug-store yellow-back, but, with notable exceptions, the level of taste is abysmal. Most advertising sponsors of mass-media entertainment feel that they must make a maximal impact through the most vapidly vulgar programmes. To travel by car across a couple of thousand miles of this continent tuning in by radio on all available broadcasting stations is to be made aghast at the dreary futility of their appeal to sub-human intelligence. The CBC, like the BBC in Britain, has helped to keep the mass media from sinking completely in the swamp of illiteracy. Although its stable of political commentators has been persistently leftist, its entertainment has not lost sight of civilized values, especially in the field of music. Rare individuals like Walt Disney have also done commendable work. So far as the social service committees of our churches are concerned, hostile criticism of mass entertainment has been chiefly concerned with the depravity of some drug-store fiction and some comic books. To attempt a major attack on the mass media—from the flashy circuses of the "Ed Sullivan Show" to the nitwit circuses of "Grand Old Opery"—all vulgar but all relatively harmless—would be to lose oneself in a forest of contemporary mores.

I began this chapter with childhood recollections of Port Hope factory workers at the turn of the century. The change in their lot today is a measure of the transformation of Canada's industrial life in six short decades. The Nicholson File Company's employees, for example, now work forty hours a week (five days of eight hours each) instead of sixty. The old Cavan Street factory, run by the water-power of Beamish's Dam, is replaced by an ultramodern, one-storey, electrically operated plant on the Cobourg Road. The average wage, including fringe benefits, is $2.48 per hour, or $5,518 a year, one of the highest in Canada. There is free life insurance ($2,000 for each employee), accident and health insurance for workers and their dependents, vacations and legal holidays with pay, two daily coffee-breaks, a generous pension plan, and company contributions to workmen's compensation and unemployment insurance. They no longer tramp down Bedford Street to their daily work but drive five mornings a week in their individual cars to the Cobourg Road factory. The humblest worker is now vastly better off than the high school principal of 1900. There was no union in the plant until 1964 and the phenomenal change has been due, not to union shock treatment, but to competent management, managerial thrift, and the use of scientific invention in increasing the output per man-hour. Out of the firm's modest annual profits, the bulk of the dollars has been ploughed back into a reserve for technological improvements. This American family company, which took over the works in my childhood, has done well by the little town.

But this astonishing increase in North American well-being cannot be wholly examined in isolation. To the eyes of those in the overpopulated and underfed parts of the world, our fat comfort often seems an abomination of selfishness.

In September 1956, in Victoria, British Columbia, I listened to Dr. Brock Chisholm, late head of the World Health Organization, denounce our Canadian (and American) prosperity and demand a redistribution of food and money throughout the world. Our ancestors, he said, had grabbed off a vast chunk of natural resources under one set of rules and then selfishly changed the rules. Our prosperity was not due to any merit or virtue on our part, but simply to our having a small population in a large and well-endowed country. Hunger and the diseases of undernourishment were rife throughout two-thirds of the world and unless we shared up pretty promptly we would be swept away by the world's rising tide of population and would deserve to disappear. We were wasting on four-lane highways and golf courses and extravagantly spread-out housing, and the like, land that might be used to feed starving millions. In short, we were a bad lot.

But what are the facts that were glibly disregarded by Dr. Brock Chisholm?

In the first place, our ancestors moved into a relatively empty continent. Where Canada and the United States now spread over two hundred million people, there were only a few hundred thousand nomadic hunters. Our ancestors, moreover, endured incalculable hardship, disease, toil, and privation in order to hew out the patrimony that we enjoy today. It is our own research and development that have given value to the petroleum, nickel, iron, titanium, and hundreds of other minerals that were meaningless to the stone-age Amerindians whom we displaced. As for "changing the rules"—by which Dr. Chisholm seemed to imply controlled, rather than unlimited immigration—there is scarcely an age in history when there was not opposition to unrestricted immigration—sometimes by Roman or Chinese walls to keep out the invader and sometimes by fierce and bloody wars.

There had been a change in the rules, but it was opposite in character to what Dr. Chisholm tried to insinuate. In the sixteen years from 1940 until the time he spoke, the United States spent over one hundred billion dollars on foreign aid. This was the new thing in human history. The hundred billion dollars given away to needy countries by United States citizens through their government was equal to the total value of all residential construction in their country during the twentieth century. It amounted to nearly $2,000 for every tax-payer in the land. It was over thirty times the value of the entire annual wheat crop of North America. It was more than twice the total net value of all property, plant, and equipment owned by all American manufacturing concerns combined. It was more than all the money in circulation in the entire world. In 1965, the Americans were still giving needy countries more than five billion dollars a year.

No such generosity had ever been shown in all human history by any country to its needy neighbours. The only remote parallel was the relief given by these same slandered Americans to alleviate Soviet Russian famine and epidemic in 1921–23. By comparison, the Communist countries, so dear to so many "liberals," had given little—except promises—to anybody. The clamorous Asiatic and African countries had given nothing since time began.

And what had been the sequel to this sacrificial outpouring of American wealth? In part, an upsurge of hundreds of millions of new human beings in the beneficiary countries, more than cancelling out the almost infinite gifts. And in part, alas, black ingratitude and vilification of the Brock Chisholm type.

For the past nine years, 1958–67, I have been chairman of the corporation of Eastern Kings Memorial Hospital, founded in 1930 by the initiative and generosity of the citizens of the little town of Wolfville and the surrounding countryside. This chairmanship carries with it ex officio membership on the board and the executive, but since my coronary in 1964 I have been much less dutiful in my attendance at their humdrum but highly necessary monthly meetings to scrutinize invoices and hammer out minor details of supplies and repairs.

Through the years the hospital has been able to gain and maintain accreditation. A more exacting taskmaster since the establishment of provincial health insurance has been the Nova Scotia Hospital Insurance Commission. Most of the burden of our current financing was taken over, to our great relief, by the provincial scheme, but our entire operation was now under the most exacting scrutiny of officials in Halifax. Economies had always been sought: for example, we had always shared a high-priced radiologist with the hospitals at Windsor and Kentville, but the provincial minister of health was now paying the piper and calling the tune. It became necessary on occasion to send our superintendent and the chairman of the executive to orientation sessions in Halifax in order that the minutiae of the new system might be fully understood.

With each year that passed, however, it became evident that our building was becoming less and less adequate for the widening tide of public medicine. Our first proposal was to add a new wing to the existing structure, but we were abruptly told by Halifax that this would not be at all satisfactory. In order to build in accordance with the latest functional principles of hospital architecture, we should have to put up an edifice that was new in every respect—at a prospective cost of $1,250,000 for a 35-bed hospital. Through the years the Corporation has saved up $148,000 from bequests and donations, and a provincial grant of $5000 per bed will add $175,000; but this leaves over $900,000 to be raised by local efforts in a poor little non-industrial town of 2500 where one-third of the merchants have gone out of business in the past five years. The advent of state medicine, instead of solving all problems, still leaves plenty of challenges for the citizens of a small Canadian community to meet with sacrificial devotion.

12

The Teaching Tradition

MY MOTHER'S IMMIGRANT grandfather, Christopher Watson, had begun life in Canada in 1819 as a teacher in "Muddy York," while her father, Thomas Watson, taught in Ontario schools, especially in Port Hope, until his retirement at the age of sixty. She herself was a teacher until she married my father—also a teacher for fifty years, forty of them as a headmaster who still carried a full teaching load. It was perhaps natural that one of their five children should spend his life in the service of education, for I was virtually reared "in the odour of pedagogy" and took in its lore along with my daily porridge.

At high school it was somehow assumed that I would end up in the professoriate. In the course of a mock trial in the Assembly Hall during my Grade IX year (1908–09), I was summoned to the jury-box as "Professor Longlegs Kirkconnell" and the nickname "Prof." followed me for the next five years. I was indeed to arrive at the prophesied destination but not by a straight course. As will be told elsewhere, the vicissitudes of war time drew me into troubled seas where I boxed the compass of prospective careers and at last returned to my original bearings by the sheerest accident.

My first teaching experience was military rather than academic. As I have explained in chapter IX, I was called on in 1912–13, while still only seventeen and a pupil, to command and instruct the cadet battalion at the Lindsay Collegiate Institute. The job was done in the gymnasium and on the campus, but it gave me a sense of discipline that has never deserted me through the years. It is the sort of thing that becomes second nature and does not depend on shouting.

My first spell of classroom teaching was in the Orillia (Ontario) Collegiate Institute in September 1913. On Labour Day, I was hotly engaged in a tennis match in Port Hope when a long-distance telephone call came through from my father. The science teacher at Orillia was ill and would not be available before October 1. Principal Lillie was desperate. Would I be willing to fill in for a month? In one sense, the proposal was fantastic. I was only eighteen and had attended neither normal school nor university. I had, however, taken all of the high school science courses as a student and was an ardent field naturalist. After a year as a cadet instructor, I had no fear of discipline. The offer of six dollars a day seemed enormous. Next morning I was in Orillia. When I enrolled at Queen's University early in October, I was considerably richer both in cash and in experience. The adventure had been abundantly rewarding. My only bad moments had been in umpiring student baseball games.

Thanks to my father, I had a chance of earning a teacher's salary again in May and June 1914—this time in the Lindsay Collegiate Institute. The cadet corps was somewhat disorganized and the teaching staff was short handed. I was therefore engaged by the Board to teach junior courses and to tune up the cadet corps for its annual inspection. My class was "3-D," an overflow pre-matriculation group of both sexes, quartered on the stage of the Assembly Hall. To them I was expected to teach all courses—languages, mathematics, and sciences—and once again I had an enjoyable time.

From 1916 to 1922 came my period of *Sturm und Drang*, when one dream-castle after another arose only to collapse and disappear. I almost got started in the fall of 1919, when I was registered for a Ph.D. in education at Harvard, had paid my deposit on a room in residence, and had spent most of the summer reading a shelf-full of books recommended by the head of the department. Alas, when the term opened I found myself in a hospital in London, England, and when I re-crossed the Atlantic in mid-November I was in no shape to consider going on with my course. In the spring of 1921, I sat down with a blank sheet of paper and made a trial balance of my training, aptitudes, and ambitions. I still hankered after an academic career but now felt that I was too old for the necessary postgraduate training. In any case, I had very little money, and after World War I the government was not educating veterans. Journalism, which did not demand a Ph.D., seemed the logical item to balance the melancholy account.

Hence it was that I enrolled with the London School of Journalism and acquired its diploma. Hence also came my decision, when unexpectedly awarded an IODE overseas scholarship at Oxford University for 1921–22, to study economics there—since this subject, so central to editorial interests, was one of which I knew nothing.

Early in September 1922, I was back in my father's home in Lindsay, putting the finishing touches on the manuscript of my *International Aspects of Unemployment* (for the London publishers, Messrs. Allen &

Unwin, and the New York firm of Henry Holt) before proceeding into a full-time life in a newspaper office. Knocking at the door came Arthur L. Phelps, professor of English at Wesley College, Winnipeg, who had been summering at nearby Bobcaygeon. His second-in-command, Fletcher Argue, had just resigned at the eleventh hour, after a thundering row with President Riddell, and the latter had wired Phelps to try to pick up an emergency replacement. I declined at once: my university field had been Classics, not English, and in any case I was going into journalism. Two days later Phelps called again and renewed his exhortations—and I accepted. It was one of the major decisions of my life, for I was to be permanently identified thereafter with higher education.

Since I had had no formal training in English beyond the sophomore year, I had no predilections as to the courses I should teach. In the two-man department, therefore, I simply taught whatever Phelps did not want. He chose the poetry of the first two years, the Shakespeare, the Milton, the Romantic Poets, and the Twentieth-Century Poets. To my lot, therefore, fell the prose of the first two years, the Old English, the Middle English (including Chaucer), the history of the language, the evolution of the drama and the novel, Restoration and Eighteenth Century Literature, and Victorian Prose and Poetry. As the book manuscript for London and New York kept me busy until about four days before college opened, I arrived in Winnipeg on the brink of the session, with no lectures prepared, to face classes in a field for which I had no specific training. I had indeed read most of the texts at one time or another. I was well versed in Latin, Greek, French, German, and Italian literature, and I had travelled on four continents, but my acquaintance with current commentaries on English literature was almost non-existent. For the first two years at Wesley College, I was always just one jump ahead of the student wolf-pack.

My knowledge of the various courses, however, steadily broadened and deepened. I supplemented Old English with Gothic (for grammatical reasons) and with Old Norse, Old Irish, and Old Saxon for a wider knowledge of the European literature and culture of the period. The Eddic poems (my own alliterative translations of some of which I published in 1930 in my *North American Book of Icelandic Verse*), the *Tain Bo Cualnge*, and the *Heliand*, for example, threw light on *Beowulf*, the *Battle of Maldon*, and the "Caedmonian" *Genesis*. The Icelandic sagas were a world in themselves.

Even more richly satisfying than Anglo-Saxon was the Middle English period. Chaucer led one back to Eustace Deschamps and Giovanni Boccaccio. In Middle Welsh it was a thrill to find in Dafydd ap Gwilym a great contemporary of Chaucer, with a feeling for nature that was beyond the reach of the London vintner's son. The mediaeval romance was stretching as far north as Iceland. In the colleges of that time, Latin was awakening to a new spring in the songs of "the wandering scholars" and especially in the haunting verse of the "Arch-poet." A Czech friend at Harvard (A. R. Nykl) helped me to bridge the gap between the troubadours and the poetry of the Arabs and also directed me to the Hebrew poems of Solomon Ibn Gabirol and Jehudah Halevi. An interest in comparative philology even led me into the labyrinths of Sanskrit accidence, among the Minotaurs of optative, benedictive, and precative moods. I was never satisfied merely with "books about books" and insisted on probing back to original literatures in various languages in order to see the resemblances and relationships for myself. Needless to say, I did not inflict all of this comparative literature on my unfortunate students. I feel sure, however, that my primary researches must have added something of value to the curriculum.

In 1933, President Riddell, who had himself been professor of Latin, offered me the chair. I promptly accepted, for the shift seemed to give me an opportunity to refresh and deepen my knowledge of the classics. Moreover, I was interested to see how eleven years in the Department of English could enrich my teaching of Latin, even as my earlier acquaintance with the classics had cross-fertilized in teaching with English literature.

There followed seven of the most satisfying years of my life. At the University, I was adopted into a new professorial fraternity—Fred Clark, Skuli Johnson, and W. M. Hugill of the University's Department of Classics, Archdeacon Matheson and Canon Seeley of St. John's, and Father Eric Smith, S.J., of St. Paul's—with whom I helped to shape the curriculum and set and mark the papers in Latin. Cicero, Livy, Lucretius, Vergil, and Horace now took on nobler proportions than they had borne in my undergraduate days. Catullus and Ovid, on the contrary, failed to recover the magic that had set me, at nineteen, declaiming their amatory verses to the waves on lonely stretches of the Lake Ontario shore. By great good fortune, Cicero set me on the track of the letters of Erasmus, with their incomparable mixture of style and intellectual zest.

The University of Manitoba worked in close harmony with the high schools and the provincial Department of Education, especially through the Manitoba Educational Association. By 1938, I found myself the chairman of a committee set up by the MEA to recommend new textbooks in Latin for the high schools. After long and careful study, we voted for *Latin for Today*, by Gray and Jenkins, a truly admirable performance, based on the "reading method" in which the pupil is reading Latin directly from the very first page. Hugill and I prepared a high school Latin reader based on the daily life of the Romans rather than on the frontier wars of Caesar, but unsympathetic publishers told us that our "vocabulary density" and "syntax density" were excessive. To stir up interest in my own classes, I sometimes used the Linguaphone records prepared by Dr. W. H. D. Rouse of the Persse School, Cambridge, but curriculum planners in Canada did not grant Latin enough high school class-hours per week to make the "direct method" feasible.

In 1940, Chancellor Howard P. Whidden of McMaster University offered me the headship of his Department of English, a chair being left vacant by the retirement of Dr. W. S. W. McLay. The salary was much higher than that on which I was scarcely supporting a wife and four children in Winnipeg, and my acceptance was immediate. Not least among the inducements to move was the opportunity to teach some of the courses that had long been the private property of Brother Phelps—the Shakespeare, for example, the Milton, on which I had been doing basic research for several years, and Spenser and the other non-dramatic Renaissance poets. I also set up new courses of my own in "creative writing," both prose and verse, and in "great books," on a seminar basis. At the postgraduate level, I again picked up Chaucer and Middle English. With a staff of four (George Haddow, Roy Wiles, Marguerite Roberts, and myself), we each took a section of freshmen English.

When I became president of Acadia University in July 1948, it was assumed that I would be a full-time administrative officer. The vicissitudes of the years, however, have occasionally drawn me into the classroom. In September 1950, for example, Dr. W. H. Thompson, professor of Classics, died suddenly; no adequate replacement was available; and I myself took on most of his load for the year. In October 1951, our professor of economics suffered a nervous breakdown that took him out of circulation for eight months and during the entire academic year I shared his load with two other instructors—my quota being a class of ninety students in Economics 4 (Labour Problems), the field in which I had studied at Oxford in 1921–22. The illness of Dr. Arthur Jewitt for the whole spring term of 1963 led to my taking over his courses in "Romantic poets" and "contemporary American poets." Since my retirement from the presidency of Acadia in August 1964, I have taken on a half-load of teaching, with advanced courses in "mediaeval literature" and "Renaissance non-dramatic literature: Spenser to Milton." In 1966–68, as an emergency arrangement, I became head of the Department of English.

A minor form of teaching has been a number of posts as "visiting lecturer." In 1938, for example, I lectured on Hungarian literature at the summer school of the Stephen Tisza University in Debrecen, Hungary. Out of sheer madness, I promised to give one of my lectures in Magyar and almost sweated blood over the ordeal. I shall never try it again. Nem, nem, soha! Eight summers later I taught a postgraduate course in "Milton" at the summer school of Laval University. As most of my students were members of French Catholic teaching orders, I set them tracing Milton's theological ideas through Augustine, Aquinas, and other fathers of the Church and left them suitably impressed with the range of his erudition. Still later, in 1950, I was invited to the University of Pittsburgh to speak on Hungarian poetry in a series of public lectures in comparative literature. I had dinner with the president and supper with the local Hungarian community and altogether was treated royally. In July 1963, I gave a lecture at the University of Iceland on the Icelandic poets of North America.

The past sixty years have seen profound changes in the theory and practice of education. One great laboratory of pedagogical experiment has been the United States of America, with Teachers' College, Columbia University, as its hottest test-tube. Another, and much less familiar, laboratory has been the Soviet Union, where a totalitarian state has been able to decree experimental changes by ukase for the entire Communist area. The United Kingdom has likewise been active in educational "reform," but with less dogmatism and a greater range of variety. Canada, as in most other matters, has shown little creative originality and has tended, in primary and secondary schools, to borrow American ideas wholesale a decade or so after they have gone stale south of the border. In higher education, our connections with the universities of the Commonwealth have kept us from complete absorption into the American system.

The river of American pedagogical theory into which I almost stepped in 1919 was heavy with freshets from the teaching of John Dewey and William Heard Kilpatrick. The former was the philosophical oracle of a new "progressive" movement; the latter was the pedagogical mechanic who misinterpreted and misapplied the Master's pragmatism in ways that were inordinately popular with a cloud of witnesses who were similarly incapable of comprehending Dewey's recondite epistemology. Thus Dewey had said, "We learn by doing." As ultimately applied in the progressive classroom, this made for incessant "projects," a great deal of doing and very little reading. But to Dewey, a boy reading a book was also "doing." The important thing was that he should not be required to read something beyond his comprehension. To quote Dewey in opposition to his progressive disciples, "Theory is, in the end, the most practical of all things." A youth who is taught automechanics in

1957 only in terms of the repair and manipulation of 1957 machines may find himself in 1977 faced with machines of an entirely different sort that are nevertheless obedient to theories and principles that he ought to have been taught.

Or again, Dewey said, "Education is growth," and many professors of education proceeded to assume that this mystic word absolved them from an understanding of the learning process. "Maturation" and "learning," however, are two different things, and Dewey merely meant that a child cannot learn Greek or binomials before he has reached a certain stage of development. Learning is dependent on maturation, but it is a separate, superimposed process.

Although Dewey said that "Education is a social process," all too often this was interpreted to mean that all educational processes must be social in nature and that the introverted child must be dragged out of his contemplative seclusion and forced into social activity. Carried into universal application, this could well give us a community of socially adjusted super-salesmen, without any of those self-sufficient personalities who bring rich gifts of invention, art, literature, and philosophy to their generation out of the profound thought of their fruitful solitude. The highly gifted pupil became not merely "the forgotten child" but even the persecuted child, chivvied into sterile conformity by a doctrinaire pedagogy.

Finally, Dewey declared that "Education must concern itself with the whole child." This was laudable enough as a mild protest against an education that was too exclusively intellectual, but it has tended to degenerate into an assumption that all subjects, from square dancing to philosophy, are of equal importance. Social adjustment, healthy emotions, physical culture, music, manual training, recreation, leisure-time activities—all these are alleged to have just as much right on the school time-table as traditional academic subjects. In fact, to believe in "subject matter" and "discipline"—along with any unwillingness to agree cheerfully with the new dogmatism—is one of the unpardonable sins.

In the 1940's, I had dinner with Mortimer Adler and heard him expound another philosophy of education—the neoscholasticism of the Chicago group. This smart young man seemed to have all the answers, but to an old classicist he savoured too much of the dogmatism of Aquinas and not enough of the questing mind of Socrates. Perhaps my own mental patterns had already hardened. At any rate, it was from England rather than from New York or Chicago that my father had taught me to draw my pedagogical thinking. My mentors have been Sir Richard Livingstone, Sir Fred Clarke, M. V. C. Jeffreys, F. R. Tennant, H. A. L. Fisher, A. N. Whitehead, and their fellows.

But before I go on to discuss my own philosophy of education, let me insert some mention of the colossal experiments in Soviet Russia. My knowledge of Soviet education has come as a by-product of long study of the Soviet state, buttressed by many years of subscription to *Pravda*, the use of much additional source material in Russian in the New York Public Library, and assistance from correspondence with (and, of course, the books of) Max Eastman, William Henry Chamberlain, and "Manya Gordon" (Mrs. Simeon Strunsky). Perspective for all this miscellaneous information came from several books by Professor George S. Counts, of Columbia University, especially *The Country of the Blind* and *The Challenge of Soviet Education.*

At the time of the 1917 Revolution, the Bolsheviks inherited a good but limited school system with nearly eight million pupils, a well-trained staff of teachers, and an idealistic pedagogy that was fully and sympathetically aware of theory and practice in Western Europe and the United States. The All-Russian Teachers' Union openly opposed the Communists and the teachers went on strike in Moscow, Petrograd, and several other cities. During the next few years, the teachers were either exterminated or terrorized into conformity by flying squads of Young Communists, who promptly reported hostile teachers to the police for liquidation. Pedagogically, the period from 1921 to 1931 was given over to romantic experiments in project methods and "socially useful work" through activity programmes, with the school organized as a "collective" in which pupils and janitors had equal authority with the teachers. On the negative side came the abolition of all marks, subjects, examinations, textbooks, homework, and discipline. With the launching of the Bolsheviks' great programme of industrialization, it became obvious that while the Party, through its Komsomol, had captured the schools from the teachers and the parents, it had not succeeded in teaching anybody anything. To transform the Soviet Union into a great industrial state called for a mastery of science and technology, and it therefore became necessary to revert to a system of education that would bring results. As of January 1, 1932, every school in the country was called on to restore a curriculum of separate subjects, with clearly defined content to be mastered by the pupil. Stable textbooks were prescribed and the curriculum was made uniform from Grade I to Grade X (the end of the secondary school). This is the system that has now prevailed for over three decades and by 1960 was providing free elementary and secondary education to every boy and girl in the Soviet Union. Every mother's son (and daughter) of them (apart from some millions of drop-outs) now emerges with ten years of mathematics (a course including trigonometry), ten years of rigorous physical culture, six years of geography, six years of biology, five years of physics, four years of chemistry, one year of astronomy, ten years of Russian language and literature, six years of at least one foreign language (begun in Grade V), seven years of history, six years of drawing (followed by four years of drafting), six years of singing, one year of psychology, and one year (in Grade X) on the Constitution of the Soviet Union. The school week embraces six days (instead of the North American five) and the school year thirty-four weeks. All this is taught under a rigorous system of marks, examinations, promotions, and awards. A decree in 1944 set up special examinations at the end of Grades IV, VII, and X. In 1946, final state examinations were ordained for every school and every grade. Students with unsatisfactory marks in basic subjects (language, history, mathematics, and science) repeat the grade. At the end of Grade X there are gold and silver medals for "excellent scholarship and exemplary conduct." In 1943, there had already been issued a formidable code of "Rules for School Children," calling not merely for cleanliness, neatness and obedience at home and at school, promptness, truthfulness, helpfulness towards little children, the sick and the aged and politeness to his teachers and his elders, but even abstinence from smoking and bad language. Homework is obligatory and theatres, concert halls, and circuses are placed out of bounds in the evenings for children under sixteen. Students who are disciplinary problems are simply expelled and put to work. Each pupil has a school uniform and carries a "card," premonitory of the internal passport of adult society. Thirty million Soviet children are enrolled today in these schools of general education, and the abler graduates (and only these) by the hundreds of thousands, are passing on almost automatically to the universities and higher technical schools. Such is the system that startled the North American businessman into a sudden awareness that his country's scientific predominance is threatened with eclipse by this giant of Soviet pedagogy.

Certain aspects of the system remain to be mentioned and they are far more significant than its prodigious success in turning out scientists and technicians. The leaders of the Bolshevik state, from Lenin to the present, have referred to education as a "weapon" in their struggle to conquer the world and make it Communist. In pursuit of that distant goal, they have not only sacrificed human welfare and the Russian standard of life to the Red Army and the creation of heavy industry, they have sought to use every agency of education—not merely schools and universities but also books, newspapers, radio, television, cinema, theatre, art, and music to mould the population of their entire empire into a new breed of human beings. The same ruthlessness that has wiped out tens of millions of Soviet citizens by bullet and forced labour camp has been applied to this plastic surgery of the Soviet mind through education. Each school course in each grade has one textbook (and only one) authorized for the entire Soviet Union and carefully vetted before publication by the Ministry of Education and the Central Committee of the Party. It is the function of these texts and their teachers to supply Soviet boys and girls with the myths by which mankind is nourished and sustained. Hence there comes, especially in subjects like history, a system of incessant lying that alters its mendacity at every change in the hierarchy of the Party and every shift in the Party line. Similarly in the universities every academic department is subject to the inquisition and censorship of the Department of Dialectical Materialism (the theology of the new era) and no book may be published without the *imprimatur* of the Communist censors. Political and moral conditioning of a very special type, as part of the universal system of education, has been applied to the entire population for nearly forty years. Canadians who imagine that the Soviet schools have been undermining the Bolshevik régime know nothing about Soviet education. The results of the programme have already permitted the Red tyranny to survive the ordeals of the early five-year plans, the revolt of the peasants against collectivization, the purges of Party, police, and army in the late 1930's, and the sufferings of World War II. That Soviet Communism, at the pinnacle of its success, should suddenly retreat, is as likely as the transformation of Niagara into a "reversing falls" on the Saint John model.

As we compare the Soviet Union and the United States, we see two great secular systems of education, the one based on dialectical materialism and the other on a garbled form of pragmatism. One looks back to Lenin and Marx, the other to Dewey and Kilpatrick. One has repudiated God and the other has forgotten Him. Each professes to shape young life towards an ideal called "democracy" and each is confident that human nature can be changed by the techniques of psychology and pedagogy. A Canadian spokesman for the American point of view is Dr. Brock Chisholm, who, in his William Alanson White Lectures, called for "the re-interpretation and eventual eradication of the concept of right and wrong which has been the basis of child training, the substitution of intelligent thinking for faith in the certainties of old people."

In their logistics of education, the Americans have let their tactics dictate their strategy, while for the Communists their over-all strategy controls their tactics. The Americans begin with a child-centred pedagogy and are concerned with his happiness in learning, the adaptation of the curriculum to his personal interests and cranial limitations, the removal of all unpleasantnesses in discipline, difficult subject-matter, and competitive examinations that might be psychologically harmful, the development of healthy emotions, and, above all, extrovert social adjustment to the community. The vaguely assumed goal is a "democratic" community in which all men and women are happily and tolerantly adjusted to one another in political freedom and economic comfort. Job security and social *savoir-faire* march hand in hand on a continent where mathematicians and scientists are in short supply—because in most states and provinces mathematics and science, being difficult, are made optional in the secondary schools. This is, of course, not everywhere the case; neither have all teachers, or perhaps even the majority, accepted the more extreme forms of the "progressive" pedagogy. The Protestant schools of Quebec, for example, have a superb curriculum. It is because there has been no clear and dominant alternative among most of the educationists that I have taken the most aggressive school as the typical one.

For the Bolsheviks, the ultimate goal of conquering and ruling the entire world sets the strategy of education, and this the day-to-day tactics of the classroom. They seek to create a type of man whose chief volitional qualities are "purposefulness, resolution, persistence, initiative, courage, and endurance." Discipline, which the Americans have rejected, is made the corner-stone of the Soviet school. Without discipline, they say, one cannot study, one cannot work, one cannot conquer in war. Therefore, above all things, get discipline. Life for the Soviet pupil may be harder than for the North American pupil. Even the most difficult subjects are compulsory for all Soviet pupils, and school honours go, not to the athlete but to the outstanding student. He is, however, challenged to sacrificial struggle for a great cause, he is commended for resolute bravery in the great task of carrying science and triumphant "socialism" to the ends of the earth. His curriculum-centred school may actually give him greater joy than the pupil-centred classrooms give to the cushioned North American, for his life is given a disciplined purpose transcending himself. That Communist cruelty, terror, and death may touch his home apparently fails to destroy the myths that command his heroic assent.

It is conceivable that, in the conflict of the next half-century, North American civilization will not survive, precisely because its lack of discipline and lack of faith will leave it with less power to suffer. The soft pedagogy of North America lacks a clear belief about the nature and destiny of man; that of the Communist world, while rigid and warped by mendacity, has the cleaving edge of a well-defined purpose. The relativism of the liberal West may well be its undoing in a world where the camouflage of "peaceful co-existence" masks a life-and-death struggle between two ways of life. One can already detect a fatal weakness in the readiness of some "liberals" to doubt our right to survive. They are more conscious of the moral bankruptcy of the West than of the implacable evil of the myth-masters in the Kremlin.

We in the West seem at times to be witnessing the disintegration of our civilization. The popular culture of Shakespeare's day—in which songs, games, country lore, and, above all, religion were factors in creating a community—has failed to survive the Industrial Revolution and no coherent culture has emerged to take its place in a scientific and industrial age, if we except the escapist trivialities of the cinema and the popular magazine. The central problem of our time is that of freedom in a planned society. One of our major tensions is that between the "haves" and the "have-nots," with pressures by organized groups that produce a persistent erosion in the value of money in Western countries. Another is the tension between the individual and the state, in which the community makes an ever higher claim on a man while he in turn fails all too often to realize his responsibilities on a personal level of reason and morality. Freedom is thought of as freedom from control rather than as a gladly spontaneous living in accordance with principle (in Kant's sense). Hence comes a preoccupation with educational techniques (often impressively effective) rather than with the ultimate purposes of education. We seek to produce people of maximum adaptability rather than to work out the meaning of their environment and the reason for adaptation to it. Even contemporary Western philosophy, instead of looking for a comprehensive answer to the totality of existence, busies itself with a sterile, pettifogging dissection of language. In the absence of any world view, we drift into a relativist chaos of values.

In the West, moreover, there are some who, out of fear of being left to rely on a self that has lost the compass of eternal values, desert the ship of freedom and camp on icebergs of collectivism. On the Soviet icecap, where these originate, there is no choice, no private life, no opportunity even for "subjective deviation," but this annihilation of personality is actually welcomed by some of the orphans of relativism. They are ready to escape all other problems by losing themselves in the collective mass. They are afraid of freedom.

Herein lies the crux of our pedagogical problem. Really free choice springs from principle and conviction. A free society needs a faith. It is the lack of faith that sends so many North Americans whoring after the Baalim of Moscow. We need nothing less than a two-fold redemption—to save the individual from depersonalization and the planned society from despotism.

The first ingredient in that faith is an understanding of the complex, difficult world in which we live. At every point, the relevance to ourselves and to our environment of the thing taught should be kept in mind. This does not mean that the curriculum must be wholly contemporary. Cicero's *Pro Milone* can throw new light on modern urban gangsterism, and Thucydides or Livy illuminate the meaning of the wars of the twentieth century. The *Old Testament* or Greek tragedy can give us a far truer analysis of present-day man than Dashiel Hammett or Ernest Hemingway. The humanities of all ages can come to a profound focus in the present.

A second necessity is direct experience of community living. Here our Canadian schools are often helping greatly with vocational guidance and a demonstration of the meaning of employment in local industry. "Home and School" groups promote a fruitful partnership of parents and teachers in comprehending the personalities, habits, aptitudes, and motivations of each individual boy and girl. Parental responsibility is still more fully exercised in homes where books, music, and intelligent conversation abound, and the family is an organic unit. It would be still more fully realized in a community that recognized Aristotle's "good life" as the objective of human society and insisted on a place for such an ideal in the schools. All education is in a sense vocational, but all education can with equal validity envisage values that will set the vocation in a truly human framework of living.

A final need in education is what Sir Richard Livingstone has termed a "vision of greatness," the introduction of young people to the great lives, the great ideas, the great literature and art that all mankind has begotten since history began. Such a vision is not the same as a faith to live by, yet without it any faith may well be a valley of dry bones. This is especially necessary in an age when the vulgarian tastes of mass-man dictate more and more the "standards" of art, literature, and religion. There is little hope of levels rising through the mass-medium entertainment industry, whose values, drawn by profit motives from the masses, are always on the ebb. Our main hope is in the schools, where universal education can set true greatness before each new generation and draw slowly upwards the tides of their intellects and their emotions.

There is no perfect political or economic system. In seeking such abstract formulas and constitutional blueprints during the past two centuries, mankind has, in part at any rate, been pursuing an *ignis fatuus* across the Serbonian bog. The moral failure of human individuals can corrupt the best of states, while a high level of community rectitude can make do with a sorry constitution. Political systems can find an enduring transformation only through the inward development of the personalities of their citizens, by the victory of good over evil in the souls of men.

Where, in this spiritual sense, are we to find a *Weltanschauung* that will give coherence, force, and survival value to our "liberal democracy"? Plato and Socrates are mighty allies against both degenerate relativism and idolatrous totalitarianism, for they have essential humility, natural piety, and a respect for human dignity. With them, personal values are neither lost in a pragmatic fog nor washed out in blood. But we need religion to join with the wisdom of the great pagans in giving us a faith in which personal freedom is central and the human soul is of infinite value.

It may seem strange to reserve for a postscript the universities in which I have spent some fifty years of my life. Cynics may say that this disproportional emphasis arises because I *know* something about universities and have irresponsibly babbled on about the schools, where my ignorance is greatest. The reason for my longer discussion of the schools is, however, I would submit, the fact that the basic conflicts and contrasts of our day are found much more openly in our elementary and secondary schools and affect almost our entire population. University problems are chiefly the material ones of finance, buildings, and staff, while school problems go deep down into the very principles of pedagogy.

Thus, the universities still have enough autonomy to insist on standards of performance. The sluggard and the hooligan, against whom the community now leaves the schoolteacher almost defenceless, may at times filter through matriculation into the university, but they do not stay long. They have (as yet) no theoretical and clamorous right to an education that they will not earn by their own hard work. The several subjects of the college curriculum are still appropriately known as "disciplines."

My lifetime has seen some major structural changes in the Canadian university. At the turn of the century, the faculties of arts (and science), medicine, law, and theology dominated the field. Queen's had begun to experiment with extramural courses and was the pioneer in this work of carrying the college to the community. The M.A. was the highest degree in arts and science. Canadians who wished for an advanced research doctorate in science went to Germany, or, less frequently, to the United States, where graduate schools on the German model were beginning to flourish. For advanced work in the humanities, our graduates would go to England, Scotland, or France, and there were wholesale importations from overseas into our own faculties.

Fifty years have brought a transformation. Research has come on a large scale, not only in graduate schools but in great research laboratories like those in Toronto (Connaught) and Ottawa (NRC).

Doctoral degrees by the hundred, earned by sound course work and investigation, are conferred annually at Canadian convocations. Another profound change has been the proliferation of technical faculties and "schools" under university auspices for the training of experts of every sort, from dietitians to office secretaries. In most European countries, the training for many of these professions would be in higher vocational schools, but in Canada nearly all of them, *more Americano*, are brought under the university roof. Still another change has been the almost universal extension of university services to the community through evening and correspondence courses and itinerant platoons of libraries and lecturers.

As already intimated, the greatest problem faced by our universities is one of finance. Even with their present registration, the universities cannot attract and hold an adequate faculty because of the superior rewards in government service and industrial research. Because of an unprecedented tide of youth now flowing upward through the schools, university enrolment will be doubled by 1975 and quadrupled by 1987. Laboratories and residences will cost hundreds of millions of dollars, and no commensurate pool of professors is in sight. Since, moreover, the financial resources of students are often in inverse proportion to their industry and ability, the horde that reaches the university will fail to include many of our ablest young men and women unless still further money is found for scholarships, bursaries, and loans to enable them to attend. Soviet Russia claims to be spending ten per cent of the national income on education and opens its universities, free, to all of its ablest young people. In Canada our expenditure is closer to two per cent. We spend more on tobacco or cosmetics than we do on the training of our young people. And there is no university in the country that hasn't already got money trouble, even before the enrolment blizzard envelops us.

13

The President's Desk

"I SAT WHERE THEY SAT," said Ezechiel, "and remained there astonished among them seven days." My shift in 1948 from a professorial chair at McMaster University to a president's chair at Acadia University filled me likewise with amazement and soul-searching. As a professor for the previous twenty-six years, I had assumed, like most of my colleagues, that I knew a great deal about university management. I now suddenly realized that I had almost everything to learn concerning the long-suffering brotherhood of prexies that I had just joined. When presently my Board of Governors gave me a welcoming dinner and asked me to expound "my plans for the University," I replied meekly that I knew too little yet about either Acadia or the Maritimes to start making pronouncements of that sort.

I had, of course, heard long since that this university was probably the first in Canada to write freedom of race and faith into its constitution. I had also long known that Acadia University had had an enviable reputation in the production of eminent scientists and scholars, and in 1954–55 research statistics confirmed the tradition in a remarkable fashion. Wesleyan University, of Middletown, Connecticut, had produced a monograph on *Origins of American Scientists*, listing in the case of each of the 34,000 entries in *American Men of Science* (American Council of Learned Societies, 1944) the institution in which each man had taken his first degree and then dividing the total for each university by the number of its graduates during a base period (1924–34), so as to arrive at an "index of productivity." The results were revealing. Reed College, Oregon, a small institution that admitted only high honours matriculants, led all the United States in its incubation of scientists, while large state universities were at the bottom of the list. Dr. William Noble and Dr. David Haley undertook the same research for the 1669 Canadian scientists in the same reference work and found that the Universities of British Columbia, Saskatchewan, Acadia, and

Mount Allison (in that order) led the Canadian roster. Since some Canadian critics questioned the selectivity of the reference works of the American Council of Learned Societies, I wrote to the general editor, Dr. Jaques Cattell, who assured me as follows: "We think that we have been as careful in selecting those from Canada as we have those from the United States. . . . In other words, exactly the same method is used in both countries and, as far as we are concerned, we treated the whole continent as one group."

I then proceeded to analyse the ACLS's 1951 *Directory of American Scholars* with precisely the same method that Dr. Noble and Dr. Haley had used in their analysis of *American Men of Science*. In the case of eminent scholars, the productivity index showed the same four universities heading the Canadian roster, but in the reverse order: Acadia and Mount Allison were tied for first place, followed by Saskatchewan and the University of British Columbia. The reasons for such eminence are not obvious. None of the four had set up rigorous standards of admission and the general quality of the faculty was not demonstrably superior, although a single professor like Horace G. Perry launched twice as many biologists as any other professor in North America. Maritimers may emphasize the intellectual virtues of the Bluenose stock, but comparisons are again debatable. The most plausible explanation is that in large institutions (and even the University of British Columbia and Saskatchewan were small in 1924–34) the multitude heads for the loaves and fishes of professional training, while in small colleges an appetite for pure science and pure scholarship may still prevail. If it were not for advanced students from the smaller institutions, the big graduate schools might have to close down. Certainly the academic tradition of Acadia was a sobering consideration to its new president. One was evidently not called upon to preside over the liquidation of such a reputation.

Acadia's administration, as determined by the Nova Scotia Act of Incorporation in 1840 and worked out in more than a century of experience, was fairly typical of the North American pattern, although the smallness of the institution concentrated more duties and toil in the person of the president. To begin with, the appointment was a life sentence, so long as his morals and his arteries held out. He was a voting member of the Board of Governors and of its Executive, the chairman of the Academic Senate, and the chairman of the General Faculty. He was thus the only man to be a member of all three bodies, saddled with the full burden of intercommunication. In the matter of recruitment, only the president (after consultation with deans and department heads) could nominate a new member of Faculty, while only the Board (or its Executives for the lower ranks) could approve his nomination. If his nominee were not accepted, it was then his task to propose another man. This recruitment of new staff was perhaps the most critical and important of my responsibilities, since the teaching faculty makes or breaks a university. It was also the most frustrating of all my tasks, for our poverty gave us the lowest salary scale in Canada; qualified instructors were therefore almost unobtainable; the categorical specialization of a modern university department meant, moreover, that in, say, biology, we would need not just a biologist but a geneticist *or* a bacteriologist *or* a vertebrate anatomist *or* a plant physiologist *or* a wild life ecologist, all of whom were in short supply and none of whom could substitute for any other; and the man whom months of search and miracles of negotiation had finally secured might presently be denounced on non-academic grounds by critics in the sponsoring Baptist denomination. No man was ever dismissed in response to such name-calling, but the air was sometimes a bit heavy. My own intransigence under such pressures could arouse displeasure, and in 1955 a petition was actually circulated among New Brunswick churches, calling on the Board to dismiss me. My offence on that occasion was that I had conferred honorary degrees on two Acadian French Catholics, Judge Vincent Pottier and Dr. Flavien Melançon and had cordially welcomed, in French, in the university dining hall, several hundred descendents of the Acadian French Catholic expellees of 1755, assembled under our hospitable roof (though at their own expense) for a bicentennial banquet. When the Board of Governors and the Convention Executive both upheld my judgement in the matter, the storm blew over.

In routine administration, I found myself closely involved in most of the major committees of the Board and the Executive—the budget committee, the investment committee, the committee on future policy, the committee on buildings and grounds, the theological bursary committee, the faculty salary committee, all planning committees for financial campaigns and a succession of planning committees for each of the many new buildings that became necessary.[1] Other campus committees on which I served were a military studies committee, a "University Christian Council," a library committee, a grievance committee, a "cut-off committee" (that decided when to lower the boom on further registration

[1]Erected during my régime, at a cost in excess of $3,000,000, were a campus heating plant, Elliott Hall (for chemistry), Chipman House (a fifth residence for men), Dennis House (a fourth residence for women), and the Manning Memorial Chapel. Planned and on the drawing boards in my time, for another $3,000,000, were the Vaughan Memorial Library, the Wheelock Hall refectory, and Eaton House, an additional new residence for 208 men. These paralleled a student body increase from 480 in 1953 to 1350 in 1964 and a trebling of the academic salary scale.

each year), and an extension committee that arranged for extension courses and an annual summer school. Matters that I found were the sole responsibility of the Acadia president were the preparation of an annual calendar, the drafting and placing of all advertising, the approval of all faculty travel grants, the handling (for many years) of all scholarships and bursaries, making arrangements for a series of public concerts and lectures, making all preparations for convocations (and even conferring the degrees myself, since we had no chancellor), the preparing of all reports to the Governors, the Senate, the Convention, and the Dominion Bureau of Statistics, entertaining all sorts of visiting VIP's, holding house receptions for graduating classes, and even assigning professorial office quarters (a nettle that no one else would consent to grasp). In matters of university discipline, there was a student judicial committee (which rarely functioned, because students would not lay charges or give evidence against each other), a faculty discipline committee (held in reserve for emergencies, but again handicapped by a student conspiracy of silence), and a provost, with a provost corps, to maintain the peace. The president was the penultimate authority in matters of discipline, but on one notorious occasion I quietly took the rap, in the press and over the CBC, for a disciplinary decision that had actually been made at a still higher level.

The president also represented the University on the Board of Governors of the Nova Scotia Technical College, the Board of the Atlantic Summer School for Advanced Business Administration, the Board of the Maritime School of Social Work, the Board of the Acadia University Institute, and the Board of an interdenominational Institute of Pastoral Training. He was also an active representative on the Central Advisory Committee on Education in the Atlantic Provinces, the National Conference of Canadian Universities, the Canadian Universities Foundation, the Association of Commonwealth Universities, and the Association of Atlantic Universities. He had also to be ready to speak at meetings of alumni branches, academic events at other universities, luncheon meetings of service clubs, financial campaign rallies, annual meetings of the Canadian Manufacturers' Association and all its cousins, and church occasions of all sorts.

My office door was always open to every member of the academic community, not only to governors and professors, the treasurer or the plant superintendent, but even to the humblest bewildered freshman or the most incoherently disgruntled janitor. When a whole day was swallowed up in interviews and committee meetings, it simply meant that I worked all the later at night. Labour unions might be reducing the industrial worker's load to 44 or even 40 hours a week, but I often worked 80 hours a week for months at a time. Had I not believed in the importance of higher education, I would certainly have pitched the job over. It had its rich satisfactions, moreover, and was a challenge to every phase of experience that I had ever undergone—as an army adjutant, an army paymaster and accountant, joint organizer of the Humanities Research Council of Canada, of the Writers' War Committee of Canada, of the Federal Nationalities Branch, and of the Baptist Federation of Canada, a writer, a singer, a field-naturalist, a journalist, and a professor. Throughout my sixteen years as president, for the sake of my batteries I took every July off, went to a quiet cottage in the woods, and worked there ten hours a day on tasks of scholarship that had been temporarily smothered under the blanket of administration. This one month of intellectual freedom helped to sweeten the eleven months of executive toil. I simply went incommunicado, seventeen miles from the nearest railway station and telegraph office, and reverted for a blessed interval to the delights of creative scholarship. The complete change, even to hard labour of another sort, was as good as a tonic. A by-product was the publication of five substantial volumes, totalling 2300 pages, by the University of Toronto Press.

I would not have it thought that as chief executive I was a mere paper-pusher, multiplying documents for documents' sake. In the beginning, some of my ventures were purely exploratory, as when I secured from every employee of the University his *curriculum vitae* and (on request) his suggestions for improving the institution. I also set up fairly early a curriculum committee to make a study of the B.A. course, not with specific changes in view but as a form of self-audit. The committee consisted of all department heads and myself. We met once a month for two years. We analysed the calendars of the major universities of Canada and the United States; we considered the rationale underlying each Arts curriculum; we were filled with theories to the gills. However, the only change resulting from this arduous biennium was the hotly contested shift of an introductory course in psychology for sophomores from a mandatory to an elective status. The net result of our great decision was that all Arts sophomores, though now of their own choice, continued to take Psychology 100. I could not help thinking of Oscar Wilde, working hard at a manuscript, whose one change in a whole morning was the removal of one comma and whose one change in a long afternoon was the restoration of the same comma. Perhaps part of the explanation of the professorial impasse was that in a small faculty each department was so jealous for the prestige of its own tribal gods that it was unwilling to give up any shred of status or privilege.

It was worth noting that our B.A. curriculum was substantially that of Yale, from which some of our older professors had taken their doctorates. Its structure was (*a*) two years of thorough training in an explicit range of traditional departments, designed to level up after the vicissitudes of the secondary schools, and (*b*) two years with a rigorous major in one traditional discipline and a minor in a second discipline. We had little use for a bargain basement curriculum that was all electives, for its customers would never have studied any one subject in depth. Neither would we approve an undergraduate degree in regional studies, where a wide range of associated departments collaborated in the study of a geographical area, for we feared that the result would be a loose bundle of unmastered disciplines.

Still another of my would-be innovations had to do with the Board of Governors and its Executive. In the later years of my presidency, mimeographed copies of all Executive minutes (as well as Board minutes) went out from my office to all members of the Board, and I myself wrote up all these minutes with the inclusion of a great deal of background material, explanations of the pedagogical and institutional reasons for decisions taken. This meant a great deal of extra labour, but I felt that it was steadily helping the thirty-man Board to know where the ship was going and how its compass worked.

On one occasion I confronted the Executive with an appalling list of Board and Executive committees appointed over the previous ten years, some of which were dying on their feet, while others, though palpably dead, were not yet buried. The result was a Board decision that all *ad hoc* committees not reappointed at an annual meeting would automatically cease to exist.

One fine morning three members of the Faculty's small cocktail brigade came jauntily into my office to demand that the campus be thrown wide open for the use of alcohol by students in all residences. In their view, the drinking of alcohol was the consummation of gracious living and I was a mangy old social diplodocus to forbid it. My defence of my dry policy began by pointing out that ninety per cent of our students, male and female, were under the age of twenty-one, when drinking becomes legally permissible. The Board of Governors, moreover, had unanimously directed me to insert an anti-drinking clause in the Calendar, so that the "gracious livers" would be warned and would stay away. Finally, I assured them that the prohibition carried my own wholehearted support. In a residential, co-educational college we had enough problems without pouring unlimited alcohol on an inflammable generation. In the case of one recent expulsion, a senior with a flask of whiskey had slipped into a girls' dormitory at a late hour and had spent the night in the arms of Morpheus, Bacchus, and a freshette. To pull down all barriers would be to invite a far wider range of drunken promiscuity. The parents who placed their under-age daughters in our care would never stand for an alcoholic campus.

The same arguments, and a number of others, entered into my treatment of an attempt to bring Greek-letter fraternities to Acadia. When I was approached by the American organizers, I explained in some detail my reasons for locking their racket out: the small student body was already a well-adjusted brotherhood and the proposed fraternity would introduce a factor of snobbishness and discrimination; it would require a nucleus of Canadians to go to a foreign country to be "pledged" and would funnel Canadian funds to that same foreign country; it would superimpose an alien loyalty on our own local loyalties; it would clutter up the campus with new social activities, where we already had more than enough; and finally, judging by my observation of fraternities in Winnipeg and Toronto, it would bring no profit to anyone except beer salesmen.

Several years after my arrival at Acadia, the founding in the central provinces of a nation-wide professorial "union," the Canadian Association of University Teachers, brought a hitherto unknown scrutiny of the relations between our Board and Administration on the one side and our Faculty on the other. The CAUT was, in a sense, long overdue. World War II, Federal fiscal policies (echoing the American) and the pressure of labour unions had cut the value of the Canadian dollar in two. Industrial wages had much more than kept pace with the inflation, but professorial remuneration across Canada had lagged far behind, leaving net salaries in 1939 dollars at a fraction of their former value. The national organization mobilized units on every campus and supplied them with the ammunition for an assault on the Administration. Acadia was no exception. In 1958, a very detailed brief was mailed to the president and the executive and was followed up by an expository delegation.

With the primary demand of the Faculty group—for very much higher salaries—we could all sympathize. The treasurer, the chairman of the Board and I had agonized over the problem, in season and out of season, and had already managed to boost our rates by sixty per cent, at the price of annual deficits. But we were still—as always in our history—at the bottom of the Canadian list. The arguments brought forward by the Faculty deputation and by the head office CAUT brain trust at McMaster that had drafted the brief pilloried Acadia, not merely for paying salaries far below the national average but still more for not announcing, as some of the provincial universities had done (in collaboration with the provincial governments whose appropriations alone made their budgets possible), a long-term programme of progressively higher increases. Scornful comparisons were made of our wage scale as against those at six other small universities, all of which were vastly wealthier than Acadia, but no mention was made of a relatively comparable institution like Mount Allison. Even there, government aid and endowment income were $208,000 a year beyond Acadia's help from these sources, and the salaries were correspondingly higher at each rank. Another anomaly was that three-quarters of our instructional staff had been given premature tenure and ranks higher than would have been accorded to them at any other university, simply to hold them and to give them higher incomes, and these stipends should have been compared with the salaries of the lower ranks that they would indubitably have held elsewhere. It was standard practice, for example, for our associate professors to transfer to assistant professorships at other universities and to gain financially by the move.

One of the home-grown complaints was that whereas my energetic predecessor had, in twenty-five years, secured $575,000 from the Rockefellers towards a building and $250,000 from the Carnegie Corporation towards a pension fund, my régime was failing to secure from such sources comparable sums *every year for salaries.* One can only suppose that the pangs of hunger had little recourse to logic. As a matter of policy, the Rockefellers and Carnegie had never underwritten academic salaries and had now virtually ceased to give to Canadian universities for any purpose. Industrial and mercantile corporations, in both Canada and the United States, had always given, a year at a time, to buildings (the need for which they could understand) rather than to salaries. To the business mind, a firm that could not meet its salaries from its own operations had no right to exist. Since corporations, moreover, performed on an annual *profit and loss* basis and some years were very lean indeed, college salary help, if once begun, could be cut off entirely in a deficit year. Our only hopes for a much larger *assured* annual income lay in doubling our tuition fees (and losing our student body in a highly competitive field) *or* in quadrupling our endowments (I had merely doubled them) *or* in gaining a large annual subsidy from government, firmly assured regardless of boom or recession.

Our fees were already the highest in the Maritimes and among the highest in Canada and constituted a dangerously excessive percentage of our budget. Our cost in administration, in proportion to our budget, was almost the lowest in Canada, and was achieved by overworking the president and the business manager. Salaries, on the other hand, were the highest percentage of our budget in comparison with all other institutions. Our simple, fundamental need was money, on a large, assured annual basis. Our reply to the CAUT delegation could have been a terse *non possumus*, but we tried to temper the facts of life with assurances that every attempt would be made, short of bankruptcy, to improve the professorial lot.

All administrative problems were conditioned by the long-term tide of student enrolment. In 1948–49, the tide was just beginning to ebb from the flood of 1947–48, when the vast wave of returning veterans, added to the ordinary stream of high school graduates, had brought a temporary crest of unprecedented height. Enrolment dropped rapidly as the veterans graduated, and by 1951–52 had fallen to one-half of the 1947–48 figure. Since that time it has risen, all across Canada, in an ever-mounting curve to nearly four times that minimum, and is expected to double yet again by 1975.

At the beginning of the period, emergency measures strove with the flood on a temporary basis. My predecessor, Dr. F. W. Patterson, had secured old army huts as extra laboratories and classrooms, had arranged billets in homes for ten miles around, and even had secured quarters for married veterans and their families at Aldershot Infantry Camp, beyond Kentville. Extra faculty members were mobilized on interim contracts. Then, during my first five years, as the tide ran rapidly out, the fee budget was cut in two and we lost, of course, the supplementary grant for veterans that had come from the Department of Veterans' Affairs. Supernumerary members of the faculty had to be dropped and financing became so grim that only the most urgent repairs on our thirty buildings could be attempted. The rivalry among Maritime universities seeking to enrol enough students to remain solvent took on for several years a rather sinister intensity.

Presently the tide of enrolment turned, and that with a completeness that was ultimately to overflow all ancient landmarks. In June 1955, I presided at a session of the National Conference of Canadian Universities, held in the new physics theatre of the University of Toronto, at which Dr. E. F. Sheffield, then of the Dominion Bureau of Statistics, became a prophet with an alarming text from the Book of Numbers. The college student population of the next eighteen years had already been born and could be reckoned in cohorts and in terms of a steadily increasing percentage of the age group. On this basis, he forecast that Canada's 1954–55 college registration of 67,100 would almost double, to 128,900, by 1964–65. As a matter of fact, it had already passed 140,000 by 1962–63, and a total of 325,000 is confidently expected for 1970. Canada's population, through a phenomenal birth-rate and heavy immigration, has risen from 11,507,000 in 1941 to over 20,000,000 in 1967. The portion in the lower age groups is very much higher than before, and an ever-increasing percentage of the college age group in every modern country is going on to university. This was the impending crisis with which Dr. Sheffield quietly confronted the university administrators in 1955, and his median extrapolations have proved in subsequent years to be less correct than a still more alarming higher range that he gave us as an alternative. The administrative problems are fantastic. University staffs must increase from 5000 in 1954–55 to 25,000 in 1970–71. Even in the quinquennium 1960–65 some $750,000,000 was spent on new buildings (with only $50,000,000 of this total coming from the Canada Council) and the annual operating costs of universities were in the neighbourhood of $420,000,000. All of this would more than double by 1970–71.

A primary problem was financial. Student fees rarely cover more than one-third of a university's operating costs, for to make them carry the full load would limit enrolment to the children of the very wealthy. Most Canadian endowments are small. Funds for erecting new buildings commonly had to be sought from the general public (alumni, corporations, wealthy, and less wealthy citizens), and high pressure campaigners, on behalf of three or four universities every year, went pounding on doors from Dan to Beersheba. Education was supposed to be *ultra vires* for the federal government, while some of the provincial governments, through poverty or lack of interest, had rarely given anything to universities, apart from driblets to two or three professional faculties. The system in the United Kingdom by which the national government supplied over seventy per cent of all universities' funds, both operating and capital, was virtually unknown in Canada. Mr. Duplessis, of Quebec, insisted angrily that only provincial governments could legally contribute to universities, and many of the provincial governments refused to do just that. On one occasion, when despairing Nova Scotia prexies appealed to the federal Prime Minister for help, he replied that he had just given their provincial government an extra $18,000,000 for that purpose but if (as had happened) the provincial authorities had insisted on spending the money in other ways, there was nothing he could legally do about it.

Back about 1950, when the annual DVA grant began to dry up, a systematic national campaign had been launched to save the universities. I took my place in committees of the National Conference of Canadian Universities, drafting out programmes to mobilize public opinion in favour of federal help. I was a party both to the NCCU brief to the Massey Commission in 1950 and to the application to Mr. St. Laurent's government for the grant. In 1951–52 federal funds were made available on the modest basis of fifty cents per capita of population, with this provincial quota then divided among degree-granting colleges in proportion to enrolment. Since Nova Scotia handled most of the professional faculties for the Atlantic area, nearly half of its college enrolment came from outside the provincial area, as compared with less than ten per cent in most provinces. As a result, the Nova Scotia grant per student was one-sixth that in Newfoundland and one-half that in Saskatchewan. For Acadia this meant a pittance of about $44,000 a year. In 1957, the federal subsidy was raised to $1.00 per capita to each province and the newly formed Canada Council was given $50,000,000 to be doled out in matching grants for new buildings at universities. As the planned construction for the next quinquennium was $750,000,000, or fifteen times the capital subsidy, the quota for each college had to be thinned out in terms of enrolment. Acadia got half the cost of one new residence and about one-tenth the cost of another. In 1958, the operational dole was raised to $1.50 per capita, and there it stuck. The iniquitous formula of division by provinces (by which Nova Scotia has fared so badly) was designed to placate the anti-federal bellowings of Mr. Duplessis. Although it became clear in a year or two that nothing would reconcile him to federal grants, the formula still survives, fifteen years later, with catastrophic results for Nova Scotia colleges.

Almost from the beginning of my term at Acadia, I sought to secure provincial help for Nova Scotia's universities. All of them were private foundations, but they, and only they, were performing unaided in this province the functions of higher education that were recognized as a public responsibility in provinces like Saskatchewan, Alberta, or British Columbia. The only exceptions were the two final years of a five-year engineering course, the two first years of an agriculture course, and some help for Dalhousie's schools of law, medicine, and dentistry. The cost of all higher education had soared since World War I and the universities were in desperate straits. The churches that had founded and sponsored six out of Nova Scotia's seven universities could not supply more than token payments. At Acadia, at the close of my régime, the Atlantic United Baptist Convention was contributing $17,000 to a university budget of over $2,500,000, or much less than one per cent, and this was sacrificial giving for the churches.

Part of my problem was to secure any sort of united approach to government from all seven universities. Dalhousie was inclined to live up to the old African proverb: "Every man for himself, as the elephant said when he danced among the chickens." I found more backing among the other "denominational" colleges, including King's, but also a fair degree of political scepticism. Said Father P. J. Nicholson, the jovial president of Saint Francis Xavier: "The trouble, Kirkconnell, is that there are too damned many Catholic colleges!" The first little breach in the Treasury dike came with a small grant in aid of teacher training, to help us prepare B.A. and B.Sc. graduates for pedagogical duties in the schools of the province. For Acadia this brought in from $5000 to $9000 a year, depending on the registration in our School of Education. The turning point in my campaign came when I persuaded President Kerr of Dalhousie to join with the rest of us in a common appeal to the provincial cabinet. My winning argument with Kerr was my assurance that we would incorporate in our brief a special request on behalf of Dalhousie's Graduate School. I drafted the brief (vetted twice by the presidents) and was the spokesman for the "group of seven" that paraded before the Executive Council one sunny morning. Then each of the prexies was polled and they all backed me up handsomely. This phenomenon of presidential unanimity so impressed the cabinet that a special grant of $250,000 was voted to the lot of us, divided in proportion to each institution's number of non-theological students beyond the freshman level, but with a graduate student (M.A., M.Sc., Ph.D.) weighted at three times an undergraduate. The help was enthusiastically received, yet in the light of exploding registrations and exploding costs the grant was only one lamb chop to seven starving tigers. Within a couple of years we were back on Premier Stanfield's doorstep, asking for more. His shrewd response was to appoint a provincial University Grants Committee to make a detailed study of the financing of higher education in Nova Scotia. *Pari passu* with this development, my presidents' committee, in part influenced by some structural planning by the Catholic colleges, became the consultative body of an Association of Atlantic Universities, expanded to include all four Atlantic provinces and buttressed by a research body of deans and professors from all of the colleges. In the current year (1966–67), Acadia's grants from the federal and provincial governments combined is $1,300,000, a sum equivalent to the endowment income on twenty-six million dollars. My share in bringing this about is perhaps my chief claim to remembrance by the University.

Acadia has had a sound tradition of work at the M.A. level dating back to 1854 (before even B.A.'s were granted by any Maritime universities except King's and the University of New Brunswick) and had awarded hundreds of master's degrees since that time. There was therefore no inclination to abandon our master's degree work in Arts, Science, Music, and Education. On the other hand, with the proposal of the Premier and the University Grants Committee that all Ph.D. work in Nova Scotia should, for the foreseeable future, be concentrated at Dalhousie, I was very ready to agree, although there were whispers of protest from junior members of our faculty. At Acadia we had a tiny teaching staff of only thirty-four in Arts and twenty in Science, and they were all underpaid. Our facilities were inadequate, even for undergraduate work. The cost of lifting them, and the faculty, to a level satisfactory for a respectable Ph.D. would be fantastic. For a really good graduate school, one needed a large and diversified staff in each department to provide an adequate three-year programme of courses at the pre-doctoral level and to supervise research and the resulting theses. One also needed a sufficient number of graduate students to sharpen each other's minds in the daily interchange of the common room. McMaster, which was just launching out into Arts doctoral work, was spending half a million dollars for extra library books for the department of English alone and was adding several new professors to the staff in English. This was being repeated all along the line. Our library budget, on the other hand, was less than $30,000 a year for books for all faculties and schools combined. For one aggressive science department to make itself adequate for Ph.D. work would be to gulp down a shark's share of the budget, to the financial impairment of every other department on the campus. If an angel from heaven were to give us twenty million dollars, much might be possible, but the omens for a celestial visitation were lacking. One querulous sophomore whom I met on the campus assured me that unless Acadia acquired a graduate school and a doctoral programme it would pass into academic eclipse. I tried to explain to him that poor Ph.D.'s could wreck a university while honest B.A.'s and M.A.'s could be matters for pride. The calculus of university staffing and financing were beyond his comprehension, however, and he could only keep on whining for a status symbol.

Good fellowship among the universities of the Atlantic region had long since been assured by the establishment in the 1920's of a "Central Advisory Committee on Education in the Maritime Provinces." This was an informal one-day gathering, every November, of representatives from all of the universities and colleges, the teacher-training institutions, and the provincial departments of education. It had been financed for an initial five-year period by the Carnegie Corporation of New York, after its almost complete failure to lure all the colleges of Nova Scotia, New Brunswick, and Prince Edward Island, with golden bait of one million dollars each, into consolidation in a single university complex on the Dalhousie campus in Halifax. Only King's, which had just been burned out at Windsor after more than 130 years there, accepted the exhortation (and lived to regret it). The Carnegie brain trust of 1921 could scarcely have foreseen that the total intramural registration of full-time students would be 12,600 by 1960–61, with a minimum extrapolation of 25,000 by 1970–71 and of 50,000 by 1980–81. Long before that intolerable concentration on the Dalhousie campus had been reached there would have been a frantic cry for devolution back to the more manageable regional units that have survived financial famine and have worked out in experience a very marked elimination of overlapping. All medicine, pharmacy, dentistry, and oceanography are at Dalhousie; all law is at Dalhousie and the University of New Brunswick; all degree work in music is at Acadia and Mount Allison; all forestry and anthropology are at the University of New Brunswick; all Ph.D. work is at Dalhousie and the University of New Brunswick; all fine arts are at Mount Allison; all social work is at the Maritime School of Social Work; and all home economics is at Acadia, Mount Allison, and Mount Saint Vincent. Almost all of the other disciplines are a comparatively simple and traditional pattern of courses in Arts and Science carried on more economically at a dozen campuses than in one monstrous urban complex.

The Carnegie Corporation hoped in 1923 that by fellowshipping for a period of years the Maritime universities might learn to grow together. When the quinquennial subvention had run out, there was still no trend towards organic union, but the annual conference seemed so worthwhile that all of the participants agreed to finance their own share in it thereafter. Meetings were held at the various universities in rotation and college heads were elected in due succession as chairman for the year.

At the annual sessions, each provincial department of education and each university reported on significant changes in the previous twelve months. The matter of maximum common interest was the articulation between secondary school and university. The heavy casualty rate among undergraduates set us searching for a possible improvement in predictors of student capacity. A major research project was therefore undertaken jointly by the members of the CACEAP in 1957–60, with a subsidy of $85,000 from the Carnegie Corporation and a heavy use of computers. A battery of tests, equivalent to those of the College Entrance Examination Board in the United States, was given to all provincial students in Grades XI and XII, and a follow-up record was made of their marks on the provincial examinations and on the university examinations of their first two years at college. When all of the scores had been worked out and correlated, it was clear that the provincial "matriculation" examinations were a much better predictor of college aptitude than the College Entrance Examination Board tests.

It might seem invidious to single out even a few from the great roster of friends that I acquired in these annual conferences, but memory insists on recalling the extrovert high spirits of Ross Flemington, the unextinguishable cigar of Frank MacKinnon, Alex Kerr's tenacity of purpose, Hugh Somers' insight into the currents of provincial and federal politics, Sister Francis d'Assisi's strong business sense, the youthful impulsiveness of Colin MacKay, the gentle optimism of Jim Puxley, the lawyerlike reservations of Ray Gushue, the unjesuitical simplicity of Fathers Malone and Fischer, the quiet geniality of Fathers MacDonald and Cormier, and the keen scientific zest of Colonel Holbrook.

Acadia's charter membership in two academic parliaments—the National Conference of Canadian Universities (founded 1911 and meeting annually) and the Association of Universities of the British Commonwealth (founded 1913 and meeting quinquennially)—gave me stimulating contact with a wide range of national and international university life. The term "parliaments" is not strictly accurate, for these were deliberative rather than legislative bodies. Each university remained completely autonomous but the interchange of experience in our assemblies was invaluable. Almost every conceivable problem in academic administration had been faced in various ways at various universities with varied success or failure, and the advice of hundreds of veteran scholars and administrators was deeply appreciated.

What impressed me most in the National Conference of Canadian Universities was the good fellowship between the French-language and English-language institutions. On the whole, it was our French colleagues who usually went the generous second mile, for their English was far better than our French. Memory brings back the mellow wisdom and impish humour of Sidney Smith, Claude Bissell, Cyril James, Bill Mackintosh, Ed Hall, Walter Thompson, George Gilmour, and Larry MacKenzie. The issues were seldom novel. At the fiftieth anniversary conference, held at McGill in 1961, Cyril James dug up the programme of the founding fathers in 1911 and found that they, exactly like ourselves, had been arguing about admission standards, student drop-outs, and a uniform matriculation for all Canada.

But it was in the Association of Universities of the British Commonwealth that we got our widest sweep of university problems. In 1953 we met at Cambridge University, in 1958 at McGill, and in 1963 at the University of London. In each case there was an ancillary conference of university heads only, held respectively at the universities of Durham, Toronto, and St. Andrew's. At each conference, moreover, some ten really top-flight people from the greatest universities of the United States were present as guests and their uninhibited contributions were among the finest things we heard. By way of reciprocity, in 1958, the Association of American Universities supplied the Commonwealth university heads with a free safari by special train from Montreal to Washington, where the red-carpet treatment included meeting President Eisenhower at the White House and a priceless luncheon address by Chancellor Kimpton of Chicago.

At Montreal, the most exciting session was an off-the-record exposition of South African university problems from both the Boer and the English point of view. At the University of London, the problems of the developing nations cropped up in every discussion. More than 500 delegates, from 130 Commonwealth universities, were present. India, with its million university students, had grave problems of finance and conflicting claims for the language of instruction. In the developing countries of Africa, almost everything seemed lacking except a consuming desire for education. From both English and American speakers I gained reassurance as to the value of locating a university (as was the case with Acadia) in the seclusion of a small town. Thus the Lord Bishop of Chester declared that smaller towns could very well provide the right atmosphere for academic study and he thought the idea heretical "that training people to take their place in the maelstrom of life today necessarily meant teaching them within the centre of the tornado." President Goheen, of Princeton, also affirmed that it was "desirable that students should have the opportunity of stepping outside the world of bustle and crisis for a few years and learning to take the long view that would later be necessary to them."

While this reaffirmed the advantages of rural Acadia, it took no thought of the disadvantages. Located in a tiny country town, some sixty-five crooked miles from the nearest city, it could look for no municipal subvention and was more likely to hear the grumbling of ratepayers over our statutory exemption from local taxes. The neighbourhood had long since, moreover, been supersaturated with students as lodgers and no further academic growth was possible unless we ourselves added still more dormitories to our existing ten—not to mention extra dining hall accommodation, more gymnasium, office, class, and laboratory space, and more heating plant boilers to keep the whole establishment from freezing. To build dormitories, we ourselves would have to put up the first ten per cent of the cost and the federal government would then lend us the remaining ninety per cent, to be repaid by us (with interest of 5¼ per cent per annum) out of enhanced student residence fees. For all other buildings, we could not even get loans, but had to raise the money by canvassing a public that was already being badgered for help by forty-six other hungry Canadian universities. It was evident that we could not expect to grow at the same rate as our affluent contemporaries in central and western Canada, which not only received up to seventy per cent of their operating costs from governments but handsome capital gifts as well. Nova Scotia's cohorts of children might be proportionately greater than the Canadian average, but the penury of the area and a tradition of governmental hitch-hiking at the expense of seven private universities put the future of the Bluenose colleges under a cloud.

Between tasks assigned by the Nova Scotia Research Foundation and those of the National Research Council, our science departments had all of the summer research that they could possibly handle. No similar encouragement was available for professors and graduate students in Arts, and it was on behalf of these that I became for a short time the interim chairman of an "Acadia University Institute" that we incorporated provincially as a research foundation loosely associated with the University. Its first act was to sponsor the establishment of a "Fundy Mental Health Clinic," with quarters on the campus, to take care of psychiatric referrals from the counties of Hants and Kings—and, of course, the university community. The Institute then launched out on a wide pool of interdisciplinary research on various phases of the socio-geography of the area, with studies of population complexes in rural Kings, forestry and farm practices in Hants, the use of sand plain country in Kings, the economic and social basis of a largely segregated Negro community in rural Hants, and so on. Acadia professors and their M.A. and M.Sc. students in economics, sociology, psychology, and biology supplied nearly all of the personnel, working in each case under a planning seminar. I could not help comparing all this with the interdisciplinary study of the Lower Swansea Valley, in South Wales, undertaken by the University College of Swansea, but in each case the initiative was spontaneous and owed nothing to the other project.

Two or three of our keenest science men presently conceived the idea of cross-fertilization among the science departments of the Maritime universities. I was persuaded to grubstake these missionaries in Christmas week, 1959, so that they might visit their opposite numbers at the University of New Brunswick, Mount Allison, Saint Francis Xavier, and Dalhousie and try to arrange for brief interchanges of professors in special fields of competence. There was some hope that support might be forthcoming from the National Research Council, Ottawa, and from a Research Foundation in New York. There was an enthusiastic response, especially from Dalhousie, and without too much delay the Atlantic Provinces Inter-university Committee on Science (APICS) was formed. This gave science students on all campuses the stimulus of contact with some of the best men in the whole Atlantic region. The men who designed the ship modestly left the captaincy to others, but they deserve credit for its conception and for the drive that brought it into being.

The only real novelties added to the curriculum during my régime were courses in clinical pastoral training, commerce and wildlife biology, and none of these emerged as the result of long-range planning. One of our theological graduates, Rev. Charles Taylor, joined the staff as a chaplain after taking his master's degree in clinical pastoral training at Andover-Newton. As a result of his competence and initiative, courses in this field were added to our B.D. and B.Th. programme, clinical summer sessions were set up, and an interdenominational Institute of Pastoral Training was founded. Commerce, as a subdepartment in Arts, came as a result of sheer demand in the field. I was none too enthusiastic over this sort of professional training, but we were able to get its curriculum strongly undergirded by mathematics and economics. Wildlife biology, solely at the Master's level, was the resultant of several forces—the grave public need for wildlife biologists, our possession of a very strong biology department, the accessibility of an ideal part-time instructor at nearby Kentville, and the spontaneous gift of three wildlife sanctuaries to the University—on Brier Island (Digby Neck), at Hemmeon Head (South Shore), and in the Daniel's Lake area on the Windsor–Chester highway.

My university education had consisted primarily of the study of Greek and Latin—which meant, after some competence in the languages had been achieved, daily converse with some of the world's greatest minds and greatest works of literature in a context unadulterated by the prejudices and misconceptions of our own time. From that education I derived, for better or worse, a theory of pedagogy that called for a rigorous mastery in depth of two or three major disciplines along with a "vision of greatness" in arts, literature, science, and religion. I could subscribe to Aristotle's assertion in his *Laws*: "We should not listen to those who tell us that human beings should think like men and mortals think like mortals, but we should achieve such immortality as we may, and strain every nerve to live by the highest things in us. They may be small in substance, but in price and power they are far beyond all else." On the other hand, I trembled to see the *pleonexia* of Athens ruin the city's soul and wreck the Hellenic world, even as internecine warfare and revolution, comparable to those of Europe's twentieth century, corrupted the whole public life of ancient Greece. Thucydides described in bitter detail the spiritual catastrophe of his generation: "They dared the most awful deeds and sought revenges still more awful." Greed, cruelty, and lying were like a trial run for the even vaster greed, cruelty, and lying of 1914–64.

Along with the models of excellence and the warnings of corruption found in ancient civilization went the importance of religion, especially the vital experience of Christianity, as an integrating force in the human spirit. Depth psychology, and especially the version of Carl Gustav Jung, was here a major factor in my pedagogical theory. One found that the conscious "rational" self is only one-half of every personality, while equal reality and even greater power must be conceded to the "shadow," the dark, subconscious instinctual self that lives by archetypes and is capable of unspeakable cruelty and horror. Instead of painfully facing this black *alter ego* as active in our own hearts, we are universally moved to project it into an existence in other groups or nations (who thus tend to be feared and hated as "the enemy") or into a master personality in a world of spirits (identifiable as "the Devil" or "lo imperador del doloroso regno"). The power of religion, as distinguished from cold credal formulations, is that its purpose and meaning lie in the relationship of the individual to God or to a path of liberation and salvation; in other words, to a deep involvement of both the shadow and the conscious self. The desiccation of living religion into theological systems can return the black monster to its den, from which, without the daily fetters of faith, it is liable to break forth into evil ways. When such unintegrated individuals are mobilized by slogans in the mass-state, they and their power-hungry rulers become capable of infinite atrocities. The past fifty years of world history are full of examples, especially in the deeds of the white men in almost all countries. The shadow, on the other hand, if joined with the conscious self by some affection of *caritas*, can contribute its dynamism to a movement towards world renewal rather than world destruction. As Carl Jung emphasizes, however, this becomes effective only when achieved in humility in the individual life as a good in itself and not as an organizational mass-project.

Early in the 1950's, some of our theological professors, emboldened by my account of a small interdisciplinary philosophy club at McMaster in which nine or ten of us had sought to "draw out Leviathan with a hook," launched a rather more ambitious faculty discussion group at Acadia to examine matters of faith in the light of modern reason. To the consternation of the sponsors, on the battlefield of dialectic the sons of Belial showed more skill and dash, and even more up-to-date weapons, than the sons of Bunyan. It was also rather frustrating to find that each side tended to deny, or still more to ignore, the major premises of the other. In general one may say that such confrontation was a healthy sign, for a university has surely the function of trying out opinions. All would subscribe to a passion for truth, thoroughness in its pursuit, precision in analysis, a willingness to learn, and insistence on freedom of utterance. In this arena of ideas it is obviously important that the Christian faith should bear its witness.

My one contribution to the curriculum at Acadia was the introduction of a mandatory course in English Bible for all Arts sophomores. I had no thought of any sacramental effect, not even an *opus operantis*. It

The Kirkconnell Country, from Criffell, 1955.

Home left by Great-grandfather Walter Kirkconnell, 1819.

Kirkconnell House, near New Abbey, Scotland.

Birthplace of Watson Kirkconnell (1895–), Port Hope, Ont.

John Kirkconnell (1824–1898).
Father's father.

Agnes Allison Kirkconnell
(1823–1903). Father's mother.

Thomas Watson (1826–1912).
Mother's father.

Margaret Green Watson (1830–1904).
Mother's mother.

Thomas Allison Kirkconnell (1862–1934). Father.

Bertha Watson Kirkconnell (1867–1957). Mother.

Watson Kirkconnell, aged 20.

Watson Kirkconnell, aged 68.

Helen Kirkconnell (1890–   ), aged 24. Sister.

Walter Kirkconnell (1893–1918). Brother.

John R. Kirkconnell (1900–   ), aged 22. Brother.

Herbert Kirkconnell (1900–   ), aged 19. Brother.

A trio in 1899: Helen 8, Watson 4, Walter 6.

The Matriarch (Bertha Kirkconnell), aged 86.

Lindsay Collegiate Institute, 1910.

Arts Building, Queen's University, 1913.

Fort Henry, Prisoners' Gardens, 1916.

Kapuskasing, Forest Fire, 1917.

Watson Kirkconnell, at ease, 1919.

Watson Kirkconnell,
at Boshkung Lake, 1920.

Lincoln College, Oxford University, 1921.

Appian Way, near Rome, 1921.

The Acropolis, Athens, 1921.

Sphinx and Pyramid of Cheops, 1921.

Staff group, United College, 1934.

Isabel Peel Kirkconnell (1902–1925).

Hope Kitchener Kirkconnell (1900–).

Family around fireplace, Winnipeg, 1938.

Canadian Authors' Association convention, 1930.

Stephen Tisza University, Debrecen, Hungary, 1938.

Budapest, Hungary, 1938.

McMaster University, Arts Building, 1940.

Baptist Federation Council, 1945.

By Boshkung Lake, "Three Acres of Vacation."

A. S. P. Woodhouse (1895–1964).

Séraphin Marion (1896–).

Maurice Lebel (1909–).

C. H. Andrusyshen (1907–).

With E. J. Pratt (1882–1964).

Lulu and Béla Payerle (1904–).

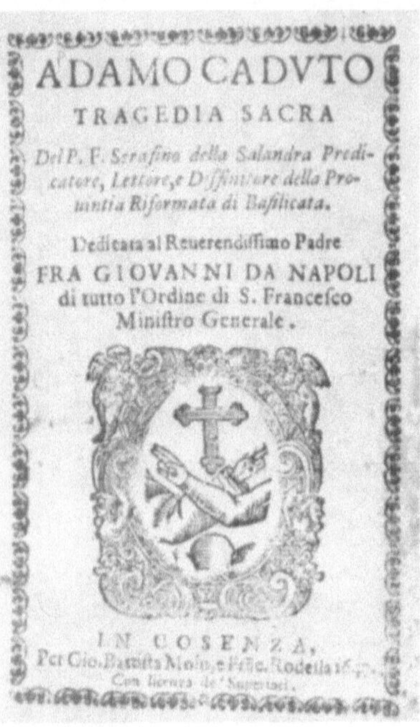

ADAMO CADVTO
TRAGEDIA SACRA
Del P. F. Serafino della Salandra Predicatore, Lettore, e Diffinitore della Provintia Riformata di Basilicata.
Dedicata al Reuerendissimo Padre
FRA GIOVANNI DA NAPOLI
di tutto l'Ordine di S. Francesco
Ministro Generale.
IN COSENZA,
Per Gio. Battista Moio, e Felic. Rodella
Con licenza de' Superiori.

Title page, *Adamo Caduto*, by Salandra.

TRAGOEDIA
SACRA: QVA TOTVM
FERE SIMSONIS HEBRÆORVM IVDICIS CVRRICVlum continetur.
M. ANDREA VVUNSTIO ECCLESIAE
1604.
ARGENTORATI.

Title page, *Simson*, by Wunstius.

Jacket of Polish epic, Pan Tadeusz (1962).

Jacket of The Poetical Works of Taras Shevchenko (1964).

Acadia University, Administration Building, 1948.

Self, wife and daughters, President's House, 1948.

Football kick-off, Acadia, Raymond Field.

Campbell–Kirkconnell wedding, July 1956.

Conferring hon. DCL on Rt. Hon. Vincent Massey, 1957.

Farewell to Dr. Malcolm Elliott, 1957.

Orchids in Iceland, July 1963.

Home on retirement, Wolfville, N.S., 1964.

Susan (1945–), Watson, Hope and Janet (1936–), 1964.

Son James (1925–   ) and family, Don Mills, Ontario.

Son Thomas (1925–   ) and family, Montgomery, W.Va.

The children of Gordon and
Helen Kirkconnell (1934–   ) Campbell, Weymouth, N.S.

was to be, in part, a renewed acquaintance with our greatest treasure-house of spiritual vision and moral teaching at a level far above the piecemeal adolescent and pre-adolescent simplifications and obfuscations of the average Sunday School. It was also hoped that this would help many to integrate an adult faith with the adult grasp of scientific, historical, and sociological truth that was emerging from their secular studies. Since example is much more potent than precept, an attempt was also made to maintain what Toynbee would call a creative minority of Christians in a predominantly secular civilization. It was out of some recognition of that need that I found myself chairman of a University Christian Council, dedicated to co-ordinating and nurturing such a core of religious concern. This ran the risk of hostility from those who might mistake it for a bad case of sanctimonious egotism. It was also in danger of saturation with students who had never grown up theologically and could make faith on the campus of no reputation with the intellectually mature. A university chaplain who stressed the ecumenicity of his ministry and a beautiful Manning Memorial Chapel (a gift of the Fred C. Manning Charitable Trust in 1960) as a focus for university worship helped to stabilize the setting of religion on the campus. This seemed to be a minimum contribution of religion to university education. For a college founded in faith by the Baptist pioneers of the Valley, no less would do.

Looking back over the years of my presidency, I am grateful to many who helped me to avoid calamities and to achieve whatever is on the ledger for good. President Emeritus F. W. Patterson could not have been kinder had I been his own son and was an invaluable collector of funds in the quadrennium 1948–52. His financial prospecting was then taken over by Dr. C. B. Lumsden as "executive secretary to the Board of Governors" (1952–58), Dr. Thomas B. McDormand as "executive vice-president" (1959–61) and Mr. Norman Moore as "vice-president for development" (1961 to the present). Dr. Malcolm Elliott, having been chairman of the Board during the hungry thirties and the difficult forties, watched lynx-eyed over the budget during the hard years of shrinking enrolment, 1948–54. His successor, Dr. Harvey Crowell, was more willing to take a chance on plant expansion as the tide came flooding in in 1960–64, yet worked indefatigably on campaigns for funds. Dr. Earle Hiltz was a princely chairman of planning committees. On Fred Elderkin, the treasurer and business manager, I leaned perhaps more heavily than on anyone else, and never knew him to fail me. His analysis of fiscal trends and of the comparative costs of our various departments helped me to maintain solvency in the face of the enthusiasms and clamours of professors and departments. Robie Roscoe, the Admirable Crichton of the Maintenance Department, and Ronald

Longley, provost, dean of Arts and Science, and ultimately academic vice-president, were also among the architects of the newer Acadia. To these, and to scores of other colleagues, my thanks are due.

In August 1965, a year after my post-coronary retirement, the Atlantic United Baptist Convention, on the recommendation of an *ad hoc* "Committee on Higher Education," passed two startling resolutions: (*a*) that a university governor who had served for six years was not eligible for re-election and (*b*) that the Acadia faculty must be made up of "professors who have a personal belief in and commitment to Jesus Christ."

The six-year rule for the Board could only mean a resolute desire to sack the governors who had appointed a non-Baptist as my successor and to replace them with a Board that would concur obediently in directives from the denomination. The effect on administrative competence would have been lethal. By 1971, some twenty of the thirty governors would have been new men with no experience whatever, while the remaining ten would have had one year of experience. At a time when the academic ship faced the most difficult navigational problems in its history (with the doubling and soon the quadrupling of Canada's students and professors, and the financing and erection of many new buildings), the new rule would have made all of the ship's officers walk the plank and would have replaced them with unskilled landlubbers.

I could see, moreover, that the Convention's proposal that Faculty members must be committed Christians was (*a*) impracticable, (*b*) a breach of the Act of Incorporation, (*c*) discriminatory, and (*d*) contrary to the principles and practices of all other church-related Maritime universities. As a septuagenarian in retirement and still under the care of a heart specialist, I held my peace pretty well, for I felt that plenty of others were active on behalf of Acadia. Stirred up by the Alumni, the Faculty, and many of the clergy, the Board of Governors presently applied to the Nova Scotia legislature for a new Act that would reduce Convention appointees to a minority position on the Board. Fur flew in the denominational and the daily press for several months, but without any statement from myself until I learned that questionable pressure was being brought to bear on individual legislators in an attempt to kill the Bill. Thereupon I wrote a personal letter to every MLA and contributed a full length article to the front page of the Halifax *Chronicle-Herald* for February 24, 1966.

After explaining how staff appointments are made at Canadian universities (see above, p. 149), and how highly specialized today's recruits must be, my exposition continued:

To bring in, on grounds of piety, some person with inferior qualifications would be like hiring a devout second year medical student to be the chief surgeon in a great hospital. Patients would be gashed to death and the reputation of the hospital would sink to zero. . . .

In my sixteen years as president, I preferred to hire a practising Protestant if a competent one were available, so as to have as many men as possible who were congenial by faith and temperament to the traditions of the institution. Unfortunately, with the lowest salary schedule in Canada and faced by a dire scarcity of trained instructors for all departments everywhere, I sometimes had to recruit men who had been brought up in other traditions. But the men whom I had sought . . . almost invariably chose the more abundant loaves and fishes at some other university. For instance, several years ago I had set my heart on getting in philosophy the brilliant young son of one of our Convention ministers. Since he was finishing up a Ph.D. at Queen's, I journeyed all the way to Kingston, Ontario, to confirm my impression of the young man and make him an offer. The offer was made and promptly refused. He explained quite honestly that he would have less work and more pay elsewhere, and I could not blame him.

What the Committee's Report disregards is that candidates for academic posts are not standing around in the market-place waiting for us to pick out one who is a professed Christian. There are far more academic openings in Canada today than there are qualified men to fill them. To secure each new man (and we need about fifteen a year), we must either lure him away from some wealthier institution or seek out some uncommitted man in a graduate school, only to find that he has already had several more attractive offers. About 1960, after searching in vain for several years for a competent mathematician, we imported one, with his wife and child, all the way from Israel. The difficulties will become incessantly greater. There are retirements due to age and the constant resignations of men who have accepted better jobs at any other university. The growth in student enrolment will further require a large absolute increase in staff. The problem presently will be to secure any staff at all. To make our requirement an assurance of Christian commitment as well as academic competence would seal us off from the employment market.

But the Convention's proposed rule also violates Article 8 of the Act of Incorporation, which merely states that professors, teachers and officers should be "competent persons of any religious persuasion whatever." It is as sweeping as that. For 125 years that article has been cited as proof of the wide vision and liberal character of the founding fathers.

The Convention's Committee may declare that its much narrower definition carries no hint of discrimination whatever. But what of the five Jews who now serve on the Acadia faculty? They are practising Jews and have formed a small community of their own for the worship of the God whom Jesus worshipped. They are now told, however, by the Convention resolution, that they are serving Acadia in breach of its new basic principles and that no Jew must ever again be appointed to the staff. At a time when the Church of Rome has just voted overwhelmingly to show tolerance towards the Jew, the Baptist Convention tells him bluntly that no matter how devout this kinsman of Isaiah, Paul and Jesus may be, they will have none of him. He cannot possibly, they imply, be "a person of any religious persuasion whatever." This is discrimination with a vengeance.

Such a rule, moreover, is unknown at all the other church-related universities of the Maritime provinces. The officials of Mount Allison, St. Francis Xavier and St. Mary's all assure me that they have no rules as to the religious commitments of Faculty members. Confronted by two equally qualified candidates, they would choose the one in their own tradition, but the best qualified man gets the job regardless of his religious affiliation. Thus the Vice-President of Mount Allison reports that "we have on the staff some Jews, some Roman Catholics and some Hindus, all of whom seem to fit into our context very well." St. Francis Xavier reports Hindus and a Jew for 1966–67 and St. Mary's tells me that it has a small minority of Hindus and Turks "and just about anything else you could mention." The Convention rule would reduce Acadia to the ignominy of being the only intolerant university in Canada—after long years of pride in our tolerance. And I prophesy that unless this shocking proposal is blocked by the passage of the present Bill, most of the Faculty will resign in protest and no self-respecting scholar or scientist will ever again accept an appointment here.

The true supervisory authority over the Board of the University is not the Convention but the provincial government of Nova Scotia. Article Seven of the Act of Incorporation specifies "That so long as any sum of Money shall be paid out by the Provincial Treasury towards the support and maintenance of the said College and Academy, the Governor, Lieutenant-Governor or Commander-in-chief of the said province for the time being may from time to time enquire into the proceedings of the said Trustees and Governors, and of the Committee of the said Education Society [the forerunner, in this context, of the Atlantic Baptist Convention] . . . and if, after just enquiry and due proof had, they find that any of the said Trustees and Governors, or of the said Committee, have conducted the proceedings of the said College or said Education Society in a manner inconsistent with this Act, or with the professed objects of the said College or Society . . . the Governor, Lieutenant-Governor or Commander-in-chief, with the advice of Her Majesty's Council, may remove the officers or members so found offending and may, on that occasion, appoint in their place an equal number of new members." The terminology may change somewhat with the years, but the intent is clear. The founding fathers, in their wisdom, foresaw the very sort of threat that has now materialized and therefore wrote the right and duty of Caesar into the very Act of Incorporation.

In keeping with that provision and in view of the unprecedented assault by the Convention on the basic principles of the Charter, the competent governing body of the University (the Board of Governors) is appealing to the competent over-riding authority of the provincial government to intervene and save the University from disaster.

In a new constitution for Mount Allison University, adopted some three years ago by the New Brunswick Legislature, the United Church of Canada is reduced to a minority position in a composite Board of Regents, in order that no single group should control the Board. The United Church has cheerfully accepted this arrangement as keeping Mount A. "church-related" but also protected from all threats to its academic freedom. The proposed Act Regarding Acadia University seeks identical safeguards for the beleaguered old institution in Wolfville.

My share in the provincial decision can only be conjectural, although many MLA's wrote to assure me that I had convinced them. Overwhelming legislative approval was given to the second reading of the Bill, and when its text came up for public review on March 8, 1966, before the Private and Local Bills Committee, a compromise was reached that took control out of Convention hands but not as categorically as had at first been proposed. The Convention and the Alumni were each to elect fourteen governors, the Lieutenant-Governor in Council would appoint six, and the Board itself would choose two more, conceivably members of the Faculty. The president of the University remained an ex officio governor with voting rights.

I should be less than fair if I did not give the Convention spokesmen full marks for sincerity and good intentions. On the other hand, the majority of those who fought for the Bill were also Baptists and men who, while wishing to save Acadia from disastrous church interference, wanted it to remain "church-related." A providential balancing of forces has been achieved, in which the church may influence but cannot dictate to the University Board and administration. A denominational tiger may continue, as in my day, to breathe down the president's neck, but its teeth have been pulled.

14

The Political Pendulum

THE SCOTTISH COMMUNITIES in Argenteuil and Prescott counties have a tradition of political Liberalism that has been consistent for over a century. Whether by conviction or by assimilation, my great-grandfather, Walter Kirkconnell, shared piously in that political faith. When his son, John Kirkconnell, my own grandfather, migrated in 1873 with many of his neighbours to Bruce County on the Lake Huron shore, they took this same Liberal persuasion with them and helped to make Bruce one of the Liberal strongholds in the province. The Toronto *Globe* was their political Bible, and every election was a declaration of faith. In my father's home, first in Port Hope and later in Lindsay, my own youth was suckled on the same editorial doctrines and nurtured in like opinions at the breakfast table.

In neither town was my father politically happy, for they lay in strongly Conservative ridings and the faith of his own youth was trampled down at almost every election. To his sons in their boyhood, of course, politics could not mean very much. No memory survives from elections in Port Hope (1895–1908) except the derisive slogan: "Vote for Aylesworth and get the canal! Vote for Ward and get the sewer!" (Sir Alan Aylesworth, Liberal, who had again urged an almost legendary canal over the old portage route from Lake Ontario to meet the Trent system ten miles north at Rice Lake, was defeated by Harry Ward, a Conservative lawyer in town, who had more realistically stressed local improvements.) More vivid are my recollections of the gloom that settled down one evening over a "Lost Heir" game in our parlour in Lindsay when the results of the 1911 federal election became disastrously clear.

My first and only political campaign speech was made at the age of seventeen in support of Mr. C. E. Weeks for the provincial House. The meeting that evening was being held at Bryson's schoolhouse, about four miles northwest of Lindsay, and Thomas Stewart, a local Liberal lawyer, drove me out to give the farmer audience a speech that I had already given, with some reverberations, in an oral composition class at the Collegiate Institute. It was dull enough stuff, I am sure, for I had based it glibly, as a boy of my age was ready to do, on an article in the *Queen's Quarterly* that was extensively critical of Ontario's system of education. I dimly gathered that I was helping to keep the meeting going until the candidate arrived. The real excitement came later, when the chairman announced with great satisfaction: "Wicks'll now come for'erd!" The meeting was finally a success but the Liberal, as usual, lost the election.

I went to Queen's University next year with few political convictions and emerged with an M.A. in April 1916 and still no assured political label. Compressing four years of advanced classics into three left little time for anything but the curriculum. Of this the most clearly political subject-matter was found in Thucydides, Plato, and Aristotle, consumed in large quantities in the original Greek. My professor, Thomas Callander, was a devout Conservative, and I found to my surprise that conservatism as a political principle often bore little relationship to the political parties and programmes in Canada. Plato, indeed, often had his Socrates talk like a Marxist, ready to push mankind around in the fulfilment of doctrinaire blueprints. Aristotle, on the other hand, gave one a balanced analysis of the forms of government practised by the political animal. Thucydides was equally stimulating in his presentation of the Peloponnesian War and the motives of strongly political communities undergoing wartime pressures and compulsions. I became sure that an interest in government at all levels was a highly important duty for the individual citizen, but at the age of twenty I was still foggy as to what an individual Canadian could do about it all.

After three and a half years in uniform, I found myself back in my father's home, convalescing from a bout with pleurisy. Here I devoted nearly a year and a half to writing the history of the Ontario county in which I lived. This *Victoria County Centennial History* first appeared in weekly instalments in the local *Watchman-Warder* and was brought out about December 1921 as a 261-page book.[1] It involved fundamental research in the archives in Ottawa and Toronto and a study of the complete files of the local press back to about 1860, but more important still was my attempt to understand and interpret the stages and legislation by which the pioneer frontier of 1821 had become the modern municipality of 1921. It was political science and sociology applied to a single local unit of Canadian government. On the basis of it, Professor J. L. Morison, professor of history at Queen's University, asked me if I

[1]In 1966, at the request of the Victoria County Council, I updated it for publication in February 1967 as the County's centennial project.

would consider becoming a lecturer in history under him, but I had hardly more than given my assent when he himself went from Queen's to Armstrong College, Newcastle-on-Tyne, and my own appointment lapsed.

I spent the academic year 1921–22 at Lincoln College, Oxford University, as Ontario's first IODE overseas postgraduate scholar. I spent the year on research that issued in a 217-page volume, *International Aspects of Unemployment* (London and New York, 1923), a book that purported to be economic but was at least fifty per cent political, for its major thesis was that the world's economic machine had been fouled up by wartime damage and post-war political policies. During the year, I had visited ten of the countries of Europe, as well as portions of North Africa and Western Asia and had become increasingly conscious of the political stresses and strains that made true prosperity almost impossible. Undergraduate life at Oxford was vastly more political than in Canada, and I was astonished to find how far to the left, by Canadian standards, even the young Conservatives were in England.

On the strength of my *International Aspects of Unemployment*, I was elected in 1926 to membership in the Royal Institute of International Affairs, London. Meantime, in Winnipeg, I became associated with one of three special discussion groups of a national organization known as the "Canadian League." Among its chief members were Edgar J. Tarr, president of the Monarch Life, John W. Dafoe, editor of the *Winnipeg Free Press*, and Principal John MacKay of Manitoba College. Our papers and discussions dealt chiefly with Canadian problems. Meanwhile in 1925 an Institute of Pacific Relations had been formed at a conference in Honolulu, and six interested Canadians had attended as observers. When a second IPR Honolulu Conference was planned for 1927, a Canadian delegation of eighteen under the chairmanship of Sir Arthur Currie attended, as did also a group from the Royal Institute of International Affairs headed by Sir Frederick Whyte. To avoid overlapping in international studies in Canada, it now seemed wise to launch an organization that would be affiliated both with the IPR (which had American support) and with the Royal Institute in London. In the autumn of 1927, a tentative constitution was drafted and branches were formed in Montreal, Ottawa, Toronto, Vancouver, and Winnipeg. In the case of Winnipeg, the "Canadian League" groups seemed to offer a natural nucleus and Sir Robert Borden met us all at a supper meeting in the Manitoba Club and carried through the reorganization. The local branch of the new "Canadian Institute of International Affairs" thus started off with a vigorous roster of fifty members. Two months later, on January 30, 1928, representatives of all five branches met in Ottawa at the home of Sir Robert Borden and set up the national council of the Institute.

As secretary of the Winnipeg branch of the Institute for nearly ten years, I came to have the highest regard for John W. Dafoe, its chairman, and Edgar Tarr, its vice-chairman. Both were Liberals of the highest type and gave a sense of character and principle to all that they touched.

In 1932, with an election in Ontario coming over the horizon in the following year, the provincial Liberal machine sought vigorously to enlist my father as a candidate for election—to become minister of education after the impending victory. He had just retired at the age of seventy, after fifty years as a teacher and thirty-six as a high school principal, and the party felt that his rich pedagogical experience would be of great benefit to educational policy in Ontario. By the same mail one day in November 1932, letters reached me in Winnipeg from prominent Liberals urging me to persuade him to accept and from my father himself begging me "to hit the project between the eyes with a bludgeon." He realized all too well his slim lease on life, although he still looked vigorous to his friends, and he therefore refused to run. The Liberal party swept the province in 1933, but not with his help. He died of a cerebral thrombosis in April 1934.

In the summer of 1938, I was to visit Hungary and lecture on Hungarian literature at the Stephen Tisza University at Debrecen. To help pay for the expenses of my wife and myself I undertook to write a series of press articles from the numerous countries that I was to visit. Unfortunately, I found that Mr. Dafoe had just signed up a man to give him exactly that sort of material for the same period. Nothing daunted, I went to the local Conservative daily, the *Evening Tribune*, sold the prospective series there, and then, at the suggestion of Dr. W. T. Allison, bargained successfully with the other five papers of the Southam chain in Ottawa, Hamilton, Calgary, Edmonton, and Vancouver. It may have appeared like a sudden switch of political allegiance but was well understood by Mr. Dafoe.

Most of 1939 went to my study of the political attitudes of Canada's two million European-Canadians towards Hitler and Mussolini as revealed in the foreign-language press in this country.

For the three previous years I had been reporting on the poetry, fiction, essays, and drama in these papers in an annual survey for the *University of Toronto Quarterly* and now a special grant of one hundred dollars from the Canadian Institute of International Affairs enabled me to extend my subscription coverage to forty newspapers in fourteen languages. A large-scale volume, *Canada, Europe and Hitler*, was in the hands of the Oxford University Press and of the Toronto research committee of the Institute just after the outbreak of the war in September 1939. The research committee protested that my condemnation of Hitler was too vigorous for an academic researcher. My publishers, who backed the volume without reserve, refunded the Institute its hundred dollars and rushed the book through the press. In re-reading it today, I have not a single sentence to retract—except to amend the date and occasion of an authentic speech of Stalin's quoted on page 91.

In December 1940, I was summoned to Ottawa for a small meeting of interested officials (Norman Robertson, Commissioner Wood of the RCMP, the Hon. Joseph Thorson, T. C. Davis, and Dr. Tracy Philipps) to discuss the setting up of a special nationalities branch under the Department of National War Services. Not only was this new branch set up, supported by a strong advisory "Committee on Cooperation in Canadian Citizenship" (consisting of G. W. Simpson, N. F. Angus, the Honourable C. H. Blakeney, Major J. S. A. Bois, Jean Bruchesi, Donald Cameron, S. D. Clark, Robert England, J. M. Gibbon, Mrs. R. F. McWilliams, Mrs. O. D. Skelton, and myself), but the Wartime Information Board, then in the resolute hands of Herb Lash, had me write a 48-page booklet entitled *Canadians All*, in which the cultural and historical achievements of all the main national groups in Canada were described, and arranged for a series of radio broadcasts on the same theme, with myself as a consultant. Some 396,000 copies of the pamphlet were distributed and the CBC broadcasts were enthusiastically received. The National Film Board also prepared a documentary film based on my theme and on one occasion, on December 6, 1941, when I spoke to the Royal Canadian Institute, Toronto, on "The Peoples of Canada," the film was run as a prelude to my address.

Quite early in the war I was frequently made the voice of Canada's public conscience. Thus, early in December 1939, four thousand people crowded the Civic Auditorium in Winnipeg to protest the Soviet attack on the gallant little Finnish nation—not in defence against Hitler but by actual agreement with him—and I was made the main speaker at the great rally. In February 1940, I organized a public protest against the German depopulation of whole areas of western Poland (see page 270). On May 3, 1940, I spoke over the CBC in tribute to the Polish nation in its martyrdom at Nazi and Soviet hands. On May 17, 1940, the CBC again had me give a full-length address in honour of the martyred Norwegian nation, so recently seized by Germany. From 1938 to 1941, I averaged one hundred public addresses a year, most of them on political issues and in defence of the European-Canadian communities in Canadian life.

When, however, on June 22, 1941, Hitler double-crossed his faithful Communist ally and drove eastward against the Soviet Union, a sort of madness seemed to descend upon the White House in Washington and presently spread to all of the Western belligerents. Franklin D. Roosevelt was not only prepared to give physical aid to Stalin. He also promised that evil man and his evil régime that he would undertake to present them to the Western world as angels of light. This mendacious programme was in due course transmitted by Mr. Roosevelt to his good friend Mr. Mackenzie King and it became increasingly impossible for an honest man to do business with the Liberal government in Ottawa. Part of the story is told in another chapter, but some phases of my ordeal may be summarized here:

(*a*) In a second large edition of my pamphlet, *Canadians All*, all criticism of Soviet Russia was carefully expunged by the Wartime Information Board.

(*b*) A League for Canadian-Soviet Friendship was launched in June 1943. The Prime Minister himself was chairman at the inauguration meeting and the sponsors included Anglican and Roman Catholic bishops and archbishops. I myself was invited by Sir Ellsworth Flavelle to be a sponsor but made my acceptance conditional on the League's not being used to whitewash Communist treason. My caveat was not accepted and my name did not appear. Some months later, when the League's secretary came to organize a branch in Hamilton, several of us agreed privately with one another to attend the organization meeting in the Royal Connaught Hotel in order to block the movement. We succeeded in referring the question to an investigating committee that never reported.

(*c*) In 1942, the Canadian Authors' Association, whose national president I had become, appointed a "Writers' War Committee," with myself as chairman, to put the abilities of all Canadian authors at the disposal of the Wartime Information Board. Its story is told in Chapter XXIII.

(*d*) Insidious pressures were brought to bear on all the foreign-language communities in Canada. Apparently out of deference to the new Soviet Embassy in Ottawa, it now became government policy to insist that the loyal non-Communist majority in each foreign-language community accept the seditious Communist minority as equal partners in all war efforts and relief efforts. In fact, the Communist leaders, many of them fresh from hiding or Canadian concentration camps, received undue hospitality at government hands. It was as if Judas Iscariot, instead of hanging himself, were made by Pilate the triumphant spokesman to Rome on behalf of the infant Church while the other eleven apostles were cold-shouldered into obscurity. Our advisory committee to the Nationalities Branch, having been loudly denounced by the Communists as unsympathetic to our noble Soviet allies, was allowed to die away. Polish relief committees, which had once felt happy to carry the names of their Canadian champions, Lawrence Burpee and myself, as "honorary chairmen," were placed by Ottawa in the hands of organizers who, to placate the Communists, dropped us both from their lists.

(*e*) I was told by Ottawa friends that Fred Rose, MP, was now a welcome visitor in the East Block as a consultant on policy. The *Canadian Tribune* boasted that when the Canadian government wanted men to parachute to Communist partisan positions in the Balkans, it had come to the Communists of Canada for volunteers.

(*f*) The CBC dropped me from its list of broadcasters and on one dramatic occasion denied me the air at a Canadian Club luncheon in Toronto. On February 1, 1943, I was to speak to the Canadian Club of Toronto on the subject "Our Communists and the New Canadians." My script was in CBC hands a full week in advance and might have been amended at any point to make it acceptable. Instead of this, a note was handed to the chairman of the meeting, two minutes before I was called on to speak, announcing that the scheduled all-Canada broadcast would be replaced by music and that only those in the room would hear me.

(*g*) It became clear that the Liberal government, on the eve of the 1945 federal election, intended to hand back to the Communist Ukrainians the 108 community halls that it had closed in June 1940 as assured centres of revolutionary indoctrination.

The intellectual immorality and political folly of all this alienated me quite early in the game and destroyed whatever Liberal allegiance I might once have felt. Hence when my old friend, Cecil Frost, of Lindsay, organizing a Conservative caucus at Trinity College School, Port Hope, in order to draft a platform for an impending national rally in Winnipeg, invited me to attend as a consultant, I was ready to accept. The section of that platform dealing with immigration, as accepted by the Conservatives in Port Hope and in Winnipeg, was drafted by me in its entirety. My intimacy with leaders in the party grew, and a couple of years later, while visiting at the home of Gordon Graydon in Brampton, I was assured that in case of a federal victory at the polls, the Conservatives intended to draft me as minister of external affairs. In one unidentified year, I actually wrote a speech for the Leader of the Opposition in reply to the Speech from the Throne.

And yet, in all this, I was far from happy. For one thing, I had hints at Ottawa that the pro-Soviet pose of the Government was not assumed with any conviction. In January 1944, I was called to the Department of National War Services for three days, to undertake, along with the Deputy Minister, Chester Payne, Dr. George Wilfred Simpson, and Dr. Tracy Philipps, to reorganize the Nationalities Branch in the form that it still preserves today. In a private interview at that time, the Minister of National War Services, Major-General L. R. LaFleche, under whose department we were operating, gave me an old soldier's blessing regarding my attacks on the Communists: "We can't say this to you publicly, but we want you to give the bastards hell!" I also found, to my grief, that some of the Conservative leaders were frankly without principle in their choice of issues on which to criticize the Government. Expediency, rather than logic or fundamental belief, dominated their day-by-day political thinking. From about this date I find in my files the carbon copy of a memorandum on the bankruptcy of social planning in Russia which I supplied on request to the Hon. Ian Mackenzie, Minister of Veterans' Affairs, as ammunition for the Liberal party in its debates with the CCF.

It had, I think, become evident that in 1946 the Liberals had been slapped wide awake by the espionage revelations, although at the time I was equally disgusted with Mr. King's craven unwillingness to receive any evidence from Igor Gouzenko against the government of a "friendly power" and with the Conservatives' eagerness to make political capital out of the preliminary investigation, whose methods had been concurred in by Mr. Bracken at the very outset.

My groping after principles was met in January 1948 by a letter from the British Liberal International Council (President, Professor Gilbert Murray; vice-presidents, the Earl of Perth, the Viscountess Gladstone, Sir Richard Livingstone, Miss Rose Macaulay, and the Right Honourable H. Graham White). My articles in *Saturday Night*, Toronto, had impressed English readers as in harmony with a "Liberal Manifesto" drawn up at Oxford in the previous April and I was invited to organize a Canadian affiliate.

The gospel there laid down caught my complete conviction and my membership fee, but my political affiliations were vague and the Governors of Acadia University, to which I was now the president-designate, had breathed a hope that I would not be actively political. As a trial balloon, I made the "Liberal Manifesto" central to an address that I gave on February 16, 1948, to my old friends of the Canadian Club, Toronto, on "The Crisis in Education." The Right Honourable Arthur Meighen, who was present, was indulgent enough to say that it was the greatest address he had ever heard. But when I turned to the Canadian Liberals in Ottawa and elsewhere and sought for some support in setting up a "Canadian Liberal International Council" I met with evasive answers and no readiness to underwrite the proposition. By the end of 1948, I had come to the conclusion that Arthur Meighen, Grant Dexter and I were just about the only serious champions of Liberal philosophy left in Canada.

At Acadia, my political position has, on the whole, been scrupulously neutral. On December 10, 1948, I was called on, as chairman of a three-party federal by-election debate in Convocation Hall, to act as referee in a platform boxing-match between M. J. Coldwell, leader of the CCF party, and the Hon. George Drew, leader of the Progressive Conservative party. My gentle hands, placed on each of the two raging political lions, might not have sufficed to break up the clinch had I not reminded them that each had been guilty of unparliamentary language and must retract and clear the record. The familiar parliamentary rebuke brought immediate obedience from the veterans of the House and the brawl was over. The only ones to profit by it were the Honourable Douglas Abbott, who represented the Liberal party and smilingly remained non-controversial in his talk, and a local photographer named MacAulay, who had snapped a picture at the critical moment and sold it to the Toronto *Star* for one hundred dollars.

My next nearest approach to political participation came in a year, here to remain undesignated, in which the then premier of Nova Scotia sought me out in Wolfville and invited me, some weeks before a general election, to become the provincial minister of education. He would have me sworn into office immediately and would dot the "i's" and cross the "t's" after the election was over. At that time no Nova Scotian party had acknowledged the need for giving substantial help to the universities of the province. My response to the unexpected overture was the proposal of a *quid pro quo*: if the premier would publicly pledge his party to give this urgently needed help to higher education, I would join his cabinet. He refused, and the deal was off. I had been willing to sacrifice myself for the welfare of Acadia University, but I had no political ambitions on my own account. An identical invitation came from the Liberal party machine in April 1967, but like my father in 1932 I begged off.

Looking back over seventy years of Canadian politics—and looking about me at the present political state of the nation—I have no grounds for unmitigated optimism.

In my early childhood, Canada was a semi-independent small power of 5,000,000, or not much more than the present population of amputated Finland. Today it is an alleged "middle power" of 20,000,000, roughly equivalent in numbers to Egypt or Burma. When I was a graduate student at Oxford, students from the Dominions felt no qualms in belonging to a "Colonial Club." Today, we travel with Canadian passports, have our own ambassadorial or equivalent representatives in some 87 capitals, and sound off freely as to what ought to be done in every corner of the world.

The character of today's population is not just the pattern of 1895 "writ large." A demographic anaemia of the rural extremities has developed concurrently with hydrocephaly of the cities. Even the province of Quebec, whose public image was long that of the *habitant* with his huge family and simple pieties, is now some seventy per cent urban, and the birthrate in Montreal is lower than that in Toronto. The ingredients of the Canadian pudding have changed, moreover, with the influx of millions of men, women, and children from countries other than France and the British Isles. While *les Canadiens* remain unchanged at thirty per cent of the whole, the Anglo-Canadians have dropped from nearly seventy per cent to less than forty-four per cent, and every nationality of Europe has contributed to the remaining twenty-six per cent.

Nor can one forget our living cheek by jowl with an equally diversified nation of 200 millions whose dynamic industrialism has endowed it with two-thirds of all the world's wealth. Canada was originally set up *a mari usque ad mare* in order to outflank the westward thrust of the American economy and to create a non-American state in defiance of geography. Increasingly, however, and especially since the Paley Report, forecasting in 1950 the requirements of American industry for the next quarter-century, pointed an inexorable finger at Canada's undeveloped resources in minerals, wood pulp, power—and, we may now add, fresh water—the inpouring of American capital and the outpouring southward of Canadian exports have made us a Siamese twin of the American giant. United States capital holds a controlling interest in Canadian petroleum, mining, chemicals, and electrical apparatus manufacture. The American market takes two-thirds of our exports.

Our rapid development could never have taken place without this American investment, and on the whole this is not a ground for outcry. *Pecunia non olet*, and we have needed the money. It is folly, however, to borrow abroad for non-productive purposes, such as federal, provincial, and municipal operating costs, which create no means of repayment. Nevertheless, most of our economic griefs come to us in another way, from the nature of American politics. United States economic policies tend to be decided by Congress as the resultant of competing Washington lobbies, the diagonal of fiercely competing sectional interests. American national interest, no less than Canadian national interest, is frequently sacrificed to the pork-barrel policies of farm subsidies, food dumping, timber tariffs, and other regional rackets.

The technique of Canada's recent federal elections is a prostitution of psychological gimmicks. As a starter, pulse-taking "specialists" are hired to ascertain everything that the public could conceivably want from parliament. "Public relations experts" are then asked to prepare a list of these legislative goodies in the order of their presumed electoral appeal. Finally, these promised benefits, no matter how ridiculous, are dangled before the public as the convictions of the party and the assured road to personal happiness. On the platform, the candidate thus takes the stance of a tipsy Santa Claus. "Pie in the sky" is to be brought down to the living after the election regardless of the financial and moral cost. The results of all this chicanery, for all parties, has been a parliament made up of ineffective fragments. James Coyne, that brother of Cassandra, who tried to tell the public the truths denied it by the parties, was forced to resign—to avoid dismissal. The late Ken Eaton (Acadia '22), who resigned in 1958 after 24 years as a senior official in the federal department of finance, became thereafter outspoken in his philippics. His remarks at an Acadia Founders' Day dinner in 1962 are a fair sample: "I believe political morality has sunk to a lower level today in Ottawa than ever before in our history. To me it is utterly discouraging. It used to be recognized *on all sides* that there had to be some restraint *on all sides* in order for our democratic system to work. Restraint seems to have gone completely overboard these days and one is left wondering."

We have talked glibly of new, little African nations suffering shipwreck through a "revolution of excessive expectations," but this is precisely the fate that is overtaking our affluent Canadian nation. Our people have been led to expect ever-increasing comfort and freedom without paying the price in personal economies, higher taxes and greater productivity. The nation came close to disaster in June 1962, and on an unending programme of deficit financing we may even yet be sucked down the drain.

The psychological basis of the predicament was stated long ago by Thomas Hobbes: "I put for a general inclination of all mankind, a perpetuall and restless desire of Power after power, that ceaseth onely in Death." One may couple with this the highly reprehensible opinion of Plato: "Then the rulers of the State are the only persons who ought to have the privilege of lying, either at home or abroad; they may be allowed to lie *for the good of the State*." This unethical precept is perverted still further when Canada's political leaders, of all parties, dupe the public, not for its own good but in order to sate the electoral candidate's lust for power.

Yet another expedient that is too often seized on to win votes is an appeal to xenophobia, especially to prejudice against the United States. Because that evil counsel of the Conservatives won them the election of 1911, campaign planners in our own time have all too often lit a brushfire down the wind against our neighbours, hoping thereby to win votes from an inflamed Canadian electorate. Such would-be cunning is disastrous. Sound policies can never be based on hatred. To infect the national bloodstream with that bacillus is to poison its consciousness for generations. "The Kingdom of Hell is within you," as well as the Kingdom of Heaven, and we do ill to conjure up its devils in order to give power to some politician.

All this has sent me back to review my earlier political reading among the Greeks and Romans and the most masterly of recent thinkers in seeking to reforge my own philosophy of politics. Thucydides, Plato, and Aristotle were still basic in their analysis of man and the human community, for while their state-forms differed from ours, they were not straitjacketed in nineteenth-century dogmas of the modern nation-state and their exposition of human nature remained valid. Among contemporary writers I have been indebted to Bertrand de Jouvenal, Robert M. MacIver, C. G. Jung, Walter Lippmann, Ernest Barker, F. A. Hayek, Arthur Koestler, Sidney Hook, Ernst Cassirer, and above all to *Systematic Politics: Elementa Politica et Sociologica*, by George E. Gordon Catlin, that masterpiece of lucid and temperate exposition.

Over against all this diversified political science of the West stood the formidable political metaphysics of the Communist camp. As Chapter XXIV will make clear regarding Communism in action, I have systematically denounced its entire programme of revolution and merciless enslavement. It would be folly, however, simply to disregard this militant doctrinaire gospel that seeks to shatter our world to bits and remould it nearer to the Moscow (or Peking) blueprints. Its philosophy is often even more dynamic than its armaments, and we must seek to understand its rationale if we are to wrestle with it intelligently. This I have long sought to do. Many years ago I bought and studied volumes by Marx and Lenin and still other books by Stalin that drew on the chameleon scriptures of Marxism–Leninism to justify any new squiggle in the Party line, but it was not until I secured Gustav Wetter's massive *Dialectical Materialism* that I could see the mountains of dogma in clear perspective. The books of George S. Counts of Columbia also helped to expound the *Weltanschauung* of "the Country of the Blind."

I had found an intriguing prelude to the gospel in action in Werner Hahlweg's *Lenins Rückkehr nach Russland 1917*. For Ludendorff it was a gamble (*Abenteuer*) to invite Lenin and his revolutionary band of 253 to travel in sealed railway coaches from Bern via Germany, Sweden, and Finland to St. Petersburg. Lenin's statement of intent is quoted as: "I will travel through Germany in Ludendorff's railway-coaches and will pay him back *in my own way* for this service." Which, of course, he did—with a vengeance.

As a Canadian of the fourth generation, I cherish deep hopes for my country. As soon as our federal government made it possible for the native-born to register formally as Canadian citizens, I lost no time in doing so. But I am loath to see Canadian nationalism taking an arrogant and hostile attitude towards other nation-states or even seeking, like some gorged and irate amoeba, to divide by bitter fission into the two main "founding races."

It has been the supreme tragedy of twentieth-century politics that, while the world's system of trade, transportation, and communication has made the five continents more of a single parish than an English county in the Middle Ages, the rise of militant nationalisms, each seeking to be viable and endowed with absolute sovereignty, has threatened the survival of the whole human race. The *pleonexia*, or arrogant greed, of the so-called great powers led to the dividing up of Africa and the ganging up of aggressors—as Woodrow Wilson saw it—to eliminate an enterprising business rival. The natural aspiration of each smaller nationality to enjoy cultural independence of its own, complete with all the pomp of absolute sovereignty after a model already obsolescent, worked out in the 1919–23 peace treaties into a drawing of boundaries by the vindictive victors so as to cut across linguistic and cultural frontiers, and leave unhappy minorities under the heel of ancient enemies.

My *International Aspects of Unemployment* (1923) stressed this aspect of a sick civilization: "A war inspired by mad nationalism has slashed and mangled the delicate economic system by which modern civilization was sustained. A peace dictated by mad nationalism has infected the wounds and prevented all healing. And currency disorders, sprung voluntarily or involuntarily from mad nationalistic policy, are driving the patient crazy." Nearly two decades later, in *The Ukrainian Canadians and the War* (1940), I was warning my Ukrainian friends that history might be moving beyond them:

> Another sobering consideration is the possibility that the absolute sovereignty of which most Ukrainians dream may be already outdated. The aggressiveness of the Third Reich has shown that nationalism for its own sake can be a devastating anachronism in a world that needs to co-operate or perish. The League of Nations failed largely because it was based on the assumption of absolute sovereignty for every member state; and much Allied thought today is looking forward to the need for smaller or larger federalisms, extending even to a partial United States of Europe. It may be that the Ukrainian vision of nationhood will need to adapt itself to this more advanced

trend in world politics, and be content with autonomy in some great European federation with adjacent autonomous areas—Baltic, Polish and Balkan.

Alas, the mad sell-out of Roosevelt to Stalin at Teheran and Yalta brought political captivity to the nations of Eastern Europe, but the development of a European common market farther west has demonstrated by its economic triumphs the benefits of even a mild sort of federation. The hedge-hog nationalistic urge of Charles de Gaulle shows how hard the old emotions die.

On the one hand, we need to recognize that the emotional drive of modern nationalism has often very little connection with the physical facts of race. This I tried to emphasize in my *Twilight of Liberty* (1941):

> We must recognize the dangerous dynamic of national consciousness as perhaps the most perilous and belligerent factor in European life. . . . The motivating principles of this nationalism are linguistic, not racial . . . the verdict of all the assembled information as to stature, pigmentation, skull-shape and blood-grouping is most illuminating. The Germans, for instance, are hopelessly heterogeneous, affiliated physically in Western Germany with the Dutch and the Belgians, while in the East a very different German-speaking population merges without any perceptible physical boundary into the Polish and Danubian populations. . . . In blood-group and hair-colour the Czechs are identical with the Germans of the Sudetenland. . . . The average Magyar coincides in blood-group with the German of Vienna. . . . National consciousness, nevertheless, does exist, as a bitter and explosive force.

On the other hand, I had urged in *Canada, Europe and Hitler* (1939) that liberal democracy, securely founded on "the sober counsels of reasonable men tested in the open sunlight of free discussion" was "the only air that can permanently sustain life in the free institutions of Canada or in that ampler world of international peace and federalism for which we strive beyond the war." And my *Seven Pillars of Freedom* (1944) stressed a national loyalty that must be merged, but not lost, in the loyalties of a co-operative world order:

> Obedience to a vision of world service is the supreme political need of today, but if it is to be shared in at all by Canadians it will be by men whose primary loyalties to home, country and Empire have not been lightly denied but have been nourished well on the natural food of the human heart and so strengthened for the exacting duties of world citizenship.

It was reassuring to find Professor Catlin, nearly twenty years later, stressing in the concluding chapter of his *Systematic Politics* (1962) the very principles that I had emphasized all my life:

> The present state, in so far as it is machinery, is obsolete, decrepit and dangerous. It is itself provocative of friction and war. . . . The state in its present form must be abolished. It is the prime threat today to peace. . . .

It does not, of course, mean that the national communities should be abolished. On the contrary, the theme has been to emphasize the importance of community, both national and churchly.

The key to that peaceful federation of world communities does not lie in a "peaceful coexistence" of two armed camps, one of which is actively pledged to the destruction of the other through "wars of national liberation," aflame now in Vietnam but blueprinted for every non-Communist state in the world. Part of the predicament has been trenchantly phrased by Salvador de Madariaga: "The trouble today is that the Communist world understands unity but not liberty, while the free world understands liberty but not unity. Eventual victory may be won by the first of the two sides to achieve the synthesis of both liberty and unity." At the present hour, the mood of the Leninist leaders is unfortunately close to that of Ivan Karamazov's Grand Inquisitor, rejecting human freedom in their absolute conviction that their slavery will win the allegiance (and meet the need) of a weak and baffled humanity: "They will be glad to believe our answer, for it will save them from the great anxiety and terrible agony they endure at present in making a free decision for themselves." The mental confusion of Western leaders in the face of this iron-willed offensive makes our peril all the greater. Countless peace-marchers, found only in non-Communist countries and in denunciation of non-Communist policies, seem ready *propter vitam vivendi perdere causas*. West European politicians, watching the American colossus at his lonely task, can think of nothing but abuse. The future in such a world is as black as in Yeats's forecast in "Second Coming":

> Things fall apart; the centre cannot hold;
> Mere anarchy is loosed upon the world, . . .
> The best lack all conviction, while the worst
> Are full of passionate intensity.

As prolegomena to any future politics of world peace-in-freedom we may postulate certain necessary principles:

(*a*) The crisis of our times calls for a fundamental rethinking of political principles, by calling in the insights of sociology, economics, anthropology, and above all psychology. Instead of worshipping such obsolete concepts as absolute sovereignty, we shall need to probe down again to the enduring realities of the individual man and his community, analysing the springs of human motive and the nature of human greatness. This is no slick task for the cynical planners of election programmes but the desperate search of wise and learned men for a solid foundation on which to build a new world.

(*b*) We cannot bring in any Kingdom of God by preaching a gospel of hate. This has been a fundamental weakness of Marxism–Leninism, which is based on hatred of the bourgeois and the capitalist and a record of stark extermination wherever it has taken over—totalling perhaps 25,000,000 murders in Europe and another 25,000,000 in China. Catlin suggests that free-world propaganda against Bolshevist Marxism might actually succeed "if it can explode this fissionable and unstable thesis of hyper-aggressive Marxism by logic from within in terms of modern psychology," but he does not spell out the sort of psychological counter-offensive that he has in mind.

(*c*) Our new philosophy of politics, if it is to have any validity, must be based on reason rather than on instinct, emotion, or prejudice. Mr. Justice Frankfurter, whom we university presidents met on a visit to Washington in 1958, has spoken judicially with regard to the virtue of a sound Thomistic rationalism: "You've nothing else except that poor reed of reason to lean on in order to get as far away as possible from the jungle and the earth from whence we all come and a good deal of which we have in us."

(*d*) This fidelity to the life of reason is only one aspect of the wider importance of morality, for the strength and validity of a state do not depend on its political machinery so much as on the moral sense of the community. Bertrand de Jouvenal has no doubts on this score: "Political science is a moral science. . . . Montaigne truly said that the generalization of lying would, by itself, dissolve human society." This is why the cynical opportunism of our politicians is so disquieting. If our leaders cannot show responsibility towards the community of which they are a part, how can they contribute anything stable to an international community?

(*e*) The aim of the political community is not merely *koinonia* for its own sake, but the creation of the good man in a good society. This involves a cultivated aesthetic judgement in the arts, religion, and politics. On this point, Catlin is eloquent and illuminating: ". . . it is Art which provides the reconciliation between the objective limitation or *power* and the subjective desire for *freedom*, in the act of creation. This is the vindication, in the widest, most Goethean sense, of this life of art, especially music." Nearly two decades earlier I had come across an anticipation of these ideas in Ernst Cassirer's *An Essay on Man* (1944), although he in his turn ranges back over other thinkers from Croce to Plato. He sums them all up in hailing public art as fulfilling a paramount function for the happiness of man in society, revealing a vision of adequate ends and meaningful good in human life.

Carl Gustav Jung adds a disquieting postscript to this aesthetic philosophy. In our generation, he says, the prophetic spirit of art has turned away from the objective world towards "a dark chaos of subjectivisms" and has seemed incapable of finding in that darkness any of those great truths by which men may live. This cult of artistic disintegration may be only a subconscious prelude to world suicide and *Götterdämmerung*. On the other hand, it may foreshadow an unconscious metamorphosis of spiritual truth, with a new range of symbols for our ancient salvation. Does modern man know, Jung asks, "that he is on the point of losing the life-preserving myth of the inner man which Christianity has treasured up for him? Does he realize what lies in store should this catastrophe ever befall him?" It is a sombre thought for a planet adrift in the gulfs of space and of ultimate meaning.

15

Religio Grammatici

ALTHOUGH RELIGIOUS FAITH is a profoundly individual experience, its modes and patterns owe much to environment. It is not merely that an Occidental reared in an all-Buddhist or an all-Moslem community will inevitably tend to be a Buddhist or a Moslem. Even in the West, his particular form of Christianity will probably owe much to accidental circumstances of family and community. Thus my devout Presbyterian great-grandfather, Walter Kirkconnell, as a bachelor pioneer in the wilderness of the Ottawa Valley in 1819, settled among, and married into a solid community of Highland Scots Baptists and threw in his religious lot with them. Hence it has come about that most of his descendants, including myself, have followed him in the Baptist tradition. The personal experience has been individual, but the denominational allegiance has tended in each generation to remain that of the home in which the sons and daughters were reared.

My earliest recollection of religious emotion comes from boyhood—and that not from our family prayers, devout instruction at home and in Sunday School, and church services experienced in the family pew with a sort of restless boredom. It arose rather in the world of nature, standing alone on the sandy beaches and clay cliffs of Lake Ontario, in secluded spots by murmuring brooks, and above all in the dim, needle-floored chancels of old white-pine groves. It was the sense of a spiritual presence, best expressed in the Latin phrase, "Numen inest!" I was later to find my awareness hinted at in Plato's *Phaedrus* and *Symposium* and spelled out in full in Wordsworth's apostrophe of that Spirit "whose dwelling is the light of setting suns." Still later it was to be diffused through theistic theories of Divine immanence (as well as transcendence) and the metaphysical astrophysics of Jeans and Eddington. But the reality of the Divine that touched my own consciousness in those moments of solitude was one of the basic facts of experience, accepted in reverent delight unmixed with fear. Its intensity has ebbed and flowed through the years; it cannot be conjured up by any act of will; but it remains, in age as in youth, a recurring source of spiritual strength.

Near the end of my thirteenth year, this consciousness of Deity was to blend with long religious instruction and public incitement to produce a moving conversion experience. The auspices were a series of evangelistic services conducted for all of the local Protestant churches in the large auditorium of the Port Hope Methodist Church by a venerable pair of clergymen, the Rev. Dr. J. E. Hunter and the Rev. Dr. H. T. Crossley. It was not that I had been a particularly wicked youngster. I have no recollection of any conspicuous misdemeanours, and by all accounts I was a quiet little fellow, neither very holy nor very obnoxious. But, in the course of a week, the pressure of spiritual awareness kept building up behind a subterranean dam. There was an ever-increasing desire for a right relationship with the God who was at once infinite Justice and infinite Love. Suddenly, "the dawn came up like thunder." A flood of light and joy swept into my subadolescent consciousness and possessed my will and my allegiance.

Sceptics may question the psychological validity of such an experience and point to the range of visionary perception available nowadays under laboratory conditions through the use of mescalin, lysergic acid diethylamide, carbon dioxide, or the stroboscopic lamp and in earlier ages by the chemical effects on the blood-stream of fasting and flagellation. But Aldous Huxley, who had reconnoitred the antipodes of the mind by the grace of mescalin, was nevertheless convinced that in so doing he had merely "cleansed the gates of perception" and that there were spiritual realities with which the mystic and the visionary make contact. He held that both "heaven" and "hell" were potential experiences, both to the visionary and beyond death, and that "union with the divine Ground" was possible, beyond time.

At the age of twelve, I encountered no such animadversions on my newly found faith. It was an undoubted entry into a new way of life. The ecclesiastical sequel was virtually pre-ordained. As my own father was a deacon in the Port Hope Baptist Church, I naturally asked for baptism and church membership there. No alternative even occurred to me. There followed long years in which the primitive democracy of the Baptist congregation became more and more second nature to me as the most appropriate and salutary polity for a religious community. In my experience, ninety-nine per cent of all our credal uproar and factionalism has been the mischievous work of the Baptist clergy, fighting among themselves and usually with zeal in inverse proportion to their knowledge. The voting equality with the pastor of every member of the congregation is one form of protection against this ministerial gangsterism. Whether a hierarchy of wise and learned bishops would be a better safeguard for the flock, I do not know. I recall Kirsopp Lake's sour comment: "In life, as in chess, bishops move obliquely." But I am familiar at first hand only with the merits, as well as the drawbacks, of congregational democracy.

On the doctrinal side, I was reared in the liberal Baptist tradition, which believed in the competence of the individual believer to frame his theology in his own terms. This was not, of course, to believe just anything at all. If one did not accept theism, Trinitarianism, the atonement and lordship of Christ, a Zwinglian interpretation of baptism and the Lord's supper, a "gathered" membership and the priesthood of all believers, one belonged to some other denomination and ought to leave the Baptist fold. On the other hand, one's definitions of basic terms were one's own right and any insistence on a uniform credal statement was an act of tyranny. Nominal Baptists who made such a demand were spiritual brothers of Torquemada and were really aliens among us.

Queen's University during my student days had become officially secular, but the Presbyterian atmosphere lingered on in the theological college, whose probationers, with groanings unutterable, shared my undergraduate Greek classes to the end of the sophomore year. More stimulus came from a habit of visiting around among the churches of the community. Every Sunday morning I sang in the choir of the Kingston Baptist Church and listened to the rather prosy sermons of the Rev. Dr. Laing. Every Sunday evening, I shopped about among all the churches of every denomination. The Anglican cathedral was emotionally satisfying but provided little for the mind. The Roman Catholic cathedral had wonderful antiphonic singing by choirs of men and boys, but the sermon menu was even thinner, except on one occasion when, to my surprise, we got a simple Gospel message that might have come from a Baptist evangelist. At the Free Methodist (Hornerite) church one could always be sure of excitement, with the Holy Ghost descending almost visibly from a ceiling trapdoor and worshippers wallowing in glossolalia on the floor. Three Presbyterian churches had doctrinal beefsteak but the musical *hors d'œuvres* and dessert were not always of the same standard. A Sunday afternoon service in Old Convocation Hall was invariably good and often provided some excellent preacher from another city or university. I became aware of an almost infinite variety in Christian faith and order but felt no compelling desire to change my own group allegiance.

The real temptation was to drop every form of faith. The scientific studies that I had abandoned for a course in Classics still entered into my reading and thinking and gnawed away at the roots of conviction. I took elementary courses in psychology and philosophy but found them for the time being more unsettling than anything else. As an M.A. student in Classics, I continued to read my Greek Testament diligently, but somehow it no longer made doctrinal sense. An interlude of despair came on, described more fully in another chapter.

The malady was almost entirely intellectual. Though college was followed by over three years in the army, I still lived as strictly as a fifth century anchorite. Church attendance was as regular as opportunity offered. The only struggle was in the sightless chasms of the mind and of this there was no outward evidence. Suffice it to say that in due course the feeble knees received strength and faith was built up once more, never to falter again. But the faith of seventy-two is not the faith of seventeen.

In the long process of reorientation, two factors entered pre-eminently —Biblical studies and general philosophy. Somehow, as a layman, I have never been subjected to even an elementary course in systematic theology. I am grateful, as a matter of fact, that I did not start on my Christian journey with six trunks full of dogma neatly packed by somebody else and tagged with my name. It was not that I threw all dogma into the ditch. It was rather that, starting from basic religious experience and philosophically made aware of the inadequacies of "matter-moulded forms of speech," I saw the whole fabric of dogma as a finite attempt to adumbrate the ineffable and the infinite in their contact with the human. I was not using William of Occam's "razor" to shave an Absolute whose credal beard I already knew to the last curl. Orthodox dogma I was prepared to accept as a tentative formulation of man's relationship with God, but I must strive unceasingly to rebuild it, for my own inner life, on foundations of my own comprehension. If I have ended close to the point of beginning, it is not through sluggish contentment with a dictated creed. It is rather that a pilgrimage through a thousand valleys and mountain ranges has convinced me that the official road map, while only an approximation, is valid enough for the journey. Even words are only a parable but they can be a parable of the truth.

One phase of this growing conviction came from long years of systematic Bible study. During some twelve of the eighteen years of my stay in Winnipeg, I taught an adult Bible class at the First Baptist Church. Instead of following any standard set of lessons (International, Graded, or the like), such as were used by the younger classes, I took my adults direct to the Bible, and systematically covered whole areas of it in their entirety. Thus we spent three or four years on the life of the Apostle Paul (based on Acts and on my own visits in most of the

Pauline territory in both Asia and Europe) and brought in each of the epistles in full in its assumed chronological place. Then followed Hebrews, the general epistles of James, Peter, John, and Jude, and the Apocalypse. We then moved back to the Old Testament for all of the major and minor phophets, the Psalms, and the Wisdom literature. We even spent a year on the Apocrypha and a year on history, archaeology, and the story of the manuscripts behind the modern translations of the Scriptures. One might say that we covered everything except the Gospels and the historical books of the Old Testament. These were omitted because they had always been the sole concern of Sunday School lesson planners and had been covered several times over in the experience of my class.

My study of archaeology, by the way, had been made more actual by a visit to Egypt and most of the Middle East in 1921–22, as well as descents into the Catacombs on the outskirts of Rome. The chronology of Archbishop Ussher vanished like a grotesque dream before the evidences of continuous urban civilization stretching back unbroken for millennia beyond Noah, the Tower of Babel, or even the primal March morning in 4004 B.C. I bought a grammar of Egyptian by Budge and one of Assyrian by Sayce in order to gain a better knowledge of these more massive civilizations that bordered on the little realm of Israel. As for the five hundred miles of catacombs chiselled through Rome's tufa, my chief impression was not of the charnel-house for millions but of the confidence voiced in numberless funeral inscriptions, all "nursing the unconquerable hope" of a life to come.

At my disposal in 1922–40 were all the commentaries in the theological library at United College, Winnipeg. I had had my own Greek New Testament ever since my high school days but now bought a big "marginal" edition and worked my way through the text again from cover to cover, with pencils and inks of various colours for marking the analysis of the Synoptic and similar problems (with James Moffatt's big New Testament manual at my elbow) and with a watchful eye for the hundreds of Semitic errors in the grammar and idiom of the Apocalyptist's barbarous Greek. I also had, of course, my Hebrew Old Testament, as well as the Septuagint Greek version, and the Latin of Jerome's Vulgate for both Testaments. My class may have been indifferently fed but in the long hours that I spent alone each week on ancient languages my own acquaintance with the Scriptures improved. Even in a matter like Greek style, one could not help noting the bald simplicity of Mark, the flowing suavity of Luke, and the tortured syntax of Paul in his more argumentative passages. Instead of the archaic uniformity of the King James Version, which had been homogenized in the translation machine of a large and learned committee, one found in the original languages the warm personal differences of individual contributors. Incidentally one found tens of thousands of variant readings amongst the numerous manuscripts behind our present printed texts of the Septuagint, the Vulgate and the Greek New Testament. Clamorous talk about verbal inerrancy became incomprehensible when there was no authority as to which among the multitudinous readings were the inerrant ones. I should admit that I once encountered a Numeric Greek Testament in which a devout crank named Ivan Panin had used a system of "numerics" to work out a divinely inspired Greek text, but by using the same technique on an abundant critical apparatus I could just as easily prove that the Deity had written a doctored version of the plays of Euripides.

Still another matter that became clearer in the ancient tongues was the prevalence of a first century climate of thought that differed from our own as much as the steaming dinosaur marshes of Mesozoic Saskatchewan differed from the temperate prairies of today. Demonology was a universal obsession. Devils were everywhere and the universe was a cosmic battlefield between infinite legions of good and evil spirits. The "principalities and powers" of Ephesians and Colossians were simply two of nine angelic categories of being, celestial or infernal. Women were to wear a covering on their heads in church as a warning to devils that they were under the superior protection of their menfolk. Demons were the cause both of sin and of disease. In the final rites soon devised by the Church, oil that had been made sacred by driving out the devils lurking in it was used to anoint all apertures (eyes, ears, nostrils, mouth) in the dying man, who, after prior confession and absolution, was thus protected against any further diabolic entry into his body. Astrology and thaumaturgy were equally matters of faith. The stars were living witnesses of human destiny and miracles happened every day in the next village.

Those who ignorantly or deliberately disregard these late Zoroastrian elements in Hebrew thinking are just as prone to condemn the first century Greek and Roman religion as a morass of degradation, waiting hopelessly for a new evangel. Such men are noisy without knowledge. Obscene fertility deities, like "Diana of the Ephesians" and the Black Aphrodite of Corinth, were importations from the Asiatic world and were light-years distant from the lofty principles of Pythagoras, Socrates, Plato, Aristotle and the Stoa. To judge the Greeks by these scandalous cults would be like judging the Middle Ages by covens of devil-worshippers and not by St. Bernard and St. Francis—or judging our own age solely by the sensational press and its diet of "the matutinal rumour and the vespertinal lie."

When I moved to McMaster University in 1940, I found in its library a most redoubtable resource for study in the hundreds of large, black, quarter-leather volumes of Migne's *Patrologia*, both the Latin series and the Greek. Here it was possible to go back to the early Fathers of the Church and to follow the steps by which they, too, groped after a theology to match the implications of the New Testament experience. Especially noteworthy seemed the Christian Platonists of the third century, A.D., Clement of Alexandria and his successor Origen, mellow scholars with an almost modern awareness of an infinite space-time cosmos and of man's place in a scientific universe. I also found in still earlier Alexandrian philosophy a deeper significance for the Fourth Gospel as a further interpretation of the Divine impact in the terminology of a Neoplatonic metaphysic—a study superbly analysed in C. H. Dodd's *Interpretation of the Fourth Gospel* (1953), where the very symbols and language of Saint John are quoted again and again from the prior treatises of Philo and the *Corpus Hermeticum*.

Two men whom I have found most suggestive in their hints at the evolution of the Christian tradition are Arnold Toynbee and Alfred Loisy. The former, in the sixth volume of his *Study of History*, devotes a 164-page "Annex" to an analysis of some eighty-seven identities of circumstances and a host of specific verbal correspondences between the Gospel versions of the Passion of the Christ and the anterior stories of pagan heroes (Agis, Cleomenes, the Gracchi, *et al.*) and suggests a folk-memory dimly at work among primitive minds for whom "the waters of this subterranean mental stream serve as waters of Memory." The mental states portrayed in Pär Lagerkvist's *Barabbas* are closely akin to these obscure currents of faith and recollection. Loisy is much more positive in a dissection of the New Testament *textus receptus*, where he finds basic poetic formulas, hymns of the early church, and the verbal crystallization of this and that gnosis regarding the mysteries of the new religion. All this does not add up to a categorical description of the process by which the New Testament material took shape but only makes one more keenly aware of the eager and diversified audience to whom its authors spoke.

A comparable but still more systematic phase of Biblical studies that has met me during the past two decades has been "form-criticism," particularly in its preoccupation with the morphology of the various units of narrative and teaching that make up the Gospels and in its related concern for their *Sitz im Leben*, in terms of those who begot or arranged them. A Canadian example has been the work of the Anglican archbishop, Philip Carrington, whom I came to know in Quebec City. As recently as 1952 he has sought to prove that the narrative pericopae of *Mark* were organized to meet the lectionary needs of the primitive

Christian calendar, assuming that a liturgical year of the Hebrew type was well established before the end of the first century A.D. Here there is certainly no thought that Christianity began as a social revolution in disguise. It is regarded as a religion, with its *didache* and its *kerygma.*

It is significant of the very small part that I have played in denominational life that only twice did I come under the lash of the great castigator, the Rev. Dr. T. T. Shields. On the first occasion, the Pontiff of Jarvis Street had come to Winnipeg to conduct meetings for a small schismatic group that had seceded from the First Baptist Church. I had preached in that church the previous Sunday evening on the Book of Jonah, analysing four different levels of significance, none of them literal. Since for Dr. Shields the literal story was the only one, he devoted several minutes of his next public service to a mocking attack on "the little professor," who was blind as a bat and couldn't even see a whale. The second attack came in the 1940's, when I had roused his ire by speaking several times under Roman Catholic auspices in my attacks on Communism. He accordingly accused me in his *Gospel Witness* of being "a secret member of the Jesuit Order." Since the Jesuits are celibates, my wife and five children at once scolded me for two-timing the Order—or them.

On the evening of Sunday, March 14, 1943, I preached for Bishop Renison in St. Paul's Anglican Cathedral, Toronto. The good will of that Anglican prelate in inviting a Baptist layman to preach from his pulpit (not merely the reading-desk) will be obvious to any churchman. Alas, I muffed the whole affair. I was frantically busy, not merely with a full teaching schedule but also as chairman of the Writers' War Committee and of the All-Canada Committee organizing the federation of all Canadian Baptist conventions, and as a key member of the Advisory Committee of the Nationalities Branch in Ottawa. I also gave eight addresses to clubs in that fortnight. Hence I did not write out my sermon but merely spoke from notes on "The Social Message of Christianity." Everything went wrong. Once started, I could not get myself halted and droned on insufferably for nearly fifty minutes. At last my brain ran down and I stopped. After the service, I said abashedly to Bishop Renison: "Well, I fear that that was not a very usual sort of sermon." "No," he said candidly, "I never heard anything like it."

That was that, and as I drove penitently back to Hamilton I resolved that I would never, never, never again preach a sermon that I had not carefully written out for the occasion.

Apart from English poets—Wordsworth, Coleridge, Browning—and a stripling acquaintance with German thought through Carlyle's *Sartor Resartus* and Goethe's *Faust*, my first real introduction to philosophy came in the original Greek texts of Plato and Aristotle, prescribed in the course in Honour Classics at Queen's University. In the case of Plato, the long-winded dialogues were often tedious in form but their flashes of poetic insight were as inspiring as their clarification of fundamental principles. Aristotle has no such beauties of Greek style but his treatises are solid meat—not without gristle.

I took only one formal course in philosophy with Dr. John Watson, who regularly opened his class with prayer and for the rest of the period inflicted dialectical mayhem on his students. Our daily assignment was twenty pages from his two Gifford Lectures volumes, *The Interpretation of Religious Experience*, which we read at home and on which we were subjected to merciless cross-examination in class. It was an awe-inspiring use of the Socratic method but it was challenging enough to drive some of us back to the classical philosophers, ancient and modern. None of us knew enough to attempt to wrestle metaphysically with the old Master Idealist and for the time being, at any rate, we were stunned into almost complete acquiescence. I say "almost" because I felt somehow that whole areas of intellectual significance were omitted from his synthesis, and that aesthetics and such modern sciences as I had encountered in biology, geology, astronomy, and anthropology were simply shouldered aside or ignored. I was even more dissatisfied when I presently encountered Thomistic philosophy in a massive manual by Cardinal Mercier, for while the mighty amalgam of Aristotle and Christian dogma had been so brought up to date as to include diagrams on cell mitosis, yet it seemed a mass of inert ideas that refused to come alive. At the other extreme were the books of Henri Bergson, which I encountered soon after graduation and devoured with avidity. Here the evolutionary data of palaeontology became profoundly suggestive in their analogies for the historical emergence of the epistemological "situation" and its framework of reference. Bergson, however, while he proved of absorbing interest, was too anti-intellectual to win my allegiance as a systematic philosopher. For a time I was fascinated by the biometrists, with Karl Pearson's *Grammar of Science* as a bedside book, and was led back to appreciate the dry incisiveness of David Hume's intellect. The American pragmatists left me cold, however, for they seemed to reduce man to a social animal and destroyed all vision of greatness in human character and human destiny. Marx–Leninism, though based on a perverted Hegelianism, went a stage further in depersonalizing man until "social engineering" and the deliberate extermination of human millions became a cool axiom of policy.

Back in the 1920's, still another ingredient entered my ruminations from a serious study of anthropology, a field in which I did a small amount of research—digging up Indian pots and measuring skulls—and earned a fellowship in the Royal Anthropological Institute in 1926. A man's thinking is inevitably modified by ploughing through such a major work as Frazer's *Golden Bough* or by keeping abreast of current anthropological thinking in *Man* and the *Journal* of the Institute. It was evident, for example, that many of the experiences of an evangelical Protestant Christian were far from unique and could be found in modified forms in many religions and in many ages of history and pre-history. But the psychological and metaphysical implications were something else again.

Reading in Oriental philosophy was marginal to all this. The perfumed swamps of anthroposophy merely repelled me and the Koran seemed a farrago of unorganized outpourings. Western attempts by men like William S. Haas to achieve some sort of Oriental–Occidental syncretism left me cold. Ancient Buddhism fascinated me most by its formidable systems of logic, psychology, and epistemology, and also by its treatment of a problem that had long tormented me, viz., how can that which is immortal have its beginning in a point of time? How can the immortal soul of man have its finite origin in the casual union of an egg and a spermatozoon? Must not immortality, by its inherent nature, run backwards as well as forwards? Buddha believed in such a sequence of existences, without beginning or end, but was not happy about it and was confident that he could terminate it. In the perspective of astronomical time, however, this anterior extrapolation of existences, even to the Pre-Cambrian, seemed a *reductio ad absurdum*, and I turned again to the West for answers to my questioning.

Mathematical and astrophysical problems raised by modern astronomy, and especially by Einstein's hypotheses, increasingly engaged my attention of the late 1920's and thereafter. Einstein's own discussions of philosophy struck me as relatively unoriginal but his famous theses in physics and those of Planck and Bohr raised issues in epistemology that have not yet been fully faced by our metaphysicians. Russell, Jeans, and Eddington have glanced at them, but not many others.

Among the Canadian philosophers I have known, those who have impressed me most are G. S. Brett and Rupert Lodge. In Brett I found one of the most universal and comprehensive minds of our times, convinced that to arrive at the fullest possible significance in reality one has to include to the utmost the insights of science, of philosophy, and of literature. Science needed to be humanized, philosophy must be enlarged by the inclusion of science, and both should be imaginatively set forth in the symbols of literature and art. The aim was not a neat monism but a comprehensive awareness of all the evidence of the human experience. Lodge, on the other hand, in a similar search for completeness, assumed that every thinker is by temperament a realist, an idealist, or a pragmatist. Each such man's insights are valid, yet each needs the other two to round out life's totality of meaning. He professed to find that Plato was the real founder of this school of "comparative philosophy," which he himself proceeded enthusiastically to apply to one area of modern society after another.

Three Anglican philosophers have successively caught my interest—Dean Inge, Canon Streeter, and Canon Raven. Dean Inge's Neoplatonism was cogently argued but, like the general public, I preferred the grim comments of his *Outspoken Essays*. (Sometimes, however, he was failing in common courtesy. At Oxford, in my student days, he publicly referred to G. K. Chesterton as "an obese mountebank.") Canon Streeter's *Reality* was a formidable attempt but seemed to me to break down in the middle. Canon Raven's Gifford Lectures, however, proved an unexpected delight in their awareness of the existence of a world of science. Style and imagination, rare among Catholic philosophers, I found in Jacques Maritain.

A special paragraph ought to go to the late Charles de Koninck, *paterfamilias magnificus* and philosopher extraordinary, whom I came to know and appreciate while I was teaching in the Laval University summer school. In his home I met his gracious wife and some of his twelve children and on the platform I admired the dialectical skill with which this Flemish knight of the syllogism jousted in two foreign languages—English and French. I had a standing invitation to come and lecture in his Faculty of Philosophy on any metaphysical topic of my own choosing. But alas, I remembered that even the Leninist philosopher Umansky, when challenged to doctrinal debate with de Koninck in Mexico City years ago, had declined the joust. I had read, moreover, the vehement and erudite debate which de Koninck carried on with Father Eschmann in the pages of *Laval Théologique et Philosophique*. And why should an undisciplined amateur like myself expose his tattered ignorance to a trim battalion of professionals? Why should a rheumatic old plough horse enter himself in a motorcycle race?

One of the most stimulating of my mental experiences was some five or six years as a member of a "Metaphysical Club" at McMaster University in the period 1942–48. The organizer of the group was Dr. H. L. MacNeill, emeritus professor of New Testament literature, but it included some nine men from the natural sciences and the humanistic disciplines. Dr. MacNeill had an absorbing interest in trying to arrive at some sort of monism, some synthesis of all the intellectual evidence that would be organized (he trusted) about some basic religious principle. He recognized that a metaphysic that disregarded the sciences was hopelessly incomplete; he admitted that the sciences tended to speak a different language and to live in a different dimension; but he hoped that a long study of fundamental problems by both scientists and humanists might achieve a single solution that would be recognized as valid by both sides.

Our programme for 1944–45 will help to illustrate our endeavour:

Nov. 2, W. Kirkconnell, The Varieties of Human Certainty
Nov. 30, A. E. Johns (mathematics) and H. S. Armstrong (geology), The Deductive Approach to Certainty
Dec. 14, Emerson Warren (biology) and L. H. Cragg (chemistry), The Inductive Approach to Certainty
Jan. 25, F. W. Waters (philosophy), Philosophical and Logical Certainty, especially in Epistemology
Feb. 22, A. P. Martin (German), Aesthetic Certainty
Mar. 29, R. J. McCracken (philosophy of religion), Religious Certainty
Apr. 26, H. L. MacNeill, Résumé and Comment

I need hardly add that in six years of papers and interdisciplinary arguments, with no holds barred, we did *not* arrive at a new *Summa*, embracing all reality. The best we could achieve was an admission by the professors in Arts and Theology that science had aspects of reality that were beyond the ken of religion, art, or morality and a correspondingly frank admission by the scientists that science had no monopoly of truth. It remained our duty to strive for a maximum of comprehensiveness in a sort of dynamic pluralism in which no aspect of reality was disregarded in science, religion, art, or literature. It was also important to embrace the whole history of human thought and culture, so far as finite and stumbling individuals could, so that the insights of the past might illuminate the present.

One or two extracts from my papers before this club will help to suggest my own position:

There are apparently two tendencies in the universe. By the one, expressed in Carnot's Second Law, all higher forms of energy tend to break down to simple heat and be dissipated in the cold vastness of space. (It is interesting to note that it is precisely in the phenomena of atomic disintegration that the Heisenberg–Dirac formula of "probabilities in chaos" becomes most obvious.) The second principle is one of building up higher and higher forms of energy, with their culmination in the moral, esthetic, rational and religious experience of man. By the mechanistic interpretation, all this is the product of causality, but the long grand chain of causation has neither First Cause nor Sustaining Cause. Neither has it meaning nor direction. The rational demand for steam in the boiler of causation, the rational insistence that the justice, faith and love created in the universe are at least as important as its toe-nails and intestines—these requests are shrugged off by a science that insists that its particular brand of reality is the whole of reality. . . .

The physicist rarely turns back to epistemology to realize that the source of his concept of causation is in the human consciousness and not in the outer world.

This is not to deny the objective reality of that world nor the existence in it of an apparently fixed order of events. But we need to remember, as David Hume shrewdly pointed out two centuries ago, that the idea of effective cause is contributed by the human mind to the flux of sense-data by which it apprehends the world, and is not inherent in the sense-data themselves. . . .

To seek to dispose of free will by rejecting the consciousness in which it occurs as an epiphenomenon, an unessential by-product of neural structures and activities, is to cut the ground from under causality as well, which also has its validity in consciousness.

As a life-long inhabitant of church-sponsored colleges, I have been inevitably aware of changes in the theological weather. During the 1920's and 1930's, for example, there was a low pressure area over the mountains of dogma and a "barometric high" over the plains of sociology. During the past two decades, however, in Canadian Protestantism as in that of the United States, the fair weather has shifted to the plateau of neo-orthodoxy, whose streams are Barth, Brunner, Niebuhr, and Tillich. Apostles of the social gospel had found their rabbis among such philosophers as Rauschenbusch and Dewey. Metaphysically they might rate a dubious pass. They contributed an invaluable element of conscience to Canadian life but their "philosophy," where they had any, was closer to positivism than to Christianity.

The leaders of the neo-orthodox school are frankly and deeply metaphysical, but their thinking, while far more intellectual than that of the Christian socialists, is just as fragmentary in its philosophy. I have a conviction that they are concerned with helpful irrigation around an oasis in the desert, but without any glimpse of the mountains, let alone of the galaxies. These men are so obsessed with ontology that they have little use for epistemology. They do not seem to be aware that a battle of epistemology is raging in the field of physics, all the way from the abyss of the atom to the gulfs beyond Orion, and that the loss of that battle could mean the loss of the entire campaign, including their own ontological skirmish. The theological existentialists do not even know that there is a major struggle, in which, for the minds of mankind in general, the loss of the rational front line would mean the ultimate extinction of their own little pockets of imaginative resistance. I even fear that many neo-orthodox camp-followers dimly assume that Barth and Tillich have by some miracle removed all necessity for metaphysical ratiocination and have thus validated almost any superstition with regard to revealed religion.

The "interim ethic" regarded by Schweitzer and some others as adequate for our leading in the jungles of Africa or Europe, is now, however, no longer seen by some as intellectually adequate, and a search is on for a primal "kerygmatic social ethic," unclouded by the mentalities and enivronments that had made the Christian ethics of Aquinas, Calvin, and Luther unscriptural. The ethical archaeologists are digging down through Jewish folklore, Iranian demonology, obsolete cosmogony, eschatology, and Hellenistic sacramentalism, confident that beneath the rubble of centuries they will find the shining ramparts of the City of God. The Social Gospelers are in search of the Holy Grail. It is worth while, however, to recall Augustine's verdict on the limitations of our comprehension: "In Scripturis per hominem, more hominum, loquitur Deus." In reading St. John and St. Paul, we still see through a glass darkly, for they were mentally conditioned no less than Aquinas, Calvin, and Luther. It would seem that we need to look forward as well as backward if we are to bridge the ideological gulf between the first century and the twentieth, to transpose the primal theme of faith into a modern key of meaning.

One may suggest, in passing, the importance of performing the same task for eschatology. Recent years have witnessed a pandemic of eschatological speculation, based on the idea of the primitive church as an eschatological institution, rapt in anticipation of the imminent coming of the Son of Man in the clouds of heaven. Not the least significant of current developments in the field has been the concept of "realized eschatology," introduced by C. H. Dodd, to the effect that the ministry of Jesus is not a prelude to the Kingdom of God: It *is* the Kingdom of God.

That unadulterated ontology might be demonic as well as angelic dawned on me through the French existentialist, Jean-Paul Sartre. On first reading his stories and plays, I was not shocked so much as bemused, and it was not until I had worked my way through the seven hundred pages of his *L'être et le néant: Essai d'ontologie phénoménologique* that I realized that his imaginative works were the belletristic sublimation of a pretty formidable metaphysic. Here was a thinker who was equally at home in classical Greek, mediaeval Latin, and modern German philosophy but rejected them all in favour of his own closely reasoned system of thought. He arrives at the complete absurdity of the world and society as we know them. Good and evil, God and Satan, these are meaningless nonsense. Existence is a hopeless monstrosity, an object of utter despair, except as the universal absurdity justifies a man's complete freedom. At the outset of each man's life, he has no character, no nature, no essence —only the freedom to shape an essence for himself by his decisions and actions. It is the duty of this freedom to repudiate all traditions, values, and principles, for these are the black chains of the enslaved. There are no ultimates, and only the man who by his own free choices "makes himself" can in any true sense be said to exist.

As a lifelong student of linguistics, I have naturally found great interest in the "linguistic analysis" or "logical analysis" inaugurated in 1921 by Ludwig Wittgenstein. Here we have a minute, logical dissection of metaphors and philosophical propositions in search of their innermost anatomy of meaning. Wittgenstein out-Occams Occam. He does not merely shave reality; he skins it; but the victim always dies on the operating-table and the surgeon ends in a world of ghosts.

Philosophy for Wittgenstein is not an organized system. It is entirely a matter of analytical activity. *Logical* thought, he says, can always be thought clearly. It is the task of the philosopher to elucidate all propositions, to analyse out their thoughts into complete and absolute clarity. Unfortunately, that which can be deduced or empirically verified is tautological and yields no insight into the nature of reality itself. Probable inference is only an argument from analogy. In Wittgenstein's own words: "That which expresses *itself* in language, *we* cannot express in language. . . . What *can* be shown *cannot* be said. . . . Whereof one cannot speak, thereof one must be silent." In the last analysis, he recognizes his own expository propositions as senseless. To see the world rightly, one must climb to mystical heights above the muddy flats of analytical elucidation. The logician of language has followed an inexorable path upwards into mysticism.

In the United States, a comparable but much less intelligent school, typified by Charles W. Morris of Chicago, has developed a new science of *semiotic*, analysing language in terms of its semantic, syntactic, and pragmatic functions. In the course of this performance, it eliminates not only universals but cognition itself. It husks the corn and then brazenly declares that the shucks are the only reality. This barren positivism was also found in the early work of I. A. Richards, but by 1936 this more penetrating thinker had begun to irrigate the desert: "Without his mythologies, man is only a cruel animal without a soul. . . . Myths . . . are no amusement or diversion to be sought as a relaxation and an escape from the hard realities of life. They are these hard realities in projection, their symbolic recognition, co-ordination and acceptance. . . ."

Yet as I grow older, I turn increasingly from philosophy back to the overflow of human experience in the compelling art of great literature. Poets who appealed to my youth for relatively superficial reasons now grip me deeply because I find that they subsume and transcend whole libraries of metaphysics and dogmatics. The closing cantos of Dante's *Paradiso* speak more clearly to the heart than a thousand pages of

Aquinas. Goethe's *Faust*, and especially the close of Part II, goes beyond whole generations of German theologians, from Schleiermacher to Tillich. This is not to confuse an image with a definition or to disregard the fact that behind and beneath all great art and literature are foundations of great ideas critically examined and imaginatively conceived. It is rather to recognize the alchemy of art in transmuting the lead of hypotheses into the gold of experienced values. It is to call down the lightnings of God, as Elijah did on Carmel, to set the mind's damp altars of dogma on fire.

A congenital preference of symbol to syllogism has driven me again and again to try to incarnate metaphysics in poetic form, usually with dubious results. Thus in the early 1930's I sought in "The Hall of Mirrors" (*The Eternal Quest*, I, i) to set forth a modified "Kantian" Platonism in somewhat elaborate imagery:

. . . Gravely on they paced
To where a mighty mirror, poised awry,
Bore on it, through a skyward window traced,
A vision of the outer world and sky—
The hill, the slumbering plain, and cloud-shapes drifting by.

"Behold," she said, "the semblances of earth—
So firm to seeming, yet so fugitive!
Here shalt thou learn to test their fleeting worth
In this, the Hall of Mirrors where we live."
Thrill'd, he beheld the radiant pier-glass give
Reflection towards a mighty gleaming prism,
Passing its beauty through that crystal sieve
In sunder'd light, thence casting all that schism
Of colour to a consort mirror-mechanism.

He gazed upon this second sheet of light;
He watched his world resolving, flake by flake,
To rainbow glories, ranged from violet night
Through green to dawning scarlet. "Hark," he spake,
"These colours laugh, breathe perfume, throb and shake!"
"Yea," said his guide, "these are the garbs of sense
In which we clothe perception. Here we take
The illusive raiment off, to seek intense
The stark reality within intelligence.

"Below the spectrum, and above, we find
Two essences that cheat the naked eye.
The grey, vague universals of the mind
Spread ghostlike here; in yonder darkness lie
The imponderable *Ding an sich* and shy
Shapeless hypostases of utter things.
And now, mark well the art by which we try
To win for life the lore this mirror brings,
Yielding the heart of man immortal nourishings!"

Just where the consort speculum drew line
Between dim dark and colour, craft had bent
Its glassy face, keen-angled to decline
The darker unseen essence, while it sent
All colours and the phantom element
Of concept through a prism, converse-curved,
And laid their light, mysteriously blent,
Upon a final mirror, which conserved
Grave, shining characters that neither shook nor swerved.

"These are the sacred Grammata," she said,
"A fusion, in imaginative flame,
Of thought and feeling, radiantly shed
In holy signs, immutably the same. . . ."
. . .

Or in "Spinoza's Eye" (*The Eternal Quest*, II, iii) I took the wave-mechanics of Heisenberg and Dirac and for the star-gazing Mathetes used undulatory imagery to embody the mental shift from a Newtonian universe to an Einsteinian one, and beyond:

Then light dissolved to waves; the lucent stream
Flow'd through infinities of space with all
The soundlessness and lustre of a dream
Where tides of shadowy splendour rise and fall
Along the ledges of a deep-sea hall;
And still he gazed, and still that glory grew,
Swelling to symphonies majestical,
Music of colour, red, green, gold and blue,
In fugues of pulsing fancy ever bright and new.

Then, by degrees, the lambent light grew less;
The universe swung ghostlike in its course,
A bubble blown of radiant emptiness;
The world had weight no more; the suns, no force,
Dark Time from three-fold Space knew no divorce,
But, misty all, they swayed in spectral dance,
Baseless, ascending from some spirit-source,
A shadow-show of moving circumstance
Whose essence was of Mind through all its vast expanse.

Then, last, he reach'd across the gulfs of space
To tear aside that vision as a veil
And gaze upon its Weaver, face to face.
But his hand shook, his cheek grew ashy pale,
Gazing on Darkness Absolute. "I fail,"
He murmur'd. "Yet perhaps the fault is mine.
For how can finite intellect avail,
Itself within the Web, to break the line
And know if some Grey Spirit spins in ways divine?"

Or yet again, in "The Vision Splendid" (*The Eternal Quest*, III, ii), I tried to capture the aesthetics of existentialism, Pre-Raphaelite style, in a net of metaphor:

Then all things merged and melted, sound and sight,
Strange hues, rich odour, attitude and tone.
He seem'd a moving focus of delight
Amid a drift of sense; he pass'd alone,
A solitary wisp of soul and bone
On which the flooding eddies ever beat—
Unstable, flickering, burning forces, blown
Into brief gem-like flame and joyous heat.
And through each perfect mood Apollo's song ran sweet.

Bird-song and flowers, temple, love-song, dance—
All essences of beauty and of art—
Wove and unwove themselves across his trance,
A flux of fleeting rapture through his heart.
"Ah, stay!" he cried, grown conscious, with a start,
Of life's dark brevity. . . .

In the preface to *The Eternal Quest*, I explained that (like Brett and Lodge) I was giving several different approaches to ultimate reality, some on the metaphysical level and others, of necessity, in the world of action. That I had failed either in the definition of my plan or in my achievement of it was suggested in a letter from James Cappon: "I like your scheme of treatment . . . but I should not call it a 'pluralistic approach to life', for the principle of judgement and ethical standard are —so far as I have read—always morally the same." Cappon was on his way to Italy, or I should have enjoyed arguing with him that the diversity I sought was not ethical but metaphysical. Laurence Binyon, on the contrary, accepted my philosophical purpose but felt that the performance was uneven. Of "The Way of a Scholar" he wrote me: "The vision of the cruelty of life in Part III, which is very powerful, remains in my mind with a rather disproportionate vividness. This is perhaps due to the fact that the picture in it has more detail." The section to which he refers consists of eleven Spenserians that systematically itemize the suffering of the world, from the attacks of bacteria up to the Crucifixion. The stanza on the heartlessness of birds runs as follows:

A shrike sat spitting sparrows on a thorn,
Alive and shrieking; then a vulture swooped
Upon a hare, and raised it, clutch'd and torn,
In greedy talons, while wing'd fellows trooped
In haste behind, and, snatching as he stoop'd,
Tore at the writhing prey; a-swarm with flies,
A fawn stood, caught in mire, its weak neck droop'd,
And on its head, unmindful of its cries,
Crows croak'd with pleasure, picking out its staring eyes.

As a matter of fact, the burden of the world's suffering and malevolence has often seemed intolerable. In 1944, I had seen the Poles of Warsaw stirred into blazing revolt against the Nazis by radio exhortations from the advancing Soviet army, only to have Marshal Bulganin halt his troops for weeks on the east bank of the Vistula while the Germans exterminated the heroic population of the city. Bulganin was as guilty of that mass murder as if he had cut half a million throats with his own hands. With the passage of the weeks, it became evident that Russia would remain idle in the north and would sweep in on Hungary from the south and blot out human freedom there—this with American acquiescence, for Hungarian friends in the United States informed me that the programme of briefing American officers (at Indiana University) for occupation tasks in Hungary had been abandoned. It was with this devastation of familiar lands and friends in mind that I penned a brief lyric outcry as a Christmas commentary:

THE ROAD TO BETHLEHEM

Above the road to Bethlehem
When I was very young,
A twilight sky of tender blue,
With golden stars was hung;

And kneeling at the stable-door,
I happily confessed
My humble worship of the Child
Who slept at Mary's breast.

But now the road to Bethlehem
Seems cold and steep and far;
It wanders through a wilderness
Unlit by any star.

The earth I tread is frozen hard;
The winter chills my breath;
On either hand rise evil shapes
From valleys dark with death.

The air is tense with moans of pain,
Mingled with cries of hate,
Where bloodstained hills and shattered stones
Lie black and desolate.

How can the sacred heart of God,
Heal all this guilt and grief?
Lord, I believe. And yet, this night,
Help Thou mine unbelief.

Purge Thou mine eyes, that they may see
Thy Star across the gloom!
Touch Thou my heart, that it may lose
These agonies of doom!

Now in the darkness guide my feet,
Give holy strength to them
To walk with childlike faith once more
The road to Bethlehem!

Another element in the faith of the evening years is a deepening sense of the continuing reality of those who have gone before. For a time, forty years ago, I believed in immortality as a "deathless" quality in the human spirit rather than as a post-mortal extrapolation of experience. In the face of bludgeoning bereavement I could find strength rather than consolation in the words of Lucretius:

illud in his rebus non addunt 'nec tibi earum
iam desiderium rerum super insidet una.' . . .
illud ab hoc igitur quaerendum est, quid sit amari
tanto opere, ad somnum si res redit atque quietem. . . .

The return of the tide up the "naked shingles of the world" has issued in such a poem as the following, penned in 1951:

Here by the Christmas hearth, the heart remembers
The loved ones, now no longer in the flesh,
Who shared with us the joys of far Decembers,
Whose glances, in the fancy, shine afresh.

Their shadowy forms surround us in our musing;
Their unseen hands upon our shoulders rest;
The sense of their affection comes suffusing
The unforgotten anguish of the breast.

I see their dim, familiar faces smiling
Upon our children whom they never knew,
Thus by their benediction reconciling
The years that flow between us as they do.

It may be to their eyes' untroubled dreaming
The youthful figures yonder are our own
As once we were, there in the firelight seeming
Unchanging effigies from days now flown.

But no, these presences are not unwitting,
In the high realm of their ongoing life,
Of all that passes with the ceaseless flitting
Of time in our low world of finite strife.

We cannot see them, but their eyes are on us;
We cannot touch them, but they touch us still;
Through joy and sorrow their deep glances con us;
They watch our lives in love through good and ill.

Are these the spirits who have shared our living?
Then still more close must be the Heart of Love
That in the climax of Creation's giving
Came as a Babe, in pity from above.

The birth of God Himself in human fashion
Hallows this season beyond word or thought,
For in his Birth we also see His Passion
And an atonement for his loved ones wrought.

And so enfolding all the glad endeavour
  In which, with the departed, we take part,
We feel God's living presence bless forever
  The peace of Christmas to the human heart.

"Call no man fortunate until his end," said the Delphic oracle to Croesus of Lydia. Not until one faces the ultimate challenge of death can one be sure that one's valour will endure the test. Even Saint Paul feared that he might "be a castaway," and I recall that two of the most distinguished scholars at University College, Toronto, were reduced to whimpering pusillanimity as they looked over the final edge of life into the outer darkness. One of them horrified his colleagues with a bitter harangue in favour of suicide, framed in the gloomiest mood of Theognis. Very humbly therefore must I say: "Scio enim cui credidi, et certus sum quia potens est." Braggart boasting is the privilege of the young. Age becomes less certain, not of its faith but of its courage, as it draws closer to the black River at the end of the pilgrim Way. If any brash youth marvels at this, I would refer him to the closing pages of *The Pilgrim's Progress.*

16

Towards Baptist Unity

IT WAS A BAPTIST MINISTER, the Rev. John Fawcett (1740–1817) who wrote our greatest Baptist hymn:

> Blest be the tie that binds
> Our hearts in Christian love . . .

yet the voice of theological hatred has never been raised more loudly than by some Canadians who have called themselves Baptists. Were it not that this is my parents' denomination and that, on balance of account, it has achieved a deeper and fuller fellowship through the years, I should long since have sought peace in some less turbulent branch of the Christian church. In my lifetime, I have repeatedly seen the body of Christ (after the Baptist witness) torn by the fangs of heresy-hunters. It is probable, indeed, that these zealots, by a Gresham's Law of church membership, have helped to account for the reduction of Canada's Baptists from 5.9 per cent of the national population in 1901 to a scant 3.2 per cent in 1961. If the wolf-pack continues to howl, the Baptist witness may well be extinct in Canada a century from now. Fortunately, I have also witnessed a widening unity among Baptists of good will. It is this, and only this, that has kept me a Baptist in a generation so given to rancour and persecution.

When I was born into an Ontario Baptist home in 1895, there was little evidence of any "fellowship of kindred minds" among Baptists across Canada. Those in the Maritime provinces had grown up in two separate camps, the Regular Baptists and the Free Baptists, each with a name that implied that all other groups were "irregular" or "enslaved." The Baptists of Ontario and Quebec, who had presumptuously incorporated themselves in 1880 as "The Baptist Union of Canada," had settled back in 1888 to the more modest and accurate appellation of "The Baptist Convention of Ontario and Quebec." The Baptists of the Prairies were the "Manitoba and Northwest Convention of Regular Baptists," while those on the Pacific Coast were "The Baptist Convention of British Columbia." Baptist consciousness was largely limited to the parish or the province. Foreign missionaries were sent out on a regional, not a national, basis.

Apostles of unity were not unknown, however, and in 1900, when I was five years old, Baptists from all over the Dominion met in Winnipeg and formed a "National Baptist Convention of Canada," with the Honourable Henry Emmerson, M.P., of Moncton, as its president. The blossom was premature; heavy frosts wiped it out almost over night; and that particular plant never bloomed again.

The year 1905, when I was a boy of ten, was a memorable time in the annals of Baptist fellowship, for in that year the Baptists of the Maritimes, both "hard-shell" and "soft-shell," agreed to an organic regional union in the "United Baptist Convention"; in that same year, Baptists from all over the world gathered in London, England, to form a "Baptist World Alliance"; and in 1905, likewise, the Rev. H. F. Laflamme, after eighteen years of missionary work in India, was brought back to Canada to promote an all-Canadian union, in the faith that foreign missions would benefit thereby.

The United Baptist Convention of the Maritime Provinces, which began operations in 1906, carried almost complete unanimity into its amalgamation. A small group of "holiness Baptists" had withdrawn from the Free Baptists and survive today in the Reformed Baptist Alliance of Canada, with eleven churches in Nova Scotia and a "seminary" at Yarmouth. In 1934 there was a forced secession of a handful of dissidents who, among other things, had vainly tried to claim possession of Acadia University on the ground that it was apostate to principles to which they alone were allegedly faithful. This group has two churches, and a Bible School at Kingston, N.S. The Maritime (now "Atlantic") United Baptist Convention has remained relatively monolithic, however, and reported some 609 churches at its 1965 Convention. The equilibrium of its pillar of testimony may at times have seemed precarious, but it has thus far avoided any shattering fall.

The achievement of fellowship, and only fellowship, was the aim of the first world Baptist congress, which met in London, England, on July 17, 1905. It was to be a voluntary association of unions, conventions, and associations of Baptist churches and was to exist (as the preamble to the Constitution declared) in order "to manifest the essential oneness in the Lord Jesus Christ, as their God and Saviour, of the churches of the Baptist order and faith throughout the world, and promote the spirit of fellowship, service and co-operation among them, while recognizing the independence of each particular church, and not assuming the functions of any existing organization." In other words, the resulting Baptist World Alliance was to have no legislative, administrative or judicial powers. On occasion, it was to centralize relief work and speak with the voice of the Baptists of the world in championing the rights of small groups suffering from religious persecution, but its main purpose was to manifest Christian unity in fellowship.

The worldwide fellowship was well-founded and destined to prosper. The contemporary effort at an administrative union of all Canadian Baptists, however, was doomed to utter failure. Its shipwreck was aptly summarized by H. F. Laflamme, the chief organizer, in a letter written to me nearly forty years later (June 9, 1944):

> I secured the appointment of a committee from each of the three conventions of Canada to promote the Union: the United Baptists of the Maritime Provinces, the Ontario and Quebec Convention, and the Baptist Union of the West. Six of these were from the Maritimes, seven from Ontario and Quebec, and four from the West, or seventeen in all. I secured from the Canadian Pacific R.R. free passes over the road for all the members of the committee and return. The committee spent the time of travel in consideration of the Baptist Union of Canada. They visited right through to Victoria and saw the entire field of the Union with their own eyes.
>
> In October of 1908, for two days in Ottawa, with about ten from the Canadian West, sixty from the Maritime Provinces and some 150 from Ontario and Quebec, we met and formed the Baptist Union of Canada. But the final step in the consummation of the Union was deferred until its first meeting could be held in the fall of 1909. That meeting was never held. Owing to the opposition of a small clique of McMaster leaders, with Messrs. D. E. Thomson, C. J. Holman and Dr. George Cross, a meeting of the Board members of the O. & Q. Convention was assembled and persuaded not to proceed with the Union. The facts are that Jarvis Street Baptist Church was at that time giving fully one-tenth of all the funds contributed for the benevolent work of the Dominion and they were told that it would be withheld if the Union was perfected. Other arguments were used but at this joint meeting of the Boards a resolution was passed not to proceed with the Union. In the fall of 1909, the O. & Q. Convention met at Hamilton. When the final decision was reached, I was the only delegate who voted for the Union. The others were all scared under the barn. Holman and Cross subsequently told me that all favored the Union, but that it was premature. But the Canadian Baptist Foreign Mission Board was favored by the three conventions and I had the satisfaction of attending its first meeting and realizing my dream.

During this same period, however, a regional consolidation was being effected in that portion of Canada lying to the west of Ontario. In 1907, the Baptists on the Prairies and those in British Columbia merged their forces as "the Baptist Convention of Western Canada." Two years later, they altered their title to "the Baptist Union of Western Canada," and so it has remained.

It was to this regional "Union" that I transferred my church membership in 1922, when I went to live in Winnipeg. As early as January 1924, however, I had a glimpse of the hounds of orthodoxy running down a victim. The occasion was a special convention held in First Church Calgary, to consider major matters of Union policy, and I was a delegate from First Church, Winnipeg. Vicious attacks had earlier been made on Rev. Dr. Sweet, the recently appointed president of Brandon College, and troublemakers had demanded a summary answer from him, "Yes" or "No," on a series of "loaded" doctrinal questions. He had refused to comply, but fundamentalist delegates rose in the convention sessions with a document which they said contained Dr. Sweet's answers to their catechism. Dr. Sweet then asked to see it, and announced that he had not written it and had never seen the paper before. His accusers had, in fact, written the answers themselves as their own twisted interpretations of what they thought he believed. They were repudiated by the Convention but the strain had been severe on the gentle spirit of the man they sought to destroy. I can still see white-haired Dr. Sweet in the pulpit of that great auditorium crying out in passionate grief: "From henceforth let no man trouble me, for I bear in my body the marks of the Lord Jesus!" He fell dead of a heart attack a few months later.

Living as I did in western Canada, I missed the greater part of the denominational earthquake that split Ontario and Quebec churches wide open in 1926. At the very time that the Methodist, Presbyterian, and Congregational churches in Canada were merging their forces in the larger fellowship of the United Church of Canada, a schismatic frenzy descended upon the Baptist Convention of Ontario and Quebec. The focus of the conflict was the alleged doctrinal infidelity of McMaster University. The leader of the revolt was the Rev. Dr. T. T. Shields, a man blessed with high intellectual gifts but implacable in controversy. He was a gifted expositor and a prince of preachers, and it was a tragedy that such endowments should have been wasted in barren attacks on other men. In the resulting warfare, devoted friends in almost every community were set at each other's throats, and towns, like Lindsay, which had not enough Baptists for one strong congregation, found themselves with two diminutive Baptist groups that were not on speaking terms. Within a quarter of a century Dr. Shields' intransigent character had alienated from him nearly all of those whom he had led out into the wilderness. But "the evil that men do lives after them," and after four decades the hostility that he nourished lives on in a hundred unreconciled churches.

In western Canada there were a few secessions. I can still remember the annual meeting of the First Baptist Church, Winnipeg, from which seventeen members marched out defiantly in order to form a Shieldsite church that was itself split within two months by a further "Pentecostal Baptist" secession. Generally speaking, however, the tidal wave in Ontario became a mere ripple in the remote and thinly peopled West. There, toleration making for unity was in the air, for the "church union" movement that resulted in the United Church of Canada in 1926 had been operating spontaneously for nearly two decades as a "grass roots" amalgamation of struggling churches. Church union (not including the Baptists) was almost an accomplished fact on the Prairies long before reluctant denominations in the East faced up to a plebiscite on an often unpopular proposal. As part of the same process, nearly all of the Baptist churches of Manitoba outside of Winnipeg, Portage, and Brandon have since been swallowed up in their local United Church congregations. In such circumstances, there was little sympathy with schismatics who sought to split the communities to fragments in the name of hyperorthodox dogma. This helps to explain how, in the period between 1931 and 1961, the United Church was the only major Protestant denomination to increase its census percentage of the Canadian population. All the others have shrunk and shrunk. In all too many cases, the man in the pew had lost patience with a dogmatic troublemaker in the pulpit and had quietly moved out.

For purposes of regional fellowship, the Baptists of the Prairies were grouped in associations, of which there were two in Manitoba. Of the more easterly of these, the "Red River Valley Association," I was elected moderator in 1937. Having survived this minor ordeal, I was thereupon elected president of the Baptist Union of Western Canada, for the biennium 1938–40, and presided over conventions in Winnipeg in 1939 and in Edmonton in 1940. On both occasions we were visited by Rev. Dr. J. H. Rushbrooke, of London, England, then president of the Baptist World Alliance, and I had opportunities for long and illuminating conversations with that great denominational statesman.

When in July 1940 I returned to my native Ontario as professor of English at McMaster University, I was promptly caught up in denominational machinery, first on the Board of Publication and then on the Board of Evangelism and Social Service. But a major task began in the summer of 1943, when the Ontario and Quebec Convention, hitherto the chief obstacle to a nation-wide Baptist body, took the initiative in proposing an All-Canada Committee to plan for national unity. Its invitation to the Maritimes and the West to elect members was promptly accepted, and on the morning of September 15, 1943, I found myself the chairman of a fourteen-man committee, sitting at a board-room table in the

Park Road Baptist Church, Toronto. The Rev. Stuart Ivison, of Ottawa, a major in the chaplain services, was the secretary. Questionnaires had already been sent out to all members of the committee, asking for their opinions as to the name, structure, and functions of a national organization, and the results of this preliminary survey were now laid before the meeting.

The term "Baptist Union of Canada" was the one most favoured. There was general agreement that matters at present being satisfactorily administered by the three Conventions should be interfered with as little as possible. To bring matters to a focus, it was moved by Dr. G. C. Warren, seconded by Dr. A. C. Archibald, and carried "That we proceed to draw up a national Baptist organization to recommend to our respective Conventions."

The afternoon session sketched in the main outlines of the proposed organization. There should be an executive, a council that met annually, and an assembly that met every three years. The council should consist of approximately thirty members, seventeen in a representative capacity and thirteen elected at large from the regional Conventions. Numerous functions of the council were discussed, including the study of matters of a national, international, and interdenominational nature.

At the close of the meeting it was moved by Dr. Herb Bingham, seconded by Mr. K. A. Wilson, and carried, "That Dr. Kirkconnell, Major Ivison, Mr. Smalley and Dr. Longley be a committee to arrange for the next meeting and to prepare a draft report to be considered for presentation to the three Conventions."

Following a directive from the All-Canada Committee, the chairman prepared and mailed to the three denominational papers on October 27 a very full article on the general nature of its proposed solution. Suggestions and criticisms were solicited from all Baptists everywhere.

I soon found myself, as chairman, backed into a tight corner by circumstances. The small subcommittee of Ivison, Smalley, Longley, and Kirkconnell had planned to meet in Toronto in December, but Major Ivison was called on for active chaplaincy duties overseas and was lost to the committee, and wartime conditions of travel became so constricted that the three remaining consultants agreed to fall back on His Majesty's mails. Faced by this situation, I undertook to draft the report single-handed, including the proposed constitution of the national organization. As a preliminary step, I studied carefully the constitutions of the Baptist Union of Great Britain and Ireland, the Presbyterian Church in Canada, the United Church of Canada, the Church of England in Canada, and the Northern Baptist Convention, for any light that these might throw on the problems faced by our own denomination in Canada.

Helped by their diction, but adhering in principle to the decisions reached by the Committee in its September session, I drafted out a detailed constitution and a proposed Act of federal incorporation. This lengthy document was then mimeographed and more than one hundred copies were circulated early in February 1944 for discussion and revision. Dr. Longley looked after this circulation in the Maritimes and Dr. Smalley in the West. I myself sent it out to some scores of individuals in Ontario and Quebec, stressing particularly the Convention executive, the officers of all the Convention boards, and certain individuals who might ordinarily be counted on to block any All-Canada project. If I could carry these people along with me and get them to feel that they were co-architects of the new edifice, it seemed likely that we would not be ambushed at a later stage. The chief objection was anticipated from vested interests in incorporated boards, and it was important that these should understand our proposals and should be able to assure themselves that we were not going to upset their applecarts.

The critical suggestions that poured in were copious and helpful. All told, there were some hundreds of proposals, some of them duplicates, dealing with matters of phraseology and matters of principle. The Honourable Albert Matthews stressed the importance of leaving the two universities, Acadia and McMaster, clearly in the domain of their regional conventions. Mr. Justice Kellock, later of the Supreme Court of Canada, pointed out that membership should consist of "the members of the churches," since the individual churches were not legally "persons." Dr. A. C. Archibald insisted on the addition of evangelism and foreign missions to the concerns of the new organization, and Rev. Harold O. Eastman and Rev. Harold Lang asked for the inclusion of social service. Dr. Edgar Tarr and Rev. Arch Ward were anxious to remove rigidities from the constitution, as where a vice-president would be regarded as president designate three years before succeeding to the throne and where notices of motion in the assembly would have to wait three years before coming to a vote. At least a third of my correspondents insisted that a full-time general secretary would be necessary and an equal number objected to the term "Union" as likely to cause confusion. I had very helpful counsel from Dr. J. H. Rushbrooke, of the Baptist World Alliance, and from Dr. Joseph B. Hazen, corresponding secretary of the Northern Baptist Convention, United States. My McMaster colleague, Professor R. J. McCracken, took three periods of his class in church polity for a seminar discussion on my draft constitution, clause by clause and phrase by phrase, and passed along the results of this analysis.

Almost as arduous as the preparation of the original draft was the new task of weighing and comparing these hundreds of new ideas and incorporating the more valuable and practicable ones in a revised constitution. The most conspicuous alteration was the change of the name to "Federation," a change suggested by several as unambiguous and more applicable than "Union" to a system that left such complete autonomy to the local conventions and boards, but there were minor changes in almost every second line and some sections were completely rewritten. The contentious issue of a full-time national secretary was left to a distant future, lest financial critics of the proposed Federation veto the whole project at the outset as an expensive luxury. Legal counsel led me to drop the idea of incorporation. On April 10, 1944, I sent out 150 copies of a second draft and solicited further advice. These further suggestions were incorporated in a third draft, which was considered by the All-Canada Committee at a second (and final) meeting, held in Toronto on May 9, 1944. Three days later I sent a fourth and final draft to the three regional conventions for consideration at their annual meetings that summer. After all of my labours, carried on without secretarial assistance, it was gratifying to have all three conventions endorse the Committee's report without amendment and call on me to convene the first meeting of the council in the Germain Street Baptist Church, Saint John, on December 7, 1944.

Those who gathered on that historic occasion may, I suppose, be termed "the fathers—and mothers— of the Federation." They were as follows:

From the Maritime Convention: Rev. Dr. A. Gibson, Wolfville; Rev. R. E. Whitney, Wolfville; Dr. R. S. Longley, Wolfville; Rev. Dr. G. C. Warren, Wolfville; Rev. H. C. Olsen, Amherst; Rev. John Linton, Sussex; Mr. K. A. Wilson, Saint John; Mrs. C. T. Clark, Saint John West; Rev. J. A. R. Tingley, Dartmouth; and Rev. Dr. Waldo C. Machum, Saint John.

From the Ontario and Quebec Convention: Rev. Dr. H. H. Bingham, Toronto; Rev. Dr. C. H. Schutt, Toronto; Rev. Leland Gregory, Toronto; Rev. Arch Ward, Toronto; Rev. Dr. J. A. Johnston, Westmount; Dr. Watson Kirkconnell, Hamilton; Rev. Dr. A. C. Archibald, London; Rev. Dr. Neil S. MacKechnie, Port Hope; and Mr. Thomas Camelford, of Dunnville. (Rev. Dr. S. H. Farmer, Toronto, was unable to attend.)

From the Western Union: Rev. Dr. Elbert Paul, Vancouver; Rev. Dr. Wm. C. Smalley, Edmonton; Rev. Dan Young, Edmonton; Rev. H. E. Nordlund, Calgary; Mr. E. H. Crimp, Saskatoon; and Mrs. J. R. McDonald, Winnipeg. (Dr. A. C. Campbell, Winnipeg, was unable to attend.)

From the Foreign Mission Board: Rev. Dr. John B. McLaurin, Toronto; and Rev. Dr. W. H. Elgee, Fredericton.

From the Women's Dominion Committee: Mrs. E. G. Blackadar, Ottawa.

Rev. Dr. W. O. Lewis, of Washington, secretary of the Baptist World Alliance, was present as a fraternal delegate.

Since by the constitution the national officers for the first triennium were to be Maritimers, Rev. Dr. Gordon Warren, dean of the School of Theology at Acadia University, was elected the first national president, and Rev. Dr. Waldo Machum the first secretary-treasurer.

The initial meeting of the council was largely given over to organization. Some nineteen committees were to be set up, but it was at once realized that before the personnel of the committee could be properly chosen, the objectives of the several committees would need to be carefully and fully defined. I therefore found myself, as chairman of a committee to define committees, spending nearly all of my waking hours with pencil and paper drafting out these terms of reference, and as fast as these were agreed upon, in instalments, by the council, a second committee, with Neil MacKechnie as chairman, supplied names to fit the functions. In the end, some 131 names, representative of all parts of Canada, were assigned to the nineteen committees, while the constitutional requirement was observed that each committee chairman must be a member of the council. Then, with the work of organization completed, the council adjourned.

While the main purpose of the Baptist World Alliance, founded nearly forty years earlier, had been Christian fellowship, the chief aim of the Baptist Federation of Canada was united planning for denominational tasks. We had haemorrhaged badly through fundamentalist rebellion and secession and through the quiet withdrawal of countless others who could not stomach the schismatic uproar. We also suffered more than the larger denominations from the sheer vastness of the national territory, with approximately one Baptist per six square miles, and with a continual flux of population breaking the ties binding the individual to a local congregation. If we were to survive as a national denomination, we needed not only to reinforce our morale by fellowship on a national scale but to pool and conscript the best Baptist brains in Canada in solving our denominational problems.

Whether we have found this unity too late remains to be seen. The risk is no excuse for our failing to support to the utmost the only organization through which we could hope to succeed.

It is twenty-three years since we launched the Federation's ship at Saint John, New Brunswick. What have we accomplished during this period? First and most important has been the setting up of uniform standards and machinery for ordination all across Canada. A second has been the drafting and publication of a pamphlet, *Basic Baptist Beliefs*, mainly the work of Dr. Warren, setting forth the Baptist position in faith and polity. A third has been the preparation of a handbook embodying rules of common order that are acceptable to Baptist clergymen across the country. Projects under way but not yet completed are a general history of the Baptists of Canada (apart from a "pocket book history" written by myself), a year book, and an all-Canadian Baptist paper. Federation committees have co-ordinated studies of almost every phase of our work and have given national leadership in campaigns of evangelism and stewardship. Ministerial superannuation on a national scale has been subject to advanced planning. Our social service committee has repeatedly spoken to the federal government in the name of all Canadian Baptists. Our representatives on a Dominion-wide scale have shared in the sessions of the Canadian Council of Churches.

In July 1955, I had a glimpse of the Baptist Federation of Canada joining for a heart-warming week in the Golden Jubilee of the Baptist World Alliance. To the Royal Albert Hall, London, England, came eight thousand five hundred representatives of the world's twenty-two million Baptists. The largest group was from the United States, with three thousand five hundred delegates. Great Britain was second with sixteen hundred, and Canada third with five hundred.

The delegates ran the whole human gamut of costume and colour. Women delegates from Germany and the Scandinavian countries came in a wide range of vividly hued peasant dresses. Baptists from India and Burma wore the gracious and colourful garb of their native lands. A thousand American Negroes came dressed in Palm Beach suits. A half-naked believer from the Sudan wore little beyond war paint, feathers, and a leopard-skin and stalked about carrying a shield and a spear. Meanwhile the daily stream of London traffic passed by with the most imperturbable indifference towards the strange legion of foreign visitors.

One impressive feature on the opening day was the "Roll Call of the Nations," spread over both afternoon and evening, at which one representative from each of sixty-eight national delegations brought brief greetings. It was my privilege to call the five hundred visiting Canadians to their feet and to address the Congress on their behalf. My script, scribbled on the back of an envelope, is still in my files and may be quoted in part:

In terms of mere size, Canada is a vast territory, larger than China or Europe or the U.S.A. Our central southernmost tip is in the latitude of California, Barcelona or Rome. Our shores are washed by three oceans. Southern Ontario can have whole weeks in July at above 100 in the shade. The winter temperatures in our far north have dropped to 86 below zero Fahrenheit. In a total population of fifteen millions, Canada has half a million census-Baptists, one-third of them active on the church rolls. Our Baptist tradition in the New World goes back nearly two hundred years. Until eleven years ago, our work was carried on in three independent conventions—the Maritime Convention, the Ontario–Quebec Convention and the Baptist Union of

Western Canada. Since 1955, we have spoken with a single voice in the Baptist Federation of Canada, which today brings affectionate good wishes to our Baptist brothers and sisters of all lands. . . .

The weather for the week—and indeed for the whole month of July—was most un-Londonlike. Day succeeded day with fierce sunlight pouring down out of a cloudless sky, and noon-hour space was at a premium in the London parks for slumbering on the grass in the leafy shade of their ancient trees. All the more remarkable, therefore, was the fidelity with which the thousands of delegates—with wilted collars or with no collars at all—rallied to the crowded sessions of the Great Week.

There is only one still larger organizational fellowship in which the Federation would be eligible to participate. This is the World Council of Churches, a non-organic assembly of most of the world's Christian denominations except the Church of Rome. We are not now members and indeed may never become members. It has not been for lack of discussion. Most members of the Federation Council felt, as far back as 1947, that the Baptist Federation of Canada ought to carry the Canadian Baptist witness into the World Council of Churches, where we would sit side by side with the Baptists of Britain and the American Baptist Convention. A motion passed at that time, however, recognized that "all three Conventions must take favorable action before the Federation is able to join the World Council of Churches." The Ontario and Quebec Convention voted in the affirmative in 1949, but a negative vote (vigorously organized and mobilized by a faction in the Maritime Convention) prevailed in the Atlantic region in 1951. I viewed this result with mixed feelings. As chairman of a Convention committee that had studied the question carefully for two years, I felt that our participation would cause more good than harm and so had myself introduced the formal 1951 motion in its favour. Nevertheless I have always had some reservations, based, not on the alleged heterodoxy of some individuals who have attended the World Council (for every church has both its liberals and its conservatives and both fulfil a useful function), but on the risks of imperilling our distinctive principles and evangelical freedom. The late J. H. Rushbrooke, who on balance of account was in favour of ecumenical fellowship and had himself been present at Oxford and Edinburgh, wrote to me thus on October 26, 1943, regarding the World Council:

You will have a further peril to consider. While the constitution of such a Council excludes organic union, the main body of its members are interested in just that. The pressure for ecclesiastical union is ceaseless; and not a few—this is frankly avowed—desire to make the World Council of Churches merely a stepping-stone to a single visible organization.

If we are ever to present an effective Baptist witness as an autonomous partner in a wider fellowship, it may be that our first need is to attain a sound grasp of fundamental Baptist principles on a national scale. The old issue between freedom and authority is still far from settled among us. What would our Baptist witness be in a world council—literal inerrancy and dogmatic finality? or the right of private judgement under the Lordship of Christ? We have emotionally charged convictions that both versions are "the traditional Baptist position."

During the past five or six years, an even wider perspective of Christian fellowship has opened up with the statements of Pope John XXIII in the course of the Second Vatican Council. In a dramatic break-through in the dogmatic curtain, forgiveness was asked for, and given, for the wrongs that Catholics and Protestants had suffered from each other during more than four centuries. "May the heavenly Father," he pleaded, "design to hear our prayers and grant us true brotherly peace." He also called for understanding and good will towards the Moslem, the Jew, and the Hindu. The sequel has been public services of ecumenical witness in towns and cities across Canada. In my old home town of Lindsay, there have been interfaith dinners, a large interfaith rally entitled "The Hour of Many Faiths," and the formation in 1966 of a Lindsay Area Association of Churches, made up of two laymen and one clergyman from each congregation. The president of this latter group is a Presbyterian, the first vice-president a Catholic, the second vice-president a Baptist, the secretary an Anglican, and the treasurer a United Church member. All but the Baptist are laymen. An interdenominational project has brought out two refugee families from Europe and settled them in the town.

Meanwhile, of course, there has been dialogue between the United Church of Canada and the Anglican Church of Canada, looking towards organic union. There have also been friendly but less purposive conversations between the Church of England and the Church of Rome. On the other hand, there have been no attempts toward a relaxation of those conflicting rigidities of dogma that Catholic and Protestant respectively regard as fundamental. The current move towards fellowship among all Christians is a welcome rebuke to ancient intolerance, but the confrontation in faith and order gives no promise of "unconditional surrender" by either side in the foreseeable future. The problems faced by Canadian Baptists have become more complex but have not lost their meaning.

17

The Milton Project

ONE OF THE LARGEST single academic enterprises of my career has been a 33-year study of the analogues of John Milton's chief poems. The first instalment was published in 1952 by the University of Toronto Press in a 729-page volume entitled *The Celestial Cycle: The Theme of "Paradise Lost" in World Literature, with Translations of the Major Analogues.* The second quantum was issued by the same press in 1964 as *That Invincible Samson: The Theme of "Samson Agonistes" in World Literature* (again with my verse translations of the more important specimens). Analogues of *Comus*, *Lycidas*, and *Paradise Regained* have been collected on two continents and a volume on their significance, now about half written, will complete my survey of works that parallel the major poetry of Milton.

This colossal project—almost fatally reminiscent of Mr. Casaubon's Key to all Mythologies—came into existence by a series of accidents. I should never have thought of it by myself, and its "onlie begetter," my friend Arthur Woodhouse, never dreamed at the outset that our literary dew worm would grow into a twenty-foot python.

The genesis of the undertaking goes back to a final paragraph, added almost as a postscript, in a long letter sent to me by Woodhouse on January 14, 1934:

> A minor project has suggested itself, which, I think, is a sound one and which I am incapable of carrying out alone even if I were willing to give the time to it. As you doubtless know, there are a number of analogues of Milton (sometimes regarded as sources) which *as analogues* are extraordinarily interesting. In one or two cases translations exist but are not easily available. The project is this: that I should plan a volume of these things and write an introduction comparing their theological ideas and treatment of Satan with Milton's; that where possible we should use existing translations, that you should check these with the originals (Latin, Italian, and Dutch) and note major errors, and that you should furnish *new verse translations* for one or possibly two of Vondel's Dutch dramas. I think that

(1) the book would be very useful to students of Milton, (2) would have good prospects of tempting a publisher, and (3) failing this, that it would probably be accepted by the University Press here (in which case we should make nothing, but it would cost us nothing).

The fly was irresistible to a philological salmon and I rose to it immediately. In a letter of February 4, Woodhouse then proceeded to explain his enterprise in greater detail. A few excerpts will show a task apparently within the compass of a year's work, or two at the outside:

(1) Grotius, *Adamus Exul*, in Barham's excellent (as English) translation. Printed nearly a century ago, it is long out of print and scarcely procurable outside the very largest libraries. One would not, I think, alter the text, but you would check it with the Latin and supply a note wherever (if anywhere) he had gone badly astray. . . .

(2) Vondel's *Lucifer*. There was an English verse translation pub'd in N.Y., 1898. It strikes me as rather mediocre and is probably still in copyright. I wonder if you would care to do your own version?

(3) Andreini, *Adamo* (1613), translated, but not very faithfully, by Hayley in Cowper's edition of Milton (Hanford) Here you could, I think, either adopt the method suggested for Barham's trans. of Grotius or simply revise Hayley's trans., incorporating your changes in the text. . . .

(4) I have not read Vondel's *Samson* as it is accessible only in the Dutch, but I mean to see what I can make of it next summer. If it looks interesting as an analogue of *Samson Agonistes*, why not add your version of that? . . .

The introduction, however, I would take completely off your hands. There would be *no* thrashing of old straw about Milton's plagiarism from the above (or some of them). The texts would be treated as *analogues* pure and simple. . . Grotius and Vondel are interesting as sincere Christians as well as humanists (Grotius in the Christian rationalist tradition like Milton, and both, like Milton, Arminians). The introduction might run to 30 or 40 pages . . .

Modest as the task appeared, we were some time in getting mobilized for it. For one thing, the only text that I had to work on before 1936 was a copy of Vondel's *Lucifer*. Moreover, a baby daughter arrived in our home in January 1934 and another one in September 1936. My father died in March 1934, and I threw myself into the writing of a book-length biography, *A Canadian Headmaster*. Five other volumes were also on the stocks, and were published in the period 1934–36, namely *The Eternal Quest* (a long philosophical poem), *Canadian Overtones* (annotated translations from forty-seven European-Canadian poets), *A Golden Treasury of Polish Lyrics*, *The Death of King Buda* (with Lulu Putnik Payerle), and *A Primer of Hungarian* (published serially), and there were at least three score contributions to periodicals. Letters from Arthur Woodhouse in 1935 reflected his anxiety to have me clear the decks for the Milton enterprise. Thus he wrote on May 27:

"I hope that you are not forgetful of our project. I am not, and have accumulated a considerable body of material for the introduction. We sail for England on June 21, and I expect to return there by January 1 for a half-year's leave of absence to finish my books on Milton; and I may be able to knock off the introduction at the same time." And another letter was written on October 27: "If the translations were done by the middle of summer (1936) I might, I think, be able to give the last 6 or 7 weeks in England to the introduction and to trying to find a publisher—or would you rather postpone completion until the early summer of 1937?"

These letters gave hints, however, of the need for raising our sights. Woodhouse had become aware of Vondel's *Adam in Ballingschap*, a Dutch play on the Fall, and Mario Praz had told him of Salandra's *Adamo Caduto*, much touted by Norman Douglas as the assured source of *Paradise Lost*. In March 1936, he passed along some excerpts from Douglas and also expressed the opinion that "We should print the Latin text of *Adamus Exul* facing the English, as it is so important and so rare. For the rest, the English alone."

That summer saw the beginning of large scale labour and the revelation of unanticipated difficulties. Thus I wrote Woodhouse on July 2, 1936:

> The photostat of the *Adamus Exul* arrived today, and I am aghast at the disparity between the Latin of Grotius and the alleged English translation by Barham. For example, lines 13–15 in Grotius read thus, in literal translation: "Through this hope, because I fly from the one greatest evil, I shall attain to heaven. Am I deceived? Or does the whole world assuredly tremble, shaken by my weight?" These few words are expanded into nine lines of Miltonese by Barham, reading thus:
>
> So forth I fare; and, hoping 'gainst belief,
> To eclipse intensest misery, by the shade
> Of miseries more intense, shall I not gain
> Supremacy of ill, and so become
> Sole despot, tyrant, and o'er all extend
> The immense emblazed autocracy of Hell—
> A god of gods! Ah, can I be deceived?
> Even now methinks this poised and stedfast globe
> Reels, rocks, beneath my incumbent weight.
>
> This may have passed as translation a century ago, but I fear it would be useless for our purpose. The chief trouble is that it confuses the issue and makes it impossible for the non-Latinist to estimate the differences (and resemblances) between Milton and Grotius. Phrases and reminiscences of Milton are woven into the fabric of Barham's version. Worse still, he is quite casual in disregarding the meaning of the little Latin that he does work in. E.g., in the very first line, the "stern Thunderer" of the original becomes the "sacred Thunderer," thus blurring the effect of the opening.

In view particularly of the fact that you wish to print the original Latin and the translation on opposite pages, I fear that the only alternative is for me to work out an English verse rendering that will correspond as nearly as possible, line for line, with the original.

On August 25, I could report a productive summer but a formidable estimate of the task. Instead of merely checking three existing translations and adding a fourth of my own, I faced the prospect of translating all these full-length plays myself, single-handed. I wrote in part:

You will be relieved to learn that I have this summer done some serious work on our *Miltonic Analogues*. The photostat of *Adamus Exul* went with me on my alleged vacation, and I have almost completed a new verse translation of the whole play. . . .

I also received from Stewart Wallace last spring the complete plays of Vondel, and have been skimming through the three in which we are interested: *Lucifer*, *Adam in Ballingschap*, and *Samson*. I had already done some work on *Lucifer* last year, but the other two were quite new to me. Vondel's portrayal of Lucifer, which seems to combine traits of William I of Orange and of Cromwell, in settings reminiscent of the Dutch and English revolutions, is intensely interesting. In the case of *Adam in Ballingschap*, Vondel's own introduction acknowledges his debt to the Latin play of Grotius, but his treatment is much more free, characters are multiplied, and the metre is that of contemporary French drama. The same is true of the *Samson*, which seems a much better stage version than Milton's but much inferior as poetry.

Our volume promises to be a rather formidable one. The *Adamus Exul*, at 28 lines to the page, amounts to 76 pages in the original. Even if one crowded it in at 36 to the page (40 is the absolute limit) it would run close to 60 pages. The three plays by Vondel will total at least another 160 pages. The poem by Salandra is listed as "251 pages, small octavo", which probably means about 30 lines to the page and at least 220 pages in an English version. I do not know the length of Andreini's *Adamo*, but it is probably good for another 60 pages. A rough estimate is therefore 500 pages of translation, with approximately 15,000 lines of verse, the length of Homer's *Iliad*. The late Mr. Pope, who didn't have to lecture sixteen hours a week or bring up a family of kids, took from 1713 to 1720 for his version of the *Iliad*. I therefore don't expect to have the whole job finished up by next spring! I only wish I could afford a stenographer to save me long days of drudgery on the typewriter. The 500 printed pages would represent 750 typed sheets, for me some six weeks of continuous typing, during which time I could grind out nearly a hundred pages of versification.

Lectures begin here three weeks from tomorrow, and a new baby is due about the end of September. Translation will therefore be a bit cramped for a few months to come.

A month later, I rendered a further report:

Your letter of the 4th is very heartening, with its news that your mother will ride my white elephant of typewriting. It will be a real advantage to have her do both the original and the translation of Grotius, as the two can be made to match carefully, page by page. I cannot say how grateful I am. . . .

There is another analogue still which I think we ought to consider, viz.: the Caedmonian *Genesis B*, one of the best things (a relative term, of course) in Old English poetry. It has considerable dramatic force, and in its portrayal of the character of Satan and the content of his speech to the fallen angels is not without some parallels to Milton. As you know, of course, it is often cited as a possible influence, as Milton and Franz Junius, the owner of the manuscript, were on friendly terms.

On February 9, 1937, Woodhouse, who had just been a visiting lecturer at Northwestern University, wrote me with great enthusiasm:

I talked, in confidence, to Hanford (the great Milton man) about the volume. He is enraptured with the idea, says it will be used by generations of Milton students. We may use that opinion when the time comes.

I leave for England on May 14, and I want to collect the material for, and plan—perhaps write, the introduction (as well as get the illustrations) during the summer. Milton will form the *centre* of the introduction. For my knowledge of the translated works I shall have to rely mainly on your translations. Would it be feasible to make a carbon of your roughly pencilled prose rendering of the remaining Vondel and the Salandra, so that I could get to work before you versified? . . .

I am busy for the next few weeks finishing up my *Puritanism and Liberty* for Dent's. Then I will go at my mother's copies of Grotius (Latin and English), and your *Lucifer*, get her to make a copy of that, and return to you copies of Grotius and Lucifer with my animadversions (if any!).

I am really excited about our volume—or rather your volume, for only the idea and the introduction will be mine. . . .

In spite of a heavy teaching schedule and home duties as the father of four small children, I rounded up most of the Vondel during the winter of 1936–37 and in the spring of 1937 read a paper on "Miltonic Analogues in Holland" in Section II of the Royal Society. That same spring, however, I received a clearer idea of Salandra's play, for I wrote thus to Woodhouse on May 13, 1937:

I got Salandra's *Adamo Caduto* out of the Customs this morning, and have been glancing through it. It is a morality play and appears at first sight to be a prolix expansion of the *Adamo* of Andreini. The dramatic value is nil; there are almost interminable soliloquies by such abstractions as Goodness, Mercy, Malice, Sin, and Death; and the whole show (7,400 lines!) would take some seven hours to put on, if indeed it were ever acted. The two Italian moralities will, however, make an instructive contrast to Vondel, Grotius, and Milton, in demonstrating the disparity between the humanist inspiration in the latter three and the more purely ecclesiastical inspiration of the former. I could wish that Salandra were less long-winded. Merely to copy out 257 pages (29 lines to the page) twice over would be something of a task; but when the first copying means translation and the second means versification, the prospect is rather formidable. I may be able to clear up the prose draft in June, although I have some other irons in the fire as well.

In view of the bulk of the material in hand, it will probably be well to limit our volume to the six dramas now under way. Even these, in ordinary format, would amount to nearly 800 pages of translation, plus preface and introduction and perhaps a few notes on metres. As you say, there are limits to what a publisher will stand! There is one other analogue on which you might possibly check up in the British Museum (though not for translation). I was reading last night Ettore Allodoli's essay on "Adamo e il Paradiso Perduto" (prefixed to the U. of T. edition of Andreini), and found that he cited one Valvasone along with Grotius, Andreini, and Du Bartas among the alleged "sources" of Milton. I wonder if you could track down the Valavsone-bird, apparently a 17th century Italian?

The summer of 1937 and much of the following winter were spent in drafting out my version of the prolix Salandra in pencil, with a carbon copy for Woodhouse. The most conspicuous result of this exhaustive study was the proof that Norman Douglas's claims for it were arrant nonsense, based on a dishonest essay by Francesco Zicari. There was neither resemblance nor relationship of any sort between Salandra's play and Milton's epic. In June 1938 a distinguished overseas visitor came to see me and I wrote Arthur in some excitement on the 10th:

Sir Herbert Grierson, the Emeritus Professor of English at Edinburgh University, who has done more than any other English scholar in the Dutch field and whose work on Milton you will know well, has been visiting a brother in Winnipeg for the past week. I have had three good sessions with him by the fireside over Milton, Vondel, Grotius et al. and he has been reading my translations—the *Lucifer* carefully, the rest more cursorily. He is most enthusiastic over the whole project, but has certain rather definite advice to offer. First and foremost, he feels sure that to approach any publisher with a single MS of over 800 pages is to be blocked before we start, unless, of course, we are prepared to pay the full costs of publication. He therefore urges that we bring the Analogues out in two instalments: Vol. I being *Adamus Exul*, *Lucifer*, *Adam in Ballingschap*, and *Samson*, and Vol. II the *Adamo Caduto* of Salandra and the *Adamo* of Andreini. Volume I, for which the translation is all complete, could be brought out almost immediately; while the issue of Volume II could follow at such an interval as might be dictated by the success and rate of sale of Volume I.

Woodhouse objected promptly and strongly. He feared that if we divided the book into two volumes, the second (and weaker) instalment might never struggle into print. His solution was rather to print one volume but to include only the more significant parts of my versions of Salandra and Andreini, with brief prose links summarizing the omitted portions.

On July 2, I wrote to accept his suggestion and to explain my temporary enthusiasm for the other alternative:

Motivating my enthusiasm for an immediate first volume was also perhaps a blending of weariness at the seemingly interminable Italians and of desperation at my own academic extremity in Winnipeg. With a home to support and four children to feed and clothe, my situation at United College becomes rapidly more and more impossible. Budgets simply will not balance, and I shall soon have exhausted the borrowing power of my insurance policies. The present summer's trip to Hungary is being financed with borrowed money, with a gambler's hope that the academic honours impending there will compel some university president to realize my capacity. To bring out *The Theme of Paradise Lost* in the near future would be another strong argument in my favour, either in English or in Comparative Literature. If it is not out by the end of 1939, I fear it will never be published, for all of my energies will have to be absorbed in heart-breaking hack-journalism in order to ward off bankruptcy.

Publication did not come in 1939. In the meantime, the threat of impending war led me to undertake a major research enterprise for the Canadian Institute of International Affairs on the Nazi impact on Canada's foreign-language communities, especially as revealed in some scores of foreign-language newspapers. This appeared in the fall of 1939 as *Canada, Europe and Hitler* (Oxford University Press). Then I was appointed in 1940 to the staff of McMaster University at so enhanced a salary that my wife's martyrdom and my own stomach ulcers were things of the past. Academic readjustments and wartime responsibilities (for example, one hundred public addresses in 1940) mortgaged my time heavily, but by November 6, 1941, I found myself once more in harness for Woodhouse and writing to him about Andreini:

> Many thanks for sending me Andreini's *Adamo* and the Cowper–Hayley version in the Bohn library.
>
> I have been doing some cross-checking between the two, and find the English rendering not bad. Unlike the fantastic travesty of Grotius by Barham, it follows the Italian fairly closely, line by line. Its chief fault is an eighteenth century tendency towards poetic diction of an ornate but rather vague sort. For example, "al Fattore eccelso" (to the high Creator) becomes "to this creative Sire." Or the line "Salamandra infernal, talpa d'orrori" (infernal salamander, mole of horrors) becomes "inhabitant of fire and mole of darkness." This slight tendency to blur the meaning is, of course, far better than a Miltonizing of the style (as in Barham) that compromises the whole basis of comparison. If you concur, however, I shall be glad to undertake a new translation of the relevant parts of Andreini, on the same principle as the translation of Salandra.

Access to the ampler libraries of southern Ontario, however, opened up unsuspected phases of the whole Milton project. The University of Toronto Library had copies of the complete catalogues of the British Museum Library and the Library of Congress which put me on the trail of scores of poems dealing with Milton's themes. Even the McMaster University Library possessed a complete set of Migne's *Patrologia*, both the Latin series and the Greek, from whose hundred of massive volumes I dredged out still other scores of analogues of *Paradise Lost*, particularly in the hexaemeral literature. The idea occurred to me of writing to scholars in all literary fields, asking for suggestions as to analogues of Milton in Erse, or Hungarian, or Russian, or any one of a score of other literatures. My thought was not to supply representative translations from all these other poems, but to include a descriptive catalogue of them all in the impending volume of translated extracts. I became aware of the existence of microfilm, purchased my own projector, and bought great quantities of microfilm from the larger libraries of the world. McMaster University paid part of the bill but most of the cash came out of my own pocket.

In September 1942, there came a major change in planning. Woodhouse had been seriously ill. He had also been awarded a Guggenheim Fellowship to enable him to take a year off and write a book on Milton. He therefore proposed that our joint volume should cease to be a joint enterprise. His introductory essay was rapidly becoming a full length book in itself. My own collection of analogues had already passed all bounds. To try to present the gargantuan combined work to a publisher could only bring a refusal. To this dissolution of an eight-year partnership I consented with regret, but continued through the years that followed to share with him all products of my further research. He on his part continually sent me news of further analogues that he encountered in foreign libraries.

In 1943 and 1946 I read two further papers to the Royal Society as by-products of the big project. The former was "The Earliest Paradise Lost," analysing a fifth century epic in Latin hexameters by Bishop Avitus, and the latter "Some Latin Analogues of Milton," an analytical essay to which I appended a dated checklist of 225 analogues of *Paradise Lost*. Offprints of this latter were sent to Milton scholars everywhere, petitioning for extra titles to make the checklist complete. Among those who generously came to my aid were Douglas Bush, James Holly Hanford, William B. Hunter Jr., Roy Wiles, Helen Darbishire, F. T. Prince, Grant McColley, Molly Mahood, Merritt Y. Hughes, Malcolm Ross, Charles G. Osgoode, J. Milton French, William R. Parker, Theodore Silverstein, Harcourt Brown, and J. F. M. Sterck. Meantime I myself ransacked all accessible libraries and ordered from foreign libraries in microfilm all titles that seemed to have the slightest relevance. There were many false trails, but the total of authentic items grew to more than three hundred—instead of the four with which we had begun in 1934.

The linguistic implications of this attempt to read and analyse all analogues in all languages were likewise staggering. The original roster called for only Latin, Italian, and Dutch; but my final *catalogue raisonnée* involved the reading of some fifty thousand pages in all of the languages of Europe and a few from Asia and Africa. I had facilities for handling all European languages except Old Church Slavonic, but Sumerian, Babylonian, Arabic, Armenian, Syriac, and Ethiopic lay beyond my linguistic orbit and had to be judged in translation.

Much time was consumed in my dealings with the libraries of the world in tracking down and securing rare books in microfilm. It was a polyglot range of correspondence—writing in German to German libraries, in Italian to those in Italy, and even in Latin to the Vatican Library, from which an answer once came in the dubious Latinity of "Libelli recensiti in epistulis a te datae [*sic*] non reperiuntur . . . in Bibliotheca Vaticana." From the Bavarian State Library in Munich came the sad news that certain books that I wanted badly "sind aber während des Krieges bei den Bombenangriffen auf die Bayer. Staatsbibliothek mit grossen anderen unersetzlichen Verlusten zerstört worden." In spite of continual disappointments of this sort, my list of books found and filmed grew in phenomenal fashion.

The process might, it seemed, have gone on forever, but the strippings grew rapidly thinner and thinner, and as I told Woodhouse early in 1950, one has to stop somewhere. I therefore submitted a manuscript of 850 pages to Dr. George W. Brown, of the University of Toronto Press, in the hope that his readers might recommend publication. It presently transpired that the real difficulties were not those of scholarly acceptability but those of hard cash. A series of strikes by the typographical unions in Toronto had pushed the cost of book publication to astronomical heights. One thousand copies of my book would take several thousand dollars to produce, and even if the whole edition sold, the necessary retail price, allowing for the retailer's margin, would put the book beyond the reach of students. Woodhouse worked feverishly to find a way out of this impasse. It was he above all others who helped to persuade my old friends of the Humanities Research Council to come through with a grant of one thousand dollars in aid of publication. And it was he who counselled George Brown to try publication by a process that would by-pass the stratospheric wages of the linotypers. This was the use of the "multilith" sheet, a sort of "super-mimeograph plastic stencil" that could be typed by my own secretary, Beth Brinton, on an electric typewriter, and used at once for press work. In this way, there would be no linotyping, no proof-reading and no revision. With such a reduction in its costs, and in its possible losses, the University of Toronto Press agreed to publish; my secretary and I spent many long months, in the margin of university business, in preparing the multilith sheets; and at last, in the fall of 1952, the ponderous volume came off the press. In its printed form, it consisted of 479 pages of analogues (mostly in my own verse translation), 200 pages of descriptive catalogue, and sixty pages of introduction and index. As with most academic projects of this kind, there seemed not the slightest prospect of the author, who did almost all of the work, making a cent out of the publication or even recovering any of his fabulous outlay on microfilm. As a matter of fact, the whole edition sold out; the generous subventions were repaid; and a small royalty cheque to the author was duly shared with his hard-working ex-secretary (by then a housewife and a mother).

The power of the Milton project to extend its roots and send up vigorous new suckers from them was shown in connection with the theme of Milton's *Samson Agonistes*. It will be recalled that in 1937 I had prepared a blank-verse translation of a vigorous *Samson* by Joost van den Vondel and that Woodhouse and I had intended to include this in our joint volume. As the *Paradise Lost* analogues spread out into a limitless jungle, we dropped Vondel's *Samson* from our table of contents, but I could not chase it out of my field of bibliographical research. Wherever I turned in my checking of parallels to the major epic, I kept finding analogues of the Samson drama, and salted them down, in photostat or microfilm, for future attention. In 1949, I repeated the device of a Royal Society paper—this time "Six Sixteenth-Century Forerunners of *Samson Agonistes*"—to which I appended a dated checklist of eighty-eight analogues that I had unearthed. Off-prints were sent far and wide in search of still further suggestions. Typical of the research required in tracking down individual items is the case of my search for a Latin *Samson*, published in Cologne by Andreas Fabricus in 1569. The only known copy had been in the Staatsbibliothek in what in 1946 was the Soviet sector of Berlin. As I was *persona ingratissima* to the Moscow authorities, I had a friend in London request a friend of his in the British sector to operate through a British liaison officer in East Berlin. In 1948 the news was relayed back that in World War II the holdings of the Staatsbibliothek had been dispersed for safe keeping and that this particular book appeared to be missing. Presently the National Central Library, in London, located an unsuspected second copy in the library of the Augustinian canonry at Klosterneuburg, near Vienna. When I wrote to try to purchase the play in microfilm, the film arrived in Canada with startling promptness, and with the further courtesy that the canonry refused to accept any payment.

The intense interest in the Samson analogues—on which virtually nothing had been written by English scholars—can be only hinted at here. While in the period 1540–70 plays on this theme were almost invariably modelled on Plautus and Terence, the playwrights of 1600–1640 were patently familiar with Greek drama and sought, like Milton, to write plays in the style of the great Athenian tragedians. Perhaps the most striking of these newer dramas is *Simson: Tragoedia Sacra*, by Andreas Wunstius, of Strasburg, staged and published in 1604 (after his death) with the addition of many spectacular "episodes" by other hands. The original version by Wunstius himself consists of a scant 1400 lines of Latin verse. There are never more than two dramatis personae on the stage at any one time, with the exception of a chorus of Hebrew maidens. The chief character—with whom the play begins and ends—is Eluma, the venerable mother of Samson. The only other characters are Samson, Dalila, a priest, and a satrap, and, very briefly, a herald and a messenger. Both the mother and the temptress balance the force of the tragic protagonist, but the whole movement of the plot can be outlined in terms of maternal emotion and resolution. It is an astonishingly original play.

Along with the translated plays of Vondel and Wunstius, my 1964 volume, *That Invincible Samson*, contained my English version of an Italian libretto, *Il Sansone* (1638) by Vincenzo Giattini, partial renderings of *Samson, Tragoedia Nova* (1547) by Hieronymus Zieglerus, and *Simson* (1600) by Theodorus Rhodius, both from Latin, and an analytical catalogue of 107 analogues.

The final research harvest—dealing with analogues of *Comus*, *Lycidas*, and *Paradise Regained*—is still being flailed out. The crop of authors, chiefly Latin and Italian, is much smaller, but readers who have found some interest in the two earlier books will not, I feel sure, consider the threshing-floor all chaff and no wheat.

18

Organizing the Humanities

CANADA, LIKE YOUNG OSRIC, is "spacious in the possession of dirt," but the very vastness of our geographical patrimony has been a handicap in the development of scholarship. A few million people sprinkled along the southern marches of a territory as large as Europe have difficulty in maintaining the fruitful contacts of like-minded scholars or in supplying them with the library resources on which modern erudition can be built.

Prior to about 1915, moreover, Canadian scholarship in the humanities had been based in large part on that of England and Scotland but without the libraries and the leisure that had nourished critical masterpieces in those countries. Most of our humanists had come from the United Kingdom or had received training in its universities. The tradition in the Canada of their day was one of teaching in large doses, rather than one of tutorial work (for which staffs could not be afforded) or of published criticism (for which the requisite materials were lacking). Men like James Cappon of Queen's and W. J. Alexander of Toronto were teachers of the very first rank, whose almost legendary fame still echoes down the years, but their published work is relatively insignificant.

For the past forty years, however, the German tradition of basic research, mediated to Canada through the American graduate schools, has bulked larger and larger in our university life. Professors still teach too much—that misfortune associated with lack of staff—but it has come to be held more and more strongly that the humanist ought to enrich his teaching by fundamental research in some limited area of his major field. The emphasis is intensive rather than extensive, for in my day at Queen's Cappon and Taylor in English and Morison in History knew Italy and Italian intimately, Cappon also knew Swedish, Rushbrooke Williams in History knew Arabic and Persian, and all of them took Latin, Greek, French, and German for granted. The old tradition probably produced a richer culture; the new one approaches criticism with sharper scientific tools.

In the 1920's, some Prairie scholars in English, having felt keenly their isolation from one another, decided to do something about it. Hence arose an annual "English Conference," held at Saskatoon for two days in 1926 and at Edmonton for two days in 1927. At Saskatoon, our hosts were R. A. Wilson, head of the English Department, who, as an old disciple of John Watson, had just completed an erudite volume on the metaphysical implications of language, and J. M. Lothian, a Glasgow M.A. who had taught in Italy and had studied the relations of the Italian and the English Renaissance drama. At Edmonton, Edmund Kemper Broadus, an irascible and aristocratic Virginian, whose specialties were Southern slang and the English laureateship, made us at home, but warned us not to speak to him each morning until three cups of coffee had restored his faith in the world. The conferences were a great success. As teachers, we discussed such professional matters as remedial English (referred to us by the National Conference of Canadian Universities for study), high school curricula, the proper character of examination papers, and modern philosophies of education. Equally important were scholarly papers in which individuals put some of their special research wares on the table and received the criticism and encouragement of men in their own field.

In May 1928, the delegates moved east by invitation to an "English Conference" at University College, Toronto. Our host was Malcolm Wallace, a specialist in Milton's prose and the life of Sir Philip Sidney, but the centre of the stage was taken by explosively irrepressible Garnet Sedgewick from the University of British Columbia and the punctilious but mellow scholar, Archibald MacMechan, from Dalhousie. "Archie" spoke on Matthew Arnold's *Merope*, and it was my task to supplement his paper with one on French and Italian dramas on the same theme by Voltaire, Alfieri, and Maffei (all borrowed a month earlier from the University of Toronto Library). This 1928 meeting, with representatives present from Vancouver and Halifax, marked the widest geographical extension of the "English Conferences." It was also the last of them. The financial crash in 1929 dragged universities down along with the rest of the community, and harassed university presidents, who had largely financed our meetings, were forced to withhold supply. The three golden interludes had revealed, however, that notable encouragement can come from a foregathering of kindred spirits and that a surprising amount of first-class material was in the making or vainly awaiting publication.

For many years thereafter, the only regular and comparable academic contact that I knew was in Section II of the Royal Society of Canada, to fellowship in which I had been elected in 1936. Most of the seventy-five fellows of that time were social scientists, but there were a number of humanists: in philosophy, George S. Brett (Toronto), Sir Robert Falconer (Toronto), and Herbert L. Stewart (Dalhousie); in history (which straddles the humanities and the social sciences), Charles N. Cochrane (Toronto), Arthur Dorland (Western), D. C. Harvey (University of British Columbia), Fred Landon (Western), Chester Martin (Manitoba), Duncan McArthur (Queen's), Arthur Morton (Saskatchewan), Stewart Wallace (Toronto), and George M. Wrong (Toronto); in modern languages, Milton A. Buchanan (Toronto); in English, George H. Clarke (Queen's), Pelham Edgar (Victoria), Thorleif Larsen (University of British Columbia), W. E. McNeill (Queen's), E. J. Pratt (Victoria), W. O. Raymond (Bishop's), and Orlando J. Stevenson (Ontario Agricultural College; and in Classics, W. H. Alexander (Alberta), N. W. DeWitt (Victoria), W. Sherwood Fox (Western), Carleton Stanley (Dalhousie), and myself, more strictly comparative literature (United College). In addition there were a number of men of letters not holding academic appointments, such as Duncan Campbell Scott, Frederick George Scott, W. D. Lighthall, B. K. Sandwell, J. M. Gibbon, and Sir Charles Roberts. The wide range of disciplines in the section made for greater variety of discussion, when a crowded programme left any room for it, although it lacked the more concentrated interest and specialized knowledge that we had found in the "English Conferences." The annual fellowship with many fast friends in almost every non-scientific field has been one of the greatest privileges of my life.

Unfortunately for the encouragement of the humanities across Canada, however, only a few scholars can ever hope to be included in the limited circle of the Royal Society and that rare election usually comes towards the end of man's career. This gives no help to the younger scholar who is struggling with an unfinished masterpiece or has a manuscript of scholarly research that no press will touch without the help of a subsidy. This problem remained unsolved until the formation of the Humanities Research Council of Canada in December 1943.

The HRCC was a by-product of World War II. The chain of circumstances that brought it into being has never been completely traced. As one who shared in its founding. I believe that the story should be told.

Canada had been in World War II since early September 1939, but had adopted towards its universities the policy of Great Britain by which high-grade students in all faculties were allowed to continue their courses for a time, on the assumption that it would be a long war and a scientific one, and that they would in the long run be of more value to their country as well-trained mathematicians, scientists, and scholars than as indifferent infantrymen and sailors. When the United States finally joined the War two years and three months later, its administration, with the precipitate energy of the latecomer, decided to make a short war of it and put all of its younger men into uniforms, emptying the universities of most of their regular students and using their facilities for the training of military personnel.

In the autumn of 1942, the principals of McGill and Queen's proposed that the National Conference of Canadian Universities approach the federal government and suggest the closing down for the duration of the war of all university faculties of Arts, Law, Commerce, and Education. A special meeting of the NCCU was to be held in Ottawa on January 9, 1943, to discuss the proposal; editorials in papers like the Toronto *Globe and Mail* (cf. Dec. 24, 1942) were insisting on its adoption; and it was understood by the grapevine that the Prime Minister was ready to implement the scheme immediately thereafter. All other university heads took alarm, but felt that utterances from the threatened disciplines were of vital importance.

With the social sciences, there was no organizational problem, for a Canadian Social Science Research Council had been set up in 1940 and was able to memorialize Mr. Mackenzie King in November on behalf of history, political science, political economy, sociology, psychology, geography, and all related subjects. The humanities, however, had no organization and hence no official spokesman. Harold Innis was president of Section II of the Royal Society of Canada, which includes both the social sciences and the humanities, and at once set up a small humanities committee to canvass the relevant university departments for their opinions. Its members were Sir Robert Falconer, George S. Brett, Milton Buchanan, Arthur Woodhouse, and myself as chairman. Woodhouse, Buchanan, and I held a meeting (to which the others could not come) at my home in Hamilton in order to prepare a tentative draft of a memorial. This I sent at once to fifty-five department heads across Canada, as well as to senior university heads like President H. J. Cody of Toronto and President Sidney Smith of the University of Manitoba. I also got in touch with Camille Roy, Arthur Maheux, and Emile Chartier, who were notable French representatives of the humanities in Section I of the Royal Society and heartily endorsed our document.

All criticisms and comments were carefully consulted in preparing a revised draft and on December 30, 1942, the resulting version, signed by forty-one anxious humanists, was forwarded to the Prime Minister, with a copy to Sidney Smith as that year's president of the NCCU for use at its fateful Ottawa session. Lest any casual reader assume that we were seeking mass wartime exemption for college students in the humanities departments, I give the text of the Royal Society memorial hereunder verbatim and in full:

MEMORIAL ON STUDIES IN THE HUMANITIES IN CANADA

The scholars and professors listed beneath, representing departments of the humanities (English, Classical Languages, Modern Languages, and Philosophy) in universities in all parts of Canada, beg respectively that in any consideration of Canada's man-power problems the vital importance of these studies be kept in mind, both for the War and for the period of reconstruction.

A survey of the universities shows that most of these departments have already been seriously depleted of male students in honour courses and in graduate work, leaving them largely with women students and with men who are ineligible, through youth or infirmity, for military service. The majority of men eligible or soon to be eligible for service, now enrolled in the universities, are either (1) beneath the draft age, in the first and second years, or (2) concentrated in the fields of science, natural and applied, in preparation for subsequent war activities.

We recognize that the man-power needs of the nation at war are of paramount validity, and that no fit student of draft age has any inherent right to exemption. We submit, however, (1) that even if the few remaining draftable students in the humanities were to be called up immediately, these departments would still have important wartime functions to fulfil, (2) that there are military grounds for urging some small measure of exemption for certain students, and (3) that the present and future welfare of Canada requires that these departments should be held intact and in the highest possible state of efficiency.

Even in wartime the primary and secondary schools of the country must be kept going, in order that a democracy may continue to become educated; and for this purpose the continued training of women students in the humanities maintains an essential supply of teachers to take the place of those who die, are retired, or enlist for war service. Moreover, in addition to training specialists, the humanities form an integral part of the university science courses, since (1) they teach languages essential to science study, (2) they teach power of expression, essential in preparing scientific reports, and (3) they supplement purely technical training by making good its deficiencies on the humane and social side. All this makes the scientific graduates more effective in whatever wartime work they may undertake. Likewise of wartime importance are the contributions of these departments in maintaining and enhancing public morale by lectures, broadcasts, articles and books.

It may be further urged that draftable young students in the humanities may be of greater value to the army as the result of temporary exemption. Arts students have proved to be excellent officer material and are often better equipped to handle problems of personnel than are technically trained men. In this regard, it might be well to follow the example of the British universities, which, in spite of military urgencies much greater than ours, have tried to hold the Arts man at least until he is 19½ years of age or thereabouts. Such exemption should, of course, as at present, be conditional on his passing all examinations and on his undertaking regular military studies and training.

Still more important is the maintenance of these Arts departments in a strong state of efficiency for the tasks of the post-war world. The work to be performed by the Canadian universities in the rehabilitation period will be very heavy. In that work—and the returned veteran is already among us—the humanities will have a large share. To disband the present Arts faculties, or even to weaken them seriously, would be disastrous in the face of these national responsibilities; for a strong Arts faculty is the slow achievement of wise administrative choice over a long period of years, and its sudden dispersion would entail irrecoverable losses. This is particularly the case in the humanities, where personality, judgement and scholarship have so important an intermingling.

In urging this maintenance of strong staffs in these departments, we are thinking in the perspective of civilization itself. Implicit in the foregoing recommendations is the conviction that the humanities are profoundly important in any long-range view of higher education. If the civilized values of the race are to survive, we shall need to have at least a fair number of men in our communities who have a strong grasp of principles, and whose minds, while appreciating practical details, can rise above these details to a sense of their broad, human significance. Much of the greatness of British political life lies in the fact that so many of the nation's leaders—men like Burke, Fox, Peel, Gladstone, Asquith, Grey and Balfour—have been classical scholars or philosophers, or have, like Bright and Churchill, steeped themselves in the finest of English literature. It is the purpose of the humanities to train men in the greatest thoughts of the human race, not merely in mechanical techniques or the arts of the market-place.

Canada, moreover, as a custodian of the literary legacies of England and France, needs especially to see that both of these humane traditions are maintained in full force for the enrichment of our national life. We would also urge that in the post-war era, when the Slavic peoples and those of China will play a large part in the development, along with us, of a new world order, a special effort should be made to encourage Slavonic and Chinese studies in our Canadian universities.

It is significant that in Germany, after the First World War, there was a rush of university students into vocational training. Instead of developing personalities or humane philosophies, this movement developed men who thought of others only as machines. We, too, unless we safeguard the humanities, both now and in the post-war world, will be in danger of coming close to the educational objectives of Nazi Germany. Everyone recognizes the inevitability, and even the necessity, of an increase in natural and applied science in the new world. Yet science brings its own hazards to the human mind, and requires its antidote in social and humane studies. As the scientific trend increases, therefore, the antidote ought also to increase. We urge accordingly that the humanities should receive equal treatment with the sciences in all that is done for the returned men and in all that may hereafter be possible in the way of national scholarships and fellowships in the post-war period.

It should be remembered, moreover, that on the North American continent the tradition of the humanities is a much more delicate plant than in older countries and that any damage done to it now might later prove irretrievable. Guarding against such damage now is therefore essential to the maintenance of our national culture after the War.

The foregoing memorial may be briefly summarized as follows: (1) we recognize the primacy of the war effort; (2) we urge the maintenance of strong university staffs in the humanities, both as important for the war effort and as essential for the period of post-war rehabilitation; and (3) we urge the strengthening of the humanities in our post-war system of higher education.

All of which is respectfully submitted.

It would be a mistake to ascribe too much importance to any one document, but one may assume that this memorandum was one of the factors that persuaded both the NCCU and the government that it would be unwise, for the sake of drafting a few surviving male students away from their mathematics and languages, to close down four university faculties for several years, turning their women students into factory hands and their professors into farm labourers.

All in all, the scholars of Canada had had a bad scare. Many who were closest to the situation in Ottawa gained the impression that a few civil servants in the Department of Labour had almost demonstrated their power to determine university policy and shut down the colleges, and that only a resolute handling of the matter at the highest level had saved the day. Still more obvious was the inarticulate plight of the humanities, apart from such *ad hoc* committees as the one set up in 1942 by the Royal Society. The need for some permanent, co-ordinating body was clear.

At the annual meeting of the Royal Society of Canada, held in Hamilton, May 25–27, 1943, the following resolution was therefore passed by Section II: "Resolved that the President of the Section appoint a committee to consider the desirability of organizing a Humanities Research Council in Canada." On June 11, Harold Innis, the outgoing president, wrote asking me to be chairman of this committee, with Woodhouse and Buchanan as members along with others to be co-opted. Dr. R. H. Coats, the Dominion Statistician, now took over as the new president of Section II, and he and Innis joined in tightening the cinch-straps on the hapless Kirkconnell packhorse. The three of us met in Toronto in September and worked out a tentative membership for the projected Council. This was no easy job. The Social Science Council, of which Innis had been founder in 1940 and of which Coats was 1943–44 chairman, was based on existing national organizations in history, political science, psychology, and other social sciences. The humane disciplines, however, had no such national groups whatever and hence their Council had to be made up of individual scholars selected directly on a national basis. All disciplines were to be represented; all important universities, both French and English, were to have their spokesmen; and each delegate was himself to be a *bona fide* researcher.

Decisions were at last hammered out. A meeting for organization was to be held in the Faculty's Upper Club Room in Hart House, University of Toronto, at 10.00 A.M. on December 29, 1943. Kirkconnell was to draft out a constitution for the new Council and a substantial memorandum on its aims. This was to be sent to Coats before October 23, so that he might then present it to the Canadian Social Science Research Council and ask them to grubstake us until funds became available from other sources. Coats, as from the Royal Society, was also to ask the prospective Humanities Council members to serve. Finally, Mrs. Pereira, the assistant secretary of the Royal Society, was to mail them out invitations from me for the organization meeting, along with copies of the memorandum and the proposed constitution.

Most of the sixteen accepted membership but only nine were able to attend the constituent gathering. Those who settled luxuriously down into the upholstered armchairs and sofas in that quiet top-floor room on the historic December 29 were: Milton Buchanan, the scholarly, well-groomed and somewhat pessimistic professor of Spanish in the University of Toronto; J. H. Brovedani, a plump, white-haired little Spanish specialist from Queen's; W. E. Collin, professor of French at Western Ontario, swarthy and handsomely piratical-looking; James Francis Leddy, a tall, curly-haired Irish-Canadian, with ironic wit and an Oxford doctorate in Classics, who was professor of Greek in the University of Saskatchewan; Rupert C. Lodge, a bespectacled product of Oxford and Heidelberg, an authority on Plato and chamber music, professor of philosophy in the University of Manitoba; Theophile J. Meek, erect, sensitive, indefatigable in research in Orientals, drawing blood at every sword-thrust in debate, professor of Semitic languages in University College, Toronto; William O. Raymond, a solidly built, deliberately spoken authority on Robert Browning, professor of English in Bishop's University; Arthur Woodhouse, a double for Dr. Samuel Johnson in bulk, forthrightness and intellectual gusto, professor of English in University College, Toronto ;and myself, professor of English in McMaster University. Also present at the birth of the new Council were three obstetrical representatives from the CSSRC: Harold Innis, its founder, tall, rumple-haired, with a fine blend of enthusiasm, shrewdness, and caustic comment, professor of economics in the University of Toronto; R. H. Coats, its chairman, belligerent of chin and emphatic of speech; and John Robbins, its secretary-treasurer, deliberate in manner and laconic in utterance, head of the educational branch in the Dominion Bureau of Statistics.

The meeting lost no time in getting down to business. Between 10.00 A.M. and 3.50 P.M., it decided to proceed with organization, made some very minor revisions in the draft constitution, and selected the following sixteen Canadian scholars to form the Council: E. Chartier, J. W. Cohoon, W. E. Collin, R. K. Gordon, W. L. Graff, G. B. Harrison, H. W. Hilborn, Watson Kirkconnell, M. Lebel, J. F. Leddy, R. C. Lodge, T. J. Meek, G. B. Phelan, W. O. Raymond, G. G. Sedgewick, and A. S. P. Woodhouse. As a quorum of these members was present, the founding fathers agreed to dissolve the preliminary meeting and reconvene the group immediately as the Humanities Research Council of Canada.

By 4.00 P.M. the Council was in full session. The name, constitution, and membership were promptly adopted and an Executive elected: Kirkconnell, as chairman, plus Lodge, Meek and Woodhouse. John Robbins was added as secretary-treasurer. By the constitution, the chairman of the CSSRC was to be an ex officio member of the HRCC and so Coats became a welcome supernumary on the humanities roster. Before adjournment at 5.30 P.M., plans were made for an Executive meeting in Toronto on February 26 and for a full Council meeting in Montreal on May 26 and 27, the final session on May 27 to be a joint one with the CSSRC.

The chief business at the February Executive meeting was the appointment of two committees on grants-in-aid—one for research and the other for publications. This was merely a gesture of faith, as there were no funds for either committee to dispense and even the infant Council was being bottle-fed by the social scientists. More important than this elaboration of machinery was a sortie made into American territory in mid-May by three humanist Musketeers—Arthur Woodhouse, Father Gerald Phelan, and myself. We were first to visit Washington and learn from the American Council of Learned Societies its techniques in making grants to scholars, and then proceed to New York to solicit funds in large quantities from the Rockefeller Foundation and the Carnegie Corporation. The trip was generously financed by John Marshall of the Rockefeller Humanities Division, who had visited Toronto and Hamilton early in the spring.

Dr. Waldo G. Leland, director of the American Council of Learned Societies, put the Canadian trio up at the Statler Hotel for May 16 and 17 and showed us hospitality as warm as the pre-summer sunshine in Washington after a very late Canadian spring. On Tuesday, there was a noon luncheon at the Cosmos Club with members of the ACLS staff with whom we had spent the morning on grants in aid of research and publication (Dr. Goodchild), the development of area studies (Mortimer Graves), and the intensive language programme (J. M. Cowan). After lunch came a drive to the George Washington estate at Mount Vernon, to the Lee home at Arlington, and to the slowly growing mass of the capital's great Gothic cathedral. On Wednesday we went through the Library of Congress (where we had a pleasant chat with Archibald MacLeish, then chief librarian as well as poet), the Federal Archives and the Folger Shakespeare Library.

The peak of American courtesy was a dinner at the Statler Hotel on the evening of the seventeenth in honour of the three visiting Canadians. There were some thirty of the "top brass" in Washington's academic circles, including Professor Emeritus Edward K. Rand of Harvard; George F. Zook, president of the American Council on Education; Solon J. Buck, U.S. Archivist, who had already shown us through his formidable domain; Joseph Quincy Adams, director of the Folger Shakespeare Library, and his assistant, James G. McManaway; Dean Henry Grattan Doyle, chairman of the ACLS committee on intensive language instruction; Lewis Hanke, chairman of the joint committee on Latin-American studies; Ross G. Harrison, chairman of the National Research Council; President Emeritus Guy Stanton Ford, secretary of the American Historical Association; S. Whittemore Boggs, geographer and secretary-treasurer of the ACLC; and John W. Studebaker, U.S. Commissioner of Education. The three Canadian visitors had to "sing for their supper," each in a brief after-dinner speech, but what I remember best is the mellow, classical wit of Edward K. Rand and Henry Grattan Doyle's zest for his language programme.

We took a night sleeper for New York and spent the following morning with John Marshall of the Humanities Division of the Rockefeller Foundation. The man who had so generously financed our trip now seemed adamant against any contribution towards the general objectives of the Humanities Council. It appeared that the needs of the humanities in Canada were still to be proven in detail. Our new-born Council had no assured standing as yet. He ended by giving us a first-class lunch—but no funds. The somewhat dejected trio then trudged across to Fifth Avenue to call on Dr. Robert M. Lester, secretary of the Carnegie Corporation, and received only a genial lecture on the sad fate, in his experience, of all foundation-supported organizations. They began, he explained, with a paid secretary; then added a stenographer and an office; and then the expense of a periodical of some sort. The secretary next acquired a wife and a baby. No other sources of support were sought out, and when, after five years, or ten, the Carnegie Corporation withdrew its grant, the organization folded up, and four unhappy people found themselves on the street. He was unwilling to cause all this grief to four innocent Canadians, and dismissed us with urbane cheerfulness. Our egos, which had expanded gloriously in the sunshine of Washington's hospitality, shrank into frost-bitten melancholy as we left New York empty-handed.

Yet I resolved to try John Marshall of the Rockefeller Foundation once more, and on May 22 I wrote to him in the strongest terms possible, asking him to underwrite our expenses for a couple of years and to finance a full-dress survey of the humanities in Canada. Meantime we would canvass Canadian sources for some permanent income to carry our routine costs. This firm undertaking to do serious work in the Canadian field brought due results, and the Executive Committee of the Rockefeller Foundation, on Mr. Marshall's recommendation, voted us $8000 to cover the costs of a survey of the state of the humanities in Canada and to finance general support for the two-year period estimated as necessary for the task. We had faith that if we could prove our case in this major project, both Rockefeller and Carnegie would be willing to assist with grants-in-aid for research and publication.

Three further contacts with the ACLS should be mentioned briefly in passing. On June 17, 1944, its "Committee on Slavic Studies" was to hold sessions at the Harvard Club of New York City, 27 West 44th Street, and Waldo Leland invited me down to report on the state of Slavic studies in Canada. Intellectual co-operation with Soviet Russia was in the air and I was interested in watching the temperate hopefulness of Sam Cross of Harvard, the bouncing enthusiasm of Ernest Simmons of Cornell, and the dry scepticism of Leland himself, who had once seen a whole prospective delegation of Soviet scientists "purged" in the 1930's before they could leave for the West. Oscar Halecki, the Polish historian, was present at the luncheon and proved a quiet but deeply learned man.

Another ACLS project was to be a bilingual conference of scholars, to be held in Montreal for a week in 1944 or 1945 at American expense, with equal numbers of French-Canadians, Anglo-Canadians, and Americans, perhaps five of each category. The subject of the supercolloquium was to be the advantages and problems of a bilingual culture (Canadian style) and all those present were to be effectively bilingual in performance. I worked out many of the preparations for this gathering with Dr. Emile Chartier, dean of the Faculty of Letters in the University of Montreal, and Prof. Maurice Lebel, of Laval, but wartime pressure on railways and human time-tables ultimately forced the Americans to cancel everything.

Finally, I was invited to the twenty-fifth anniversary meeting of the American Council of Learned Societies, in Boston, Massachusetts, January 25–26, 1945, in the House of the American Academy of Arts and Sciences. At the anniversary dinner, the highlights were addresses by Howard Mumford Jones, then president of the American Academy of Arts and Sciences, and President James B. Conant of Harvard University. From my own feebler contribution I would cull only two or three paragraphs:

I appreciate this opportunity of visiting Boston, where on this occasion every branch of learning is lined, not with tame villatic fowl but with Minerva's own birds, with supersized owls of erudition. To bring still another owl—and a wild, Arctic one at that—into such a company, is surely to bring an owl to Athens, *glauk' eis Athenas.* Be that as it may, I am happy to convey Canadian greetings to this esteemed Parliament of Fowls and to express the hope that relations between our fields of scholarship may be still more intimate and fruitful with the passing of the years.

We have similar ideals, but our methods of approach are sufficiently different to be of mutual interest. I suggest one instance only: The United States has been at war for slightly over three years. Canada has been at war for nearly five and a half years. In proportion to our population, we Canadians have raised armed forces and produced war material as great as those of your republic. We, too, instead of accepting Lend Lease material from anyone, are supplying it to others by the billion dollars' worth. Canadian troops have fought in the Far East, in Italy, and now, beside the Americans in France and Belgium. Yet throughout all this, Canada has kept its universities and Arts colleges intact. Not a single course in the humanities has been interrupted and our registration, now augmented by a return flow of disabled veterans, shows only a slight drop from pre-war figures. Two provisions, and only two, protect the system from abuse. The first is that at the end of the Freshman year the lower fifty per cent of the class, regardless of pass or failure, are taken over by the army and war industry. The upper fifty per cent are free to continue to graduation, provided they pass each year on a full year's work. In the second place, all of our male undergraduates must take systematic military training throughout the college year, plus a spell of military camp or naval service in the summertime. From the outset, over five years ago, it was assumed that this would be a long war and that in the long run young men with university training would be more useful to their country than those who went direct from high school into the forces. It was also assumed that the sort of civilization we were fighting for required a strengthening, rather than a weakening, of humane studies. Our system is a logical sequel to such assumptions. We fear that it is possible to conquer in the battle of tanks and planes and yet to sell out to the enemy in that war of ideas that is far more vital, that war of the spirit that should never know a truce.

The survey of the humanities across Canada was the task to which we now turned all the energies that could be spared from a full load of academic work. All of us were full-time professors in busy universities and the most that any of us could hope to "scrounge" from our long-suffering presidents was leave of absence from the campus for two or three weeks in term-time in order to visit other universities while they were also under full sail. The rest of the work had to be done in our evenings and throughout two summer vacations.

A full description of the scope and methods of the survey will be found in the preface to *The Humanities in Canada* (1947), the 287-page octavo volume in which our results were finally published. In retrospect we realized the importunity with which we demanded answers to five different and almost interminable sets of questionnaires sent out to all university presidents, deans or registrars, heads of humanities departments, librarians, and all individual scholars in the humanities. The return of many thousands of pages of answers was followed by personal visits to all universities in term-time. Because of the obstacles of time and geography, we divided Canada into four areas and sent a team of two (supplemented by a social scientist) into each area. The four teams were as follows: *Western Canada*, J. F. Leddy and Arthur Woodhouse; *English universities of Ontario*, Rupert Lodge and Jean Houpert; *English universities east of Ontario*, MacGregor Fraser and Gerald Phelan; *French universities and colleges*, Maurice Lebel and Watson Kirkconnell.

The final report was written three times over. The first draft was worked through by the entire Council at Kingston in May 1946; a mimeographed revised draft was circulated to two hundred university officials and scholars for criticism and was worked through again by the full Council in December 1946. The printed edition was a still further revision. Apart from Chapter II (The Humanities in the High Schools) by J. F. Leddy and Appendix B (Music, Fine Arts and Drama) contributed by Arnold Walter, Robert Ayre, and Herman Voaden, its twelve chapters and four appendixes, evolved from the chaos of questionnaires and visitations, were entirely the work of Arthur Woodhouse and myself. We split between us the opening historical chapter and Appendix A (The Humanities in Professional Faculties). Of the rest of the report, Woodhouse wrote chapters III, IV, and VII (Pass, Honours, and Graduate Courses, English-speaking Universities) and Chapter X (Aids to Scholarship in the Humanities), while I wrote the Introduction and chapters V (Collèges Classiques), VI (French Graduate Studies), VIII (Academic Libraries), IX (Faculty Research), XI (New Provinces), XII (Recommendations), Appendix C (Bibliography on Education), and Appendix D (List of Canadian Publications and Works in Progress in the Humanities). John Robbins helped with the press work in the Ottawa printing shop. I was never more thankful to see the end of a book. The effect on the American foundations was marvellous, however, and helped to repay all our toil.

Before noting those results, I must record another achievement that seemed to impress the said foundations just as much as our big red-bound volume.

The sustaining funds of the Rockefeller Foundation were for two years only and were to expire at the end of 1946. It was clear from both Carnegie and Rockefeller that for permanent administrative expenses we must not look to foundations or to American sources. Something had to be done about putting the HRCC on a solid financial footing in Canada.

It was Garnet Sedgewick of the University of British Columbia who, at a Council meeting in 1945, came up with the fertile suggestion that we appeal to Canadian universities for our running expenses. Séraphin Marion then coached us on the technique of our tactical approach. We could argue that largesse from the Foundations would be showered on their professors, and since all university presidents had been talking sonorously of the plight of the humanities, this was a chance to ask for presidential works as well as oratorical faith. Woodhouse was to canvass President Sidney Smith of Toronto; Father Phelan was to round up the heads of the federated colleges in Toronto; and Graff, with such Arts allies as he could mobilize at McGill, was to put the landing-net under Principal James. If these prospectors struck oil, the rest of the campaign across Canada was to be left in my hands for action, either by direct appeal or, where deemed strategically more effective, through any local Council member on whom I cared to call.

To the great credit of Canada's universities, almost every one of them agreed to make a small annual contribution, ranging from fifty dollars in the case of small Maritime universities up to five hundred each from Toronto (including the federated colleges) and McGill. The total has grown steadily, moreover, from $2650 in 1946 to about $6000 today, and has usually covered routine costs. This proof of independent vitality and assured survival made its due impression on the big American foundations, and from 1947 to 1958 the Rockefeller Foundation gave the HRCC $115,000 and the Carnegie Corporation, once so reserved, gave it over $80,000. Up to that time, over three hundred awards had been made by the HRCC in aid of research and publication.

A bold new chapter opened in 1958, with the mobilization for action of the Canada Council for the Encouragement of the Arts, Humanities and Social Sciences, with the annual income from $50,000,000 at its disposal. Since *The Humanities in Canada* and the HRCC brief based on it had been written large into the decisions and recommendations of the Massey Commission (1949–51), it was to the HRCC that the new

Canada Council turned for a definition of its tasks in relation to the humanities and for untold labour in the implementing of the proposed programme. Even though the American foundations abruptly terminated their aid in these new circumstances, the financial help from Canadian sources was so greatly increased that the tide of applications rose sharply. In 1958–63 there were 2993 candidates for grants in the humanities and the social sciences. All of these were processed by the HRCC and the CSSRC, and 989 awards were made. The sheer amount of administrative work had so increased, however, that in 1963 the Canada Council announced that henceforth it would itself manage the appraisal of all candidates for aid. This has not meant that the HRCC is now *functus officio*. Its general leadership in the humanities, especially in the planned co-ordination of research and publication, remains as important as ever. A second edition of *The Humanities in Canada*, updated by F. E. L. Priestley, was published in 1964, and a further supplement, prepared by Roy Wiles, was published in 1966. Systematic visits by senior scholars have also stimulated and encouraged research at the individual universities.

My administrative connection with the HRCC ended in 1948, when I became a university president and ceased to be eligible for membership. My own scholarly researches continued, however, and I have twice been the grateful recipient of large grants in aid of publication, first for my *Celestial Cycle* in 1952 and later for *That Invincible Samson* in 1964 (see Chapter XVII). Large bronze medals were also bestowed on me and other past chairmen at a special dinner at the University of Montreal on May 26, 1964. Likewise present, and recognized, on that occasion was the late Arthur Woodhouse, the true founder of the HRCC's auxiliary corps, the Humanities Association of Canada. In the early pages of this chapter, I stressed the value of contacts among professors in the same or closely related fields—a contact briefly realized in the old "English Conferences" and experienced on all too small a scale in Sections I and II of the Royal Society of Canada. Grants in aid of research or publication helped the individual researcher but did nothing for the rank and file of the humanities departments across Canada. Hence came Woodhouse's vision of a "Humanities Association of Canada," instigated and in large part financed by the HRCC. The proposal appears in one of *my* chapters in *The Humanities in Canada*, but the idea was his in the first place and his was the enthusiasm that pushed it on to achievement in the years after our first objectives had been reached. Suffice it to say that the "Association" has existed since 1949–50, that it has some eight hundred members scattered across the

Dominion, that there are local or regional branches for mutual stimulus, and that annual meetings have been held on a national scale ever since 1949.

Nor is this all. Thanks to the new university budgets of a more affluent society and to the readiness of university presidents to help subsidize professorial participation in annual meetings of professional bodies on a national basis, some thirty-five "learned societies" now meet each year at the same host university as the Royal Society and spread their overlapping schedule of sessions over more than three weeks in late May and early June. The Canadian Historical Association (founded 1922) and the Canadian Catholic Historical Association (founded 1931) date from an earlier period, but our HRCC cat can claim paternity for some ten equally healthy humanities kittens: The Classical Association of Canada, the Association of Canadian University Teachers of English, the Association of Canadian University Teachers of French, le Centre d'Etudes Canadiennes-Françaises, the Canadian Association of University Teachers of German, the Canadian Association of Hispanists, the Canadian Association of Slavists, the Canadian Philosophical Association, the Canadian Linguistic Association, and the Canadian Association of University Schools of Music. Each of these societies joyfully discusses the problems of its subject-field, each has a feast of research papers contributed by its members, and each concludes its annual sessions with a banquet.

Machinery is not an inevitable cause for satisfaction. If it becomes a mere end in itself, it can be a menace to intellectual and spiritual growth. It is my own feeling, however, that all this organization of the humanities for which a few of us laid the foundations in 1942–47 has had a profound influence on these disciplines in Canada and that its greatest achievements are still to come.

19

The Masonic Brotherhood

I FIRST LEARNED of the Three Ruffians and the seafaring man of Joppa on a December night in 1920. The town was Lindsay, the lodge was "Faithful Brethren," No. 77, A.F. and A.M., and the worshipful master was Alex Birchard. I was later to have contact with lodges elsewhere and even to become the master of a lodge myself, but no other lodge-room is quite so haloed with remembrance as that in which I was "raised" by an indubitable grip and joined the company of the brethren.

Instruction between the degrees was in the hands of Worshipful Brother Phil Morgan, a guileless soul who all his days was a lamb caught in the thickets of speculative investment, but his devotion to the Craft was so real that it inspired his pupils to a faithful mastery of the Emulation ritual. So thorough indeed was his training that when, some thirty years later, I affiliated with a York Rite lodge in Nova Scotia (St. George's, No. 20) and went through the chairs, I had to jettison the verbal cargo of my early manhood and acquire an entirely new book-load of phraseology. The ritual of the old was just sufficiently out of focus with the new to make it impossible to depend on it at any point. A completely new start was therefore necessary.

A propos of Masonic instruction, an unusual story was told me by Worshipful Brother David Upton Hill, Ph.D., D.Sc., master of St. George's Lodge in 1926. During his term of office, he did considerable coaching of candidates in the privacy of his own home and there the practising of "signs and tokens" was repeatedly witnessed by a bright young tomcat of the Hill ménage. Thereafter it was a notable fact that whenever the tomcat was especially hungry, he would come to Dr. Hill, sit erect, and give the Due Guard or hailing sign of a master mason. This he always did for his master alone and never when women or outsiders were around.

It was during my term of office "in the East" of St. George's Lodge that the brethren, after slowly accumulating funds by bequest for forty years, at last boldly decided to purchase a building lot on which to erect a "temple" of their own instead of renting quarters up two long flights of stairs above a Main Street grocery store. My own enthusiasm fizzed up in the "Trestle Board" for April 1955 in a poem whose opening lines were full of jubilation:

> Sound the loud timbrel by Minas' mud flats!
> The brethren have spoken, and not through their hats!
> Four decades of waiting have ended in praise.
> Come, thump a big drum for life's wonderful ways!

My mother lodge in Lindsay was founded in 1857, the year of the incorporation of the little town, then the backwoods terminus (population 1100) of a railway line from Port Hope. The dispensation of "St. George's Lodge, No. 20, R.N.S.," with which I affiliated in Wolfville in 1952, dates back to 1784 (warrant as No. 11, R.N.S. in May 1785), when it was organized among the New England colonists who had settled on evacuated Acadian French territory near the mouth of the Cornwallis River. Grand Lodge Masonry in Nova Scotia actually goes back to 1738 when the Provincial Grand Master of Massachusetts appointed as Provincial Grand Master of Nova Scotia a certain Major Erasmus James Philipps of Annapolis Royal, the great-great-great-grandfather of Dr. James Erasmus Tracy Philipps (born 1890), one of my closest personal friends two hundred years later. Today, there are grand lodges in each of the provinces of Canada and the total membership has risen by fifty per cent in three short decades.

Yet the significance of any institution does not depend on numbers. Its survival value finds more eloquent testimony in evidence that it has found validity in human experience throughout thousands of years. Elements in Masonry bear proof of such antiquity.

Perhaps at this point I ought to make a confession. When I was first made a Mason in the old home town in Ontario, I had only the vaguest idea of what was meant by an "Ancient, Free and Accepted Mason." I knew something about "Freemasons" and had a general notion as to "Accepted Masons," but this matter of "Ancient" left me, I fear, in a mood of growing scepticism.

It may be that I had some grounds for that attitude. I turned to Josephus, that contemporary of the Apostle Paul who wrote a famous history of the Jews, and I found that Hiram Abif, the Masonic master and artificer, instead of dying a violent death, was apparently building Solomon's palace long years after the completion of the Temple. I studied the Book of Ecclesiastes, so familiar in Blue Lodge ritual, and learned that the language and general character of the original Hebrew text assign it to a period at least eight centuries after Solomon. I turned to books on the Craft itself, and found that most of its ritual lecture material was composed in England in the eighteenth century by Dr. James Anderson, Dr. J. T. Desaguliers, George Payne, and William Preston. I had grave reasons for suspecting that Free and Accepted Masons were not much more "ancient" than the establishment of Grand Lodge Masonry in London in 1717.

Evidence as to all this was obvious in the language that was woven into the authorized work of the Blue Lodge ritual. Thus the Middle Chamber lecture quotes in full a poem by Joseph Addison (1672–1719), beginning:

> The spacious firmament on high
> And all the blue ethereal sky
> And spangled heavens, a shining frame,
> Their great original proclaim. . . .

The same lecture even refers to "the plaintive strains of 'Home, Sweet Home,' " a song that was not written by J. Howard Payne until 1823. It also echoes in the "pearly gates," a well-known nineteenth century hymn. Another passage recalls the *Essay on Man* by Alexander Pope (1688–1744) and his familiar line:

> An honest man's the noblest work of God.

Two quotations from William Shakespeare (1564–1616) are also patched in, one from *Hamlet*:

> That undiscovered country from whose bourn
> No traveller returns. . . .

and one from *Henry VIII*:

> This is the state of man: today he puts forth
> The tender leaves of hopes; tomorrow blossoms
> And bears his blushing honours thick upon him;
> The third day comes a frost. . . .

Quotations from the Bible are invariably in the language of the King James (1611) translation. Thus the ritual refers to "Faith, Hope and Charity" and adds that "the greatest of these is Charity." William Tyndale, in his earlier (1534) translation of the New Testament said rather: "Now abideth fayth, hope, and love, even these thre : but the chefe of these is love." Or the ritual says: "Peace on earth, good-will toward men" where Tyndale in 1534 wrote: "peace on the erth and unto men rejoysynge."

If one is to think of the ritual as handed down from Solomon's time, there are a host of other anachronisms. There is mention of the roar of cannon, the din of musketry, old cathedral airs, the art of printing, the seven liberal arts (of mediaeval education), and such mediaeval orders of chivalry as the "Golden Fleece," the "Star," and the "Garter." Older than these but still much later than Solomon are the the Holy Bible itself, the Holy Saints John, the prophet Ezekiel, synagogues, the Book of Revelation, and the Greek science of geometry.

There are also absurdities that would never have been perpetrated by Solomon. Before the days of the Suez Canal, the Ruffians would never have sought ship-passage from Joppa to Ethiopia. Solomon is represented as paying wages to 80,000 Fellow Crafts on the evening of the sixth day of each week in the "Middle Chamber" of the Temple, but Scripture describes only an outer chamber (60 by 30 feet) and an inner chamber or "holy of holies" (30 feet by 30 feet) and this relatively tiny building could not have begun to accommodate 80,000 Fellow Crafts (plus 3300 Master Masons and 70,000 Entered Apprentices) and the vast quantities of corn, wine, and oil needed to feed them and their families. The Fellow Crafts alone, at 400 to the hour, would require over eight days and nights, without pause for sleep or food, for Solomon to pay them for one week's work. As a matter of fact, in another context, only fifteen names are on the several rolls. When we consider again the diminutive proportions of the Temple, it is hard to see how it could have had 1453 columns and 2906 pilasters, "all of the finest marble." It is also disconcerting to find the "Eureka" episode of Archimedes erroneously ascribed to Pythagoras, and to have the Greeks given credit for originating architecture when the Egyptians had a priority of several thousand years and even the so-called "Doric style" is found in a temple of Hatshepsut nearly a millennium before the Greek's refined still further this architecture that they borrowed. Such were some of the modernities and confusions that left me, at one time, highly dubious as to the antiquity of the Craft.

As the years went by, however, I saw something of the world. I visited Egypt, Palestine, Syria, Cyprus, Crete, Asia Minor, and most of the countries of Europe. In the course of these travels, I found Masonic evidences that were puzzling, if not bewildering, in terms of their antiquity. I found, for instance, that in the island of Crete, in ruins of the palace at Cnossus several centuries *earlier* than Solomon, there were hundreds of little clay figurines, whose various postures embodied some of the signs of the first three degrees of Masonry. What were these doing in the Minoan land, from which, hundreds of years *later*, the Philistines migrated by sea to vex the coasts of Israel?

The apparent answer I found in Egypt, the country from which the Cretans learned the craft of working in stone. On a chilly afternoon in late December 1921, two Arab guides had helped to boost me up the battered sides of one of the pyramids of Gizeh, in Egypt, and at last I stood panting on the wrecked summit of the rocky mass. The view in every direction was breath-taking, but what caught my eye more than anything else, nine miles across the desert to the south, was a huge geometrical hill of masonry, obviously still mightier than the pyramid on which I was perched. What I gazed at was the great step-pyramid of Sakkara, not strictly pyramidal like those at Gizeh and Medum but rising in successive ledges of man-wrought stone.

Here lingered the bold topic sentence that had begun a whole chapter of human history. Prior to this, all buildings in Egypt had been reared of mud or sun-dried bricks. Then at one stride and apparently through the genius of one man, the art of stonemasonry came into being. The pyramid itself was the tomb of King Zoser, of the third dynasty, roughly 3000 B.C., reared by his prime minister, physician, and architect, Imhotep, one of the most gifted men who ever lived. He is recorded in inscriptions as "Chancellor of the King of Lower Egypt, First after the King of Upper Egypt, Administrator of the Great Palace, Hereditary Nobleman, High Priest of Heliopolis, Imhotep, the Builder, the Sculptor." As the inventor of stonemasonry and one of its greatest architects, he deserves to be held in reverential remembrance by all subsequent masons, whether operative or speculative. The secrets of his skill became the possession of the priests of Ptah, the god who was himself the Creator and Supreme Architect of the Universe. The high priest of Ptah was "the chief of the artificers," and in the inscriptions of the old monuments there is a frequent reference to the "three chiefs of the stone masons," a sort of adumbration of "the three who open a lodge."

The "house of eternity" first framed for Zoser was the centre of a "vast monumental complex, built of fine limestone blocks that were carefully smoothed and matched in regular courses." Two thousand years before King Solomon of Israel, Imhotep had erected of stone a structure more than two thousand times as large as Solomon's puny temple. At its focus was earth's first pyramid and one of its greatest. By it, Imhotep sought to defy the tyranny of death and to give the soul (*Ku*) of Zoser a regal court in which it might rule throughout eternity. This was the meaning of each pyramid. Each was the tomb of a single monarch, and sought, like the 3rd degree of Blue Lodge Masonry, to proclaim on man's behalf a passionate protest against the mortality of human life.

Each Egyptian temple shadowed forth much Masonic symbolism. It was square, or rectangular, because the Egyptians so envisaged the Earth. Its orientation, in terms of sun-worship, was to the east and west. The square, the cube, the triangle, the circle, and the cross were all full of sacred meaning. At the entry to the temple of Ptah, at Amenta, were two pillars, akin to those two brazen pillars, Boaz and Jachin, that Hiram the Master later set up in the porch of Solomon's temple. When an obelisk of the fifteenth century, B.C., misnamed "Cleopatra's Needle" by phrase-hungry journalists, was taken down in 1879 to be transported to Central Park, New York, all of the emblems of its masonic builders were discovered in its Egyptian foundation: the rough cube, the polished cube, the plumb, the trowel, the square, the arc of a circle, even a stone trestle-board! These bear witness to the antiquity of a symbolic faith.

Masonic experience in ancient Egypt seems also to have been associated with religious ritual of a highly dramatic character. The greatest passion play of the ancient world was the liturgical presentation of the "mysterium magnum" of the Egyptian Trinity—Osiris, Isis, and Horus. Here the believers portrayed the murder of the beneficent Osiris, the search for his corpse by his faithful wife Isis, and his ultimate triumphant "raising" as Saviour and Redeemer in the glory of the spring season. Here was a quest for an answer to the spiritual problem of human death, and here was an ultimate shadowing forth of a doctrine of human immortality.

As the art of architecture spread out from Egypt into the rest of the ancient world, there seems to have gone with it the same sort of union of masonry with a religious drama of faith. Thus in Asia Minor the so-called "Dionysian Artificers," a craft-guild of temple-builders, had likewise the same religious "mystery" of murder and resurrection, except that Osiris is here renamed "Dionysos." And when one crossed to European Greece, one found this same legend of Dionysos shadowed forth in annual ritual at Eleusis, about fourteen miles west of Athens. For every Greek who was able to follow the philosophical subtleties of a Plato or an Aristotle there were hundreds who could imbibe deep spiritual truth from the symbolism of these Eleusinian Mysteries. Masonry seems at a remote time to have drafted the unmurdered Hiram the Master for the central role in a kindred drama of religious loss and a quest for spiritual meaning in the face of death. It is a transmuted Osiris and not an historical Hiram whom millions of Freemasons have impersonated in the ritual parable of man's rebirth after death into the invisible lodge of master builders. The very sprig of "acacia" is ancient Egyptian in name and origin, and the Pyramid Texts tell how the dead Osiris is raised from death to life by the strong grip of the lion-god.

I visited Jerusalem, and found little of relevance to the Craft except an old stone quarry, deep under the rock of the hill, where Solomon's operative stonemasons are alleged to have held sessions. I journeyed north past the realm of Hiram of Tyre and farther up the Lebanon coast to Beirut and Tripoli. Hereabouts I learned of the Lebanese tribe of the Druses, who today declare themselves to be the descendants of the Phoenician builders of Solomon's temple, who have temples like lodges, with three degrees of initiation, who have signs, grips, and pass-words, and who use building tools as emblems of moral truth.

I returned by way of Cyprus, Smyrna, Istanbul, and Athens to Italy once more, and here I found the ancient record likewise significant. Masonry and a secret cult initiated into the practical secrets of building, came early to ancient Rome. Even today in Rome you will find the great sewer, the *Cloaca Maxima*, built with masonic skill about 500 B.C., still giving massive service to the region of the Forum. Throughout most of Rome's history we find evidence of *collegia* or guilds of stonemasons, which bore striking resemblances to a lodge of practising masons. There was a Master and his two Wardens (*Magister* and *Decuriones*), as well as a secretary, a treasurer, and a chaplain (*Sacerdos*) and numerous symbols of the Craft. If you go, as I have, to the ruins of Pompeii, you will find there, not far from the so-called Tragic Theatre, the lodge room of an old Roman operative lodge, duly dug out of the ashes of the great eruption of A.D. 79. There are two columns in front, interlaced triangles on the walls, and on a pedestal in the room an altar with a symbolic design of rare beauty.

During the reign of the Emperor Diocletian (A.D. 284–305) four Master Masons and one Entered Apprentice suffered atrocious deaths in the persecution of the Christians, and the "four crowned martyrs" (*Quattuor Coronati*) became in far later centuries the patron saints of Masons in Germany, France, and England. In London, England, the supreme research lodge of the entire Craft bears their names today.

The link between the old *collegia* and the mediaeval guilds of masons would seem to be the "Comacine Masters," whose retreat on an island in Lake Como I glimpsed in my travels. As early as A.D. 643 one encounters an edict of the Lombard king Lotharis recognizing them as "free masons," and we learn from an inscription of A.D. 712 that they were organized as Masters (*Magistri*) and Apprentices (*Discipuli*), under a *Gastaldo* or Grand Master. They had oaths, tokens, grips, and passwords; they had masters and wardens; they wore white aprons and gloves; their emblems included the square, the compasses, the level, the plum-line, the arch, King Solomon's Knot, and the Lion's Paw; and they gave special reverence to the Four Crowned Martyrs. From this Coma-cine Order came the great cathedral builders of the Middle Ages. And from the rituals of the various English branches of these masonic guilds came in due course those "Old Charges" that were duly studied by speculative Masonry in the early eighteenth century and made the cornerstone of the much more elaborate ritual that we know today.

Such was my period of historical re-education as I passed from my early scepticism over into a growing sense of the profound age of the Craft. We are compassed about with a very great cloud of witnesses, not merely Anglo-Saxon but Roman, Greek, Cretan, Syrian, Palestinian, and Egyptian. There are elements in Masonry that are nearly as much older than Solomon as Solomon is older than Winston Churchill, but the long endurance of a secret fraternity, conveying deep religious truth from generation to generation, has not only left behind it a majestic record of monumental architecture but has grown increasingly in spirituality.

No comparable antiquity could be ascribed to the twenty-nine degrees of the Scottish Rite through which I passed in "the Valley of Halifax" in 1950–52. Dramatically they were well staged, with a discreet subordination of the spectacular to the didactic, but a critical eye could see that their highly edifying lessons were secondary rather than primary in origin.Thus the Lodge of Perfection was chiefly given over to spelling out large the lessons of Blue Lodge Masonry; the Rose Croix Chapter's symbolic degrees gave a highly formalized picture of Persian Mesopotamia; and the historical degrees of the Consistory could be as recent as A.D. 1765 (the twenty-fifth anniversary of King Frederick "the Great" of Prussia) and reached their allegorical climax in the thirty-second in a Cathedral in Flanders in A.D. 1300, a degree with its closest analogue in the mediaeval morality play *Everyman*. The roots of the Scottish Rite, and some of its degrees, go back to the Chivalric orders that took part in the Crusades and set up their chapter-houses in Europe. Suppressed in the early fourteenth century in a dastardly plot by the papacy and the French monarchy, many of the leaders fled to Scotland, where they took refuge with King Robert the Bruce and united with the Masons of Kilwinning. The ideals and philosophy of this new "Scottish Rite" gradually became more Masonic than military. When the cause of the Stuarts, which they espoused in 1688, 1715, and 1745, was defeated, they fled again to the Continent and flourished there, not least under the leadership of Frederick the Great. "Grand Constitutions" were approved in 1762 and 1786, and the first Supreme Council in the Americas was set up under the latter authority in 1801 in Charleston, South Carolina. The Scottish Rite degrees of our day owe much to the inspired and erudite revision of Albert Pike, head of this Southern jurisdiction (the "Mother Council of the World") in the years 1859 to 1891. Their language, however, is often prolix and involved in syntax, and I myself wrote on invitation in 1962 a new lecture for the 6th Degree that was at once authorized as official for all Canada. The materials of the Rite come from many sources. The builders quarried much of their stone from many ages. The ceremonial "mass" of the 14th is not a parody of the eucharist but a survival of the still earlier commensality of Mithraism. The allegory of the "rosy cross" shows intimate familiarity with the ritual of Rosicrucianism, which in turn seems to stem back through Arabic and Neoplatonic mediation to Hermes Trismegistus *alias* Thoth, the old Egyptian god of wisdom. Those who framed the degrees also show smatterings of Hebrew scholarship, in many of the "mystic words." Far from being mere abracadabra, the formulas of the Rite have been heavily loaded with significance from the past.

Certain basic facts emerge, however, from any candid study of Freemasonry. It is deeply religious and all of its sessions are opened and closed with prayer, *but it is not Christian.* The Holy Bible has its invariable place on the altar of Masonry in the English-speaking world, but its basic texts are all from the Old Testament and not from the New. The Jew can accept its teachings as readily as the Christian. The Incarnation and the Atonement are unknown to it. Nothing in masonry is repungent to Christianity but to the Christian it cannot take the place of his own religious faith nor does it aspire to do so.

In my forty-seven years of Freemasonry, I have never heard any hostility towards Roman Catholic or Jew expressed in any Masonic Lodge. On the other hand, I have never met a Catholic Mason, although Catholics are not excluded by statute and Cardinal Cushing has recently been fraternizing with the Masons of Connecticut. I have often wondered whether the overwhelming preferences of Protestants for Freemasonry goes back to basic psychological principles. New Testament Christianity was starkly simple but with the passing of the centuries an astute hierarchy took over and reconsecrated the more compelling aspects of the *mysteries* and the pagan state religions. Protestantism, by insisting on the austere simplicity of the primitive church, left an emotional vacuum in the lives of its worshippers. Naturam expelles furca, tamen usque recurret. Into this void, to replace the subconscious need for the *mysterium magnum* of the Mass and a host of other ministering rites of bygone centuries, came the ritual of the Blue Lodge. In many respects, it was pre-Christian or sub-Christian, but its morality was that of the Old Testament at its best, and its ritual, saturated, like Catholic ritual itself, with a host of elements from man's remote religious past, ministered to deep-seated needs of the spirit. As the Chorus mysticus comments profoundly in the closing lines of *Faust*, Part II:

> Alles Vergängliche
> Ist nur ein Gleichniss. . . .

and the capacity of the spiritual imagination to see symbols of truth in things transitory has incalculably enriched the religious experience of mankind.

Nevertheless, Masonic ritualism has its own dangers. Unimaginative and full-blooded brethren may stoop to levity and horse-play. Snobs may be unduly impressed with the inflated titles of the Scottish Rite degrees. The sober and deeply spiritual drama of these same degrees may be smirched with the "Hollywood touch." Kindheartedness towards a delinquent brother may paralyse the hand that should discipline him. The lodge devotee may even run the risk of letting the good supplant the best by failing in his higher responsibilities to the church of Christ.

There is another danger, to which Freemasonry in Europe has often succumbed. This is zeal for political revolution in a spirit both anti-Christian and conspiratorial. The Freemasonry of the English-speaking world, which today comprises over ninety per cent of the fraternity, has carefully avoided political partisanship, which in a secret order would justify its suppression, in self-protection, by all the legal powers of the state. On this score, there are Masonic groups in the world today which Canadian Grand Lodges refuse to recognize, on the ground that they are atheistic and politically minded. The Canadian Freemason, as a Mason, is pledged to religious faith and fundamental morality. His ideal is a fellowship that can rise above nation, race, and creed in its brotherly tolerance. Loyalty to one's own is not denied, but it is held to be consistent with fraternal good will towards men of every origin who have been initiated into faith in God, purity of life, discipline of character, and a hope of immortality.

20

The New Canadians

IN THE SUMMER of 1922, when the time came for my return to Canada after a postgraduate year at Oxford University, I was so "flat" financially that I sold my bicycle and a pair of German field-glasses to raise the price of steerage ticket on one of the CPR boats. Close to a throbbing propeller in the bowels of the ship, I found myself a mess mate of hundreds of Ukrainian, Polish, and Belgian immigrants. Rather to my surprise, I learned in conversation that some of the most dilapidated among them were cultured fugitives from Bolshevik terror in eastern Europe. Often they were well versed in three or four languages and literatures and their musical talents were prodigious. Thus it was that we of the steerage put on a high-class benefit concert in aid of sailors' orphanages and had as our guests the affluent but unmusical passengers from upstairs. As chairman for the occasion, I made a polyglot appeal for a generous collection.

This little episode was a foretaste of the new life that opened up for me when I joined the staff of Wesley College, Winnipeg, in September of that year. Western Canada was peopled with a very different ethnic mixture from that of the Anglo-Celtic communities of my Ontario youth or the Ottawa Valley Scotch-French symbiosis of my pioneer ancestors. To the French of the Red River Valley and the Ontario farmers' sons (especially from "Huron and Bruce") who had opened up the prairies there had been added scores of other strains, until the Bible House on Alexander Avenue could assure me in 1922 that it sold the Scriptures locally in fifty languages.

In 1967, forty-five years later, Canada's "European-Canadians" total over four millions in a population of twenty millions. They are collectively more numerous than the combined populations of Newfoundland, Nova Scotia, Prince Edward Island, New Brunswick, Manitoba, and Saskatchewan, or about equal to the total citizenry of Eire plus Northern

Ireland. They are thus a far from negligible factor in the Canadian equation. Like the French, Scotch, Irish, and English pioneers in our land, they have survived a major transplanting from an older continent, but the conditions under which the transfer was made have frequently been bloody and tragic, and the difficulties of adjustment have been enormous.

In Chapter VII, I have discussed their polyglot Canadian poetry as a revelation of the traumatic experience through which they have had to pass. In some cases the wounds never heal, and the exile's grieving spirit either drives him back to a troubled homeland or renders him forever a hopeless misfit in the New World.

For some tweny-six years (1922–48) it was my fortune to live in communities where the process of acculturation was active and to have intimate contacts with scores of ethnic organizations by which the newcomers have sought to cherish the values that they have brought with them from their past. An atomistic existence is painful and dangerous for these orphans of the storm and they seek comfort in fellowship with others of the same language, the same habits, the same political or religious faith. They are neither angels nor devils but three-dimensional human beings like the rest of us, striving to build themselves a new existence in a new country.

The most basic institution among them is the church of their ancestors, whatever that may happen to be—chiefly Lutheran among the Scandinavians and Balts, Presbyterian ("Reformed") among the Dutch, Lutheran or Catholic among the Germans, Catholic among the Poles, Uniate or Orthodox among the Ukrainians, and so on. Block settlements of immigrants with the same language and faith, originating in the same area of Europe, have naturally accelerated the building of churches in the new land as centres for community activities of all sorts. As the years passed by and the sheer struggle for economic survival slackened, other types of organization bourgeoned out in all directions.

Literary societies undertook the building of community halls and in them established libraries, arranged for lectures, and sponsored concerts and dramas. Orchestras, choral groups, folk-dance groups, handicraft groups, and drama clubs multiplied. Athletic clubs became active. Farmers' co-operatives flourished. As supplementary to the English-language schools of the Canadian government, informal schools were set up to preserve in the children of the settlement a proud knowledge of the cultural legacy of their past. Mutual aid societies (in a generation long before "medicare") gave benefits in case of illness or accident and provided for the funeral expenses of deceased members. Foreign language newspapers came early, sponsored by the various churches, by secular organizations, or by Canadian political parties.

Generally speaking, the organization of the several foreign language communities was a spontaneous grass-roots development, assuring the survival and then encouraging the evolution of a new Canadian population that was nevertheless strengthened by its past.

The greatest single factor making for the integration of the ethnic groups into a Canadian nation was the English-language school, supplemented at a later date by radio and television. At a somewhat more advanced stage of affluence, the sons and daughters of the immigrant communities passed on into the universities, and proceeded to give a good account of themselves. I remember one year in the 1920's when, although the registration at the University of Manitoba was more than half Anglo-Canadian, ten of the top twelve students in general proficiency were "European-Canadians." They had a zeal for knowledge that was prodigious.

As the second generation became completely Anglicized by the schools, a chasm all too often opened up between these young people and their parents, who had been left behind in their grasp of English and of Canadian issues. The foreign language newspapers stood in a curious relation to this problem. At a time when the first generation would have been unable to comprehend English-language instruction in Canadian farming methods or Canadian municipal politics, the ethnic press supplied all this information in assimilable form, but wherever there was no continuing flow of new immigration the demand for the foreign language press faded away. In the Icelandic community, for example, there were once two healthy weeklies; at last they were forced to amalgamate in order to survive; and now the combined *Lögberg-Heimskringla* is a small eight-page sheet that may well be on its deathbed. Meanwhile, the New Canadians are taking a fuller and fuller part in Canadian life. They are now judges and archbishops, MP's, senators and, MLA's, members of provincial and Federal cabinets, university professors by the score, and engineers by the hundred.

Living through the experience of Canada at war was a great integrating force making for a Canadian consciousness. Thus in World War I the Icelandic-Canadians had an enlistment record greatly above the Canadian average, while over 10,000 Ukrinians were in the CEF. In World War II, between 35,000 and 40,000 Ukrainians volunteered for service overseas and there was a comparable response in other communities. In the spring of 1940, the Queen's Own Cameron Highlanders were in training at Winnipeg and used to march one thousand strong down Portage Avenue past my college, with their bagpipes skirling and their kilts a-swing, and I used to smile proudly to think that more than half of the "Highlanders" were Ukrainians, Poles, and Magyars.

Many New Canadian communities that had begun their organization at the grass-roots level of the parish church and the community hall ultimately created at least one organization at the national level, in order to perpetuate the knowledge of their cultural past and to give voice to their Canadian attitudes on world politics. I have had personal contact with most of these and can pay tribute to their strength and their integrity. Among them have been the Icelandic National League, the Canadian Polish Congress, the Canadian Jewish Congress, the Ukrainian Canadian Committee, the Czechoslovak National Alliance, and the Canadian Slovak League. Over against these may be set tiny minority organizations of Communists in each language group, including French and English, all tightly controlled by a Politbureau for the whole Dominion and dedicated to "the triumph of Soviet power in Canada."

Some of our English-language Canadian newspapers have been prone on occasion to condemn as "fascist nationalism" the hostility of the larger nationality groups towards Communism, both in Canada and in their ancient European homelands. Part of the trouble is that few Old Canadians or their newspaper editors have even an elementary knowledge of the history of central and eastern Europe. To make the New Canadian attitude clear, let us have recourse to a simple illustration. Let us suppose that a Soviet army has occupied Scotland, has looted the country of everything that could be carried off to Russia, from pocket watches to the shipbuilding machinery on the Clyde, has murdered or imprisoned all leaders in Scotland's political, religious, and economic life, has set up a Communist puppet government, and is extending everywhere, from Galloway to the Orkneys, the systematic extermination of all freedom by the bullets, torture-chambers, and slave camps of the secret police. Would not the great majority of Canadians of Scotch origin be "full of rage and full of grief" over the fate of Scotland? And would other Canadians, in such circumstances, be sneering at them as "Scotch nationalists" and telling them that as Canadians they had no business to get excited over a legitimate Soviet desire for a "friendly government" in Scotland? If a few other Scotch-Canadians were making common cause with the Soviets, were sending congratulations to the Soviet quisling government in Edinburgh, and were openly pledged to the setting up of a revolutionary Soviet tyranny in Canada, then the parallel would be complete.

The present chapter could easily mushroom into a full-length book in itself. What follows is a series of notes on some of my contacts with a few foreign language communities and with the people of their ancient homelands.

The first Canadian-born generation of Icelanders had a meteoric career and two of their Rhodes scholars, Skuli Johnson and Joe Thorson, were among my earliest friends in the West. Skuli taught Icelandic as well as Greek at Wesley College, Olafur ("O.T.") Anderson taught mathematics, and there were numerous young Vikings in my classes. As a section of the library was given over to Icelandic literature, ancient and modern, it was perhaps natural that the first volume in my huge projected series of poetries in translation was a *North American Book of Icelandic Verse*, published in 1930 to coincide with the millennium of the Althing (see Chapter VI above). In my choice of poems I was deeply indebted to Professor Sigurður Nordal's *Islenzk Lestrarbók* and to some scores of volumes of contemporary Icelandic verse that I purchased through Mr. Snæbjörn Jónsson of Reykjavik. To Dr. Nordal I was also indebted for one of his own unpublished poems, which I proceeded to translate and include. Dr. Rögnvaldur Pétursson of Winnipeg, in whose home I found a large Icelandic library affectionately bound in dark red leather, gave me scholarly advice in the matter of editing.

My anthology proved to be a key to the hearts of the Canadian Icelanders. Their doors swung open even wider in 1935, when my *Canadian Overtones* included my renderings of thirty-six poems from fifteen Icelandic-Canadian poets, together with a biographical note on each. A Royal Society paper and articles in the *University of Toronto Quarterly* dealt still further with the community's poetry. Vilhjálmur Stefánsson sent me a copy of his latest book, *The Standardization of Error*, and with it a whimsical letter. In my *Canadian Overtones* I had published my English version of a long poem in his honour composed by Thorsteinn Th. Thorsteinsson. Vilhjálmur's gift was, he explained, bait to induce me to send him a copy. In those days I was invited to speak at Icelandic occasions at Riverton, at Lundar, and, of course, in Winnipeg. I visited in the farm home of Guttormur Guttormsson at Riverton and in that of Dr. P. H. T. Thorlaksson in Winnipeg. Years later, on August 2, 1953, I was brought all the way back from Nova Scotia to speak at a huge picnic at Gimli. My address was on "Stephan G. Stephansson and North America," based on the four volumes of his collected letters. I was even invited to be the godfather of the little daughter ("Marnie") of an Icelandic physician and his wife (Dallas and May Isfeld Medd), a relationship that I greatly prize.

During the past thirty years or so, honorary memberships have brought me annually, in Icelandic, the scholarly *Tímarit* of the Icelandic National League, *Skirnir* (issued since 1826 by the Icelandic Society of Letters) and at least one other volume a year from Reykjavik in the meticulous and tireless reprinting of Iceland's historical and literary documents. Comradeship in Icelandic studies through the years also linked me with Sir William Craigie of Oxford, and Bishop C. V. Pilcher of Sydney, Australia. Some of my own fondness for Eddas and sagas is also rubbing off on my Acadia students in mediaeval literature. I have likewise made frequent contributions to the pages of *The Icelandic Canadian*, an excellent quarterly issued in English by the community since 1942. The Icelanders are certainly one of the most articulate and culturally minded of all the nationality groups in Canada.

Comparable, if less intimate, friendship grew up with the other Scandinavian-Canadian communities—Norwegian, Danish, Swedish, and (in part) Finnish. I translated poetry by Arthur A. Anderson, Justus Linderholm, Sten Goerwell, Gerhard Silver, Gustav Stohle, and Harald Bratvold. In 1938, I visited all of the Scandinavian countries except Iceland, armed with letters of introduction from Winnipeg friends. Back in Winnipeg, I foregathered with Esse Ljungh, then on the threshold of a brilliant dramatic career. I was able to recruit the Swedes for the "Heritage of Europe" series at the University of Manitoba. The consular corps of Albert Hermanson (Sweden and Finland), Carl T. Kummen (Norway), and Grettir Leo Johannson (Denmark and Iceland) were good friends. When a Viking Club was organized in Winnipeg, it made me an honorary life member, and for many years after my removal to the East it continued, through its secretary, H. A. Brodahl, to send me annual invitations to the Viking banquet and ball.

Scandinavia's political horizon darkened in the fall of 1939, when, in accordance with a treaty between Hitler and Stalin, the Germans were to seize the western half of Poland and Russia the eastern half plus the Baltic States and Finland. Soviet forces occupied their moiety of Poland in September 1938 and then turned against the tiny republic of Finland—a state of 200,000,000 against one of 6,000,000. To the amazement of the world, the diminutive victim fought the gigantic aggressor to a standstill. Relief funds for suffering Finns sprang up across the English-speaking world, and in Winnipeg, too, a Finnish relief fund was organized under the auspices of all of the city's Scandinavian societies. On Sunday, December 17, 1939, a huge rally for relief funds was held in the Civic Auditorium under the sponsorship of the Lieutenant-Governor. I myself was the speaker for the occasion and gave the Russians both barrels of my oratorical shotgun. Musical selections (including "Finlandia" by Sibelius) were supplied by various Scandinavian choirs and a large Salvation Army band, and the meeting ended with the mass singing by an audience of four thousand of Luther's *Ein feste Burg*, a hymn that in the context had profound overtones:

For still our ancient foe
Doth seek to work us woe.
His craft and power are great,
And armed with cruel hate
On earth is not his equal.

Next spring it was the turn of Denmark and Norway to suffer invasion at Nazi hands. On May 17, 1940, I gave a CBC national broadcast on "Norway's Day of Independence," a sequel to one on Poland two weeks earlier. A few opening sentences run:

In times like these, it may seem grimly as if I were providing a series of requiem masses for the souls of murdered nations—murdered by the brutal aggression of Nazi Germany. They are rather intended as tributes to nations that are destined to rise again. . . . My present talk, for instance, is in no sense a fulfilment of that venomous jibe of a recent Berlin commentator that the extent of British concern over the conquest of Norway would be a few selections of Norwegian music on the BBC.

Norway, of course, recovered its independence in 1945, but Poland remains a betrayed and conquered state under Soviet bayonets.

Back in the old, uncomplicated, pre-Hitler days, a splendid *Goethefest* was held in Winnipeg in commemoration of the centenary of the death of the poet on March 22, 1832. Rabbi Solomon Frank and I sat side by side with Hugo Carstens and other distinguished German-Canadians on the platform in Knox United Church. My one unforgettable memory of the evening is the figure of a charming young girl, beatified by two long golden braids, who declaimed in clear, ringing tones the noble utterance of "Das Göttliche," beginning

Edel sei der Mensch,
Hilfreich und gut!
Denn das allein
Unterscheidet ihn
Von allen Wesen,
Die wir kennen. . . .

The arrival of a Nazi consul two or three years later introduced a new and alien element into the community. It was in an obsessive search for an explantion of my aloofness that he presently enquired of Gladys Pettingell, our college lecturer in German, whether my wife (*née* Kitchener, and a Canadian-born cousin of the old Anglo-Irish field-marshal) were a Jewess. "What difference would it make?" retorted an indignant Miss Pettingell. My research project on the evil but ineffectual impact of Hitler on foreign-language Canadian journalism, published in 1939 as *Canada, Europe and Hitler*, was a categorical statement of my anti-Nazi position.

Knocking at my door in Wesley College about the year 1928 came a burly young Hungarian exile, Béla Bácskai Payerle, an engineer, born in Ujvidek-Neusatz-Novy Sad but now editor of the *Kanadai Magyar Ujság*, of Winnipeg. He had encountered my translations from Magyar in *European Elegies* and the *Western Home Monthly* and had come to pay his respects. Thus began one of the most enduring of all my friendships. It was Béla's enthusiasm for Hungarian literature that led me to make this the second volume in my mammoth series. It was he who linotyped the whole of my *Magyar Muse* with his own hands and printed it on paper purchased for us by Lord Rothermere. It was he who founded a monthly magazine, the *Young Magyar-American*, to which for five years, I contributed the equivalent of several hundred pages of verse translations, articles, reviews of Magyar books, and an English grammar of the Magyar language. It was with him and his wife Lulu that I collaborated on the first English translation of János Arany's epic, *The Death of (King) Buda*. It was through him that I became acquainted with the Hungarian-Canadian community, especially Consul Joseph Schefbeck-Petényi and his wife Charlotte, his *locum tenens*, Dominic Szent-Iványi, and his successor Louis Szelle, and through them with officials and scholars in Hungary.

My intimacy with things Hungarian reached its climax in the summer of 1938 when I was invited to lecture on Hungarian literature at the summer school of the Stephen Tisza University in Debrecen. Echoes of that memorable summer will be found later, in Chapter XXIV, but the main narrative finds its place here. My wife and I sailed from New York along with the Payerles, on the Polish motor-vessel *Pilsudski*, passing north of Scotland by the Pentland Firth and landing at Copenhagen. We went from Warnemünde via Prague to Vienna by rail and thence by steamer to Budapest down a Danube the colour of adulterated catsup.

Our arrival in Budapest by boat after dark was a page out of a fairy-tale. The captain had invited the Kirkconnells to the bridge. Towering above us to the right were the volcanic hills of Buda with their flood-lit palace and church of Saint Stephen; to the left were the level glories of Pest, with its flood-lit Houses of Parliament; and on the broad, dark river flowing between them bridge after illuminated bridge shone like necklaces of pearls or diamonds. Presently the boat docked, and in less than an hour we were comfortably installed in a guest suite at the Eötvös Kollegium ("the Eton of Hungary") placed at our disposal by the Ministry of Education.

The next month was a kaleidoscope of excitement diversified enough to make a book in itself. There were two rail trips to Debrecen. There was a millennial session of the Hungarian parliament at Székesfehérvár. There was my recording of a fifteen-minute interview for the Hungarian state radio. There was a trip to Szeged, where we saw Hungary's greatest philosophical drama, *Az Ember Tragédiája*, performed in the cathedral square.

But as usual, the supreme interest was in people. In the Külügyminisztérium I met Tivadar Edl, with whom I had begun to collaborate on an English translation of Arany's epic *Toldi.* Mrs. Charlotte Petényi, now back in Hungary, entertained us at dinner. Dr. Louis Szelle took us to a "posh" restaurant where we sat at the next table to Danielle Darrieux. At a meeting of an "International Club," I met a whole covey of literary birds. But perhaps our deepest satisfaction was in meeting Dominic Szent-Iványi once again, for more than any other Hungarian except Béla Payerle he had encouraged my efforts in the Magyar field. At his apartment in Budapest, we met Judge Stephen Kertesz (now a professor at Notre Dame University), Dr. Joseph Szentkirályi of the University of Budapest (later to be smuggled out of occupied Hungary in a packing-case through the help of an American plane), and Stephen Traub of the Foreign Office, now operating with a travel agency out of Buenos Aires. Szent-Iványi was one of the honest and idealistic young men whom Teleki had been building into the Hungarian civil service. He was one of a truce party sent to Debrecen early in 1945 to negotiate with the invading Soviet army. Budapest friends who saw him two years later in a "People's" courtroom told me that he was by that time the mere gibbering ghost of a man whose body and mind had both been broken by torture. Thereafter he disappeared again into a Communist dungeon at Vác.

Another good friend was Joseph Balogh, editor of the *Hungarian Quarterly*, to which I had been a repeated contributor. My wife and I had evening dinner at his apartment on August 18. His personal library was that of a profound scholar, with learned books rising on every wall to a very high ceiling. His choicest possessions were numerous Danteana and editions of the letters of Erasmus. Balogh was murdered by the Gestapo in 1944 during the Nazi occupation of Budapest. His only offence in their eyes was that he was a Jew.

At a reception at the Belügyminisztérium on the evening of August 16, I met three members of the Government of that time—Teleki, the minister of education, whom I already knew well, and two others. One of these was the premier, Béla Imrédi, whom I somehow distrusted in spite of his astonishing resemblance to Mr. Vincent Massey. He was later hanged by the People's Courts of the Soviet occupation because of his alleged collaboration with the Nazis. The other was the foreign minister, Kálmán Kánya, a quiet grey-haired man of aristocratic charm, whose nickname in the inevitable subterfuges of those perilous times was "Kánya the Fox." Unlike Imrédi, who succumbed to the inexorable Nazi pressure, and Teleki, who committed suicide rather than surrender to it, Kánya resigned from the government soon after my visit and migrated to Mexico. It is small wonder that Stephen Kertesz's volume on Hungary's foreign policy during that period is entitled *Diplomacy in a Whirlpool* (1955). Even to survive was impossible for those who stayed with the ship.

Back in Canada, our friendship with the Hungarian community continued, apart from wartime attacks on me by the Communist newspaper, the *Munkás*, of Toronto. Béla Payerle moved to New York, became secretary of the American Hungarian Relief Incorporated, and was still later the executive secretary of the American Hungarian Federation. After the Kirkconnell transfer to the East, my chief group contact was with "the Hungarian Helicon," in Toronto. On February 1, 1963, I was a guest by invitation at their Hungarian Helicon Ball, held in the Royal York Hotel under the patronage of Lieutenant-Governor Keiller Mackay. Half-way through the occasion there was a strategic break and an eloquent orator presented me with a large bronze medal from the Hungarians of Canada. Inscribed on its face was the greeting: "In gratitude to Canada for the welcome accorded to the exiles of the Hungarian Revolution 1956–61."

Sixteen months later, at a banquet held in New York City, I was awarded a Gold Medal of Freedom in company with some eight other "international champions of human liberty"—Charles de Gaulle of France, Premier Segni of Italy, Defence Minister Strauss of West Germany, Chancellor Julius Raab of Austria, Cardinal Cushing of Boston, Mrs. Bang Jensen of Denmark, former Vice-President Richard Nixon, and Senator Thomas J. Dodd. The medal had been designed by the Hungarian sculptor, Mihály de Katay, and was struck by the Supreme Council of the Freedom Fighters in memory of the Revolution of October 23, 1956. The large parchment scroll accompanying the medal was deliberately burned around the edges so as to symbolize the martyrdom through which the Hungarian people have passed.

Still another Magyar award was the George Washington medallion of the American Hungarian Studies Foundation, conferred on me, along with Hans Selye and Marcel Breuer, at a 1967 banquet at the Plaza Hotel, New York.

My fellowship with Polish groups began in 1933, when a "Polish Academic Society," organized by seventeen students of Polish origin at the University of Manitoba, elected me as its honorary president. On January 21, 1934, in the Dom Polski, I gave a public lecture on "Polish Literature" under their auspices and several hundred persons turned out for the occasion.

On February 9, 1934, about fifty Winnipegers gathered in the Convocation Hall of United College for a more ambitious project. This was the founding of a "Canadian-Polish Society," composed of both Anglo-Canadians and Polish-Canadians, whose avowed purpose was "to promote, foster and propagate closer mutual cultural, economic, educational and social relationships between Canada and Poland." After considerable free-for-all discussion, a three-page constitution was adopted and a slate of officers was elected. As reported in the *Evening Tribune*, they were as follows: Watson Kirkconnell, president; B. B. Dubienski, first vice-president; Mrs. Colin Campbell, second vice-president; Robert England, secretary; Mrs. W. Chasney, assistant secretary; B. Zeglinski, treasurer. Membership was both English and Polish and attendance remained remarkably stable at about fifty. We held some six meetings a year and sought, in our programmes, to present the achievements of both Poland and Canada. One evening had papers on Madame Curie and Sir William Osler; another evening paired Joseph Conrad and Frederick Philip Grove; on still another we had talks on Copernicus and John Stanley Plaskett. In 1935, we were fortunate in adding to our membership Miss Myrtle Ruttan (later Mrs. Earle B. Patterson), an accomplished pianist whose specialty was Chopin. As a result, the musical side of our programmes was greatly enlarged and in five years we became familiar with almost the whole range of Chopin's compositions. Her studio in the Music and Arts Building became the Society's monthly rendezvous.

At the foot of the main staircase in my home hangs a cherished souvenir of those happy days—a masterly portrait in oils of the Polish novelist, Joseph Conrad, presented to me by the artist, Jan Sikora, a member of the Society.

Each spring we rejoiced to share in the Polish Ball, "Wiosna w Polsce," staged with great magnificence at the Royal Alexandra Hotel by the Federation of Polish Societies in Canada, under the patronage of the Lieutenant-Governor of Manitoba. In a sense, it became the chief event of Winnipeg's social year. Its floor show, by a young Polish group in costume, was incomparably beautiful.

On July 18, 1940, just prior to the Kirkconnells' migration to McMaster University, in Hamilton, Ontario, the combined Polish organizations of Winnipeg, some twelve in all, together with seven Hungarian groups, summoned my wife and myself, our two sons and our two little daughters, to Sokol Hall for the valedictory presentation of a large silver tray and a briefcase. A big leather-bound volume contained farewell letters of good will from all of the organizations concerned.

After my removal to Hamilton, I became less associated with individual community groups than with such integrating agencies as the Council of Friendship and the Canadian National Unity Council. On June 18, 1948, when these groups gave me a farewell dinner on my removal to Acadia University, I was presented with yet another leather-bound volume in which specially painted manuscript pages conveyed the valedictory good wishes of the two councils, the Hamilton Women's Civic Club (which had itself already staged a dinner and a presentation), and the Armenian, Estonian, French, Hebrew, Hungarian, Latvian, Lithuanian, Polish, Rumanian, Serbian, and Ukrainian communities. The good fellowship of all these groups was a heart-warming experience.

My chief friend in pre-war Poland was Roman Dyboski, professor of English literature in the old Jagiellonian University of Cracow. Dyboski had a most striking face, like some old Roman on a coin—with the profile of an Agrippa or a Scipio. I had first met him in Toronto in Christmas week of 1929 when the Modern Language Association of America met in that city and both of us were giving papers before the Slavonic Section. My last glimpse of him was in Cracow on August 27, 1938, when he entertained Mrs. Kirkconnell and myself at evening dinner in a restaurant facing the Sukiennice. Arthur Coleman, then of Columbia University, was also one of the party. Some fifteen months later the invading Nazis were to herd all of Cracow University's professors, like animals, into captivity. Dyboski never recovered from the treatment he received and died within a year.

When World War II began with Hitler's campaign against Poland, my indignant sympathy with his victims was immediately engaged. My horror deepened two weeks later, when Soviet troops, in accordance with an agreement with the Nazis, occupied the eastern half of Poland and proceeded to deport 1,750,000 of its citizens to die in Siberia. For the time being, however, we heard more of the enormities committed by their Nazi partners in crime. February 1940 thus found me drafting a letter of protest over the driving of a million Poles from their homes in the western provinces and herding them, in mid-winter, into the war-ravaged area of central Poland. I then mobilized the signatures of a small but highly representative group of Canadians and communicated the document to the Canadian government and the press of the world. Those who signed along with me were Sir Robert Falconer, Sir Frederick Banting, Sir Charles Roberts, Sir Ernest MacMillan, Sir Wyly Grier,

Monsignor Camille Roy, Dr. H. M. Tory, Dr. R. C. Wallace, Mr. Grant Dexter, Mr. Frederick Burchill, Dr. Victor Morin, Dr. H. L. Stewart, and Dr. George M. Wrong.

On May 3, 1940, the Canadian Broadcasting Corporation had me give a national broadcast on "Poland's Constitution Day" in which I pointed out that "The Allies today are, in this war, pledged to a restoration of the Polish state. A Polish government in exile is in existence with Wladyslaw Raczkiewicz as its president and General Sikorski as its premier."

Contacts with specifically Polish organizations or Polish political issues did not cease, as a few dates will make clear. On November 10, 1940, I spoke at a Hamilton Polish Church (Barton at St. Anne's) at a banquet in aid of a drive for funds for a Spitfire plane for Polish airmen in England. On November 17, 1940, I spoke at a Polish Veterans' meeting in the Playhouse Theatre, commemorating the uprising of 1863. September 20, 1941, found me at a banquet of the Federation of Polish Societies in Toronto. My diary for December 20, 1941, records my taking relief parcels to a Polish mission in Hamilton. On May 3, 1943, I gave a radio address over station CHML as part of a half-hour Polish programme. In September 1943, I threw in my two cents worth towards the formation of a United Polish-Canadian Council—combining the Associated Poles of Canada, the Federation of Polish Societies, and the Polish Alliance. The result was the Canadian Polish Congress.

On May 2, 1944, I spoke again for Poland over CHML. In June 1944, a United Polish Relief Fund was organized in Ottawa, with my old friends Lawrence Burpee and Peter Taraska as national chairman and national secretary respectively and with myself on the national executive. On June 24, 1944, *Saturday Night*, Toronto, printed my rebuttal of a particularly vicious slander on Poland by one David D. Gatley-Philip. In late August, I joined with Lawrence Burpee in a strong protest against the inhuman Nazi treatment of Polish women and children at Pruszow Camp, near Warsaw. On September 4, 1944, I was present at a Polish banquet at the Royal York Hotel, Toronto. On the afternoon of Sunday, October 1, 1944, with the fate of Warsaw at Nazi hands a grim specimen of Soviet perfidy, the Polish Veterans' Branch of the Canadian Legion held a memorial service at the Hamilton cenotaph. I was the speaker of the occasion and did not pull my punches:

> Make no mistake. The fate of Poland will be a test case for all Europe. If Premier Mikolajchyk's generous offers of settlement are accepted and a truly independent Poland reemerges, then there is hope that this war with its infinite bloodshed has not been fought in vain. Instead of gloating with rhapsodies of fatuous optimism over all that Stalin does, the public and

press of the free nations should be outspoken in their advocacy of the principle of human freedom.

On February 23, 1945, the *Evening Telegram*, Toronto, published a long heavily documented article of mine entitled "The Crucifixion of Poland." There I gave an unvarnished story of Communist infamy:

> It is time that Canadians took a steady look at the grim sight and realized the full horror of the wholesale rape, spoliation, murder and slavery inflicted on a brave and once independent nation by a gigantic and brutal "ally." This is the country on whose behalf we went to war in 1939 while Stalin slept in the same political bed with Hitler. Today a Soviet citizen and Comintern conspirator, Bierut, is president of Poland by the grace of Russian bayonets and the Soviet political police are murdering all effective opponents by the tens of thousands.

A sequel to this frankness soon followed. Our government had insisted that all of the nationality groups in the Canadian United Allied Relief Fund must include the Communists—who had recently emerged from Canadian concentration camps or from hiding. Because of my major part in organizing the Hamilton Committee of the United Polish Relief, both Polish and Anglo-Saxon, the Committee had appointed me its honorary chairman. On March 13, 1944, however, I sent the following day-letter to Lawrence Burpee, the national chairman in Ottawa:

> All organizations United Polish Relief Committee two weeks ago ratified officers. Leftist minority after pep talk from visiting Morski now threatens to withdraw unless Kirkconnell honorary chairman dropped. Boast Ottawa will recognize them as sole agents. Majority refuse on principle to accept Leftist dictation. Please advise.

With the close of the war it became increasingly obvious that Roosevelt and Churchill had sold the Poles down the river. My surviving friends in Poland, like my surviving friends in Hungary, had been the victims of Communist brutality and of Western folly in high places.

Typical of my friendly relations with Canadian Jewry in the 1930's and early 1940's were such episodes as my being invited as a special speaker ("Historical Reasons for Jewish Survival") at the Bar Mitzvah festivities of an attractive young lad in Winnipeg and my preaching on invitation in a Hamilton synagogue, where, on the suggestion of George Gilmour, I wore my academic gown, hood, and cap as the proper raiment for an officiating Gentile. I had also been closely associated with Rabbi Solomon Frank (later of Montreal) and Sam Freedman (later to be a judge and university chancellor) as fellow officers in the League of Nations Society.

While still in Winnipeg, and on the invitation of the co-chairmen,

Claris Silcox and Rabbi Maurice Eisendrath, I joined the Board of the Committee on Jewish-Gentile Relationships, with headquarters in Toronto. In the fall of 1940 this became the Canadian Conference of Christians and Jews and in 1947 the Canadian Council of Christians and Jews. Throughout its various metamorphoses, I have served on its Board for nearly 30 years and have spoken under its auspices during "Brotherhood Week" both in Canada and as far afield as Washington, D.C., where in 1951 I spoke in a symposium with Lowell Thomas on "Education for World Brotherhood." For nearly the same length of time I have subscribed to the Jewish owned and operated *New Leader* in New York, and have annually contributed extra cash towards its operating deficits, either directly or through the S. M. Levitas Memorial Fund.

In March 1941, while I was working on my pamphlet, *Canadians All*, for the Wartime Information Board, I gave Oscar Cohen and the Canadian Jewish Congress a chance to vet my section on the contribution of the Jewish-Canadians. My one plea was that he should not try to inflate my text, since, in my effort to be generous to the Jews, I had given them more inches than any other group in Canada, including the French, the English, or the Scots. In June 1943, while I was chairman of the Writers' War Committee for Canada, I wrote and distributed to both Jewish and Gentile publications a long poem entitled "The Agony of Israel." It lamented the Jewish martyrdom in Europe and deplored the unwillingness of North Americans to accept Jewish refugees. Two letters, out of many in that year, touched me deeply. One was from Mrs. Florence Friedlander Cohen, editor of the *Canadian Jewish Review*, Montreal, who said in part: "Men like you who act under inner compulsion to bear witness to the truth wherever found make us feel befriended and I want to thank you for your kindness." The other letter came from Private S. H. Abramson, U.S. Army, "Somewhere in North Africa," who said: "I know how infinitely helpful you were during the time I was with the Jewish Congress Office in Toronto, how we valued your sound counsel and advice. This moving poem is but another manifestation of your deep concern and sympathy for the innocent victims of a cruel martyrdom." In May 1945, I published in *Saturday Night* a letter protesting the persecution of believing Jews in the Soviet Union.

There was a brief period in which my record of goodwill towards the Jewish-Canadians was maligned by a campaign of character assassination. In an address to the Canadian Club of Toronto in February 1943, I had analysed the composition of the Communist party of Canada, nationality by nationality, and indicated that one of these fractions was Jewish. In my *Seven Pillars of Freedom*, in 1944, I spelled the analysis out in full, with the names of party leaders and party publications in each nationality group, *based on the party's own records*. That there should be an outcry from the Jewish Communists themselves was only to be expected, for with the USSR now in the war they were working busily to build themselves a radiant public image as honest and loyal Canadians, and every Communist paper in Canada raised a hue and cry against me, each in its own language (see Chapter XXVII). I had not been prepared, however, to find the bloodhounds of the Anti-Defamation League baying down my trail, as they now did. It almost seemed that to label *any* political leftist as a Jew was the unpardonable sin, and that my advice to the Jewish community to repudiate its Stalinists, as all the other ethnic groups had done, was the ultimate insult.

Back in 1940, Louis Rosenberg, executive director of the Canadian Jewish Congress, Western Division, had printed in the *Israelite Press* a long panegyric on me as "unique in Canadian life." "Watson Kirkconnell," he said, "has gone out to meet us more than half way, and when he ceases to be an isolated phenomenon and becomes one of many there will be greater hope for mutual understanding in Canada." I now wrote to him (June 6, 1943) for enlightenment: "It was with surprise approaching incredulity that I heard recently from Winnipeg friends that some of the Jewish community regarded my speech to the Canadian Club of Toronto last February as savouring of anti-Semitism. . . ." Mr. Rosenberg reaffirmed his confidence in me, but the smear campaign in the community went on for years to come. The final vindication of my political wisdom doubtless came in 1957, when even the Canadian Communists' Jewish political arm, the United Jewish People's Order, publicly dissociated itself from the Labour Progressive party.

My friendship with the Poles kept the Canadian Ukrainians at a distance until they gradually learned, through their authors, that my primary loyalties were Canadian and that I was not the unreserved champion of any of the nationality programmes in Europe. After I had included my translations of seventeen Ukrainian-Canadian poets in my *Canadian Overtones* and had given an evening lecture on Ukrainian literature at the University of Manitoba, I was finally accepted as a friend and was invited to community dinners at the Institute Prosvita, where Dr. Hunter of Teulon and I ate borstch, holuptsi, perishky, and pampushky and listened to midnight flights of Ukrainian oratory.

In reviewing Ukrainian language books for the *University of Toronto Quarterly*, year after year from 1935 to 1965, I dealt with nearly one thousand volumes by scores of Ukrainian-Canadian authors. I also wrote the article on modern Ukrainian literature for the *Columbia Dictionary of Modern European Literature* (Columbia University, New York) and the article on "Ukrainians in Canada" for the *Slavonic Encyclopaedia.*

It was World War II that pushed me into close non-literary relationships with the Ukrainian-Canadians. This largest of all our Slavic communities had been split into several mutually antagonistic groups by Old World differences in faith (Catholic and Orthodox) and politics (hetmanite, republican, socialist, and Communist). The Communists, in 1939–40, were already in league with the Hitler–Stalin alliance, but how could the other five Kilkenny cats be induced to purr in unison for the sake of Canada? My *Canada, Europe and Hitler* (1939) had already made an analysis of the entire foreign-language press, including the Ukrainian. In January 1940, I published in the *Winnipeg Tribune* a series of articles on "War Aims and Canadian Unity," pleading for unity among New-Canadian groups and for a federal statement of war aims that would give coherence to that unity. The Prime Minister, Mr. Mackenzie King, who usually worked by indirection, then asked me through a personal emissary, Leonard Brockington, to write a substantial pamphlet on *The Ukrainian-Canadians and the War*, seeking to expound the issues of the conflict as I saw them and to emphasize the urgency of Ukrainian-Canadian unity. This was made a rush job and was issued before the end of April, 1940, by the Oxford University Press, as one of the "Oxford Pamphlets on World Affairs." It did not mince words in my advocacy of community integration in wartime:

> Canada is the one Allied country with a large Ukrainian population, and the opinion of the Canadian government regarding the Ukrainian Canadians is likely to have an important influence on the policies of the Allies. If these Slavic citizens of Canada show obvious appreciation of liberty and democracy here, and a willingness to co-operate in maintaining Canadian unity in a time of great national stress, it will all be counted to them for righteousness when they plead the cause of their European kinfolk. If on the other hand they remain hopelessly disrupted by political dissension and if the chief characteristic of their nationalism seems to be hatred for other national groups, then they will do a fatal disservice to the cause they seek to serve, for they will persuade the Canadian nation that Ukrainians have not yet reached political maturity.

Joe Thorson and I had meanwhile shared in a rapprochement between the Brotherhood of Ukrainian Catholics and the Ukrainian National Federation as a "Representative Committee of Ukrainian Canadians," while with Professor George Simpson as their adviser the Self-Reliance League, the Hetman party, and the League of Ukrainian Organizations had formed a rival "Central Representative Ukrainian Committee of Canada." These two mergers remained irreconcilably aloof from each other until November 1940, when at a conference in Winnipeg and through the wise counsels of Messrs. Tracy Philipps, Edgar Tarr, Victor Sifton, and George Simpson an all-inclusive "Ukrainian Canadian Committee" was agreed upon. The Communists at this time were still in alliance with the Nazis; the Ukrainian Communist organizations had been declared illegal in June 1940; and their leaders had either gone underground or had been arrested as active enemies of Canada. All loyal Ukrainians were involved in the Ukrainian Committee and their war record was a distinguished one. Its officers were: Reverend Dr. W. Kushnir, president; Very Reverend S. W. Sawchuk and W. Kossar, vice-presidents; J. W. Arsenych, secretary; A. J. Yaremovich, executive secretary; A. Malofie, treasurer; and S. Chwaliboga, financial secretary.

By December 1940, I was sharing in the formation of a "Nationalities Branch" in Ottawa. When the government offered me the post as its first director, my refusal was voiced in terms of academic responsibilities at McMaster. An even greater ground for saying no was that as a civil servant such a director would be completely gagged and could neither speak nor write on public affairs. I foresaw that I could probably guard the rights and welfare of New Canadians much better as a free agent. Relevant occasions came in due course.

On June 22, 1941, Hitler double-crossed his Soviet friends and invaded the Soviet Union. Tim Buck, Canada's Communist leader, then in hiding, issued a four-page manifesto calling for an immediate Communist revolution in Canada and the setting up of a Canadian Soviet republic. The advent of a Soviet embassy in Ottawa soon played an active part in a great propaganda ballet. Canadian Communist beetles came boldly out from under chips in all directions and their press attacked the loyal majority in every New Canadian community as "fascists." It needs to be emphasized that it was Communist onslaughts on these well-loved Canadian communities that turned me more and more into a vocal critic of the Left. I was not an addled-brained hound baying at the moon but an anxious sheepdog trying to protect the sheep of these folds from attacks by conspiratorial wolves and from betrayal by naïve politicians. Both threats were very real. More and more political leaders and high civil servants were being softened up in the spirit of the times. Respectable clergymen, judges, and journalists gladly stood sponsor for crypto-traitors seeking citizenship or demanding the return of revolutionary halls, and a giant pro-Soviet rally was held in Toronto on June 22, 1943, with Mr. Mackenzie King himself in the chair.

That very day, therefore, in the city of Winnipeg, I delivered a carefully documented 2½-hour address before the First All-Canada Congress held under the auspices of the Ukrainian-Canadian Committee. This organization had been particularly under fire and I denounced the aims of the Communist faction in no uncertain terms:

They want to make the Ukrainian Canadians a political closed shop with the Communists as sole bargaining agents. Judas, instead of committing suicide, wants to be made sole spokesman for the Apostles. Their campaign is an insult even to the hard-boiled Ottawa politician; for why any serious campaigner would want to rely on 20,000 yelping members of a seditious organization rather than on 300,000 loyal citizens (all bitter enemies of the aforesaid 20,000) is a problem in psychiatry. But the question is not merely one for the electioneer. It is a matter of the common decencies of political life. For to have politicians or civil servants dream of smiling on the sons of sedition while cold-shouldering the overwhelming majority of a loyal community would be a disgrace to any nation.

During the next three years the National Council for Canadian-Soviet Friendship rapidly disintegrated through its own intrinsic dishonesty, and in 1945–46 the evil heritage of Teheran and Yalta was being grimly implemented by the Allies in the railroading of Ukrainian and Baltic refugees home for liquidation by an implacable Stalin. On February 9, 1946, I published an article, "The Ukrainian Agony," in the Toronto *Telegram*, documenting and denouncing this appalling wickedness. On March 31, 1946, I spoke in Massey Hall at the Second Congress of the Ukrainian Canadian Committee. In this address, "National Minorities in the U.S.S.R.," I expounded the cruel falsity of the Kremlin's programme of cultural encouragement for a national area like Ukraine:

But there was manure in the bottom of the cultural milk pail. The Communists insisted that all culture and education should follow their Party line and become mere crude instruments of propaganda. Non-Communist scholars, like Vsevolod Holubovich and Michael Hrushevsky, who were lured home by promises of cultural freedom, were presently shot or imprisoned. Literature was rigorously scrutinized for evidences of political heresy, and those who showed signs of developing a Ukrainian culture, as distinct from a Marx-Leninist one, were promptly liquidated.

I also told of the Kremlin's liquidation of five "autonomous" Soviet republics in wartime, the extermination of Russian Jews *qua* Jews, and of course the post-war liquidation of Ukrainian refugees—with Allied connivance. Two outspoken articles that I wrote on subsequent developments appeared in the *Ukrainian Quarterly*, New York, as "Integrity in Foreign Policy" in 1956 and "The Shevchenko Centenary" in 1961.

Meanwhile my contacts with Ukrainian scholarship had become increasingly intimate. Back in the nineteenth century, when the tsars were suppressing all national culture in Ukraine, a sort of academy in exile, the Shevchenko Scientific Society, was set up in the city of Lemberg (Lwów, Lviv), in what was then the Austrian province of Galicia. Following World War I, a large group of Ukrainian professors who had escaped from the Red terror set up a "Ukrainian Free University" in Prague. At the close of World War II, when Communist conquest flowed still further west and engulfed both Poland and Czechoslovakia, the fugitive scholars of Lemberg and Prague, together with new academic refugees from the Ukraine itself, moved the Shevchenko Society and the Free University to the Bavarian city of Munich. A large group of them came subsequently to Canada, where they established a branch of the Shevchenko Society in Toronto and a "Ukrainian Free Academy of Sciences" in Winnipeg. I am an honorary member of the former and an active member of the latter (philological section), contributing three monographs to its series of publications under the general editorship of Dr. Jaroslav B. Rudnyckyj of the University of Manitoba. I have also been given an honorary doctorate by the Ukrainian Free University, in Munich.

In Chapter VI, I have told in detail the story of my most massive single undertaking in translation from any language, *The Ukrainian Poets, 1189–1962* (Toronto, 1963, pp. xxx, 500) and *The Poetical Works of Taras Shevchenko* (Toronto, 1964, pp. li, 563), both done in collaboration with Dr. C. H. Andrusyshen, FRSC, of the University of Saskatchewan. A sequel was my invitation to Washington, D.C., on May 22, 1965, where I recorded a broadcast interview for the Voice of America to beam to Ukraine, addressed a luncheon meeting of the Centennial Committee, gave the main address at an afternoon celebration at the Shevchenko Monument, and read an original 92-line poem at a commemoratory banquet that evening at the Mayflower Hotel. The following couplets are part of my tribute to what Shevchenko achieved for the Ukrainian nation:

> He took his people's speech, a thing abhorred,
> And forged its metal to a flaming sword;
> He took his people's visions of desire
> And raised them up, a pillar of white fire;
> He took their history, by foes ploughed under,
> And made its annals march with steps of thunder. . . .

While I had a fleeting trip through the little Baltic states in 1938 and had syndicated my resulting travel articles in six Canadian dailies, it was the murder of their national life by Stalin in 1940 that at last engaged my emotions deeply. My detailed correspondence with the Latvian Legation in Washington, D.C., began in 1944, while a Lithuanian official, Colonel K. V. Grinius, and the Lithuanian Information Centre supplied me with scores of photostats of NKVD documents, all marked "Sev. sekretno." From the very beginning of its publication in 1946, I subscribed to the *Newsletter from Behind the Iron Curtain*, published by the Estonian Information Centre in Stockholm, Sweden. A typical diary entry thereafter is my address to the Lithuanians of Toronto when a public meeting commemorating their nation's Independence Day was held by the Lithuanian League of Canada and other organizations. On February 16, 1946, the *Evening Telegram*, Toronto, published my full-scale article, "Eclipse of Baltic Freedom"; the next year saw my "Pattern for Extermination" in the *Revue de l'Université d'Ottawa* and my "Blanket of the Dark" in the *Baltic Review*, Stockholm, Sweden, and in 1948 my "Lithuanian Tragedy" appeared in *Plain Talk*, New York.

The escape of many Baltic refugees to Canada has done much to enrich Canadian life. For example, I have been exceedingly glad to welcome Professor and Mrs. Janis Kalejs, violinist and pianist of the Latvian Academy of Music, to teaching posts in Acadia University's School of Music.

On June 17, 1958, the Estonian National Council, the Free Estonian government-in-exile, graciously elected me an honorary member for my "active part in the fight against Communism," my "friendly and helpful attitude and co-operation with New-Canadians," and my "outstanding contribution to the democratic way of life in Canada."

I had translated Czech and Slovak poems in my *European Elegies*, in my *Outline of European Poetry*, and especially in my contributions to Clarence A. Manning's *Anthology of Czechoslovak Poetry* (Columbia University Press, 1929). I had visited the country in 1922 and 1938 and maintained friendly correspondence with such scholars as the Czech historian O. Odložalik and the Slovak lexicographer Miroslav Kalál. Both Czechs and Slovaks appeared in my *Canadians All* (1941) and I had checked my data with the Czechoslovak National Alliance (Karel Buzek, secretary). Early in the war, I was made an honorary member of the Publications Committee of the Canadian Friends of Czecho-slovakia Inc. On March 9, 1941, I attended a public meeting staged by the Czechoslovak National Alliance in the Hamilton Labour Temple. That same year I helped to receive the members of a Czechoslovak military mission, headed by Colonel Čeněk Hutnik, in the interests of a Free Czechoslovak army and the provisional government-in-exile under Dr. Edvard Benesh. It was about this time that I was publicly presented with a handsome gold medal struck by this régime. On the reverse side appears the Czechoslovak coat of arms, with the marginal superscription "Republika Československa, March 15, 1939." On the observe is the powerful figure of a man, with his arms outstretched and chained to two swastikaed and behelmeted posts, each coiled around by an angry snake. Beside him stands his wife, with a babe in her arms. A young son clasps his waist in grief. Behind him is the Charles Bridge and above him the old citadel of Prague. The platform on which he stands bears the message: "Czechoslovakia shall be free again."

By 1945, the Benesh régime was blindly trusting in the promises of the USSR (and was in due course to meet with inevitable betrayal), but the Canadian Slovak League, horrified at the wholesale rape and murder inflicted on Slovakia by Soviet troops, was protesting frantically against the tyranny of a small Communist minority over its homeland. My chief contact with their Canadian community was through the Reverend John Zeman, OSB.

"The time would fail me to tell of Gedeon and of Barak" . . . and of Greeks, Armenians, Italians, Serbs, Croatians, Byelorussians, and still others with whom I have had literary, personal, or political contacts. To all of these I have stood for a Canadianism that would preserve and integrate its folk legacies in a wider and richer national culture. In the Preface to my *Canadian Overtones*, published over thirty years ago, I wrote out my philosophy of the multicultural state in categorical terms:

> There is nothing so shallow and sterile as the man who denies his own ancestry. The "100%" American or Canadian is commonly one who has deliberately suppressed an alien origin in order to reap the material benefits of a well-advertised loyalty. There can be little hope of noble spiritual issues from such a prostituted patriotism. Unfortunately, it is abetted by the ignorant assumption of many an English-speaking citizen that alien origin is a natural mark of inferiority. He who thinks thus is a mental hooligan—whether he be a lawyer, a militia colonel, or a bishop of the church. What we sorely need, on the contrary, is enough common intelligence to recognize both the rich diversity of racial gifts on this earth and the strength that racial roots can contribute to the individual.
>
> We do not think less of the Scot in Canada because of his proud wistfulness towards the land of his origin. . . . As a Canadian he is not poorer but richer because he realizes his place in a noble stream of human relationships down through the centuries. His sense of the family, the clan, and the race can scarcely fail to vitalize the quality of his citizenship. He grows greater than himself by virtue of his conscious pride in the past and his determination to be worthy of it.
>
> Prophetic hopes would envisage a future Canada in which every individual would be thus inspired to fuller citizenship by his realization of his origin, whatever that might be. . . . That they should be speedily integrated into loyal co-operation with our general Canadian population is, of course, of supreme national importance. But it would be tragic if there should at the same time be a clumsy stripping-away of all those spiritual associations with the past that help to give depth and beauty to life. . . .
>
> Canada has not yet achieved any such spiritual integration as has brought Celt, Angle, Saxon, Dane, Norseman, Norman and Fleming to a unified consciousness in England, and we must realize that the integration to which we ultimately attain will be very different from that of England. If, however, we accept with Wilhelm von Humboldt "the absolute and essential importance of human development in its richest diversity," then we shall welcome every opportunity to save for our country every precious element of individuality that is available.

The fact on which I should like to close is the rapidly developing reality of the Canadian amalgam for which I desire to preserve these qualities of diversity in unity. Perhaps even more successfully than in the United States, where the census keeps no record of ethnic origins and the sociological ideal is the "melting pot," we have nevertheless succeeded in blending all strains into a single community.

The Ukrainians are a typical example. The pioneer generation, sixty years ago, began in sod huts on the prairie and endured intense privation in laying the foundations of a viable economy. Their children, surging upwards through our Canadian schools and colleges, learned the language and ways of their new homeland. The third generation is almost indistinguishably Canadian. Hundreds of them began a professional career as elementary school teachers but presently spread out into all the professions—as lawyers, physicians, dentists, engineers, architects, entomologists, geologists, biologists, chemists, home economists, librarians, druggists, veterinarians, and clergymen. They have their composers, painters, sculptors, and skilled musicians. They have taken their place in every phase of commercial and industrial life. They have played an honourable part in municipal, provincial, and federal politics. They have occupied professorial posts in almost all our universities and have carried their full weight in research, both academic and industrial. Since about 1946, the Canadian-born generations have been reinforced by a European-trained intelligentsia, a refugee remnant saved from the maelstrom of war and the NKVD dragnet of forced repatriation. If by some sinister magic one were suddenly to remove all Ukrainian-Canadians from the life of many Canadian communities, their economics would stagger and falter, and the same essential participation is true of most of the other European-Canadian elements in our population. It is the fact that they have entered so fully and enthusiastically into our national life that renders so important any effort to maintain the tinctures of their several traditions in the fabric of our national culture.

21

Les Canadiens

I THINK IT WAS Elizabeth Parker, "the Bookman" of the *Winnipeg Free Press*, who nearly forty years ago wrote of me as "the Apostle of Good Will to the Gentiles," meaning of course the ethnic groups. A few years later, Lorne Pierce pasted another label on me: "Proconsul for the Minorities." Much as I appreciated these friendly honorifics, I was a bit distressed in 1964–65 to find myself cited before the Royal Commission on Bilingualism and Biculturalism as a partisan in a multicultural counter-attack against the assumptions constantly made that there were only two "races"—the French and the English—worthy of Canadian consideration. I certainly supported the claim of the New Canadians to their own places in the national sun—I had devoted much of my life to that affirmation—but I did not want to be placed on the record as thereby hostile to my still older friends, the Canadian French.

Study of the French language had begun in my first year of high school, but without any opportunity for conversation. Hence I was dismayed, while visiting with Allison relatives near St. Eugène in 1913, to hear my cousin Willie Logan Allison engage in rapid-fire dialogue with a French neighbour and to realize that I couldn't make out a word of it. Hence it came about that as an undergraduate at Queen's in 1913–16 I arranged with Alphonse Hébert, a French engineer at the Kingston Locomotive Works, to come to my rooming house an hour a week for conversation, part time in French only and part time in English only. I also subscribed to the Montreal daily, *La Presse*, in order to soak myself in the language.

In 1917–19, while serving as paymaster of Kapuskasing Camp, I had seen the devoted toil of the French-Canadian pioneers who were surviving incredible hardships in that part of Ontario, and I had also witnessed a heavily subsidized Kapuskasing settlement of Anglo-Canadian veterans who folded up and returned to Toronto within two years.

This first-hand acquaintance with the area led me, nearly twenty years later, to lock horns publicly with a Protestant "research committee" in its legalistic version of the French in Ontario. In a lengthy letter in *Saturday Night* in February 1947, I listed some aspects of the problem that the committee had overlooked:

It should also have noted that the French population of Ontario had increased from almost nil in 1863 to approximately 430,000 today, thereby certainly creating "a new condition in Ontario" and a group not lightly to be denationalized by the stroke of a Protestant pen; that large numbers of Anglo-Saxons have failed as colonists in the subarctic Clay Belt (as witness the million-dollar settlement fiasco in the Kapuskasing area, liquidated in 1920); that the "Canadiens" by dogged endurance have succeeded in the same area and have risen in numbers in the Cochrane District to 32,744; that the Roman Catholics may just conceivably be sincere in regarding religion as an essential part of education; and that the provision of French schools and Catholic churches for this growing population, presented in the brief (pp. 29–31) as a long term conspiracy, need not bear that construction at all but might even receive their commendation as wise pastoral oversight if the beneficiaries were a growing English Protestant settlement in Northern Quebec. . . . Instead of being grateful to these French Catholics for opening up marginal country that many others will not tackle, the Protestant brief would penalize them. . . .

As I wrote that letter of protest, I could see again the interior of a French settler's shack near Kapuskasing one summer evening in 1918. I had gone with our camp medical officer and watched the settler's little daughter slowly dying of tuberculosis of the spine, brought on by exposure and privation. Thus I had seen a tiny instalment of the price that was being paid by these brothers and sisters of Maria Chapdelaine in their conquest of the wilderness.

When in 1936 I was elected a Fellow of the Royal Society of Canada, I found it a stimulating fraternity of scholars and scientists. While most of my contacts were in Section II (humanities and social sciences in English), there was a good deal of friendly fellowship with the members of Section I (humanities and social sciences in French), and ultimately attempts were made to have at least some sessions that were freely and spontaneously bilingual. Among those whom I came to know in this cultural interchange were the Greek scholars, Emile Chartier and Maurice Lebel; the historians, Gustave Lanctôt, Lionel Groulx, and Olivier Maurault; the ethnologist, Marius Barbeau; the archivist, Arthur Maheux; the French scholar, Séraphin Marion; the mediaevalist, Louis-Marie Régis; the philosopher, Charles de Koninck; and the social scientists, Georges-Henri Lévesque and Arthur Saint-Pierre.

Comparable experience, based on shared administrative problems rather than on the enthusiasms of erudition, came with my sixteen years (1948–64) as a university president in the NCCU (see Chapter X). On several occasions I heard valiant attempts at bilingualism at these sessions. I was ready to give George Gilmour high marks for a diglott postprandial oration at Duchesnay, but have to record that for sheer brilliance in both English and French Father Légaré, rector of the University of Ottawa, was in a class by himself. This *magister utriusque linguae* could travel in high gear in either tongue and could shift gears from one to the other without batting an eyelash. It was a joy to see him in action.

In 1944, a survey of the humanities in Canadian universities began under my chairmanship (see Chapter XV). The fact-finding team that visited French colleges and universities in Ontario and Quebec consisted of Maurice Lebel (professor of Greek in the Faculty of Letters, Laval University) and myself. Laval, Montreal, and Ottawa were our main concern. Of the eighty or so *collèges classiques* whose four final years constitute the Arts Faculty of Laval and Montreal we chose only a representative sample—Collège Bourget, Collège de Montréal, Collège de Saint-Laurent, Collège Sainte-Marie, Collège Jean-de-Brébeuf, Externat André-Grasset, Collège Stanislas (the Canadian branch of a Paris *lycée*), Séminaire de Joliette, Collège de Sillery, and Séminaire de Québec. Our perambulations were done at intervals in the spring term of 1945. We pried into curricula, professorial training, faculty research, libraries, classrooms, music, fine arts, and drama. I was responsible for the two chapters, V and VI, in *The Humanities in Canada* (1947), in which the French tradition was analysed in great detail, but I leaned very heavily on the expert knowledge of Lebel.

Unexpected aspects of the classical colleges were encountered. Thus we found that the Collège de Saint-Laurent, in a Montreal suburb, had built a large private theatre, seating 1500. The stage was immense and was fitted out with the best modern machinery and lighting equipment. The Séminaire de Joliette had a distinguished painter, Wilfrid Corbeil, as its director of studies, and one of the country's chief playwrights, G. Lamarche (trained in Europe, the author of twenty plays) as its drama coach. In the Quebec region, weekly courses in the appreciation of music were compulsory in all classes in all colleges. Statistically considered, language study was astonishing in an age when most Anglo-Canadian students take only one foreign language and most American students take none at all. In the academic year 1943–44 there were over 12,000 students in the *collèges classiques* of Quebec enrolled for at least four years of Greek and six years each of Latin, French, and

English. The pedagogy, however, seemed hard and brittle—more concerned with the accurate use of the four compulsory languages than with any illumination from imaginative literature.

The University of Montreal had just moved into imposing new quarters on the northwest slopes of Mount Royal while Laval was straitjacketed in obsolete buildings in the Upper Town of Quebec City—but would be transferred in the 1960's to a new *cité universitaire* (one square mile) in the western outskirts. At the University of Montreal, where Lebel and I called on Canon Lionel Groulx in his office, the fiery old historian, aged 67, introduced us to a handsome young scholar, Dr. Guy Frégault. "J'ai choisi mon successeur!" said Groulx, with obvious pride. Alas for departmental dynasty-building! Twenty years later, Dr. Frégault was in the Department of Government at Laval.

On June 2, 1945, I was offered an honorary doctorate in laws by the University of Ottawa. On June 8, a private letter from a member of the university senate passed along the grounds for the award: "The Senate of the University was unanimous when your name came up for the LL.D. We seized this occasion to express to you our profound appreciation of your good work in defending the Christian way of life." The convocation was held in the university gymnasium on Sunday evening, June 17. Honoured along with me were General George P. Vanier (then ambassador to France), Ernest C. Desormeaux, and Rev. Father William J. Kelley. The rector, Very Rev. Philippe Cornellier, presided and read the citations, while the degrees were conferred by the Most Rev. Alexandre Vachon, Archbishop of Ottawa.

Since the university was officially bilingual, I made my statutory address in both French and English. A few extracts will indicate my general theme:

> We have won a crushing victory over an evil enemy; and yet the very soberness with which we greet that event shows that we are still in danger of losing everything. In a dozen European countries today, Christian civilization is being systematically exterminated by the hangman and the firing-squad. . . . Who like the universities should wield the Sword of the Spirit against the false ideas and ideals of a darkening world? *Quis pro Domino*?

Mention is made in Chapter XXIII of an anthology of French-Canadian prose and verse, selected by Dr. Séraphin Marion (professor of French-Canadian literature in the University of Ottawa, honorary secretary of the Royal Society of Canada, director of publications for the Public Archives of Canada, and chairman of the French section of my Writers' War Committee) and translated by myself. Thanks to the sympathetic interest of Canon Arthur Sideleau, dean of letters in the University of Montreal, it was published in 1946 in his faculty's "Collection Humanitas" as *The Quebec Tradition (Tradition du Québec)*. While the anthology proper was completely bilingual, with my English version on the right-hand pages facing their French originals on the left-hand pages, each of the two editors wrote his own preface. That of Dr. Marion gives me credit for the planning of the work:

> Toutefois peu connaissent aussi bien notre mentalité et nos traditions que M. Watson Kirkconnell. Intelligent guetteur au créneau de la patrie, l'éminent professeur de l'Université McMaster apprécie à sa juste valeur notre rôle dans la sauvegarde de la civilisation chrétienne en Amerique du Nord. Aussi bien ai-je été singulièrement honoré lorsque mon actif confrère, désireux de révéler à ses compatriotes de langue anglaise le vrai visage du Canada français, me pria de lui prêter une modeste collaboration pour combler, dans notre pays, une lacune manifeste. . . .

My own foreword seeks to clarify the purpose of the volume still further:

> The present small volume . . . does not seek to make propaganda for that French tradition, but simply to make it intelligible to Anglo-Canadians who may not have realized its historic origin, its passionate loyalties, its sense of mission. Some readers may quarrel with certain aspects of that tradition; but until they understand it, they are not even competent to argue about it. Out of comprehension, however, there may come better relations. The Anglo-Canadian may grow to realize that his French compatriot is not an alien, with un-Canadian loyalties, but a member of a deeply self-conscious and enduring Canadian culture-group, numbering three and a half millions, whose character has been moulded by a struggle of nearly two centuries to maintain its identity on a continent that is overwhelmingly English-speaking. . . . He will realize how far from simple is the problem of integrating so intense and dynamically emotional a tradition into the free federal structure of a democratic Canada. Mutual understanding may, as in marriage, result in a happier measure of harmony. To that end this book is dedicated.

The Quebec Tradition was dedicated to "Our Canada," and I appended a relevant quotation from the panegyric of Rutilius to Rome: Fecisti patriam diversis gentibus unam ("You made one fatherland out of diverse peoples").

The division of the subject-matter was sixfold: La grande patrie, la petite patrie, ancestors, nature in Canada, French language and race, religion. While selections in prose and verse, went back as far as Nerée Beauchemin, François-Xavier Garneau, and Sir Wilfrid Laurier, the majority of those represented were men still living, including many of our fellow members in the Royal Society of Canada: Camille Roy, Lionel Groulx, Gustave Lanctôt, Olivier Maurault, Edouard Montpetit, Arthur Maheux, Georges Bouchard, Albert Ferland, Sir Thomas Chapais, Louis-Adolphe Paquet, and Adjutor Rivard. The separatism and bomb-throwing of the 1960's were still unknown to the generation of 1946, and although the fervour of the French-Canadian patriot was great, there was no tendency to question the permanent fact of Confederation. Terrorist refugees from French Algeria had not yet brought *la peste* to our shores.

July 1946 found me teaching a graduate course on Milton at the Laval University Summer School. Classes were held in the Faculty of Letters, but I boarded at the French home of Mme Aline Fontaine, 57 avenue Thornhill. For twelve years I had been doing research on the analogues of *Paradise Lost* and now set my two dozen students, most of them priests and nuns in French teaching orders, burrowing into assigned passages in Basil, Aquinas, Ambrose, Augustine, Bonaventure, Abelard, Origen, and many others, looking for indications as to the background of Milton's thought and language. They emerged with a wholesome respect for the erudition of the Protestant poet, for they could track him everywhere in the snow of the Fathers.

The year 1955 brought the bicentennial of the expulsion of the Acadian population from Nova Scotia—and it seemed inevitable that Acadia University (which had borrowed the name of the dispersed settlers, stood only three miles from the site of old Grand Pré, and was actually on the edge of "the Big Meadow") should not go untouched by the anniversary celebrations. I have told elsewhere (see Chapter XIII) of my conferring honorary degrees on two Acadians, Judge Vincent Pottier and Dr. Flavien Melançon, on August 16. The great day of festivities, however, was Monday, August 15. By arrangement with the University, an open air lunch was held on our lawn (following a pontifical high mass at Grand Pré park) and a regal banquet for eight hundred was scheduled for 6.00 P.M. in the university dining-hall. For a rental fee, our facilities and staff were to be used, but the bicentennial committee imported its own chef and dietitian. At the time that the arrangements were made, I explained that the non-alcoholic tradition of the University and its sponsors would have to require a "dry" dinner. Somehow this directive never filtered down to the chef, and I discovered, on receiving a printed menu about four days before the event, that five courses of wines were being provided, with the compliments of an enterprising Ontario winery. As it was too late to print eight hundred new menus, and as I refused to surrender to a *fait accompli*, a neatly printed insert was added, explaining that out of deference to the traditions of the institution the sole beverage (other than coffee) would be Annapolis Valley apple juice.

Meanwhile I had encountered on Wolfville's main street a whole fleet of buses on which our guests had come, and each carried a large streamer: "CENTENAIRE SANS BOISSON—Société Lacordière." It became evident that this militant temperance society represented a majority among the visitors and that the wine list had been slipped in by the chef and an aggressive Ontario advertiser. When at the banquet I welcomed them all, I suggested that I had deserved a large gold medal from the Société Lacordière.

Meanwhile I had written, at Easter 1955, the libretto of a light opera, "The Mod at Grand Pré," centred about the theme of the Expulsion, and Dean E. A. Collins, of our School of Music, was spending the summer composing the musical accompaniment. The plot is outlined in Chapter VII above. When the opera was staged in March 1956, special invitations went to the French bishop of Yarmouth (an Acadian) and to the father superior of the Collège Sainte-Anne on "the French Shore." When I represented Acadia University at the College's seventy-fifth anniversary in May 1965, I was still encountering expressions of appreciation from Acadian clergy who had seen the performance. Incidentally, "The Mod at Grand Pré" won the Nova Scotia Drama League's trophy for 1956 for the best play of the year "written by a Nova Scotian."

On the evening of June 2, 1962, I found myself sitting in the front row of an auditorium on Laval University's new campus. To my right sat Roger Létourneau, a 54-year-old professor of law at the University and that year's president of the Bar of the province of Quebec; to my left was Father Martin d'Arcy, a 73-year-old Irish Jesuit, for many years Master of Campion Hall, Oxford. Professor Létourneau was to receive an honorary doctorate in laws, Father d'Arcy was to have one in divinity, and I was being awarded one in letters and was scheduled to deliver the convocation address. The contrasts that marked off the three honorary graduands were so striking that in the preamble to my discourse I took time to play about with them:

> Nous sommes un trio assez curieux, nous autres docteurs honoraires—homme de Québec, homme de la Nouvelle-Ecosse, homme de l'Irlande—professeur de loi, ancien professeur de langue latine, ancien professeur de philosophie —savant quinquagénaire, savant sexagénaire, savant septuagénaire—Canadien depuis trois siècles, Canadien depuis un siècle et demi, et Canadien pas du tout—père de trois enfants, père de cinq enfants, et Père . . . sans enfants. C'est moi, le terme moyen du trinôme honoraire, qui dois parler pour tous, et j'en suis reconnaissant.

My address was built around a prose-poem by Félix-Antoine Savard that I had translated with deep admiration in *The Quebec Tradition*. A few of my convocation sentences will indicate my general rhetorical plan:

> Mais je voudrais ce soir rendre mes hommages à un des votres qui restera toujours, selon moi, parmi les âmes les plus profondes et les poètes les plus éminents du Canada. C'est monseigneur Félix-Antoine Savard dont je parle. Je ne puis jamais oublier un de ses poèmes les plus beaux, poème en prose mais en prose d'un véritable archange. Il s'appelle *Les oies sauvages* et nous décrit le vol de printemps au nord, de ces oiseaux canadiens d'un titre vrai. . . . Si j'osais donner un conseil aux jeunes gens qui vont sortir de cette université pour entrer dans la vie, je voudrais leur présenter cette vision lavalloise des oies sauvages, vision d'une foi indomptable. . . . Que nous autres, pauvres créatures humaines, nous restions fidèles comme elles aux lois encore plus profondes de notre destinée spirituelle!

The four signatures on my diploma were those of my old Humanities Research Council colleague and friend, Maurice Lebel, now dean of the Faculty of Letters; Mgr. Jacques Garneau, the secretary-general, who had frequently discussed disciplinary headaches with me at the NCCU; the Very Rev. Mgr. Louis Albert Vachon, the rector magnificus, also an old friend of NCCU circles; and Cardinal Maurice Roy, the chancellor, whom I had first met at the great apple-juice dinner at Acadia in 1955.

22

The Embattled Authors

IT WAS THE PATTERN of "challenge and response," Toynbee style, that brought the Canadian Authors' Association into being. No such organization had existed during almost five peaceful decades from Canada's first Copyright Act in 1875 down through a series of small and equally equitable amendments (consolidated in chapter 70 of the *Revised Statutes of Canada 1906*) to a sudden outbreak of printing-house piracy in 1921. In the spring of that year a lobby of job-printers from the virtuous city of Toronto had successfully slipped through Canada's unsuspecting parliament a bill that would permit them to print in Canada, whether the author was willing or not, any book, already printed abroad, that was selling well in Canada. Price, format, and conditions of sale were all at the mercy of the piratical printers. They were presumed to have their eyes on the books of Stephen Leacock, from which they hoped to make a killing. Stephen and his friends therefore sent out the fiery cross for an authors' indignation meeting at the McGill University Club. As some sixty remonstrants, male and female, rallied to the fight and overflowed the quarters, the resulting conference shifted to McGill's Old Medical Building, with a dinner at the Place Viger Hotel. At first there was no thought of setting up a permanent organization, but Pelham Edgar, then of Victoria College, Toronto, pointed out that, as the fight would probably be a long one, a "Canadian Authors' Association" was imperative. The challenge of print-shop iniquity thus called into being a battalion of belligerent writers. I already had one substantial volume of history to my credit, and joined the ranks in that militant year.

It is worth noting that the five men most concerned with founding the CAA were all Fellows of Section II of the Royal Society: Leacock (the ram caught in the thicket), Edgar, Sandwell, Gibbon, and Burpee. The Royal Society is sometimes unjustly accused of doddering senility, but its Fellows have frequently proved themselves neither feeble nor senescent.

The CAA's first national president was John Murray Gibbon of Montreal, novelist, Oxford graduate (student at Christ Church, a first class in Literae Humaniores, plus postgraduate work at Göttingen in Sanskrit and Greek archaeology), and publicity manager of the Canadian Pacific Railway. So devoutly did he believe in fighting for justice that for many years—until the Board of Railway Commissioners vetoed the happy plan—he and Walter S. Thompson (his opposite number with the CNR) supplied Canadian authors with free passes to their annual convention. As his friend for over thirty years, I had the privilege of writing his obituary biography for the 1952 *Proceedings* of the Royal Society. One of his most notable characteristics was his laconicism. In speech as in correspondence, he never used two or three sentences if one would serve his purpose.

The first national secretary was B. K. Sandwell, then at McGill University but best known to a later generation as the editor of *Saturday Night*, Toronto. It was his omniscient stenographer who had concocted the invitation list for the 1921 gathering of the clans, and it was he who at many later stages of our history poured in the oil of quiet personal negotiation to solve the crises that seemed about to wreck the machinery.

The dates of the kings of England form a convenient chronological pattern for the history of the nation. In like fashion a dated list of the national presidents of the Canadian Authors' Association may serve as a framework for any sketch of the history of the group: 1921–23, Murray Gibbon, Montreal; 1923–24, Robert J. C. Stead, Ottawa; 1924–25, Lawrence Burpee, Ottawa; 1925–27, W. T. Allison, Winnipeg; 1927–29, Charles G. D. Roberts, Toronto; 1929–31, W. D. Lighthall, Montreal; 1931–33, Duncan Campbell Scott, Ottawa; 1933–35, Rev. C. W. Gordon ("Ralph Connor"), Winnipeg; 1935–37, Pelham Edgar, Toronto; 1937–39, Leslie G. Barnard, Montreal; 1939–42, Madge Macbeth, Ottawa; 1942–44, Watson Kirkconnell, Hamilton; 1944–46, Roderick S. Kennedy, Montreal; 1946–48, Wm. A. Deacon, Toronto; 1948–50, Will R. Bird, Halifax; 1950–52, W. G. Hardy, Edmonton; 1952–54, Paul Kuhring, Montreal; 1954–56, Frank Stiling, London, Ontario; 1956–58, Watson Kirkconnell, Wolfville, Nova Scotia; 1958–60, H. Gordon Green, Ormstown; 1960–62, Don Thomson, Ottawa; 1962–64, Helen Creighton, Dartmouth; 1964–66, R. S. Longley, Wolfville; 1966–68, Vinia Hoogstraten, Winnipeg.

The first convention of which I have a clear recollection was held in the Chateau Frontenac, Quebec, in 1924, with a fine French sense of pageantry at the annual banquet. Criticism of the federal government for its copyright turpitude was so violent at this convention that Bob Stead, as a civil servant, felt moved to resign from the national presidency. He was promptly succeeded by Lawrence Burpee, another civil servant, but one with less caution or a more phlegmatic disposition. I little dreamed at the time that a year later the convention would be held in Winnipeg and that I myself would be elevated from the Winnipeg branch secretaryship to the national secretaryship.

William Talbot ("W. T.") Allison, under whose national presidency I served for the next two years, was associate professor of English in the University of Manitoba. He was a product of Victoria College (Toronto) and Yale University, with a Ph.D. thesis on Milton's *Tenure of Kings and Magistrates.* He had a rare gift of friendship and his home at 600 Gertrude Avenue was a constant rendezvous for men of books and ideas. He was the literary editor of the Winnipeg *Tribune* for a score of years. The national treasurer in 1925–27 was Robert Watson, editor of the Hudson's Bay Company's *Beaver* and an indefatigable writer of romances of adventure. He was barely five feet in height but (as a young man in Glasgow) had been the champion sprinter of the west of Scotland. He gave me my first taste of haggis. He later moved to Hollywood and was killed in a car accident. I myself was a professor at Wesley College, where I set up the CAA files (shipped by Burpee from Ottawa) in my office and dictated letters several nights a week to a young male stenographer, Conan Frayer, who later became a captain in the Royal Canadian Navy in World War II. The stenographer, of course, was paid, but the national secretary, like his predecessors, worked merely for the good of the order.

One of our chief national concerns was the unending but apparently unsuccessful struggle for honest copyright legislation. Leon J. Ladner, M.P. for Vancouver in the House of Commons, was our legal champion in Ottawa and repeatedly sought to introduce a private bill to rectify the situation. I find in my personal files a brief note that I had sent to Burpee on July 2, 1926: "Tonight's paper brings news of the dissolution of the House. Am I right in supposing that the general brawl has thrown Ladner's bill into the garbage can?" Burpee had sent it back with a scrawl of melancholy comment: "Your prognostications am surreptitiously veracious. Dat bill done gone flooey. L. J. B."

Numerous letters from "Archie" MacMechan of Dalhousie, the Halifax branch president, illuminate my early files. Of a letter in which I sounded him out as to a possible convention in Halifax in 1928, he wrote: "I must confess that it touches my conscience. I have long felt that a meeting of the C.A.A. in Halifax was due either this year or next, and that an invitation was expected of the Halifax Branch. As the curate said, 'I have a feeling that I feel we all feel,' and I ought to respond to it."

At Christmas in 1932, I sent him a brief poem of my own:

As comets by a star's high cheek
In pale parabolas of light
Might greet each other ere they seek
The vacant vastness of the night,
So may brief sparks of human dust,
Bound to some sightless avatar,
Salute each other in the august
High season of the Christmas star.

His answer was much more sombre than usual:

MY DEAR KIRKCONNELL,—

You are entirely right. We *are* comets hurtling through Space, we greet, and then we pass. How true! Chilly but true. Thanks for the kind remembrance at Christmas time. May the New Year bring us such happiness as is possible.

It brought him death. He had a coronary thrombosis that summer and died on August 7, 1933.

The 1926 convention was held in Vancouver, with a leisurely social epilogue in Victoria. As a matter of fact, the social side of the convention had tended, even in Vancouver, to crowd out the more legitimate activities of the gathering. Thus an afternoon session devoted to the basic business of authorship was simply scrapped in order to give the delegates more leisure to prepare for a tea-party at the new chalet on Grouse Mountain. More indignant even than I over this was Frederick Philip Grove, who had been asked to prepare a paper for the session and had brought his carefully written manuscript two thousand miles by car only to find it ignored in this cavalier fashion. On returning home, he expanded its ideas to book length, and three years later Hugh Eayrs, of Macmillan, issued it as *It Needs To Be Said.* The first address in this austerely idealistic volume was entitled "A Neglected Function of a Certain Literary Association." That function was to present the young author with fundamental standards of art and thought, based on the great classics of English literature and not on the popularly successful work of "E. Phillips Oppenheim, Zane Grey and Arthur Stringer." At the time of the 1926 convention, Grove was known only as the author of two gifted volumes of prairie essays, although Arthur Phelps and I, in a week-end visit at his home in Rapid City, had seen the manuscripts of a dozen full-length novels awaiting publication. Stringer presented his side of the case in *The Canadian Author and Bookman* about fifteen years later as a dialogue between a veteran author and a youthful idealist.

The last convention for which I was responsible as national secretary was held in Ottawa, June 28–30, 1927. Our sessions were scheduled for the Royal Victoria Museum, where we had two symposia—one on "My Methods in Novel Writing," by eight Canadian novelists, and the other on "Conscious Canadianism in Literature," with seven major participants—and watched Mazo de la Roche's *Low Life* put on by the Drama League of Ottawa. On the evening of the 29th, with the Prime Minister as chairman and Their Excellencies as front-seat patrons, we had a music recital in the ball room of the Chateau Laurier. Mlle Juliette Gaultier de la Vérendrye, accompanied by Milton Blackstone, sang us a most unusual programme of Indian and Eskimo native airs and French-Canadian folk songs.

By 1929, the national files had become so bulky and the duties of the secretariat so much recognized as more than a marginal activity that a salaried national secretary was hired in the person of Howard Angus Kennedy, a veteran Montreal journalist who was willing to take over the job on half-pay. The national office was thus anchored in Montreal. As vice-president for the biennium 1933–35, I might have expected a purely honorary position, but in this I was speedily disillusioned. The 1934 convention was set for the Devil's Gap Inn at Kenora and the Winnipeg branch was geographically closest to the battleground. As branch president, I was therefore saddled with nearly all of the arrangements. The year 1935 was nearly as bad. "Ralph Connor" was on a protracted tour in Australia, and as vice-president I had to preside at all functions at the convention in Montreal.

The year 1942 put me at the helm while the vessel was facing a very rough sea. There was a savage feud in progress between members in Toronto and Ottawa and the third year of World War II was piling up new responsibilities for authorship even while it multiplied impediments of lodging, transportation, paper, and extra wartime duties for everyone. I was supposed to be a safe captain for a rough voyage. I had no oratorical gifts, no social graces, no imposing presence, no spontaneous brilliance, no Socratic powers of conversation, no infectious geniality to sway an audience or a committee. On the other hand, I had a reputation for patience, integrity, hard work, and administrative competence, in other words, for being a nice tame dray horse who would not run away with the milk-wagon.

Excerpts from my second presidential address, delivered on September 1, 1944, will indicate something as to the labours of my wartime presidency:

This annual meeting is positively my last appearance in the presidential chair. . . . Frankly, it has been a most strenuous experience. The National Secretary, Mr. Charles Clay, is an old student of mine whom I conscripted for the job in November, 1942. He has been getting his revenge for classroom assignments of bygone years by thinking up new jobs for the Old Man to do; while I in my turn have been concocting new policies that swamp him with work. In his report this morning, you got a glimpse of the secretarial beaver at work. As for my share, I may simply remark that even during my vacation at a summer cottage in July I was typing letters for an average of five hours a day, and since my return home four weeks ago I have typed and mailed out another four hundred letters. Rarely in the past has the national executive ever had more than two meetings a year. We have had eleven during my term, and the minutes, typed single space, run to over seventy pages. . . .

Not the least strenuous among the developments in my biennium of office was the organization of a Writers' War Committee [see Chapter XXIII], as chairman of which I found my efforts paced by another dynamic young secretary, Mr. Nathaniel Benson. . . . Trying to keep up with both Mr. Clay and Mr. Benson has often fairly run me ragged. Of the work of this Writers' War Committee, I am to give a formal report tomorrow morning. I mention it now only because the railway trips to Toronto and Ottawa, the constant committee meetings and the endless flow of correspondence were all part of the moving picture of my presidency.

In paying tribute to the energies of Mr. Clay and Mr. Benson, I should like to add a word of appreciation to those members of the national executive who, during last year and the year before, were most faithful in attending meetings and serving the interests of the Association. I shall not soon forget the cheerful forthrightness of Frank McDowell, the alert scepticism of Rod Kennedy, the incisive practicality of Bill Deacon, the shrewd legal reservations of A. H. O'Brien and Judge Surveyer, the Maritime reserve of Mrs. Flora Rogers, the gay humour of B. K. Sandwell and the deceptive taciturnity of John Murray Gibbon. To these and to my two national treasurers, Philip Child and Milton N. Campbell, I cannot be too grateful.

I tried hard to get Stephen Leacock as banquet orator for the 1943 convention, and wrote him in urgent terms:

I particularly want some of the younger writers to meet you in the flesh, not as a legendary diplodocus from the far-off marshes of our national youth but as the only Canadian young and vital enough to publish five books in 1942, all crackling with life and energy. You could be like the ostrich egg that the farmer hung in his hen-house to encourage the hens.

Regrets came back from the Old Brewery Bay: "Please tell your committee how sorry I am that I can't attend, and convey my best wishes for a fine gathering. This noblest phase of authorship, its legs under the mahogany, is denied to me; but I still envy it."

He rightly sensed the tenuousness of his hold on life, for a year later, at our Hamilton meeting, I regretfully announced his death, along with that of such other members as Sir Charles Roberts, Archdeacon F. G. Scott, Frederick Niven, Professor W. J. Alexander, Judge Howay, and G. W. Kirby.

At the 1944 annual meeting, there was some covert fencing with Soviet propagandists. Some time before the convention, the national executive had received through the National Council for Canadian-Soviet Friendship a routine circular letter from VOKS, the Literature Section of the USSR Society for Cultural Relations with Foreign Countries. We really felt that it called for no action but foresaw that Soviet sympathizers at our national convention would try to exploit it for their own ends. As a partial antidote, I therefore wrote to New York to Kaziemierz Wierzynski, an eminent Polish poet (whose work I had translated) and president of the "Association of Writers from Poland," who in response sent a vivid telegram to our Hamilton convention, stating in part: "Today when the burning homes of Warsaw, deserted and alone, have become a witness to the lonely struggle of the Poles for freedom, Polish writers turn with outstretched hands to their Canadian colleagues ready and eager to participate in the great work of world reconstruction and rebirth."

As the destruction of Warsaw at that very time was due to the infamous betrayal of the Polish underground by the Russians, this certainly tended to offset the gobbledygook of the Soviet circular. Thanks to their press connections, however, the Reds took the rubber. Stanley Ryerson, "educational director" of the Communist party of Canada, had recently joined the CAA's Toronto branch, and now, appearing as a "delegate," moved that the CAA convention "recommend to its incoming executive to establish contact with the writers of the USSR, in order to help strengthen the ties of friendship and understanding between our two peoples as allies in war and friends in peace." Next day this juicy item was jubilantly reported in the *Toronto Daily Star* and the *Globe and Mail* as if it were the only newsworthy achievement of our gathering. Fortunately for the peace of mind of the new executive, this was only a "recommendation" and not an order, and the propaganda move went little further. Rod Kennedy, the incoming president, was nobody's fool. On the other hand, constant needling by the Council for Canadian-Soviet Friendship led to the Executive's appointment of B. K. Sandwell as the CAA's official representative in the pro-Soviet racket, until in due course its fraudulent character became evident and only a rump of die-hard dupes and dupers was left.

The skeletal structure of the CAA can be seen in a series of constitutions by which it has been administered. The *textus receptus* was a version worked out by Murray Gibbon in an all-night sitting at the 1921 convention, with the constitution of the Izaak Walton League of America as a somewhat irrelevant model. The national organization was primary, but provision was made for the local activities of branches. The head office and the national officers were to be centred, over an eight-year cycle, in Montreal, Ottawa, Winnipeg, and Toronto, two years in each. By the 1930's, the sheer accumulation of files and the need for a paid secretary led to a tacit arrangement by which the office of such an official would be stationary while the elected officers maintained the cycle. Thus Howard Angus Kennedy functioned on a Montreal base for nine years (1929–38), and Ottawa, with Eric Gaskell and Charles Clay, housed the files and the secretary for the next seven years.

A revised constitution, adopted by the annual meeting on July 5, 1939, allowed for a head office at any city in Canada approved by a two-thirds vote at an annual meeting. It also approved of an "advisory body" to be known as the National Council, meeting at least once a year and consisting of fifty members elected by the several branches in proportion to the size of their membership. A quorum at the National Council meeting was to be seven, and at a National Executive meeting, five.

As the Council proved unwieldy and unworkable, it was dropped from a new constitution adopted in 1942. There followed in 1943–44 long and exhaustive meetings of a constitution committee under the chairmanship of Murray Gibbon, and a huge revision, asking for "yes" or "no" on each separate subsection (some eighty-seven specific points in all) and printed on a sheet nearly two feet square, was mailed to every member in Canada. The new version was finally approved at the CAA annual meeting in Hamilton on September 1, 1944. Once more a "National Council" was provided for, but it was now to consist of the national president (as chairman), all past national presidents and the presidents of all branches. In this way, past administrative experience was to be preserved for the benefit of the present. The Council, moreover, was to be represented on the National Executive. The national officers were to be elected by mail ballot on the proportional representation system. Nominations might be made by any branch, any ten members, or the National Executive. The quorum was to be five for the National Council and seven for the National Executive.

By April 10, 1945, Charlie Clay, still national secretary, was writing me in ironical amusement: "You will, I am sure, be delighted to hear that the Constitution over which we labored so lovingly last year not only is full of holes big enough for elephants to caper through, but that said elephants are actually capering through them with high glee."

There followed further mending of our fences. Late in 1947, moreover, a plan proposed in 1943–44 was finally carried out by which the CAA was incorporated under part II of the Companies' Act and was given a charter by the Secretary of State. The incorporators and first directors were Deacon, Gibbon, and Kirkconnell. The CAA was now legally entitled to receive gifts and bequests, own land, and sue or be sued. Its officers were no longer personally responsible for its debts, unless acting outside the scope of their authority. The Secretary of State had insisted, however, that some specific place be named in our constitution as the head office. The Executive therefore proposed, and the national body approved, that this should be Toronto, with the proviso that this could always be amended by the CAA, provided some other definite place was named. As the files and other accumulations of forty-five years must now total several tons, it seems obvious that there will be no haste in shifting headquarters.

My personal files are full of the Association's continual attempts to secure government encouragement for Canadian authorship. In 1926–27, with the sixtieth anniversary of Confederation looming on the summer horizon, I repeatedly wrote to the Prime Minister in my capacity as National Secretary and urged the establishment of annual "Confederation Medals," each with a substantial cash prize attached, for the best books of each year. Mr. King was simply not interested. Nearly ten years later, the issue was raised again by Albert Robson, William Arthur Deacon, and Pelham Edgar, of the Toronto branch, and Edgar sought to persuade the new Governor-General, Lord Tweedsmuir, to establish and heavily endow a set of annual medal awards. There was a colossal row between the two men, the details of which lie buried with them both. It appears, however, that His Excellency thought Edgar showed unpardonable effrontery in wanting him to spend a hundred thousand dollars endowing perpetual prizes for Canadian writing, and Edgar, in his enthusiasm, thought that John Buchan could, and ought to, be generous in such a worthy cause. When the smoke of battle cleared, Edgar found that his only concession from Rideau Hall was the right to attach the Governor-General's title in perpetuity to a set of annual medals for Canadian writers. There was no cash payment available for the winner; the administration of the awards was left to the CAA, and even the annual cost of casting and engraving the medals was to be borne by the Authors' Association.

Meanwhile the government of the Province of Quebec had endowed in perpetuity the valuable David Awards, involving an annual expenditure of several thousand dollars for the best Canadian books in the French language. Believing that this was one of the factors causing the literature of French Canada to forge ahead of that of the Anglo-Canadians in power and significance, I brought heavy pressure to bear on the government of Ontario, urging particularly the Department of Education and the Provincial Treasurer to do their duty towards Anglo-Canadian authorship by matching the Quebec system of large cash prizes. Alas, the "Ontario Prizes" proved as elusive as the "Confederation Medals."

Even the administration of the unendowed Governor-General's medals proved a mighty headache. At first the CAA turned to the senior academic statesmen of the Royal Society as judges. The hope had been to announce the awards by Easter, so that the public might have guidance and the authors "honour and profit thereby." Unfortunately these learned judges dawdled over their task until midsummer and then chose books that were erudite but unreadable. For example, the fiction winner for 1936 was Bertram Brooker's highly philosophical novel, *Fruits of the Earth*, which sold exactly eight copies. Commissioning the judges and bringing them to a focus of decision was still another task that bedevilled the national officers. As president, I wrote uncounted letters to the judges in 1942–44. At the 1944 convention, which ended my presidency, a decision was reached to set up a special awards board to choose the judges and to stress the importance of giving the medals to books that were not "caviare to the general" yet had conspicuous literary merit. In 1954, the Awards Board was made completely independent of the National Executive, so that its operations might avoid even the very appearance of pressure.

In the spring and summer of 1944, the CAA, under my presidency, was closely associated with some fourteen other groups in the arts and letters (Royal Academy of Arts, Royal Architectural Institute of Canada, Sculptors' Society of Canada, etc.) in presenting a brief to a Special Committee on Reconstruction set up under the chairmanship of Mr. Gray Turgeon by the House of Commons. The Committee's terms of reference were not too auspicious, for it was to consider "the needs for new employment of the men and women in the armed forces and in industry and the opportunities that will be available to meet those needs as men and women are demobilized from the armed forces. . . ." To meet this somewhat unpromising formula, our 10,000-word brief dug down to basic principles:

The creative arts stand in a key position as regards the economy of the whole nation. The influence stems from the fine arts, extends into commercial works and has ramifications throughout the trades and services. Manufacturing is as dependent upon design as upon capital, labour and raw materials. Construction, which is the greatest single source of employment, is dependent upon the architectural arts. The printing and publishing services are dependent upon journalism and illustration. The radio, and all it implies in the way of technical employment, business promotion and public welfare, can function only because of literary and dramatic talents. Transportation and tourism, agriculture, mining and the distribution of natural resources are tied up less obviously, yet actually, through advertising, with artistic energy. . . . The absorption of large numbers of men and women into fields related to the arts would help materially in securing full employment in the post-war period.

We went on to propose such measures as the setting up of a governmental body to supervise cultural activities, the federal matching of local funds for building community centres (including auditoria, art galleries, craft work shops, and the like), and the founding or expanding of such Dominion institutions as a national library, a state theatre, a national orchestral association, and the National Gallery.

Alas, our rulers failed to be convinced, but some six years later a new investigating committee, "the Massey Commission," was set up with literature and the arts specifically within its terms of reference. Out of its monumental report (1951) came once again the proposal of a national "body to supervise cultural activities" but with the proviso that it should do this by way of encouragement and in no sense through planning. Instead of a "Ministry of Culture" in the style of many European countries, it was to be a "Canada Council." This was set up in 1957, with the annual income on fifty million dollars to distribute.

A minor headache for a national president has always been the squabbles in the branches, and even in the craft groups within the branches. The female of the species has always been more belligerent and deadly than the male, and these branch quarrels have almost always involved two or more women authors whose mutual hostility reminded me of the "baleful wrath of Achilles, son of Peleus," that brought such countless woes on the Greeks at Troy. The *casus belli* might be as trifling as the disputed use of a minute book in a branch's short story group, but both parties to the fight assailed me with long letters, full of scratching, tearing words, demanding that I "avenge her of her adversary."

A "house organ" for the CAA began in 1922 as the *Authors' Bulletin*, designed not as a vehicle for criticism and belles lettres but as a means of keeping members of the Association aware of each other's activities and of the developing programme of the branches and the national office. In December 1933 (Vol. XI, No. 2), it was rechristened the *Canadian Author*, and in April 1940 (Vol. XVII, No. 1) it absorbed the *Canadian Bookman* (the organ of a then defunct "Association of Canadian Bookmen," founded by Pelham Edgar and the publishers in 1935) and became the *Canadian Author and Bookman.* For many years, the editorship was part of the job of the national secretary, who leaned heavily on routine contributions from the branches and the annual convention, but in 1947 the collecting of advertising and articles had become so arduous that a separate editor was appointed, backed by an editorial board. Still another publication, the quarterly *Canadian*

Poetry Magazine, was founded by Pelham Edgar, with the blessing of Lord Tweedsmuir, and brought out its first issue in January 1936, with Ned Pratt as editor. I was myself editor of the *Authors' Bulletin* in 1925–27 (while national secretary) and of the *Canadian Poetry Magazine* in 1944–46. In the latter post, the chief difficulty was in persuading any avant-gardists to contribute. They tended to regard the CAA as a decrepit battalion of effete traditionalists with whom they would be ashamed to be found dead. The CPM editors have always welcomed good work in either the old idiom or the new.

Still another authors' project to which Pelham Edgar played the midwife was the Canadian Writers' Foundation, launched in 1931 and eventually incorporated in 1945. Almost all other countries had a "civil list" to support distinguished but unmonied authors, but it was not until 1933 that the Canadian government approved a grudging $2500 to be administered by the Foundation for the declining years of Charles G. D. Roberts. The federal grant for such purposes has since been doubled, but the Foundation has undertaken to raise substantial sums from private benefactors as well and for many years now has been dispensing monthly slices of financial aid to several pensioners. I have been a director almost from the outset and can vouch for the merit of its achievement.

Back in 1944, when I was led out from the buggy-shafts after two years as national president of the CAA and chairman of the Writers' War Committee, I felt that I had earned a quiet corner in the pasture for the rest of my days. One can imagine the reluctance with which I surrendered in 1956 to a move to draft me for an unprecedented further biennium in the presidency. The winning argument was that I had served my secretaryship as a Westerner and my 1942–44 presidency as a citizen of Ontario and that I had still to render some service as a Maritimer (by adoption) since 1948. Moreover, if Sir Charles Roberts had taken on the job at the age of sixty-seven, why couldn't I try it again at sixty-one? By such specious dialectic, I was lured into a further sentence of hard labour—a man without the fortitude to say no.

The chief event of the 1956–57 session was the preparation of a brief for the new Canada Council, first in exhaustive spade-work by a CAA committee consisting of Leslie Gordon Barnard, Constance Beresford-Howe, and Don Thomson, and then in a last minute emergency drafting job by myself. The following extract from this ultimate version gives the perspective of our appeal for help:

> On page 381 of the Massey Commission Report, special consideration is urged for "the strengthening, by money grants and in other ways, of certain of the Canadian voluntary organizations on whose active well-being the work of the Council will in a large measure depend." We submit that the

Canadian Authors' Association is one of these voluntary organizations "whose work is of national importance but whose resources are inadequate for their growth." For thirty-six years, we have borne the burden and the heat of the day and have struggled with the slenderest means and heroically voluntary labour on behalf of authorship in this country. The editors of our quarterlies work without reward, for we have no money to give them. Again and again our deficits have threatened to swallow us up, and only sacrificial giving has bridged the muskeg. We therefore submit that ours is one of those voluntary national organizations envisaged by the Massey Commissioners. . . .

My subsequent connection with the CAA has been somewhat tenuous, and I look back over my forty-six years of membership with mixed emotions. Of all those hundreds of authors who enrolled in the Year One, only four of us are left alive—William Arthur Deacon, Vincent Massey, Arthur Phelps, and myself. The total number of members is more substantial than ever, but the weight of barnacles has sometimes threatened to sink the ship. In other words, far too many have joined on the strength of a single chapbook or a couple of magazine articles and have given branches and even the national convention a reputation for triviality and prestige-seeking sentimentality. Publishers were allies whose collaboration in, and even instigation of, "Canadian Book Week" also made us sitting ducks for young scoffers with a catapult. The rise of an avant-garde, who denounced the CAA as effete and traditional, helped to blacken its image in the public eye.

Solid achievements remain, however, and should be placed on the record. The sound copyright laws that the brave young cynic takes for granted for his protection are the result of long years of warfare by the Canadian Authors Association. That his books now sell by hundreds instead of dozens owes much to the CAA's often unlovely propaganda on behalf of a national literature. The Canada Council owes its creation in part to the pressures on government of organizations like the Canadian Authors Association and the Humanities Research Council, and if greater prestige now attaches to the Governor-General's annual medals, each at last supplemented by a cheque for one thousand dollars, it should be remembered that it was the CAA, in all its poverty, that inaugurated these medals, bore all expenses for nearly a quarter of a century, and only transferred them to the care and administration of the Canada Council when it became clear that the cash supplement would not be available on any other terms.

23

The Writers' War Committee

TOTAL WAR, with its mobilization of all the nation's personnel for some task contributing to victory, is a relatively modern concept. Not the least modern feature of it is the government's control of all mass media of propaganda in order to condition minds towards preordained political thinking. The Goebbels machine did a concentrated job on Germany from 1933 to 1945 and the Kremlin brain trust has maintained this sort of total control of Soviet brains for some five decades, but in the English-speaking countries wartime propaganda had commonly lacked the same ministerial master planning.

Hence it was that, although Canada entered World War II on September 10, 1939, it was not until December 1939 that the government got around to thinking about the need for public information. The first Director of Public Information, Walter Thompson, accepted the post, became immediately ill, and resigned a month later without having functioned at all. His successor, for almost three years, was G. H. Lash, with Claude Melançon as Associate Director.

Conflicting currents in the character of the Prime Minister continually frustrated this new agency. One part of Mr. King shunned publicity, another craved it, and his mood of caution prevailed. His appointees were men of the utmost probity, yet he feared that he might have created a Frankenstein monster. As a result, no hand was lifted to help the little group; no guidance was given; no information was furnished from the sources that should have been supplying it.

Mr. Lash and Mr. Melançon did not remain paralysed, however, and sought bravely to help win the war. Lacking guidance and barred from information, they devised imaginative projects that could inspire and strengthen national morale. Thus without either the knowledge or the consent of the government until they were accomplished facts, they issued a 48-page booklet, *Canadians All*, written by myself, of which 396,000 copies were distributed in Canadian schools; two radio series,

"Let's Face the Facts" and "Canadians All"; the booklet "Two Ways of Life"; the famous "Votive Mass for Victory"; and, to the government's horror, the establishment of the Canadian Council for Education in Citizenship. It was typical of Mr. King's phobias that recommendations from Mr. Lash that the Canadian story should be told in the United States led to stern orders by memorandum, telephone, and personal interview, that he must not attempt any such thing.

Late in 1941 and early in 1942, press criticism of the government for this calculated policy of silence became more and more bitter. As a device for self-protection, Mr. King therefore appointed Charles Vining a one-man commission to report on the matter, but did not even bother to notify Mr. Lash of Mr. Vining's appointment. As a matter of fact, the Vining report leaned very heavily on Mr. Lash's files and views, although it recommended much more elaborate machinery than had hitherto been used and a vastly higher salary schedule. In September 1942, on the basis of this report, the government replaced the Office of Public Information with a new Wartime Information Board. Charles Vining and Philip Brais, KC (a Montreal lawyer and staunch Liberal) were to be co-chairmen. Most of the former staff resigned. The astute Mr. King, however, had changed nothing so far as effective support to the information services was concerned. He had merely appeased press criticism by an alteration in the models in the shop window. The shop behind still had no stock on the counters.

The United Kingdom, in the meantime, had a Ministry of Information under a full-time minister and member of the cabinet. As for the United States, which had not entered the war until two years and three months after Canada, its action in the matter of public information was immediate. Not only was an American Office of War Information set up, with a regal budget and warm presidential support, but the very day after the declaration of war and at the request of the Treasury Department, a Writers' War Committee (later "Board") was called into being by offering the Authors' League of America, for such a committee, free quarters, a free secretarial staff, free franking privileges for all of its mail, and an annual grant of $42,000. The offer was at once embraced with enthusiasm and an organization sprang up, headed by the detective story writer, Rex Stout, to undertake immediate action. Its stated purpose was "To serve as liaison between the writers of America and government departments which want writing jobs done that will in any way whatever, directly or indirectly, help to win the war; and to place with the proper government departments any ideas or pieces of writing collected from writers as a contribution to the war effort." In brief, it was another phase of total mobilization.

Within a couple of months, it was doing jobs not only for the Treasury Department but for the Army, Navy, and Air Force, the Office of Civilian Defense, the Co-ordinator of Information, the Office of Facts and Figures, the United Service Organizations, the Red Cross, the Maritime Commission, and several other official and semi-official bureaus. It conducted high school essay contests on a national scale for the Treasury Department, wrote articles, pamphlets, and stories for the armed services and the Department of Civilian Defense, prepared radio broadcasts for several government departments (e.g., a network broadcast by Stephen Vincent Benét on the burning of books in Berlin), and provided material for daily broadcasts by short wave to the United States armed forces everywhere. Some of the material was placed with magazines, newspapers, and book publishers, and the writers were paid the usual commercial rates. Some was placed with government departments and might even be a free-will contribution. The members of the Board itself were all professional writers, ready to give the Board a full day each week, without remuneration.

Nine months later, and three years after Canada's entry into the war, the American model of organization was proposed to the annual convention of the Canadian Authors' Association by the distinguished American novelist, Carl Carmer, president of the Authors' Guild of the Authors' League of America. Late that night, in a smoke-filled bedroom in the Mount Royal Hotel, six Canadian writers (Gibbon, Sandwell, Sullivan, Clay, Benson, and Kirkconnell) held a bull session with Carmer and drafted a resolution that was ratified the next morning at the final general meeting of the convention. By this motion, the CAA decided to set up a "Writers' War Board" (presently renamed "Committee" at Ottawa's request), aimed at providing the Wartime Information Board with a Dominion-wide reservoir of Canadian writing talent and, in general, to duplicate the American record. The Association had over six hundred and fifty members to draw upon and felt that much could be done. It was wisely decided, however, to leave the new Writers' War Committee complete freedom to organize itself and to frame its policies to meet its needs.

The following was the consequent organization:

Hon. Chairman: Sir Charles Roberts (who proved one of our most active and valuable committee members).

Chairman: Watson Kirkconnell, professor at McMaster University.

Secretary: Nathaniel Benson, publicity man with Young & Rubicam.

Assistant Secretary: Mrs. Verna Bentley.

Other members of the Executive: B. K. Sandwell, editor of *Saturday Night*; Joseph L. Rutledge, Can. editor of *Liberty*; Philip Child, novelist, Hamilton;

Frank McDowell, novelist, Toronto; John Murray Gibbon, director of publicity for the C.P.R.; and Roderick S. Kennedy, editor of *The Family Herald and Weekly Star*, Montreal.

Other Members of the Council: Irene Baird, Leslie Gordon Barnard, Bertram Brooker, Audrey Alexandra Brown, Grace Campbell, Franklin S. Carmichael, John Coulter, Leo Cox, Wm. Arthur Deacon, Mazo de la Roche, Clara Dennis, Ira Dilworth, Pelham Edgar, Wilfrid Eggleston, John Fisher, Sir Wyly Grier, Edna Jacques, Stephen Leacock, Major F. V. Longstaff, Madge Macbeth, Leslie McFarlane, Norman A. M. Mackenzie, Sir Ernest MacMillan, Nellie McClung, Dan McCowan, R. H. Mainer, J. E. Middleton, H. Napier Moore, Hugh Whitney Morrison, Frederick Niven, Arthur L. Phelps, Arthur A. Porter, S. Morgan-Powell, E. J. Pratt, Lt.-Col. Keith S. Rogers, Mary Lowrey Ross, P. D. Ross, Laura Goodman Salverson, Duncan Campbell Scott, H. L. Stewart, Kathleen Strange, Arthur Stringer, Alan Sullivan, Gordon V. Thompson, Mary Weekes, Healey Willan.

One of the principles that was hardest to explain to faithful branch officials of the CAA was that the Council was not chosen in terms of fidelity to branch meetings in their neighbourhood but in terms of serviceability to the war effort. Many of the Council were not even members of the Authors' Association but contributed invaluable skill, prestige, and labour to the tasks that we undertook. In some of these cases we needed a whole diplomatic corps to smooth the feathers of the indignant local group. In other cases, our own nominees turned out to be stuffed owls, and the local wrath was justified.

I also wrote to Mr. Victor Barbeau, president of La Société des Ecrivains Canadiens, inviting his organization to set up a French section of our Writers' War Committee. Its working nucleus consisted of Claude Melançon (Montreal, formerly Herb Lash's associate on the WIB), Séraphin Marion (Ottawa), and Leopold Richer (Ottawa). This French section worked in loose association with our English section but for the most part dealt directly with Mr. Brais of the WIB.

Toronto was the rallying point for our executive and we met at least once a fortnight in the club rooms of the Toronto Branch of the CAA on the second floor at 99 Yonge Street. Gibbon and Kennedy would come up from Montreal, Child and I crossed from Hamilton, and the Toronto group was always on hand. Only Clay in Ottawa found it difficult to get to Toronto regularly, but he was helpful in his contacts in the Capital.

Our first and most important task was the stimulation of war-time writing, especially among the 650 members of the CAA. This work had three phases:

(*a*) The appointment of regional directors across Canada to instigate and direct the war writing in the various areas.

(*b*) The sending of detailed directives to our 650 members and others to suggest helpful fields of war writing and sources of information. (In this system, writers were left to market their own work in the usual way, but three gigantic scrapbooks of the resulting clippings and radio scripts were prepared as evidence of our activity.)

(*c*) The inauguration of a WWC syndicate to send gratis to a large number of daily and weekly newspapers a series of brief, specially written items in prose and verse.

As had been the case with the American Writers' War Board, we also set up a number of subcommittees for specific phases of our work. Examples were: a committee on songs, chairman, John Murray Gibbon; a committee on radio, chairman, Nathaniel Benson; a committee on publicity in the agricultural field, chairman, Roderick Kennedy; and a committee on drama, chairman, John Coulter.

The song committee arranged for the actual preparation, publication, and widespread public use of popular war-time songs, such as "Back the Attack" (Gibbon and Adaskin), the theme song of the fourth Victory Loan campaign; "Cross of Red on a field of white" (Gordon V. Thompson), theme-song of the Red Cross Campaign; "Roll Along" (Gibbon and Abrahamson), the Navy Show song; and "I want a Share in my Country" (Thompson and Grant). Mr. Gibbon also prepared a radio series, "Songs of Freedom," in which national songs of the Allies were broadcast over CBC.

The radio committee undertook three main projects: an international broadcast in conjunction with the American Writers' War Board, a series of radio plays, and a series of Sunday evening talks under the general title "The Inheritance of Freedom."

Early in its work, the WWC selected a large number of capable writers in almost every section of the country who were willing, as a part of their war effort, to submit special confidential fortnightly reports to the Wartime Information Board, giving their impressions of the trend of public opinion, from week to week, in their own districts. These reports covered every conceivable topic, especially those associated with the war. This constant feeling of the public pulse was considered exceedingly valuable by Mr. Dunton's division of the WIB and outlasted all other activities of the WWC.

My own share of the load went far beyond chairing fortnightly meetings, paying an occasional visit to Ottawa, carrying on extensive routine correspondence and making occasional contributions to the syndicate. There were, indeed, six major projects that I undertook, four alone and two in partnership:

(i) As a basis for an intelligent assignment of tasks in writing, I prepared singlehanded a "National Service Register" of all Canadian authors and the fields in which they had published work.

(ii) As an aid to interallied understanding, I prepared a series of

All People's Readers, containing translated prose and verse from all the nations.

(iii) At the request of the WIB, I prepared a *Handbook of Canada*, designed for young Americans.

(iv) At the request of the Canadian Legation at Rio de Janeiro, Brazil, and in consultation with Sir Charles Roberts, I prepared an anthology of Canadian poetry in English for distribution throughout South and Central America. A similar volume of Canadian poetry in French, edited by Jean Désy, had already been printed for this purpose of stimulating international good will.

(v) In the interests of national unity and in collaboration with Mr. Séraphin Marion, chairman of the French committee, I prepared a volume of French-Canadian prose and verse, *The Quebec Tradition*, that would interpret the background, point of view, and real spirit of French Canada. Mr. Marion selected the French extracts in prose and verse and these were printed throughout on the left-hand pages, facing my translations, in English prose and verse, on the right-hand pages.

(vi) In still another activity, I myself wrote a long series of biographies of great Canadians of all origins (Banting, Stefansson, Laurier, Macdonald, etc.) which were mimeographed by the Citizenship Branch in Ottawa and supplied to some seventy foreign-language newspapers, regardless of their politics. I was likewise called in, on occasion, to advise the War Finance Publicity Committee on their releases to New Canadian communities.

All six projects were completed, but one or two of them remained unpublished because there were no funds to underwrite them. In the case of the *Anglo-Canadian Verse*, for example, the Department of External Affairs was unwilling to pay copyright fees, subsidize publication in any part, or even cover a small bill for typing. To my great satisfaction, however, la Faculté des Lettres, l'Université de Montréal, sponsored *The Quebec Tradition* in its "Collection Humanitas" and brought it out in both cloth and paper-bound editions.

I was also in occasional touch with the American Writers' War Board, as for example, when its secretary, Paul Gallico, who had just written his beautiful Dunkirk sketch, *The Snow Goose*, got me to approach Stephen Leacock for an article on "Britain" for a New York publication. Leacock told me that he had only recently written the very article that Gallico desired but that it was in the hands of his temperamental New York agent, Jaques Chambrun, and that he would no more think of writing to him than he would of disturbing "a sitting hen." The best that I could do was to suggest to Gallico that he "take a tactful poke at the sitting hen." Apparently it worked. Another interesting contact with the American group was a visit from its chairman, Rex Stout, on November 10, 1942, during which he had a vigorous business session with our executive in the afternoon and spoke to a public meeting in the evening in the auditorium at Eaton's uptown store.

But from the very beginning of our operations we were painfully aware how differently the Canadian Government viewed all such activities, as compared with the American Government. When I had approached Mr. Vining, as WIB chairman, and Mr. D. B. Rogers as general manager, I found cordiality and a willingness to give us any amount of confidential direction as to issues to write about, but their own budget was so small that the best they could do in November 1942 was to promise us two hundred dollars a month for postage, telegrams, and stenographic help for Nathaniel Benson, the secretary.

Not the least of our hazards was the rivalry of a very active "Communist Front" group, the Writers' Broadcasters' and Artists' War Council, organized at almost the same time. It is a question whether any "front" organization ever had a higher percentage of Communists. Thus it included five members of Tim Buck's national executive: namely, Rudolph Shohan (Raymond Arthur Davies), the WBAWC organizer; the Communist MPP, A. A. MacLeod; John Weir (born Ivan Wevursky), then editor of the *Canadian Tribune*; Edo Yardash, editor of the Communist *Novosti*; and Sam Lifshitz, secretary of the Jewish section of the Communist Party of Canada. Still others were Steve Szöke, editor of the Communist *Kanadai Magyar Munkás*, Avrom Yanovsky, staff cartoonist for the *Canadian Tribune*, Mrs. Margaret Fairley, literary editor of the *Canadian Tribune*, Max Chic, a leader of the Young Communist League, and Emil Gartner, leader of the Communist choir at all of the big Party rallies. It was a triumph in the campaign to whitewash the Reds that many eminent and highly conservative people were lured into association with these and still other Communists.

At the outset, the honest but misguided figurehead of the WBAWC had been an active Conservative, John Collingwood Reade, of the Toronto *Globe and Mail*, but he presently parted company with the War Council and within two years was making trips to Hamilton to have me brief him for attacks on the Reds. He realized that he had been "taken for a ride" and had enough integrity to make his indignation known.

Charles Vining had clearly understood the ulterior motives of the "United front" group. In a conference in his office on November 30, 1942, he therefore gave our WWC "exclusive recognition as an authors' organization" and promised "to notify such groups as the WBAWC that their collaboration would be acceptable only through the WWC." This was confirmed by an exchange of letters between the WIB and the WWC.

So long as he remained chairman, we did not have to fear backstairs intrigues against us at Ottawa.

As already intimated, we were on terms of goodwill and collaboration with many of the WIB subdivisions, such as the Reports Branch (under Davidson Dunton), the Consumers' Information Branch (under Leonard Knott), and the General Information Branch (under Ross Brown). We were also building up friendly co-operation with the Wartime Prices and Trade Board, the War Finance Publicity Committee (Herbert Richardson) and the Special Services Branch of the armed forces. The range of our active output has already been indicated.

Meanwhile there were signs that Ottawa was content to drift in many respects. A letter from an indignant artist on December 18, 1942, had expressed envy at the success of the Writers' War Committee:

> I notice that . . . the Writers' War Committee . . . has been approved and accepted by the Government. Now I wonder if you can tell me how you reached this happy condition? The Federation of Canadian Artists, with a petition carrying nearly a thousand signatures, has been trying to reach the Government for months with the idea of enlisting the artists in the war effort. We haven't been able to get an entry. . . .

Or again, on April 19, 1943, Bill Clarke, of the Oxford University Press, wrote me:

> As I look at the Ottawa situation, I feel frightfully discouraged. I scarcely know where to turn to find anyone there in any position of responsibility who has the faintest interest in books as essentials even, if not as weapons, as Mr. Roosevelt has called them. Perhaps you can help me.

Towards the end of January we had been receiving persistent reports from Ottawa that Charles Vining was retiring from the chairmanship of the WIB. On January 28, a staff release in the *Globe and Mail* reported a much more startling realignment. Vining was indeed resigning for reasons of ill health, and John Grierson, national film commissioner, had been appointed general manager of the WIB, but at the same time, four other resignations were announced, those of Philip Brais, KC, the deputy chairman, Dave Rogers, director of the Board's domestic services, Campbell Smart, director of the foreign section, and Frank Ryan, deputy chief of the foreign section. It was almost a clean sweep of the men with whom we had been working in amity.

There was also a change in structure. Professor Norman MacKenzie, of the University of New Brunswick, who was named on February 12 as successor to Mr. Vining, was merely to be the chairman of a consultative body that met briefly in Ottawa at long intervals. Management was tightened up and put firmly in the hands of John Grierson, the new general manager. Dave Dunton became his assistant and George McCracken replaced Dave Rogers. Grierson also remained chairman of the Canadian Film Board. When I wrote to wish him well in his new work, he told me that instead of merely confirming Vining's arrangement with us he would put us on trial for three months and would then review the whole matter.

Grierson was an Old Country film expert who had come to Canada only a short time before and had brought with him the orientation that then prevailed in the British Ministry of Information. In the United Kingdom and the United States in 1942, all agencies of public information were dressing their ranks "by the left" in order to supply the English-speaking world with a war-time image of Soviet Russia as a glorious and all-virtuous ally. This was deemed wise by Roosevelt and Churchill for the sake of military victory, but the facts of history were an unavoidable casualty and this was presently to stick in our own Prime Minister's crop. Thus a typical Film Board release, *Our Northern Neighbours*, was a tissue of unreality from start to finish. It begins by stating that in 1914 "scores of millions of Russian serfs" were toiling under Tsarist despotism—although serfdom had been abolished in 1861 and most of the 1914 land was owned by the peasants. It then represents the Tsarist war effort as hamstrung from the start by social discontent—although the Tsarist armies fought with much greater unanimity than the Soviet armies. (In the so-called Vlassov Army, some 800,000 surrendered Soviet troops volunteered to fight with Germany against Russia, and five autonomous Soviet republics were liquidated by Stalin for mutiny. There were no such defections to the enemy in Tsarist times.) The film then shows Trotsky and Lenin at work in Russia organizing war-time revolution against the Tsar—although Trotsky and Lenin were both abroad until after the Tsar abdicated in March 1917. It shows the Red soldiers' attack on the Winter Palace in November 1917 as an attack on the power of the Tsar, whereas the Tsar had been gone for eight months. And so the great folk tale goes on. The honour paid to Trotsky in this film led to a violent row with the Soviet Embassy. Mr. Grierson was certainly no agent of the Stalinist régime. He was too utterly independent to be any man's agent. He was also, by the testimony of those who knew him intimately, a genuinely creative person. A subsequent serious illness in the United Kingdom was happily followed by a new lease on life in the film industry, three important books, and a C.B.E. in 1961. I suspect that in 1943 he was not too much concerned over either the WWC or the WBAWC. Men who were close to him tell me that he was "obsessed with audio-visual media" and had no interest in Canadian writing except as a handmaiden to film and radio. For this, he had his own "stable" of writers from the National Film Board.

It was perhaps scarcely surprising that his assistant, George McCracken, kept throwing scares into our Ottawa liaison man, Charles Clay, that we were soon to be cut off without a shilling. The further and much more significant version that we got by the grapevine was that we might hope to survive on his payroll only if we would amalgamate with the Communist-front WBAWC. Suspecting that my own head would be the price demanded by the Reds for such a merger, and hearing rumours that some of my own executive were so influenced by Canada's growing Russia-worship as to be ready to throw me to the wolves, I had a showdown with my own group in the late spring of 1943 and demanded a frank statement of loyalty or disloyalty. There were one or two flushed faces but the assurance of devotion was unanimous. As Philip Child and I rode back to Hamilton by CPR that night, he remarked quietly that my ultimatum to the executive had been very wise and very necessary.

Confident in the backing of my own men, I was now willing to enter into personal negotiation with the WBAWC head, and to chair an informal joint meeting on July 11 at which Frank Sutherland and Margaret Gould represented the WBAWC and H. G. Kettle and L. A. C. Panton the Federation of Canadian Artists. In all our deliberations, however, we made it clear that we did not seek amalgamation but only co-ordination, with perhaps an assignment of radio exclusively to the WBAWC, of art to the FCA, and of music and authorship to the WWC.

Late in August, we received a confidential report from Ottawa (that presently proved to be true) that the Prime Minister was drastically cutting the WIB's starveling budget and that Grierson was resigning from his directorship. Meanwhile there was a complete lack of action in the War Council. It seemed clear that as they could not secure Kirkconnell's head in a basket as the price of unity, they preferred not to collaborate. Early in September, I recommended to the national executive of the Canadian Authors' Association that we ourselves cut the frayed hawser that tied us to the WIB tugboat, and there was unanimous agreement.

In acknowledging this withdrawal on our part, Mr. Grierson expressed some regret over our failure to merge with the WBAWC:

> I would draw your attention to the fact that on July 27 I wrote to you in the hope that the Writers' War Committee and the Writers', Broadcasters' and Artists' War Council might be able to co-operate in extending their sphere of usefulness. I take it from your letter that further co-operation between these two organizations was either not possible, feasible or perhaps desirable.

Our bus was now out of gas. Three weeks later, we were also to be without a chauffeur. Nat Benson, our energetic secretary, was transferred by his firm (Young and Rubicam) to its New York office. No successor was available and we simply parked our vehicle for the duration. The individuals on our Special Reports Committee still carried on and our Ottawa man, Charles Clay, continued to supply Government offices with authors for occasional projects; but generally speaking, we were through.

Probably the most significant feature of all this was the way in which Mr. Mackenzie King, fearful of the corrupting influences of an official propaganda agency, kept the WIB as his personal pet but starved it to death. The need for unremitting and skilful publicity for keeping the Canadian people united and courageous was obvious in the face of aggressive propaganda from Germany. The major danger in Anglo-Saxon countries was the infiltration of the information services by those whose ultimate aim was the destruction of Western freedom by the Communists. Rex Stout told our Executive in Toronto on November 10, 1942, that he had found the American Reds invading his Writers' War Board in such numbers and for such obviously dishonest purposes that he had had to throw them out en masse. In Canada, the Office of Public Information and its successor, the WIB, were comparatively free from Red infiltration, but the WWC was threatened from the start by a Communist-organized group whose ultimate loyalty was to our enemies. When Mr. King himself was led up the primrose path to the chairmanship of the first meeting of the National Council for Canadian-Soviet Friendship, the very thing that he had feared had at last ensnared him.

24

Confronting Communism

MY FIRST DIRECT contact with Communism was in January 1922, in Istanbul, Turkey, where I found a pretentious Soviet trade mission in the Pera quarter in flamboyant contrast to the thousands of grimy White Russian fugitives who were starving on the streets of that semi-oriental city. On the S.S. *Bulgaria*, on which I left Istanbul for Salonica and Athens, one fellow-passenger was a German carpet-merchant from Tiflis, Georgia, who had lost everything there to the Communists by fire and confiscation. Georgia was now, he said, wholly given over to vodka, violence, and idleness.[1] Two days later, Giulio, the cabin-boy, gave me a 500-ruble Soviet note as a curiosity. Its purchasing power was zero but it propaganda value was considerable. Printed on its face in all of the chief languages of the world—from English to Chinese—was the revolutionary slogan, "Workers of the World, Unite!"

In Winnipeg, where I settled in September 1922 for an eighteen-year sojourn, there had already been an attempt at revolution in 1919, when a general strike, still interpreted by many labour leaders as merely a labour dispute, was floated on a black river of revolutionary purpose among the foreign-language radicals of the prairie city. These had brought their fierce political projects from Russia among a minority of the Ukrainians, Jews, and Finns from the very beginning of the twentieth century and had published in Canada such insurrectionary news-

[1]The Soviet conquest of Georgia in February 1921 had been in open violation of a public treaty between Soviet Russia and the Democratic Republic of Georgia, signed on May 7, 1920, by which Russia recognized unconditionally "the existence and independence of the Georgian State" and agreed "to refrain from any kind of interference in the internal affairs of Georgia." On February 12, 1921, Soviet troops marched into the little country, crushed all resistance, and proclaimed a soviet republic. (Cf. Walter Russell Batsell, *Soviet Rule in Russia*, 1929, pp. 215–23.) This was one of the earliest of almost numberless treaties that Moscow has broken under Communist rule (cf. William C. Bullitt, *The Great Globe Itself*, 1946, pp. 219–32).

papers as the *Red Flag*, *Kadylo*, and *Kropylo*.[2] In May 1921, moreover, the Communist Party of Canada, "Section of the Communist International," had been organized by a well-financed agent from Moscow, a Lett named Jensen, *alias* "Charles E. Scott." Leaders of alien radicalism in Canada were mobilized by him in a barn near Guelph, Ontario, and the new arm of Moscow in Canadian life flexed its muscles.

Many years later, former members of the Party passed on to me a great amount of archival material, including complete mimeographed minutes of several conventions and countless broadsheets, pamphlets, magazines, and books. One of my most striking exhibits is a copy of Vol. 1, No. 1, of the *Communist*, an underground paper published in June 1921 and giving a very full description of the constituent convention at which the Party had been organized the month before. It is frankly stated that the chairman was not a Canadian but a visiting agent of the International. Delegates freely accepted the "twenty-one Conditions for admission to the Communist International," and a detailed constitution in which they promised to share in "destroying the entire machinery of the bourgeois state, including all parliamentary institutions." According to one of the Twenty-one Points, there must always be an underground, illegal portion of the Party (until, of course, Russia has taken Canada over), and, according to another, orders from Moscow are binding on every member of the Canadian section. The minutes of subsequent conventions, moreover, usually led off with a letter of criticism and instruction from the ECCI (Executive Committee of the Communist International) in Moscow, showing the Canadian Communists their mistakes in the preceding year and giving them detailed instructions for their revolutionary task in the year to follow.

All this documentation came to me in the 1940's, however, after my denunciation of Canadian Communism had begun to attract the fury of the Party and the goodwill of some of its former victims. During my eighteen years in Winnipeg, I actually had very little contact with the ferocious Communism that flourished in that city and was only vaguely aware that it existed. On one occasion in the early 1930's, I gave an evening lecture, under the auspices of the League of Nations Society, in Theatre "A," Broadway Building, University of Manitoba, on "How Russia is Governed," and found a solid platoon of Communist hecklers in my audience. The discussion period developed into a strenuous

[2]In an article in the *Worker*, January 10, 1931, John Weir (born Wevursky), a prominent ULFTA Communist wrote: "The Ukrainian Labour-Farmer Temple Association began its existence as the legal cover for the then underground Socialist groups, and the first hall was built to enable publication of the revolutionary paper."

argument with them on the principle of freedom of speech. I held the line in terms of John Stuart Mill's essay *On Liberty* but, of course, could not hope to convince the Red dogmatists.

In 1939, I had made a survey of the foreign-language press of Canada in terms of the efforts of Hitler to tamper with the loyalty of Canadian citizens. The reassuring results—and my vehement exposure of the evils of Hitler's régime—were published in a 213-page book as *Canada, Europe and Hitler*. Unfortunately for any accurate judgement on the current Communist party line, however, my book was in the printer's hands before a new directive from Moscow in November 1939 instructed the Canadian Communists to denounce the war against Hitler's Germany as an imperialistic fraud. Tim Buck, who on September 2 had sent a telegram to the Prime Minister urging support for the Poles, issued a leaflet on November 14 denouncing that same Prime Minister as the promoter of an imperialistic war in having supported the Poles. He then clamoured for revolution and the establishment of a people's government. By June 1940, the Party, then in alliance with Hitler through Moscow, was officially outlawed and went underground.

Opportunities soon arrived for giving them their due place in the picture of sedition. On November 4, 1940, I spoke to the Canadian Club in Toronto on "European Elements in Canadian Life" and, while urging fraternal unity amongst Canadians of all origins, I pointed out the menace not only of the Octopus of Berlin but also of the Octopus of Moscow. A further blast against the Communists came in the autumn of 1941 with a chapter on "The Fifth Column in Canada" in my book, *Twilight of Liberty*. Part of the chapter dealt with the Canadian agents of Hitler and Mussolini and some twelve pages were devoted to a criticism of such Communist papers as the *Kanadai Magyar Munkás* and the *Canadian Tribune* and the circulation of venomously anti-war leaflets in many Canadian cities. Since Hitler had now attacked the Soviet Union, the Canadian Communist party was planning to use the conflict as a lever to pry their leaders out of internment camps and out of hiding. I declared that it was folly to think of them as turned into honest men: "Whatever the outcome in Europe, they work for the break-up of the present order in North America, in order that, in the day of our confusion, they may seize power and set up the proletariat's reign of blood and steel." A sample of Communist disapproval comes from the *Canadian Tribune*: "His books and his babble are without truth because they form an adulterous alliance with the vomits of the brown python of Germany, the spews of the black snake of Italy, and slime of the sun-shark of Japan."

Conflict broke out much more violently, however, after an article that I published in *Saturday Night* on December 12, 1942, entitled "Our Communist Revolutionaries are not Russian," pointing out their active attempts to gain a false respectability by association with Red Army achievements. I stressed the fact that their "single, ultimate aim is revolution" and listed all their organizations and their foreign-language newspapers. An analysis of the last showed that they were simply mouthpieces of Communist Russia.

The reply came in a two-page assault on me by Leslie Morris in the December 26 issue of the *Canadian Tribune*, complete with a brilliant cartoon of me as a puppet in Ukrainian costume, labelled "Hetman Kirkconnell" and manipulated by strings from a swastika. Comrade Morris also had a violent letter in the January 2, 1943, issue of *Saturday Night*. Both of his attacks were duly answered by me in the *Saturday Night* of January 23. Morris had accused me of forgery. I was able to present Mr. Sandwell with authentic originals. Morris accused me of the honorary presidency of the Hetman organization among the Ukrainians (this was the alleged point of the cartoon). I showed that this was a complete falsehood. He accused me of supercilious hostility towards the "New Canadians." I pointed out that more than any other single Canadian I had sought, by book and lecture, to promote a fraternal understanding of these very communities. And so on. Mr. Sandwell ran an editorial on the controversy and declared that the Red campaign of slander would have no weight except "among the kind of people to whom epithets like Quisling Kirkconnel and Hetman Kirkconnell are more impressive than any amount of reasoned argument."

All of the dozen Communist Canadian newspapers took up the outcry against Kirkconnell, and I began to collect a large scrapbook of cartoons and vituperative articles in some ten languages. The cartoons were a special joy to me—cartoons of Kirkconnell as a jackass-head mask through which Goebbels bayed the moon of a brave new Soviet–Western world, Kirkconnell as a statue of lies melted by the sun of Soviet truth, Kirkconnell as a cur snapping at Stalin's heels, Kirkconnell with a bottle of Quisl-ink, Kirkconnell being drilled (fountain-pen on shoulder) along with the Premier Hacha and Father Tiso by Goebbels as drill-sergeant, Kirkconnell as a toreador certifying a bull named Drew as "pedigreed stock," and so on, and so on.

Generally speaking, I held my peace pretty well for the next fifteen months and let the heathen rage. During this period, however, I had in preparation a book-length study of Communism in Canada and in Russia. I called it *Seven Pillars of Freedom* and released it through the Oxford University Press, Toronto, in March 1944. For maximum effect it was issued in a 35-cent paper-back edition and the run was very large.

The answer now came in heavy artillery from Moscow itself. Igor Gouzenko has told me that a Mr. Montinov, who was assistant military attaché at the Soviet Embassy in Ottawa and who kept official watch for any Canadian daring to criticize Soviet Communism, nearly had apoplexy at my book and dutifully so reported to his superiors in the Kremlin.

The counter-attack came in two instalments. First came two blistering speeches in the House of Commons, Ottawa, on April 27, 1944, by the two Communist members, Dorise Nielsen and Fred Rose. Gouzenko's batch of documents from the Embassy shows that Rose was in almost daily contact with his Russian bosses and there is no doubt that the two speeches, delivered with parliamentary immunity, had been well vetted for the occasion. Unfortunately for the Embassy, the attack backfired. Several members of the House rose in my defence, and not merely General LaFlèche, to whose Department I was an adviser. Ralph Maybank, MP for Winnipeg South Centre (where I had lived for eighteen years) said in part: "Professor Kirkconnell was for a long time a citizen of my city and one of our most honoured citizens. The people of my city are a discriminating people, and the fact that Professor Kirkconnell was a particularly honoured citizen of Winnipeg is itself a passport that will carry him anywhere in this country or in any other country. . . . If we had many more men like Professor Kirkconnell in this country, Canada would be a great deal the richer for it."

Then in November came a full-dress article by David Zaslavsky, spread over four columns in the Moscow newspaper *Trud*. My book, said he, "should have been published in Berlin under the editorship of Goebbels" and "obediently reproduced all the dirty imaginings of the Fascists about the Soviet Union. . . . One might think Kirkconnell is a learned crackpot, but he is not a simple professor, and least of all a professor. . . . There is only one thing we don't understand, why this wild flower of the Canadian prairies flourishes in Ottawa."

The Communist press in Canada exhausted all the resources of language in their denunciation. To *Ludove Zvesti* (Slovak), I was "a fascist" and "unbalanced mentally." To the *Kanadai Magyar Munkàs* (Hungarian), I was "a mad dog" and in my book there was concentrated "all the crafty intrigue, perversion and falsehood of this notorious professor." *Novosti* (Croatian) called me "a traitor to Canada." The *Canadian Tribune* accused me of "falsehoods that make the efforts of Goebbels look pale by comparison."

Every Red journalist across Canada went into action and placed his wares wherever he could. *John Bull's Flash*, Toronto, threw weekly abuse in my direction, but even a neighbourhood sheet like the *Danforth Spotlight* and handbills left on Brandon, Manitoba, doorsteps treated me as a class-Z scoundrel. There was a Red subordinate who had joined the staff of Judith Robinson's Conservative *News* and denounced me in her columns as "an arch-muddler suffering from a fit of literary apoplexy." A zealous Red undergraduate at the University of Toronto enlivened the correspondence columns of *Varsity* with the lie that I "had received gratefully a medal from Hitler," but there was an apology the following week from a red-faced editor.

Fortunately for my ego, every responsible newspaper across Canada came to my support. B. K. Sandwell gave my book an editorial of commendation. The *Montreal Gazette* classed me "not as a narrow-minded fanatic but as a thoughtful, clear-sighted Canadian." But my favourite review came from Angus Munro in the *Windsor Star*:

> The slightly-built, outspoken academic has gone to the uttermost ends of the proverbial limb in his contentions and he quotes figures and dates and names to provide backing for his statements. . . . The book is for Communism what his *Twilight of Liberty* was for fascism, an expository blast that will bring down upon the author's slim shoulders the heavy hand of critics in high places. . . . This writer is definitely on a crusade. The way is hard for any such in the days of Russian victories on the one hand and a newly named Communist party on the other. The crusader must be like his fore-runner—an iron man and a saint—if he is to meet all his challengers on the ground that they select for the meeting. . . . The book is thorough. . . .

Grimmer times were to come. President Roosevelt had prevailed on the Western nations to undertake a vast programme of selling Soviet Russia to their entire populations as a democratic and amiable friend. Propaganda to this end had gone into high gear with the simultaneous founding in all countries on June 22, 1943, of "National Councils for Soviet Friendship." In Toronto, the Prime Minister of Canada himself chaired the inaugural session and the sponsors included nearly all the angels and archangels of our social, political, academic, and ecclesiastical heavens. I, even I, had received a personal invitation but made my acceptance conditional on the Council's avoiding "sentimental blindness to the evils of revolution and dictatorship and the whitewashing of seditious Canadian Communists." When the list of patrons was published, there were at least eight of the Communists on the shining roster, but Abou Ben Kirkconnell's name had been significantly omitted.

Over in England, labour leaders had shown scruples quite alien to Roosevelt and Mackenzie King. The national executive of the British Labour Party had warned its members against association with Anglo-Soviet friendship committees "or other activities of the Communist party." In Australia, the New South Wales Conference of the Australian Labour Party issued a similar warning to its members. In Canada, however, Mr. M. J. Coldwell, Mr. King, and Mr. George Drew were equally patrons of the dubious organization. Within sixteen months, however, the original united front of leftists and rightists had exploded in pandemonium and a Toronto clique proceeded to mould it nearer to their hearts' desire, with Communist organizer Max Chic as "national director." I hope that Canada may some day be given a full story of the Great Consult from the inoffensive citizen who was there badgered, insulted, and driven out of office, yet left to pay the deficit of three thousand dollars from the previous Red callithumpian show.

Falsification went from bad to worse. Our own CBC broadcasted daily rhapsodies on Soviet Russia from Moscow, spoken by a Canadian Communist journalist and Soviet agent. Sir Bernard Pares was sent over from London to abet the pro-Soviet line in meetings of the Canadian Institute of International Affairs. To my astonishment, even B. K. Sandwell published as a leading front-page *Saturday Night* editorial, entitled "Distrusters of Russia," an attack on his own foreign editor, Willson Woodside, and myself. My faith in his fundamental intelligence was at last fully restored some nine years later by an article (August 8, 1953) in the *Financial Post* where he stated categorically of active workers in the Labour Progressive party: "There is, it seems to me, only one possible attitude toward such a person, and that is to treat him as an enemy."

All government departments, however, were not culpable. The then minister of justice, the Right Honourable Louis S. St.-Laurent, with whom I had spent a quiet evening of discussion at the Roxborough apartments, wrote me personally in categorical terms: "I fully agree that we cannot be too cautious in guarding against the seeds of vicious propaganda which are being disseminated throughout so many of our unsuspecting fellow Canadians. Your book is very timely and I hope it will also bring real light to many who do not realize the seriousness of the problem."

I also appreciated a long letter from my old friend, John W. Dafoe, of the *Winnipeg Free Press*, asking me to send him copies of everything that I wrote on Communism, so that he might have "some ammunition in stock."

In the spring of 1945, a series of articles that I wrote for the *Evening Telegram*, Toronto, stirred up the Party to renewed attacks, this time of more than a merely verbal nature. Following one article, entitled "On Soviet Imperialism," a friend in Toronto wrote to me in some disquiet:

> The article has caused consternation in the camp of our Communist friends and I have information from a very confidential but most reliable source that the high priests of the Party are seriously thinking of prosecuting you under the Defence of Canada Regulations. Apparently your friend, Harry Hunter, is to lay the information and the suggestion has been

advanced that a "big lawyer" be engaged to handle the case. T. B. McQuesten has been mentioned as a possibility but there is nothing definite about this. To lay the information against you would depict Hunter as a public-spirited individual having the interests of the country at heart and incidentally would help him in the election campaign.

Either the big lawyer refused to act or the strategists thought better of the project. Action was demanded, however, and I promptly heard of the next chapter from the Honourable Albert Matthews and Mrs. Matthews at a reception following the spring convocation at McMaster University on May 14. Mr. Matthews who was chairman of McMaster's Board of Governors, said that he had been waited on by Joe Atkinson, proprietor of the *Toronto Daily Star*, and a lady member of his editorial staff, and that this precious pair had urged him to dismiss me from my professorship because of my articles in the *Telegram.* "Yes," added Mrs. Matthews, "and we are proud of you!"

A variant of this attack came presently through Communist indictments of me before the two main labour organizations in Hamilton, who were urged to demand that the University dismiss me as an evil man. Carefully briefed accusers came forward, both in the Trades and Labour Council and in the CCL–CIO, charging that Kirkconnell was anti-Semitic, anti-labour, and anti-democratic. I have nothing but praise for the way in which the matter was handled by the Trades and Labour Council under Mr. Bruce Doherty. The accusation was referred to their law committee and I was given a chance to appear before it. Comrade Abe Schaeffer (an old-line Communist, financial secretary of the Party in Hamilton in 1938 and a delegate to the constituent convention of the Labour Progressive party in 1943) was present as the accuser, with a laboriously drafted indictment from Communist headquarters that took him an hour to read. I had no trouble in refuting the scandalous accusations, and on the committee's report to that effect the Trades and Labour Council threw out the Communist charges. In the Councils of the CCL–CIO unions, however, where the same attempt at character assassination was made, I was at once condemned in absentia, without a hearing, and the unions' protest to the University, against its employing such a scoundrel as I, was duly communicated to the press. Sam Lawrence, the Socialist mayor of Hamilton, was quoted in the *Spectator* as favouring my internment, but luckily for me our Pink burgomaster had no authority to issue a *lettre de cachet*.

Just to keep me from sleeping too soundly there were also threats of libel action from the lawyers of some of the organizations that I had pilloried. My standard practice was to mail the same lawyers a partial list of the documentation that I had against their clients—and the rest was silence. There were even anonymous letters threatening my life,. but I consoled myself with the thought that political assassination had been almost unknown in Canadian history. Nevertheless, I avoided short cuts through back alleys after dark.

It is worth noting that shortly after the war a lawyer wrote theatening me with a libel action for my 1941 criticism of Mr. Adrien Arcand and his right-wing extremists, but here too I held a royal flush against a broken straight.

My publisher, W. H. Clarke of the Oxford University Press, met with more than threats. A recent female recruit in his office staff was found going through his private files in the interests of the Party and was immediately dismissed. Then followed two spite burglaries—break-ins through a basement window. There were no thefts but in each case his office records were thrown together on the floor in a confused pile of wreckage that took weeks to sort out.

Still another type of attack came through Red exploitation of labour unions. A front page article in the *Canadian Tribune* tells the story:

> By resolutions, letters and public meetings citizens across the country are piling up demands on Ottawa for vigorous action to round up all fascist traitors . . . and to put under ban the anti-United Nations propaganda now being circulated by Professor Watson Kirkconnell.
>
> Public meetings at Oshawa and other points urged banning of Kirkconnell's "Seven Pillars of Freedom," which is packed full of Goebbels-inspired falsehoods about the Soviet Union. . . .

In view of all these Party frustrations on the Canadian front, Moscow itself now fired a broadside at me. In *New Times*, a semi-monthly periodical publication issued in Moscow, the issue of June 15, 1945, contains a three-page assault on me by one of the Kremlin's chief hatchet-men, David Zaslavsky. A few excerpts will suffice:

> In Hamilton, Ontario, there resides a Professor Watson Kirkconnell who possesses all the principal attributes of a scalp hunter. Although the Professor wears trousers and his feet are encased not in moccasins but in modern shoes, he is a perfect savage, if not in blood, then in spirit. . . . The very mention of the Soviet Union sends him into paroxysms of rage. As, unlike his ancestors, he can write English, he gives vent to his fury in print . . . a cacophony of lies, slander and frenzied vituperation. Last year a book of his appeared entitled Seven Pillars of Freedom, which in vituperation excels anything that exists in the jungle of anti-Soviet literature of America. . . . In addition, Kirkconnell performs public war dances, which are called meetings. At these performances Kirkconnell jumps and yells to demonstrate to his audience his hatred of the Soviet Union, his longing to destroy it, to kill and scalp it. . . . Kirkconnell has as much idea about the Bolsheviks as his savage ancestors four hundred years ago had about Einstein's theory of relativity. . . . What is at the bottom of this Canadian's dread of the Soviet Union? It is as difficult to explain as the reason why dogs howl at the moon. . . .

Still another lecture that aroused the ire of the Embassy was delivered in Ottawa in February 1947. On Friday the 21st I had lectured by invitation to a class of senior officers of the RCMP, using my slide material on Soviet legislation. That same evening, I lectured at the University of Ottawa. On Saturday the 22nd I attended sessions of the Council of the Royal Society. On Sunday evening, the 23rd, I gave a closely documented public address in an Ottawa theatre on "The Situation in Russia." The chairman whispered to me that he had spotted men from the Embassy in the audience, furiously taking notes while I presented scores of documentary exhibits from *Pravda* and *Izvestia.* Sure enough, the response came over the Moscow radio on March 6 and was duly spread across Canada by the various press agencies. The British United Press cable said in part:

> The Moscow radio today broadcast a charge by *Izvestia* that . . . the pro-fascist Kirkconnell . . . gave a lecture in the Canadian capital on the subject Situation in Russia . . . affirming that his source of information was exclusively the Soviet press and official Soviet statistics. . . .
>
> Normally nobody would have paid much attention to the lecture, but this time the sponsors of the lecture, reactionary Catholic church organizations, guaranteed a suitably large audience.
>
> The pro-fascist lecturer attempted by his remarks to slander the Soviet Union, and the only feeling he could arouse was that of disgust. He was like those creatures described by Jonathan Swift, creatures whose teeth have rotted so much that they can no longer bite, but who are compensated by nature in the strength of their breath.

One of my most interesting experiences was a public debate on Sunday evening, March 3, 1946, in the Bathurst Street United Church, Toronto. Its minister, the Reverend Gordon Domm, had called me by long distance telephone and asked me to take the affirmative side of the proposition that "Soviet Russia is a menace to the peace of the world." I rashly consented and learned a few days later that my adversary was to be Leslie Morris, who had so frequently traduced me in the *Canadian Tribune.* Natural misgivings arose when I remembered the story told me by the Reverend Norman Rawson of the time when, at a similar debate in Massey Hall, the Communists had packed the place before anyone else could arrive and had put him and his partner through a terrific barrage of noise and abuse.

I need not have worried. When I came to the church I found that my friends in the Polish, Ukrainian, Serb, and Lithuanian communities of Toronto, noting the much advertised debate and wishing to assure me of fair play, had thronged the auditorium the minute the doors were open. Thus most of the Communists, who surged in at their heels, found all seats taken and were compelled to stand in the aisles. So congested did the building become that the police were compelled to push upwards of a thousand of the standees out of doors, where they milled about and shouted encouragement to Comrade Morris through the windows.

Within doors, however, the balance of the active audience was for once on the non-Communist side and attempts to heckle me were at once responded to by even louder heckling of Leslie Morris. I can still see the Communist MPP, A. A. MacLeod, white-faced and furious, leaning over the balcony-railing and shrieking at the chairman: "Tell Kirkconnell to call off his fascists!"

As I had anticipated, Morris did not concentrate on the real debate but sought to discredit me as being a forger in terms of a speech of Stalin in quoting which, in my earlier book, *Canada Europe and Hitler*, I had made a mistake as to date but not as to person. Although I had actually printed in *Saturday Night* my original source in an article by André Tardieu in *Le Gringoire*, Paris, in May 1938, the Communists had continued to parrot their "forgery" cry. I therefore brought to the Toronto debate still another source of Stalin's statement in the anti-Hitler Paris magazine, *La Petite Illustration* (No. 896, Nov. 26, 1938, Part II, p. 26), carrying from the McMaster University library in Hamilton the huge bound volume of the 1938 issues. When Comrade Morris trotted out his forgery canard, I simply set the volume under his nose and silenced his slander. Yet in at least two subseqeunt issues of the *Canadian Tribune* I encountered articles in which (in 1947 and 1955) this same Mr. Morris shamelessly talked about "Professor Watson Kirkconnell's faking of Stalin's writings which I had the pleasure of uncovering in 1943."

On August 7, 1946, the Reverend Mr. Domm invited me to a complimentary dinner on September 22 for all of the speakers on the Forum's programme for the two previous years. He also hoped that I would take part in another Forum meeting in the 1946–47 season. In replying with a firm negative, I tried to explain why I would not break bread with Mr. Domm's speakers:

> The report of the Taschereau–Kellock Commission (through whose 733 pages I have gone carefully) and the details brought out in the actual trials of certain spies have proven beyond all question that the Communists of Canada are traitors to Canada. I do not care to associate with traitors nor to collaborate in giving traitors a public platform. There are limits to what decent citizens can stomach.

One of the most strenuous experiences of all my warfare was in the city of Timmins, where I addressed a mass meeting of twelve hundred on the evening of Sunday, April 27, 1947. At least two hundred of these were Communists who had marched to the theatre in military formation and sought to wreck the meeting. Perhaps the simplest procedure will be for me to quote excerpts from the April 28 edition of the *Timmins Press*, which gave the affair extensive front page coverage:

> By any standards the meeting was a stormy one, even for this mining camp. . . . Deploying their forces strategically throughout the theatre, the Communists started heckling and booing long before Professor Kirkconnell's turn on the speaker's dais. The storm broke out the moment the chairman, Albert Aube, president of the Porcupine Adult Education group, which sponsored the meeting, stepped onto the platform . . . It was impossible to follow Professor Kirkconnell. For the first fifteen minutes of his address the entire audience was in an uproar.
>
> Cries of "Fascism", "poppycock", "go back to Hamilton", and "we don't want to hear you", filled the hall, only to be followed by wild cheering and clapping when a portrait of Lenin or Marshal Tito was flashed onto the screen. During one lull in the storm a woman's voice, speaking broken English in contrast to the Professor's quiet, well-cultured accents, exclaimed: "To hell with you, professor!" . . .
>
> Through it all, Professor Kirkconnell ignored his hecklers and his supporters alike. Acting as though he were at home before a class of his own university students, he kept his voice even and controlled. Only in conclusion did he give any indication that he had heard his hecklers. Then he said good-naturedly:
>
> "I think if this meeting has accomplished nothing more it has shown the good people of Timmins that the Communists can dish it out but they certainly can't take it."
>
> The twinkle in Professor Kirkconnell's voice and the matter-of-fact way he said this reduced his hecklers to sheepish silence which gave way to a roar of clapping and cheering from the hundreds of people who had come to see fair play. . . .
>
> Immediately after the meeting a group of Communist sympathizers held an impromptu street meeting under the watchful eyes of the police and, as a precaution, Professor Kirkconnell's friends cancelled his hotel reservations and whisked him away to private quarters for the night.

What promised to be a similar episode came that autumn when I was invited by the Windsor (Ontario) branch of the United Nations Society to give a public address in their city. A Red "fraction" in Local 200 of the United Auto Workers persuaded a rump meeting of the Local to announce that I would speak in Windsor at my personal peril. The United Nations Society refused to cancel its invitation, and I spoke as advertised. The RCMP were on hand to block any physical violence, but there was not even a word of interruption. The Red board of strategy had evidently changed its mind.

Harold Innis gave me a personal glimpse of the Moscow mind. In 1946, as president of the Royal Society of Canada, he represented this country at the bicentennial celebrations of the Russian Academy of Sciences. On his return to Canada, he told me with a chuckle of his encounters in Moscow with Soviet officials and scientists who kept telling him that Canada was wrong to tolerate so wild, irresponsible, and mendacious a scoundrel as Watson Kirkconnell. His reply had always been that he had known me intimately for twenty years and that I was quiet, honest, responsible, and scrupulously scholarly. The Moscow campaign to turn a visiting Canadian scholar against a well-known friend back home struck him as highly amusing.

So effective had been the wartime indoctrination by pro-Soviet propaganda that the detailed documentation of my *Seven Pillars of Freedom* slipped off most Canadian minds like water off a duck's back. Everything in print was capable of being specious, fabricated evidence. At times I despaired of getting honest men to face honest facts.

I therefore began to envisage a series of photostats of the actual evidence, first as an appendix to a new edition of my *Seven Pillars* and later (as the material piled up) in a large volume, *The Red Record*, consisting of nothing but such direct exhibits in photostat, with English translations where necessary. By the autumn of 1947, I had several hundred items, mounted and edited, ready for a publisher.

In securing such material, I had first of all subscribed to *Pravda*, which came to me daily from Moscow for many years by air mail at ten dollars a year. I had early learned that all laws are first published in *Pravda* and *Izvestia*. All else in these papers might be slanted, often shamelessly, for propaganda purposes, but laws are made to be enforced and hence they tell an unmistakable story. A systematic study of the current Moscow press then sent me back to the files of earlier years, available in full in the Slavonic section of the New York Public Library. Here I became a familiar visitor, checking through the Russian newspapers for significant items of law and news. I would then order photostats of the pages or issues that were relevant to my purpose. Still other Soviet Russian items, not available in New York, I located in the Library of Congress, Washington, and added to my bag.

To give here a full list of the basic information thus gathered on every phase of Soviet life would usurp book-length space in these memoirs for the contents of a large unpublished volume and negate the purpose of my present work. A few sample specimens must suffice by way of illustration:

(*a*) A decree of November 21, 1929, decreed death by shooting in case a citizen refused to return to Russia on request. This was presently extended to all who tried to escape from the Soviet Union.

(*b*) A decree of August 2, 1932, decreed death by shooting in case of theft. Clemency was expressly forbidden.

(*c*) A decree of June 8, 1934, supplemented that of November 21, 1929, by providing for the punishment of a fugitive's family with up to ten years imprisonment if, knowing of his plans, they failed to report him to the police. If they could show that they knew nothing regarding his offence they were still to be deported to Siberia for five years.

(*d*) A decree of July 10, 1934, reconstituting the OGPU as the NKVD, gave the reorganized police force authority to send any man or woman to penal servitude in Siberia for five years *without trial.* The dose could, of course, then be repeated.

(*e*) In a brief decree of December 4, 1934, persons accused of terrorism were to be tried within ten days without right of defence or appeal and then shot immediately.

(*f*) In a decree of April 7, 1935, minors accused of theft and other crimes were to bear "all measures of criminal punishment."

(*g*) In a news item of April 19, 1935, a boy named Leppe was shot, "on the basis of the new law," for stealing a briefcase.

(*h*) By Section 59 of the Criminal Code, a railway worker who by lateness or absence has caused an accident or even a deviation from the time-table can be sentenced to up to ten years' imprisonment. If his absenteeism or lateness is proved to be deliberate, the penalty is death.

(*i*) A law of October 2, 1940, introduced conscription of labour among adolescents.

(*j*) An edict of December 4, 1934, had put food supplies under the control of the factory bosses, so as to starve the complaining worker. By an edict of December 28, 1938, workers, for certain offences, were to be evicted from their homes—"without allocation of other housing accommodation."

(*k*) Electoral lists in *Izvestia* for October 17, 1945, revealed that five autonomous Soviet republics had been wiped out of existence during wartime by Moscow.

From the Lithuanian Embassy in Washington, I also secured other priceless photostat exhibits: checklists of the categories of the Lithuanian population to be exterminated by the NKVD during the grim murder-cum-deportation epoch after the seizure of 1940, a copy in Russian of the liquidation orders to the police, and a dated Soviet military map showing Lithuania as a Soviet republic a year before the actual absorption in 1940 in terms of a cheerful Soviet bargain with Hitler.

My preface to this great collection of evidence was written on the very day that Moscow and its Canadian worshippers were celebrating the thirtieth anniversary of the second (or autumn) revolution of 1917. Two paragraphs will be valid here, especially since the volume was never published:

Thirty years ago, on November 6, 1917, a tiny minority of Communists took over power in Russia, not from the Czar (who had abdicated eight months before) but from the only free administration that Russia has ever known, the Provisional Government headed by Alexander Feodorovich Kerensky. Amid the tumultuous celebrations of the 30th anniversary now being staged by the Stalinist régime—and its Canadian satellite organizations—there is some relevance in placing on the record a collection of original documents, mostly from Soviet Russian sources, illustrating the true character of the Communism that rules in the Kremlin.

Such a work is, in fact, long overdue. It is almost beyond contradiction that in Canada no editors, no clergymen, no professors of history and no members of parliament combine a working knowledge of the Russian language with an extensive survey of Soviet source material in the original. Anyone who undertook to analyse political, social and economic movements in France or Germany without a thorough-going study of source material in the original French or German would feel himself to be a dilettante or a charlatan. In the case of Soviet Russia, however, there are no such inhibitions. In our daily press and our learned journals alike, from church pulpits and radio news analysts, and from the intramural and extramural utterances of our elected representatives there is a spate of pronouncements, both rhapsodic and denigratory; and throughout it all one receives the impression of opinions held by instinct rather than a grasp of principles arising out of fundamental study. Many of the editors are doing an excellent job to the extent of their knowledge, but their material is almost invariably acquired at second or third hand. The present collection of documents attempts to supply data for arriving at conclusions at first hand.

But alas, books cost money, and the prospective cost of making cuts of several hundred photostats daunted even my good friend, Will Clarke, of the Oxford Press. He argued, moreover, that the wind of facts had begun to drive away the war-time fogs of propaganda-gas that had poisoned our radio, press, and public opinion. The Gouzenko disclosures had shown what evils the pro-Moscow mendacities had unwittingly but culpably cloaked. The long and short of it was that my *Red Record*, which had cost me so much in research and in photostat purchase, was much too expensive a proposition for anyone in Toronto to touch. It still slumbers on my shelves.

There have, however, been some minor by-products. For example, I wrote a forty-page pamphlet, entitled *The Communist Threat to Canada* for the Canadian Chamber of Commerce in 1947, using some eight of my photostats. I also wrote a whole series of anti-Communist broadcasts for Jim Hunter, which he delivered for the benefit of the miners and lumbermen of New Ontario. Two articles on Soviet law went to *Saturday Night*. For myself, a set of one hundred lantern slides, made from some of the more striking exhibits, has proved of value in presenting the truth about Communism to lecture audiences. In May 1948, I prepared a paper on "Canadian Communists and the Comintern" for my colleagues in Section II of the Royal Society, and in June, 1950, I gave them another heavily documented paper, "Some Aspects of Soviet Legislation." B. K. Sandwell said of this latter essay that I had "thrown the book at them." When in 1952, I finally brought out a revised edition of my *Seven Pillars of Freedom*, it was immeasurably strengthened by additional material. There were still, however, no photostats included.

There was little satisfaction in knowing that I was alone in this research into basic materials. I had checked carefully with the research committee of the Canadian Institute of International Affairs as to anyone else in Canada who was using Russian materials for a study of Soviet Russia today, but was assured that I was companionless in No Man's Land. Perhaps I was not quite alone. My friend Willson Woodside, although he had no Russian, had access to some excellent press summaries and seemed to me to be remarkably right for a man without primary sources.

After becoming a college president in 1948, I gradually dropped nearly all of this intimate research. For one thing, there was no prospect of further publication, and I felt that I had completed my task. For another, academic and denominational responsibilities had come to absorb almost all of my time and energies. Still more clearly, those energies were waning as I grew older and I no longer felt the inexhaustible drive towards research that had animated me in Winnipeg and Hamilton. I no longer subscribed to *Pravda* or studied source material in the New York Public Library. That this did not imply any withering in my convictions may be gathered from an interchange of correspondence. On July 18, 1956, His Excellency, Dmitri Chuvakhin, Soviet Ambassador to Canada, sent me a most graciously worded letter, in Russian, asking for detailed information on higher education in Canada. He hailed me as "one of the chief Canadian scholars" and "one of the chief experts in Canada on the Russian language" and offered me reciprocal information on higher education in the Soviet Union. Not long before this quite another version of ambassadorial thinking was passed on to me by my crony, Willson Woodside, following a conversation at an Embassy cocktail party. An Embassy official had there become confidentially communicative—*in vodka veritas*—and breathed to him: "We wish that we had that son-of-a-bitch Kirkconnell east of the Iron Curtain for just five minutes."

The information that Mr. Chuvakhin had requested was sent immediately but the first paragraph of my letter made my position clear:

> I am startled to receive your courteous letter of July 18th. From the days when your Embassy's Comrade Montinov supplied the ammunition against me and Comrade David Zaslavsky threw the Embassy's bombs in the Moscow press, I had assumed that your Government was aware of my detestation of all its works. *Timeo Danaos et basia ferentes.*

Soviet savagery in Hungary four months later merely confirmed my belief that dovelike noises in Soviet diplomacy were subtle ventriloquism by a Politbureau vulture.

But to end this chapter on such a note would falsify my philosophy of international politics. I cannot feel any sentiment other than goodwill towards any nation in the world, for we are all members of one human family. Neither can I ascribe all evil to the Communist East and all virtue to the non-Communist West. For example, the stark Soviet brutality in Hungary in 1956 was more than matched by the crime of Roosevelt and Churchill when they threw open the gates of Hungary to Stalin's legions in 1944, even as Poincaré and Grey secretly signed away Istanbul and other Turkish territory to Nicholas II in March 1915. Lord Acton said of Britain that her annals were the most sanguinary of all Christian nations. Between Waterloo and 1914, Britain waged *thirty-eight* aggressive wars. Between 1875 and 1914 she added 5,000,000 square miles to her earlier 8,000,000 square miles of territorial loot. The exploitation of Morocco, Algeria, and Syria by the French was matched by the British exploitation of Egypt. American imperialism got off to a malodorous start with the war on Spain, fomented by Hearst and Pulitzer and exploited by the Republican "war hawks."

Plato, in the ninth book of his *Republic*, analyses the character of the tyrannical man, swayed by greed for money and power, ruled by the subterranean passions that speak to all of us in dreams when "the reasoning, gentle and ruling part" of the soul is asleep. The philosopher then goes on, by implication, to indict the greedy leaders who had led the Athenians to enslave their neighbours and hence had shattered the fabric of the Hellenic world in a fratricidal Thirty Years War. Our own age has seen similar greed, from 1900 to the present, result in similar disaster. It has seen that *pleonexia*, on the part of more than one or two ruling classes, twice tear Europe to pieces and jeopardize the whole future of mankind. The conspirators of 1904–14 and 1937–41 have put a tiger in our taxes. Thus in 1957, a year of "peace," $59,800,000,000 or some 78 cents of the American tax dollar was being assigned to military services and a round forty billions to the sheer means of destruction. Our tribal gods of the past six decades have been wicked enough, and the genies that they have let loose have been malign enough, to threaten human history with an utter end, not with a whimper but a bang.

My hostility to Communism is based on the simple ground that it is a carefully organized drive for power, committed to the systematic extermination of whole strata of the population in every country that it takes over. Our so-called "Free World," intermittently cursed with spiritual wickedness in high places, has nevertheless a potentiality of liberty that is impossible in the police-driven death-camps and torture-dungeons of absolute dogmatism. The dilemma of the Vietnam war is that it is a test case for the Communists' new technique of the "war of national liberation" (complete with bourgeois extermination and Party dictatorship), blue-printed for all non-Communist countries, one by one, as a feasible alternative to the world suicide of general nuclear warfare.

25

Of Travel

MY CRUISING LIMITS in the Western Hemisphere have been from Miami in the south to Resolute in the Arctic north and from St. John's and Washington in the east to Victoria, San Francisco, and Los Angeles in the west. In the Eastern Hemisphere I have ranged from Cairo in the south to Helsinki, Stockholm, Oslo, and Akureyri in the north and from Jerusalem and Beirut in the east to Galway and Reykjavik in the west. I was fortunate to see Jugoslavia, Roumania, Hungary, Poland, East Germany, Lithuania, Latvia, and Estonia before they passed into Communist captivity, and Palestine before the Arab–Israeli dichotomy of 1948 made frontiers an embarrassment to the wayfarer. I cannot lay much claim to being a traveller, for I have crossed the Atlantic only twelve times and have never seen South America or the Far East. So far as Europe and the Near East are concerned, my chief *Wanderjahr* came in 1921–22, during the vacations of my graduate studies at Oxford, reinforced in 1938 by my travels to and from the summer session of the Stephen Tisza University at Debrecen, Hungary. Other trips were chiefly on university business.

Pleistocene geography, already described in chapter III, had dominated my early years. Port Hope was built on terminal moraine of sand and clay. Lindsay lay on clays and muck in the old bed of Lake Schomberg, a Pleistocene arm of a larger Lake Huron. In between the two towns rose a great range of morainic sand hills. I was later to spend over two years at Kapuskasing in the bed of the former Lake Ojibway and eighteen years at Winnipeg, in the red silt laid down in former Lake Agassiz. The soils of these fine agricultural areas had been scoured by four glacial periods off igneous and metamorphic rocks of the Great Canadian Shield, to the north and east, nearly two million square miles of wilderness, dotted with millions of lakes and rivers.

These were the familiar facts of geography from which I was to go out and meet a more diversified world. There were, of course, resemblances. In air flights over Finland and Sweden, I found the conditions of the Canadian Shield repeated, with countless lakes scattered among the sheep-back hills of a heavily glaciated terrain and countless islets in the Gulf of Bothnia that reminded one of Georgian Bay, Chester Basin, or the Labrador and British Columbia coasts. The counterpart of this was the morainic deposits of the Baltic States, sprinkled with numerous erratics from Finland. Sweden also had some striking eskars, and there were ample evidences of glacial till all across Northern Europe—including the scenes through which I had cycled daily for several months in Oxfordshire, Berkshire, and Buckinghamshire. Hungary, however, had been protected from the glacial thrust by a ring of mountains and was rich in loess and alluvial soils. Egypt likewise showed no sign of moraine or glacier, but the narrow limits of the Nile valley and delta were hemmed in by the dry erosion of windborne sand.

The most un-Canadian phenomenon that my travels encountered was volcano country—the millions of catacomb graves in the volcanic-ash tufa near Rome and the smoking cone of Vesuvius, still ominous beside the lava beds of Herculaneum and the cinder-buried skeleton of Pompeii. Still more appalling was the immensity of lava field formations in Iceland. The whole island was originally volcanic in origin, but at least a quarter of it represented lava flows so recent as to be completely sterile and pathless. Hekla billowed smoke far to the east of Thingvellir and throughout the southwest part of the island, larger than Ireland, hot subterraneous water oozed generously up from the depths. Great fissures, like the Almannagjá at the ancient outdoor place of parliament, testified to monumental faulting in the volcanic rocks, but the most awesome vision was the immense canyon valley of Oxnadalur through which we flew from west to east and back again, on an air visit to Akureyri. Stretching for fifty miles roughly east and west, between the grassy fields of Skagafjördur and the steep, narrow inlet of Eyjafjördur, its shadowy depths seemed like a Gustave Doré engraving of Milton's hell, lacking only colossal fiends to match its titanic barrenness. On either side indigo walls sank abruptly a mile down into a sort of perpetual twilight. Sometimes vast lateral valleys yawned suddenly to north or south in the stupendous faulting of those sterile ranges. Jagged summits, capped with snow, brooded high above the corridor through a dead Hades. It must have taken courage for the early Icelander to make his way on foot through that gorge in Niflheim. One can realize why Icelandic folklore peopled such cliffs with vast evil spirits, *karl* and *kerling* and *troll*, in the form of huge rocks.

My first river was the Ganaraska, *alias* Smith's Creek, at Port Hope—in spring flood a mighty torrent that could cut the town in two and leave huge ice-cakes stranded in the business section, but for the rest of the year a quiet little stream, six inches deep and twenty feet wide, babbling down over broad, flat shelves of limestone into a Lake Ontario so broad that we could not see the farther shore. The years brought acquaintance with the whole roster of Canada's major rivers except the Mackenzie complex of lakes and streams. The rivers of the United States were ultimately added and all the great rivers of Europe west of the Prut and the Daugava except those of Spain and Portugal. The Nile and the Jordan were thrown in for good measure.

Against this diversified background of physiography, a few travel episodes may be briefly set. While diaries could easily spin this chapter out to two or three book-length narratives, the main interest of the volume is in Canada, and the foreign wanderings of one Canadian have merely marginal relevance. What follows may be regarded as a mere succession of notes and comments rather than a connected chronicle.

DECEMBER 1921

On the afternoon of December 26, I arrived in Cairo by train from Alexandria. Reports of riots in the capital had held us up at the dockside for a couple of hours, but we had finally set out about noon. The general station at Cairo was deserted, however; there were no taxis or carriages; and the only traffic in sight was an occasional armoured car loaded with British troops. A young Arab lad offered to carry my suitcase for me, and I gave him the name and address of my hotel (the Rossmore Pension, 15 Sharia el Madabegh). He seemed a little uncertain as to the route, and after we had walked nearly a mile to the right from the station, he spoke to a passer-by who directed us sharp left from our course. After trudging another mile, we enquired again, were again directed to the left, and a mile farther on came safely to my hotel, after covering three sides of a rectangle. The point of all this, however, is that had we gone directly from the station to the hotel we should have passed through the heart of the Zaglul Pasha riots, in which seventeen persons were killed that afternoon and damage was done in excess of two million dollars.

I left Cairo by rail one evening later in the week and headed for Jerusalem. The children of Israel had once taken forty years to wander from Goshen to Jericho, but now, thanks to the railway laid down during Allenby's campaign (and a pre-war line from Jaffa to Jerusalem) I could look forward to arriving in the Holy City after a journey of only eighteen hours. At midnight we reached the Suez Canal, walked across "the bridge" at El Qantara, and mounted a decrepit narrow-gauge Palestinian train where we were to sit up all night on bare plank benches in a converted boxcar. The welcome dawn broke as the train neared Gaza. Silhouetted against the pale east as he stood on the crest of a little hill to the right was a shepherd, dressed as his kind had been dressed for three thousand years and surrounded by his sheep. To the left, as the light grew stronger, I could distinguish a rolling waste of yellow sand, stretching away towards the Mediterranean.

Amid the orange groves of Ludd we changed again, this time to the Jaffa–Jerusalem train, and struck off to the southeast over ground that swelled unevenly up to meet the blue hills of Judea. Soon the train entered the green Vale of Sorek, long ago the home of Delilah. Then the mountains began, and the valley narrowed to a canyon-like gulch, winding through towering limestone hills, many thousands of feet in height. For hours there was hardly a sign of human life—nothing but the desolation of rocky cavernous cliffs and boulder-strewn valley bottoms and an occasional herd of scrawny black goats.

As a travelling companion on my journey up from Egypt there had come a venerable Jewish rabbi from Kansas, visiting Palestine for the first time, in order to see the new Zionist settlements. It was pathetic to watch his distress, first at the sandy deserts of the coastal area and then at the stony desolation of the Judean hills. And now, as we neared the Holy City itself, a torrential shower, typical of the winter season, burst upon us, churning up the roads into mud and half veiling the landscape with driving rain. His tearful disillusionment was a moving sight.

A few days later, I was at Haifa, the seaport of Galilee, waiting for a belated steamship that was to take me on up the Syrian coast. With time to kill, I wandered up the slopes of Mount Carmel among the budding clumps of wild narcissus and to my delight chanced upon some prehistoric tombs of the sort inhabited by the demoniac in the New Testament—a tunnel into the chalk hillside to a central chamber from which stopes were hollowed out, spokewise, to house the individual corpses. It was only afterwards that I learned that the hillside was a haunt of vipers.

JANUARY 1922

On January 3, 1922, I arrived at Mersina on the little Italian freighter-mail-steamer *Montenegro*, and found three warships (two French and one Italian) and the Khedivial Line steamer *Montazah* already anchored in the shallow open harbour. Mersina was a fine-looking town, with large handsome houses and broad streets, chiefly the creation of Greek, Swiss, and German capital. Back of it stretched the malarial plain of Cilicia, towered over by the Taurus Mountains. Eighteen flat miles to the east lay Saint Paul's old home town of Tarsus. The *Montazah* was already crowded to the gunwales with Armenian refugees and we were soon to be loaded down in similar fashion. Most of these had earlier come from farther north, escaping from Turkish violence in Armenia to take refuge under the French flag in Cilicia, but the French had suddenly ceded Cilicia to the Turks in exchange for a commercial grab farther east, and the Armenians were face to face with their ancient foes again. Our vessel had arrived in port on the very day that the Turks marched in, and we sailed away to the accompaniment of rifle-fire, a distant brass band, and uproarious Turkish jubilation. Our little ship was swamped with tired and dishevelled fugitives—men, women, and children. The horrors of past experience had left its dreadful mark on their faces, and relief at their sudden rescue from imminent peril was curdled by the utter uncertainty of their future.

The next few days were full of a sense of misery. We tried to land them at Limassol, in Cyprus, but Mersina had been full of smallpox; the island's only quarantine station was at Larnaca, farther east, and we were already two days behind schedule, travelling west. We tried again at Rhodes, but the Italians were emphatic in their refusal. The weirdly accursèd ship of Coleridge's *Ancient Mariner* seemed somehow a prototype of our own vessel with its hopeless load of passengers. At last we arrived in Smyrna, then under Greek rule, and there, not through any willingness on the part of the authorities but through sheer laxity in police control, our refugees disappeared over the ship's side during the night and melted into the underworld of the city. Even there, in squalor and obscurity, there was no ultimate safety, for a few months later the city was sacked by the Turkish army and most of its population was driven into the sea.

I had a comparable glimpse of desperation in the summer of 1938, while travelling by Danube steamboat from Vienna to Budapest. Near Bratislava, where the Austrian, Czechoslovak, and Hungarian frontiers met, I saw a forlorn-looking steamer moored near the shore. One of the Hungarian sailors on our own boat volunteered to give me its story. It was a Greek steamer, he said, with three hundred Viennese Jewish refugees on board. They had been there three months. The Czechs would not admit them to Czechoslovakia. The Hungarians did not want them in Hungary. And behind them, Nazi police barred their path. So long as their money lasted, they could hope to eat. Beyond that, no one dared conjecture.

APRIL 1922

One of the happiest interludes of my life was a month spent in Dresden, Germany, during the Oxford Easter vacation in 1922. I shared a boarding-house room with Corvin D. Edwards, an American Rhodes scholar from Missouri and a member of my college, but while he ranged freely about at all hours, I had brought along a mass of research notes and wrote the complete first draft of a thesis on unemployment at the rate of ten pages a day. Whenever I had finished my diurnal quantum by suppertime, we went together to the State Opera House, for the season was in full swing and the programme was superb. When Good Friday came, Wagner's *Parsifal* was scheduled, but the house was sold out. Was there nothing left, we asked again. Well, the royal box of the former king of Saxony was still available—at a price. The charge in German currency was nominally prohibitive, but thanks to the black market value of disintegrating marks as against North American dollars we two young *Valutaschieber* enjoyed the luxury of the royal box for twenty-five cents apiece.

One sunny Sunday afternoon, as I was strolling through a Dresden park, I saw a flaxen-haired little three-year-old boy hopping happily about on the grass. Joyfully he cried out to his young mother, who sat on a nearby bench: "O Mama, Mama, ich bin ein Osterhase!" There was no premonition of the horrors of February 1945, when Anglo-American fire bombs and blockbusters obliterated the whole peaceful, non-industrial, non-strategic city and all its inhabitants.

JULY 1938

My wife and I reached Budapest after an all-day trip down the Danube by river steamer. As Hitler had taken over Austria four months before, we reached the Vienna wharf through streets disfigured by anti-semitic slogans. The "Beautiful Blue Danube" proved to be tawny and turbulent, impressive rather than sentimentally romantic. Vivid scenes on our voyage came at the towering "Porta Hungarica" at Devény, at the old Hungarian capital and coronation city, Pozsony, at the lofty cathedral and the residence of the Catholic prince-primate at Esztergom, and finally on our arrival in Budapest in the deepening dusk as tens of thousands of lights, from palaces and bridges, turned the city into a vision from fairyland.

About three days later we proceeded by train across the Great Hungarian Plain to the "Calvinist Rome," Debrecen, a Presbyterian city of 120,000, where a university had been founded four centuries before by Magyar graduates from Geneva and Leiden. Count Paul Teleki, then minister of education, came with us and we were royally entertained at an evening dinner at *The Golden Bull*. The next morning saw the opening session of an international summer school at the university. The student representatives of a dozen different nationalities brought greetings, each in his own mother tongue, and the director of the *Nyári Egyetem*, Dr. János Hankiss, replied in pentecostal fluency with a gracious response in each of the languages that had been used. Then Count Paul Teleki, as guest of honour, was called on for an address, and this he delivered, eloquently and with great freedom, in English, French, German, and Magyar. That evening, at a student reception, he taught my wife to dance the *csárdás*, an achievement on her part that won her a friendly cartoon in one of the Budapest dailies. I lectured in English the following day on Hungarian poetry, and the day after that ventured to give a lecture on the same topic using the Magyar language. With the exception of a convocation address in French that I delivered at Laval University in 1963, this has been my sole full-dress effort in a foreign tongue, and the toil and anguish that its preparation cost me made me resolve that it would never happen again.

In many respects, Count Paul Teleki was the greatest man that I have ever known. Professor of geography in the University of Budapest, Chief Scout for Hungary (known affectionately by all boy scouts as "Uncle Paul"—Pál Bácsi), sometime minister of education and foreign minister, and twice Prime Minister—this slight, wiry, grey-haired scholar had touched life with distinction at many points. His death by suicide on April 2, 1941, was a torch of protest to a world at war. After years of devoted and indefatigable service, he had reached the point where, as the living premier of Hungary, he could no longer accomplish anything for his nation. By his death, however, he could both denounce to all mankind the Nazi violation of his country's honour and at the same time issue a sobering warning to some of his countrymen who, though anti-Nazi like the vast majority of Magyars, were yet glad to accept territorial restitution at German hands. In keeping with his calculating act of self-immolation, Count Teleki, on that fatal Wednesday, attended a church service with his beloved Boy Scouts in the afternoon, held a final meeting of his cabinet in the evening, paid a last visit to his invalid wife in hospital, and then walked unfalteringly home to a waiting revolver. By his act he did what one resolute man could do to show the essential integrity of his tragic country.

AUGUST 1938

My wife and I were sitting on a park bench in a public square in Kolozsvár (Cluj), the capital of Transylvania. Between us was Sándor Reményik, the chief living poet of the region. All walls had ears under the Roumanian régime that had smashed nearly all public monuments of a thousand years of Hungarian history and subjected the Magyar population to laws of draconic assimilation. It was only amid the shadows of a public park, with an eye open for eavesdroppers, that we could venture on any discussion of the current attempt to stamp out the identity of two million non-Roumanians. Only the Roumanian language was now valid. Every personal name had to be Roumanized and was legal only in its Roumanian form. It was a penal offence, even in a poem or an historical work, to print the non-Roumanian form of any Transylvanian place-name. Offenders against such laws were brought, not before a civil court but before a military court. To criticize the administration was treasonable, and a bishop whose criticism was quoted in a Budapest paper had found himself promptly in prison. Public meetings of every sort were forbidden and even a birthday party of a dozen persons had been dispersed by the police.

Less than four years later, Reményik was to die at the age of fifty-two. Especially under the pen-name "Végvári" and often in verses that were deliberately guarded, he had done much to alleviate the anxiety and despair of his countrymen. His body was frail but his spirit was honest and intrepid. I had translated much of his poetry into English, to his great satisfaction. An excerpt from his "To the Magyars of Transylvania" will give a taste of his quality:

> Out of the flame of strawfires there is left
> A handful of red embers in our hearts,—
> A thousandfold more hot than burning worlds
> Or aught that heat imparts.
> Upon each other's heart-wall, in the night
> Of this our doom, we tap our rataplan,
> One signal in the catacombs of death:
> "We stay Hungarian!"

In June 1965 I was to encounter a still grimmer postscript in a letter from another Transylvanian poet, Albert Wass, who, as a shattered refugee from Communist Roumania, has found refuge in the University of Florida: "Sándor Reményik was lucky. He died before 1944, and so had not seen the hell on earth."

SEPTEMBER 1938

My wife and I had trudged beside Dr. Longchamps, professor of law in the University of Lwów, up the great Mound of the Union of Lublin, a tumulus erected in 1569 to commemorate the uniting in that year of Poland and Lithuania (including Ukraine) under a single crown. Its nearest English model would be the much smaller Silbury Hill, near Avebury, in Wiltshire, but the occasion for this latter memorial is lost in pre-history, under the blanket of the dark. Other immense barrows that came to my mind from earlier travel were the so-called graves of Achilles and Patroklos on the shore of the Troad or the Serpent Mound graves on the shore of Rice Lake, near Peterborough, Ontario.

"Yonder, to the east," said Professor Longchamps, pointing across the steppe towards the Soviet Union, "is the invader that we all dread. In western Poland, men are naturally fearful of the Germans, but here we live in the shadow of the Communist glacier. There are no natural frontiers between the Urals and the North Sea and the ice-fields of slavery are waiting to engulf us from the east." His prescience was all too correct.

JULY 1955

On the top of the Cheviots we (my wife, my three daughters, and I) paused in the gap at Carter Bar, dismounted from our faithful little Morris-Oxford, and gazed about. Beside us was a small canteen, near which a hungry old ram was rummaging earnestly in the garbage. To the north stretched the incredible green hills of Roxburghshire in one of the most beautiful vistas on God's earth. To the south, the Cheviots declined less abruptly but with an incessant series of downward sweeps that would presently bring us to Corbridge, the old capital of Northumbria, and the Roman remains behind Hadrian's Wall. The excavations at Corstopitum were to remind us of the Roman camp that we had seen at Fortingall, at the mouth of Glenlyon, in Perthshire, and of the Wall itself just north of Hexham. We tried to imagine the emotions of an ancient Caledonian, of say A.D. 130, standing at Carter Bar and brooding over the alien imperialism that had so recently set up an almost impregnable fortification from the Tyne to the Solway. I could even envisage one of my own remote ancestors on the distaff side standing on the summit of Criffell and gazing apprehensively across the Solway to the western end of the Alien Wall.

The five of us were ultimately to visit Avebury, Silbury, Stonehenge, and the remote "White Horse Hill" near Uffington in Berkshire. These were glimpses of a more remote epoch, only darkly understood as compared with the Roman civilization whose tongue we had all studied and into whose history we had all been initiated.

APRIL 1960

In April 1960, I received a gracious invitation from Air Vice-Marshal Bryans, RCAF, to go with a transport flight from Halifax *via* Trenton, Winnipeg, and Churchill to Resolute, on Cornwallis Island, roughly 75 degrees north and 95 degrees west. That would place us some 15 degrees from the North Pole—not quite within spitting distance but close enough to be exciting. The 7000 miles of travel had, unfortunately, to be carried out with unremitting insistence. After five days of flying in ear-shattering old North Stars, I was pretty well tired out before I got home. For having crossed the Arctic Circle, however, I had been presented with an illuminated certificate, vouching for me henceforth as "an Airborne Ice Worm of the initial degree."

One of the most obvious impressions of the trip was the contrast in temperatures. In Southern Ontario it was 65 above, at Churchill it was around zero, while at Resolute it was a gentle 20 below. About halfway between Churchill and Resolute, we crossed the DEW-line and saw the utter bleakness of one of the radar stations, Shepherd's Bay, with a small shed, some radio masts, and a landing strip. The terrain up across Boothia Peninsula, Somerset Island, and Cornwallis Island is an alternation of rolling hills, muskeg, and a labyrinth of lakes, but at this time of year the whole treeless waste was frozen solid and drifted over with an infinity of snow. In January blackness, in a blizzard at sixty below zero, it must be a fair sample of the colder parts of hell.

Resolute has two functions. On the one hand, I was given a guided tour of the meteorological, ionospheric, magnetic, and seismic laboratories, busy with their share of geophysical research. On the other hand, I saw "flying boxcars" shuttling millions of tons of fuel oil, gasoline, food, and building materials to the entire archipelago. A summer waterborne fleet piles these up at Resolute, and then for a favourable period of two or three weeks in April and again in October transport planes work twenty-four hours a day on airlifts to substations in all directions. All the extra staff for this crash programme had to be put up at the camp mess. I was amused at some doggerel painted in red on the light blue outer wall of the mess, just as one entered the building:

> You are welcome to Resolute,
> As welcome as can be!
> Our prices are high,
> But women are free.
> The grub is first class;
> The climate is hell;
> You've got to stay here—
> It's the only hotel.

Part of the jest is that, as with "the snakes in Iceland," there are no women in Resolute.

For flying in regions where proximity to the magnetic pole drives the ordinary compass crazy, the Arctic planes have to be equipped with gyroscopic compasses, fly on Greenwich mean time, and take constant sextant bearings on the sun and the stars. For that long period of the year when the sun is continuously out of sight, the navigator has recourse to a polarized light sextant, which can get its bearings from diffused light at the horizon from a sun that is itself hidden. This was a new toy for me to gloat over on our night flight back to Churchill.

JULY 1963

A few rods to the left of the Lawman's podium on the Law-mountain at Thingvellir, a small glacial river, the Oxará, topples in foam over a sheer basalt cliff and then reunites its waters to flow along the foot of the escarpment, closer and closer to the seat of justice. Just short of that august spot, it turns left again and flows swiftly down the slope, but first rests for a moment in a deep icy pool, just short of a modern highway bridge. This, "the drowning pool," is one of the grimmest spots in the whole island republic. Men sentenced to death by the Althing had their throats cut, but condemned women were drowned here in the pitiless, cold depths of the river. The arctic thyme on its rocky banks had seemed a portent of beauty, but as Dr. Ármann Snævarr, rector magnificus and professor of law in the University of Iceland, told us the history of the spot, a cold gust from the mediaeval past chilled the imagination.

Just east of the city of Reykjavik rises the long, high mass of Esja, a mountain whose infinite variety of aspect is a matter of national comment. Light and shade, cloud and sunshine, are altering it continually. Sigurður Nordal has remarked that Esja is like a vain beauty, everlastingly changing her mood and her dresses. This Cleopatra of mountains has a sister, however, in the profile of Cape Blomidon, as seen from the slopes of Wolfville, for its noble countenance is never the same for two hours on end.

In the little town of Akureyri, the chief thrill for me was not the home of the old poet, Matthias Jochumsson, nor the fine, twin-spired Lutheran church with its 48-stop classical organ, but the botanical park where labelled specimens of all Icelandic flora had been sedulously planted according to their families and genera. My wife quietly got out her camera as I knelt in long, rapt adoration before a bed of seven different Icelandic orchids, simultaneously in bloom, identical in genera with those of my native Ontario but differing enough in detail to be ranked as alien in species.

The last supper of our 1963 visit to Iceland was as guests of Dr. and Mrs. Snævarr in the roof restaurant of the skyscraper Hotel Saga. All of Reykjavik lay in sun-drenched panorama round about us, while eighty miles to the north-northwest across Faxa Fjörður rose the stern volcanic peak of Snæfell, down whose extinct lava-shaft Jules Verne, in the best of his scientific romances, sent a German professor of geology, his nephew, and an imperturbable Icelandic servant on a "journey to the centre of the earth." The tale had nourished my youth, and the mighty summit seemed worthy of the tale. After the meal, we adjourned to the great university auditorium to hear the latter part of a superb concert by a visiting Soviet pianist, Ashkenazi.

JULY 28, 1963

With my wife and our daughter Janet, I had taken a Sunday morning train from Dublin to Galway. A bus carried us another twelve miles along the north littoral of Galway Bay to the hamlet of Spiddal, where we picnicked on the shore, fronting the Aran Islands and the gentle sunlit expanse of the North Atlantic. Food, the breathless July heat, and the habits of nearly seventy years urged a siesta, but ancient glaciers and marine erosion had picked the whole coast as clean as Logie Bay or Peggy's Cove. At last we found a patch of grass a little larger than a man, and on this scanty mattress I slumbered soundly while my less drowsy companions gazed at Inishmore, Inishmaan, and Inisheer. It was hard to realize that this flat, bare, rocky coast was part of the same island as the bogs of Meath or the romantic mountain eyrie of Glendalough, full of learned echoes of Saint Kevin.

In confessing to deeper fascination in the landscapes of Europe and the Near East than in those of Canada, I would plead in extenuation the vastly greater mass of human associations in the Eastern Hemisphere. Geologically considered, all parts of the world may be equally old, but all are not equally rich in historical records. Until carbon-14 dating had been invented, Canada had no history in depth, and although Canadian pre-history now has random bench-marks back to 9000 B.C., we have virtually no linguistic or memorial instruments to survey the intervening millennia. A scientist might suggest a "coefficient of historicity," with maxima in Italy, Greece, Egypt, and Mesopotamia and minima in Manitoulin Island or the Olduvai Gorge.

To let one's imagination take the wings of the morning and sweep across the whole expanse of Europe is less to be concerned with mountain and plain, river and sea, forest and plough-land, than to envisage those tides of human life that have flowed and eddied and intermingled here since the beginning of history. Finding its continuity through the mating of individual men and women, the human stream has frequently shown an astonishing perpetuation of type. I can still remember how, on an entire tram-ride from the Piraeus up to Athens, I stared in startled admiration at a young woman whose every feature and proportion seemed to have stepped in antique Hellenic charm from a design on a vase of the age of Pericles. The strong masculine faces of old Roman portrait busts have met me again and again on the streets of Rome or

Naples. The Renaissance grace of the girls of Florence or Venice I have found not only recreated in the flesh in these historic cities but also preserved in the art of Raphael, Botticelli or Titian in galleries as far afield as Dresden, London or New York. Hans Holbein the Younger endowed a score of collections with "timeless Englishmen" and in a corner of the National Gallery in Dublin I found the circle of Samuel Johnson come more alive in some portraits by Reynolds than even in the pages of Boswell. To such a mood, the world is not primarily physiography or architecture or the fabrics of economics and politics but human beings in all their variety and wonder. "O brave new [and old] world, that has such people in't!"

26

Three Acres of Vacation

THE ANNUAL RENDEZVOUS has been "Fair Havens," an abrupt three acres of headland and highland fronting the northernmost bay of Boshkung Lake and backed by the Dorset highway in the county of Haliburton. Fifty years ago, when my brothers and I were young and used to paddle and portage back the seventy miles from Lindsay, this lake was our favourite base of operations for shorter, radial canoe trips along chains of lakes in all directions. Growing old, however, brings a willingness to abandon the tent for a cabin in the woods and to find in the natural history of a tiny plot enough exploration to brim the weeks of any summer.

At "Fair Havens" the very contours of the earth are a challenge to scientific enquiry. "Every face, however fair, is but moulded on a skull," and through the veil of tree-clad morainic sand and clay one perceives clearly the underlying skeletal form of the rocks. Even on so small a property, there are a dozen major outcroppings of grey Archaean gneiss, some of them forming precipices thirty feet in height. Here and there the shelving bands of the rock are pierced from top to bottom by dikes of snowy quartz or reddish feldspar. In this region, as in a million square miles of Canada's playground, one is among the worn roots of the everlasting hills. Sedimentary rocks, miles in height, once overlay these granites and have since been stripped away by aeons of erosion. Some of them, deep in the earth, had merged with invading plutonic masses from the depths to make a devil's batter and harden into gneissic granite. The dip and strike of the banded gneiss, conforming to that of the crystalline limestones a few miles farther south, bears witness to their subterranean kinship a thousand million years ago.

For the geological detective, there is superimposed the evidence of glacial drift, chiefly unstratified sands full of granite boulders. On the south acre, however, where we dig our garbage pits under the shade of the red oaks, the sand is clearly stratified, marking deposits in the once higher waters of a Pleistocene lake.

Nature has been busy healing all these wounds, whether of ice or of fire. The very front of the rocky cliffs has been completely covered with lichens—broad, wrinkled masses of ashen grey, like lettuce leaves from some garden in Erebus; or again, a sort of livid, creeping tetter, like a grim skin disease on the face of the rocks; or yet again, upright filaments, ranging in colour from pale silver to pale rose and endowed with all the finely branching grace of a clavaria. Hours without number may be spent with a hand lens and a microscope among these Lilliputian forms of vegetation. The same zeal can find ample scope among their green and brown neighbours, the mosses, which carpet the shadier parts of the cliff with fresh and vivid tapestries. Here I have found great patches of the giant *Bryum*, with its incredible green rosettes, the dark cushions of *Grimmia*, the lighter, sturdier masses of *Rhacomitrium*, and the delicate, ascending branches of *Thuidium*. Ferns complete the cliff-side colony, especially the cheerfully ubiquitous polypody, the graceful male fern, and the dark evergreen fronds of the marginal shield fern.

Passing from Lilliput to Brobdingnab among the botanical inhabitants of "Fair Havens," one may find over thirty varieties of trees about the place. The original stand was white pine, and vast stumps, charred and crumbling, tell how the primeval forest perished by axe and fire three human generations ago. As is so often the case with burnt-over land, the present occupants are predominantly poplars and birches. The broad-leaved aspen (a most brittle tree in a high wind) and the canoe birch outnumber all other varieties. As for shrubs, the shores are fragrant with dark-green thickets of sweet gale; the slopes bear handsome specimens of leatherwood (its bark once used for twine by the pioneers); and the rocky heights abound with staghorn sumach and low-bush blueberry.

Ferns in the darker woods are shy but abundant. Great clumps of delicate lady fern line the over-arched lane into "Fair Havens," in company with smaller stands of grape fern. Nearby, on mouldering mounds that once were stumps, lurk the triangular, light-green fronds of the oak fern. Farther on is the fragile bladder fern, and close beside it, so small as almost to escape the casual eye, are the elfin fronds of the smooth woodsia.

Flowers of the forest have their place and season. The lane itself is carpeted with blue violets in springtime and with blue heal-all in summer. At the very shore, iris and skullcap and meadow-sweet and meadow rue bloom thickly among the sedges on the sand. Twinflower and partridge-berry, pyrola and pipsissewa, starflower and wintergreen and mitrewort deck the glades nearby, in company with club-mosses in great profusion. Clintonia, Solomon's seal, twisted stalk, and trillium throng the higher slopes in their season. Fly honeysuckle and dogbane and wild sarsaparilla are knee deep in the open woods. In rich soil, the great angelica rears its dark red stem and shining umbels. In a damp glade under heavy maples, a stand of coral-root has rewarded my annual search, and only last summer, with the unexpectedness of a meteorite in one's kitchen garden, I found one healthy specimen of the ragged orchid standing boldly in damp grass beside our boathouse on the shore. I had never found it before except in Nova Scotia, and it had only once been reported in eastern Ontario.

Along the nearby road, one may botanize among the floral "hoboes of the highway," and note with each passing year how still more immigrant plant-tramps penetrate into these northern regions. Only within the past two decades has the viper's bugloss, bristly, blue, and arrogant, followed on an earlier invasion by the devil's paint brush, with its hairy leaves and lurid orange-red flowers. More welcome, as less epidemic, is the ground cherry, with its curious Chinese-lantern calyx cover for the sticky orange berry.

Following warm rains in July and August, the mushroom legions march in almost overnight, to paint the woodlands with uncanny colour. Most abundant of our July visitors is the deadly amanita, slender and angelically white, bearing a lethal dose equal to forty rattlesnakes but, unlike the rattler, fatal only if swallowed. Its poisonous cousin, the fly amanita, is still more showy, with its broad orange cap dotted with flakes of white. The August colour scheme ranges from the vivid white masses of the oyster mushroom, through the yellow of the chanterelle, the gold of the clavaria, and the reds and oranges and yellows of the cup fungi, to the dark red of the vermilion hygrophorus and the black of the deliquescent coprinus. Bracket fungi also run the gamut of colour, with whites and scarlets predominating. Even the creeping horror of the slime fungus has a chromatic fascination all its own.

Almost as interesting as the region's botany is its wide range of zoological variety. Except for biting insects, most of its animal life is shy by day. I have indeed stood within two feet of a beady-eyed little chipmunk, incontinently stuffing himself with fragments of a green russula mushroom, or have watched another, at an equal distance, biting and scratching at his fleas in evident desperation, but the porcupine that chose the dead of night for gnawing at our tool handles is more typical of the mammalian temperament. Beside the road in the twilight, I have watched a mother skunk followed by five baby skunks in Indian file, marching resolutely towards our garbage pit in search of Lucullan desserts. On or near the home base, I have seen the red fox, the red squirrel, the black squirrel, the common deer, the black bear, the mink, the big-eared deer-mouse, and the groundhog. I have heard the timber wolf in this neighbourhood, but have never seen him here.

Lacustrine life ranges from lake trout and bass in the weedy deeps, past millions of clams on shelving sand in about six feet of water, to the society of leeches, crayfish, and minnows in the shallows. Here, too, I have watched three-inch trout busily gorging on one-inch herring. An interesting sight offshore is a mother catfish guarding a school of tiny mudcats grouped in a globular swarm about the size of a football. Three weeks later, in water about six inches deep, I have watched the small individual fish, still only an inch in length but complete with spines and whiskers like the parents. Along the shore, one may stroke big bull-frogs on the head with a hay-stalk and make friends with numerous snails, worms, newts, toads, and snakes. The commonest serpents are the garter snake, the black snake, the copper belly, and the milk snake, but the most picturesque native is the hog-nosed snake or spreading adder, who on occasion has puffed himself up prodigiously but harmlessly on a flat rock a few feet from the back door.

Spiders are uncomfortably numerous. One summer day, while kneeling on dark granite by the water's edge, I nearly set my hand on a huge *Lycosa* or running spider, slightly smaller in body than a tarantula but with a leg-spread of fully four inches. She was quietly standing guard over a great mass of eggs, and was almost invisible on the dark wet stone. Farther up the slope, one encounters the orb-weavers, the crab-spiders, the wolf-spiders, and the jumping spiders. A familiar sight by night all one mid-July was a very large nocturnal orb-weaver who spun a two-foot web on the outer wall of a sleeping cabin. Invisible by day, she emerged by night as a magnificent spectacle, under the light of an electric torch, with her body of rich velvet brown ringed with a row of white dots and decorated on the under surface with a brilliant white lyre.

The insect world is almost unlimited in its opportunities for observation and identification. When it is remembered that there are three times as many living species of insects in the world as of all the other animals put together, one can realize the busy summer days that can be devoted to an acquaintance with those of even a limited neighbourhood. From the woolly aphids that swarm like mould masses on the stag-alder to the buprestid larvae boring into the pine tree, the plant world is alive with these voracious parasites. One need never fail for lack of material, whether one is poking new adult specimens into the broad mouth of the cyanide killing bottle or is gathering larvae for a "crawlery" in order to watch the wonders of metamorphosis. Some people are most interested in the spectacular butterflies and moths—the monarchs, red admirals, fritillaries, silver-spots, angle-wings, mourning cloaks, swallow-tails, sphinx moths, cecropias, lunas, and the like, all of which are found at "Fair Havens." Other people may be interested in such oddities as the praying mantis, the walking-stick insect, the leaf-hopper, and the tree-hopper. Still others are fascinated by the social life of bees, wasps, and ants.

Personally, I have found most satisfaction in the study of beetles. "Fair Havens" abounds in longicorns, those insect parodies on the ibex, with curling antennae often many times the length of the body, and in buprestids, especially those with large, bronzed, metallic wing-covers. Two varieties of carrion-beetle are very common, the large red and black *Necrophorus* and the much smaller *Siloha noveboracensis*, whose larva, common among dead leaves, looks like a wood-louse grown uncommonly supple. Scarabs, cockchafers, fireflies, lady-beetles, water scavengers, tiger-beetles, carabids, elaters—such are only a few of the families abundantly represented in the leafy glades by Boshkung Lake.

Most fascinating of all living things here are the birds. On a July night, with the Corona Borealis like a starry necklace overhead, Antares glowing redly in Scorpio far to the south, and Cassiopeia a glittering hieroglyphic in the far northeast, the weird cry of the loon far out on the lake is echoed by the mournful trisyllable of the whip-poor-will in the darkened woods and by the hoot of an owl from the western shore, nature's fluted intermezzo for a midsummer night's dream. The lake by day is also the haunt of gulls and wild ducks, especially the young mergansers, who pillage the shallows in a flotilla of diving, scuttling, splashing eagerness. Kingfisher and osprey dive into the waters from shore-side branch or lofty rampike. Throughout the boughs of the aspens and the oaks, warblers and phoebes and thrushes search tirelessly for insects, while nuthatches and brown creepers and downy woodpeckers explore the lichened tree trunks. The scarlet tanager and the brown thrasher are among our distinguished visitors. Almost every year, on almost the same date in late July, a pair of great pileated woodpeckers drum out a noisy salute on the tree trunks near the cabin and tear off bark and wood in great chunks in their strong, chiselling quest for larvae.

Humility and understanding permeate one's meditation on all this proliferous pattern of life. Here is the ant, who kept "cows" and manured his garden for millions of years before man, in his brief yesterday, learned the same wisdom. The insect's social organization is as detailed, and, alas, as rigid, as the phalanstery of a socialist state—an adumbration of a human future where intelligence will have been bred out of the race and the ineluctable net of "the organization man" will hold the community tight in an unchanging tyranny of "adjusted" behaviour. Here are the winged emotions that we call birds, passionate in love-making, each pair pugnacious in defence of its little tract of

Lebensraum. Almost equally bathed in an emotional world of odour, sound, and sight are the mammals, often as resentful as the red squirrel at any invasion of their living space. Here, in a drop of roadside water, is the microscopic miracle of *Volvox*, bringing sex and death into the world by that reshuffling of chromosomes which embodies nature's plan for variety and "progress" yet leaves a senescent parent superfluous and doomed to perish. By the same roadside, there bloom the dandelion and the hawkweed, which have abolished sex and brought one line of evolution to an end. Here is the whole teeming animal world, from microbe to mammal, depending for food on something that is, or was, alive. "The worm will do his kind" in devouring his prey and so will every other animal. If birds were not incessantly "turning caterpillars into warblers," a year's crop of caterpillars would devastate the earth. The pressure of plant life is likewise importunate as a myriad myriad seeds fall every year on each three acres of the wilderness. Animal predation and plant rivalry reduce the annual catch to a few thousand successfully adapted specimens; yet so urgent is their lust for life that the forest moves in on any corner that is left for a few years unpruned by brush-hook, axe, and clippers. All this is a sombre parable for a thoughtful man, so far as his own terrestrial permanence is concerned. *Sub specie aeternitatis*, his role here, "a green thought in a green shade," is as transient as that of any other shadow.

27

De Amicitia

"FOR FRIENDSHIP," wrote Francis Bacon in his *Essays*, "maketh indeed a fair day in the affections, from storm and tempests; but it maketh daylight in the understanding, out of darkness and confusion of thoughts." Through the years, I have been abundantly blessed with friends. Some of these have already been mentioned quite naturally in the subject-categories of earlier chapters, but for many others it would have required Procrustean violence to force them in. I have therefore written this brief chapter, made up of glimpses of a few old friends. Men still living are omitted, because it would be invidious to try to choose amongst them. From among those now deceased, I have cut back my present roster to ten—Grove, Pratt, Roberts, Lloyd, Campbell, Callander, Philipps, Hingston, Phelan, and Woodhouse.

One of my most highly prized friends through the years was Frederick Philip Grove, the novelist and essayist. When I first met him, about 1923, he was principal of the high school in the little Manitoba village of Rapid City. Son of a Scottish mother and a wealthy Swedish father, he had run almost the full gamut of human experience in many countries and after almost incredible hardships was at last anchored in a prairie hamlet—teaching by day and by night concentrating his polyglot reading and knowledge of the world on self-realization through writing. Ill health was to dog his path again and again, but fate's bitterest blow, about 1927, was the death of his little twelve-year-old daughter, May, through the ignorant obstinacy of a young doctor who, in spite of earnest paternal warnings, administered the wrong anaesthetic (for a child with a cold) and snuffed out the young life before an operation for appendicitis had even begun. A few days later I went with him to the pathetic little grave on a hillside beyond the village.

Many have professed to find Grove difficult, cantankerous, and overbearing and have told strange tales of his behaviour. On the contrary, in nearly thirty years of friendship I never found him anything but kindly and solicitous and ready to concede his own fallibility in his judgement of men and books. This is amply borne out in the letters in which he repaid with candid comment the loan of large numbers of books from my personal library. Take, for example, a letter of March 7, 1927, regarding Henri Bergson's *Creative Evolution*:

> I began to read the book with a certain exhilaration, but it soon turned into depression. That may be, of course, because I am just a dilettante—in this as in other things. . . . But how does he know what instinct *seeks*? If it is pessimism I am after, I prefer an esthetic pessimism like Schopenhauer's. But perhaps I am simply dense. . . . This long rigmarole about Bergson may make you laugh. I really don't like to speak about such things for fear of merely exposing my ignorance. Well, if you do laugh, it'll do you good.

In a letter of November 11, 1927, he was equally frank with regard to the basic philosophy of prosody (as expounded in *Rhyth*m, by E. A. Sonnenschein): "I see as I have so often seen that—for the lack of books and, perhaps, of a formal education—I had set out to discover things which others had done before me." Perhaps his reputation for *saevitas* came from occasions when he somehow felt an attitude of condescension on the part of men whose mental equipment he judged to be no greater than, or even smaller than, his own. A life of almost unmitigated hardship had worn his skin very thin indeed.

Pessimism frequently emerged regarding the plight of a literary pilgrim in the Canadian Sahara. Thus on November 30, 1927, he wrote me:

> I've done little since you were here except burn MSS. But, in putting things into order, I found that there are four volumes which I should want to publish and three more which I should release if there were any demand for my stuff. The balance—some five or six volumes more—I'd burn if I could. That's all I have done in a life of nearly fifty years.

Some nine years later (December 26, 1936), in a letter from R.R. 4, Simcoe, Ontario, the barometer was just as low:

> Canada has shown quite sufficiently that she wants none of my work. I am writing, of course; in fact I have written three or four books during the last eight or nine years. But I am producing them as I used to before that Winnipeg mirage began: to be shelved and put away. Why publish? The grapes, of course, are sour, too; I will not hunt publishers, however. . . . You know I have a farm, owing it, rather than owning? Slowly, as the years go by, I am, largely with my own hands, remodelling an old farm-house, built in 1828, to suit my needs. Likely I'll finish the job when I'm ready to lay me down in my grave.

Fortunately, recognition was still to come—in the Lorne Pierce Medal of the Royal Society and in honorary doctorates in literature from the universities of New Brunswick and Manitoba. But poverty was still so stark that the medal had to be sold for its gold content, and when I brought the D.Litt. diploma from the University of Manitoba to his home near Simcoe, a stroke had left him speechless and paralysed, but still gratefully conscious of the belated honour.

E. J. ("Ned") Pratt I first met in the summer of 1923 at Arthur Phelps's summer place near Bobcaygeon. The Pratts had a riverside cottage in the woods next door to the Phelpses, and there was constant visiting to and fro. Ned was busy at "The Witches' Brew" and was ready, when fortified with strong coffee, to chant parts of his newly created extravaganza for our delight. I also remember his indignation that a Bobcaygeon contractor, with whom he had arranged the previous autumn for the building of a private "dock" (meaning, in the Newfoundland sense, a small enclosed swimming dock for his little daughter) had completed, well before his arrival in the summer, a pier or wharf ("dock," Ontario style) big enough to moor a Kawartha Lakes steamboat—and with a price to match. Ned's poetry alternated with golf training, for he was practising chip shots in a nearby pasture field and by continual operations in a limited area had removed several square yards of divots and loam to a depth of about two feet. When we played golf together on the nine-hole course at Lindsay, I wished that I had practised as diligently with my own irons. Through the years we often foregathered; he and Mrs. Pratt were particularly kind to Mrs. Kirkconnell and myself when we moved back to Ontario in 1940 and took part in literary events in Toronto.

Thus a letter of march 19, 1941, started off:

My dear Kirk:

When your note came in, I was just on the point of writing you about Sunday evening the 28th. Vi and I would very much like to have you and your wife to dinner with us that evening and also have the two of you to stay over night. Claire is staying at the Residence this year, which gives us plenty of room.

I do hope that you can come to the recital and give us the bull or the frog. It would put beef (or frogs' legs) on the menu. . . .

On May 6, 1942, he divulged to me that he had successfully nominated me for the Lorne Pierce Medal of the Royal Society, an honour of which I had not dreamt:

Dear Kirk:

Can you do something for me? First let me congratulate you on the Medal. When I was in Ottawa last month, I put up your name and it was accepted. Now the President has asked me to read your *Citation* and present you, which I am delighted to do. Will you please let me have at once a little biographical sketch. . . .

It will be a great pleasure to see you. Bring along your clubs if you want a game.

Ned.

In his citation, which was published later in the *Proceedings* of the Royal Society of Canada for 1942, he stressed the primacy of my original volumes, *The Eternal Quest* and *The Flying Bull*: "This poetry is the effective focussing of a very full and vigorous life and is the main ground of the present award."

On February 10, 1958, he was confined to his bed but wrote to me cheerfully about some of my recent work in verse translation:

Dear old Kirk:

Your industry amazes all your friends and acquaintances. Is there any language remaining to burn up another of your multitudinous brain cells? Acadia must be proud of you.

I would write more but I am still in bed and my pen wobbles.

More power to you!
ever affectionately
Ned

A year later, his arthritis was lodging itself implacably deeper:

Dear Kirk:

Thanks for your Christmas greetings and your "free Alexandrines," which I greatly enjoyed. You are the most versatile writer in Canada, and I always admired you, even from the Winnipeg days.

I'd write you at greater length, but my arthritis is hitting my fingers as it does my hands. Still I feel better and I'm getting out a bit.

Affectionately,
Ned.

With Sir Charles Roberts, my association was long and intimate. We collaborated on a wartime anthology of Canadian poetry for circulation in Latin America, and I wrote a number of biographies for him when he was editor of the *Canadian Who Was Who*. Our backgrounds were utterly different, but we admired each other's work. For nearly twenty years I found in him the generous encouragement of an elder brother. And he was the first to spring to my support when, one Saturday afternoon in 1943, I demanded a showdown with my Writers' War Committee on the Communist issue. It was by no accident that I dedicated my *Flying Bull* volume to him. He was a man and a friend.

A tragic friend in Winnipeg was Cecil Francis Lloyd, a slight snowy-haired Welsh man of letters, who put a bullet in his own brain on July 13, 1938. Widowed, childless, still unemployed after six hungry years of job-hunting in the Depression, he was to be ejected, through mortgage foreclosure, from the little cottage to which his most intimate memories clung. On the day set for that forced departure, he closed the grey page of existence with a bloody period, *vitaque cum gemitu fugit indignata sub umbras.* By virtue of four slim volumes of lyric poetry and one of prose essays he has an assured place in Canadian literature, but the man himself was more significant than his published work would indicate. During six years of friendship, I gave him the freedom of my personal library and was richly repaid by the many scores of letters in which, since it was often difficult to meet, he poured forth abundant discourse on himself and his literary interests. In June 1951, I read a 53-page cento of selections from this correspondence before Section II of the Royal Society.

His all too true announcement of an imminent end was written early in July 1938, when I was absent in Europe, and caught up with me in Budapest:

> When this reaches you, or very soon afterwards, I shall be down the long trail, past the valley of swords and the island of the singing women, to Fiddlers' Green. I have lost home, books, pets, everything that makes life worth living and I'm not going to stay to become a nuisance to my friends and sink as I have seen too many sink. The hardest thing I shall have to do tomorrow morning will be to kill my poor pussies to save them from falling into the hands of some brute who would abuse or neglect them. . . . I shall be nearly dead before I turn the gun on myself. Now an eternal Good-bye, my very good and true friend, and may whatever gods there be bless you and Mrs. K. and the children.

Of all my Queen's professors there were only two—P. G. C. Campbell (1878–1960) and Thomas Callander (1877–1959)—with whom old friendship was steadily maintained by correspondence through the years. Campbell was not only the life honorary president of my class (Arts sixteen) but made me his adjutant when he was Commandant at Fort Henry in 1916. We also had the Scottish Rite in common. In a letter of September 28, 1924, after telling of his ordeal in a successful three-hour "soustenance" of his D. ès L. thesis in a huge hall at the Sorbonne, he went on:

> Although that is over, the consequences are now pursuing me, as the French mediaevalists are urging me to this or that research, and as you know, the material for this at Queen's, or indeed in America, is of the scantiest. I am also under a half promise to Dent's to write a book on English Mediaeval Military Architecture, but ever increasing numbers at Queen's and its "res angustae" or angustissimae forbid any proper increase of staff and prevent me from finding much leisure during the session.

On December 21, 1940, à propos of my *Western Idyll*, which had been sent to him with Christmas greetings, he wrote: "Both of us enjoyed very much your lighter touch poetically. I was somewhat startled at your command of modern Canadian slang—which usually baffles me—but my wife said at once that you had 'picked it up' from your children."

On December 18, 1948, after he had generously filled in for three emergency months on my staff at Acadia and was now safely home again in Kingston, he gave me some advice:

> And now for some 'ghostly' counsel. I trust that you are gradually learning to take things—I will not say easily, but at least steadily. I am always preaching this because I find it pretty hard—even now—to put it into practice. I seem to have more to do than I ever did—one of the fruits of being retired. I trust you got my letter in answer to yours re the Scottish Rite. I was having a chat with the Sovereign Grand Commander about it only three days ago.

Although I had not met Professor Callander since I graduated in his department in 1916, letters kept us in touch and this on a deeper level of ideas, both in theology and in politics, than the letters of any of my other correspondents. A typical comment of his, in a letter of December 23, 1952, was as follows:

> My theological reading is chiefly *The Hibbert* and I get an impression of tremendous proliferation (much cry & little 'oo) due to the vice stigmatised by Collingwood (mental laziness). Watson read T. H. Green's *Prolegomena* 75 times: the modern would be too superficial to read it through once before reviewing it. Surely there never was such a slick one as Reinhold Niebuhr, with his "interim ethic" and universe-ranging Omniscience. By the way, another friend of ours, Liddell Hart, was in Kingston also. He is no mean adept in religious controversy and believes in converging lines—all "systems" gravitating to final harmony.

Callander had participated in his youth in archaeological work in the Near East, and what he found never ceased to impress him:

> In Asia Minor it was heartbreaking to see how the Moslem hatred of images ravaged the infidel monuments. Religious intolerance has been a pest, true enough. A dose of Edward Caird would be a grand antidote, wouldn't it? Religion in every form is surely a *search*, a search for the Infinite, the reverse of dogmatic. If only our churchmen would admit it! (Dec. 12, 1953).

In spite of his advanced years, Callander spent his old age in a sustained and intensive study of the documents underlying the two World Wars and the new light thrown on their causes by men like Gooch, Butterfield, Lutz, Huddleston, Fuller, Miksche, Veale, Neilson,

Beard, Fay, and Barnes. Out of that process came a highly pessimistic insight into the true meaning of our times:

> We have entered a new phase of the big controversy since Winston, Eden and Duff Cooper have endorsed the contention of Miksche (and long ago Kuhlmann) that the destruction of the Habsburg Empire was a dire calamity. The lamentable spectacle of our tribal god groaning over the *situation immeasurable and laden with doom* which he has striven to create since he was commissioned by Asquith to go to the Admiralty to prepare for war on Germany calls for a Bernard Shaw or an Aristophanes. What an opening for budding historians! All they need how is the release of the 1,800 Tyler Kent documents. Given that, the Message of the Documents would electrify the world. One straight march from July 24 (when Winston encouraged the war-party in Petrograd to extract the ukase of July 30) to Hiroshima and Nuremberg—don't you think Winston as he *roams and peers on the rim of Hell* glimpses the meaning of his life-work? (Sept. 4, 1955)

Or again,

> Since the Kremlin bosses have said openly with reverberations what our bosses knew full well about dear Uncle Joe, you can ease off in your crusade and may even enjoy a grudging admission from the many-millioned dupes that you told them so. Or is that too much to expect? (August 3, 1956)

His book appeared posthumously in 1961 as *The Athenian Empire and the British.*

One of my closest friends for over two decades was Tracy Philipps (1890–1959), a product of Oxford and Durham with a distinguished military and anthropological career in Africa and the Middle East, who came to Canada on loan from the United Kingdom in 1940 in connection with our nationalities programme. He went to Washington in 1944–45 as chief of their department for planning the resettlement of displaced persons under the UN and spent much time in Europe in 1945–52 in close touch with this task, especially as an active member of the Halifax–Beveridge "Refugees' Defence Committee." Thus he wrote me on May 20, 1945:

> I have had a good deal to do with camps of Soviet subjects, and eventually with the Soviet officers who are gradually sent to "take care" of them. . . . Those repatriated from Normandy via British ports had often to be battened down below hatches, like the ships plying between Africa and the USA at a certain period.

This forcible deportation, to death or slave camp, of all the millions of refugees from former Russian territory had been agreed to by the Allies in a secret "military agreement" at Yalta. Philipps was witness, moreover, of the further constant attempt to shanghai into Soviet captivity all refugees from countries like Poland and Hungary that had been conquered by the Reds, and he discovered that the officialdom of the western Allies was honeycombed with Communists or fellow-travellers who were ready to help along the scandalous programme. Thus he wrote on Feb. 14, 1946, of an English colonel who had suppressed the admirable education system set up by a large Polish camp and was proposing to put their children under a Communist inspector from Warsaw. Or again, on February 8, 1949, he told of an attempt in England itself to railroad a large group of Ukrainian refugees back to a grim fate in eastern Europe. A letter of September 28, 1946, had already given his pessimistic verdict on the whole sorry business:

> I spent yesterday afternoon with Freddie Morgan, who had just been "released" by LaGuardia from directing D.P. operations in Germany. A fine fellow. He thinks that UNRRA has been made to stink (I agree) and that most honest men are long ago out of it for the very reason that they were honest. . . . The IRO will be worse than UNRRA, whose rejects, thrown out by F.M., have already been promised places in IRO!. Most international things are now thoroughly penetrated from within by cells or paralysed from without by vetoes.

The readiness of most Britons to have their country compromise with Communist foreign policy led him to sombre speculation, as on January 5, 1948:

> One of the main dangers of our modern world issues from a common belief that it is right for an individual to approve action by his country (that is, his nation) which, for himself, he would know to be wrong. This nationalist doctrine is dignified as "a sense of realism". Call it "realism" and any dastardy will pass.

He found churchmen particularly subject to this weakness of moral principle:

> All the Protestants no longer "protest too much", but on the contrary too little. They really believe that the gulf is easily bridgeable, "given" good-will and if only both worlds get round that wonderful magic ROUND-TABLE. Doubless they believe in some magic (which you and I have not discovered) in either the wood or the green baize of that round table yet to be made! I must find out what Protestant group in the U.K. grasps the position & has guts, if any, and certainly not the C. of E. Most of them won't know what the world-struggle is *about* until the shooting starts.

On November 18, 1951, I find him tracing much of our malaise back to the lack of clearly defined ideals in our Western civilization:

> It is probably true that *Ce ne sont pas les intérêts, ce sont les croyances, qui mènent les hommes.* But the beliefs must periodically be revaluated, restated in synthesis (for a wider anxious audience than Christians alone) and be made simple and crystal-clear for all. At present, to millions in Europe, Asia and Africa who are being led to see in the West only

Uniprix-values, a Chaffeur-ideal or idolatry of private gain and of machines, the belief of the West is neither clear, nor summarized, nor trusted, nor understood.

We had both been deeply concerned over the wicked attack on Freddie Voigt, of the *Nineteenth Century and After*, first by Brendan Bracken in the Commons (where such iniquity was "privileged") and then in the London *News Chronicle*, where it became liable to action. On July 12, 1945, Mr. Justice Birkett found the *News Chronicle* guilty of gross and malicious libel, and imposed heavy damages. Mr. Voigt's offence, in the eyes of these gentry, had been that he had dared to criticize Stalin and Tito. A week later, he sent me greetings through Tracy: "Will you convey a message to Watson for his comfort in case he has trouble? Merely this: *Isaiah* xxxii, 8.[1]"

When Father William H. Hingston, S.J., died in St. Michaels' Hospital, Toronto, on November 30, 1964, at the age of 87, I lost a friend of rare quality. We had first met in Hamilton, some thirty years before, just after his retirement as provincial of the English-speaking Jesuits in Canada, and we built up an enduring friendship in terms of political convictions and a love of Latin poetry.

The following extract from a letter of December 16, 1948, acknowledging my Christmas card translation of a Latin poem by Notkerus Balbulus (facing the original), is perhaps characteristic of the letters that passed between us year after year:

W. H. Hingston, sac. e Societatu Iesu, W. . . . K. . . . , praeclarissimo et doctissimo viro, poetae, scriptori, patriae canadensis defensori impavido, Christi Aeterni Regis famulo obsequentissimo atque militi fortissimo, amico suo, gratulabundus ac omnia fausta in Christo adprecans, S. P. D.

My Christmas card to you had left the day before your charming card came with that extraordinarily faithful translation that is almost word-for-word. Something awoke within me and I put down the following four lines which you will scan with an indulgent eye, praising the good intention when you may not conscientiously the effort. I really wanted to get off a few distichs, as being more appropriate, but these simply would not come, and instead I had these:

Quae monachus Notker recinebat versibus olim,
Christo nascenti quo testaretur amorem:
Haec eadem Tu, diverso sermone, Poeta
Reddis ad unguem: par stilus et pares Tibi amores.

Five years later he was writing again. My Christmas leaflet had taken thirty-two Latin lines of Hildebert, in elegiacs; "De nativitate Christi," had cut them back to sixteen, and had rendered these into two English

[1]But the liberal man deviseth liberal things; and by liberal things shall he stand.

stanzas in ottava rima, printed facing the original. Father Hingston alone among my friends seemed to sense what I was about:

> I loved your Christmas poem translated from Hildebert of Lavardin. . . . I think that you have improved the poem by omitting exactly one-half of the lines by those two judicious cuts, of eight lines each. The sixteen lines that have been retained say all that is said in the thirty-two of the original. Hildebert versified too easily and did not resist the temptation to become diffuse.

Another of my close personal friends in the Church was Father Gerald Phelan, who died in Toronto in May 1965. He was an eminent philosopher, trained in seven universities, including Cambridge, Würzurg, and Louvain, and was one of the founders of the Pontifical Institute of Mediaeval Studies, in Toronto. Along with Woodhouse and myself, he had gone on the 1944 safari to Washington and New York on behalf of the newly formed Humanities Research Council and we had been closely associated in the subsequent survey of the humanities in Canadian universities. Throughout the years our contacts had been maintained, chiefly through an interchange of off-prints and letters and some private argument as to the bearing of Artistotle's *Metaphysics* on Aquinas.

Of the life-long correspondence between the First and Second Humanities Musketeers, Arthur Woodhouse (1895–1964) and myself, some mention has been made in Chapter XVII ("The Milton Project"). One of Arthur's typical comments, in a letter dated New Year's Day 1951, craves repetition: "I am just back from the M.L.A. at New York, where I gave a paper on the Historical Criticism of Milton with (or against) Cleanth Brooks of Yale, who was on Milton and the New Critics. We buried the hatchet (as between the two schools), but I used it a little first." Of all the departed friends of a lifetime, there is none whom I miss more.

28

Tempora Mutantur

TENNYSON MIGHT WRITE of "murmurs from the dying sun" and H. G. Wells's Time Traveller, driving his frail machine forward through a vast, spectral futurity, might see in the sky only a dull red globe that now and then "suffered a momentary extinction"; but the newer astrronomy assures us that for the next five thousand million years our brave, adolescent star will actually grow in heat and light, at first very slowly but at last with savage rapidity, until it flares up as a blazing *nova* and then settles back into a new cycle as a white dwarf. The fiery vaporization of our planet in that celestial inferno is still almost inconceivably remote. On the other hand, a deadly acceleration of our fate at human hands is a contingency that could arrive tomorrow morning at half past four. While the panic fear of having a nuclear chain-reaction explode the earth no longer haunts us, the no less fatal extermination of all terrestrial life by Russian and American bombs hangs over us, like the sword of Damocles, by a hair.

Leaving aside all millennial yammering that we are those "on whom the ends of the world are come," we may yet be pardoned for pausing occasionally to ponder whether the headlong speed of human "progress" in our lifetime has been an unmixed blessing.

Change there has certainly been during the past seven decades. At the turn of the century, my parents might take me on a morning voyage from Port Hope to Toronto by the lake steamer *North King* and go with me around the tramway "Belt Line" (Queen–Sherbourne–Bloor–Spadina) for the ride. Today the very wharf at Port Hope has long since been washed away, but Metropolitan Toronto has a subway, New York style, for its two million inhabitants. Sixty years ago, my little world was bounded by leisurely travel on the roads and waterways of Ontario. Last year, I took the wings of the morning and swept by airliner from Vancouver to Halifax in a few hours. Another five hours put me in Prestwick, Scotland. As a small boy, flat on my stomach in my father's study, I read quietly but excitedly through most of Scott and Dickens. Today my grandchildren, in the same posture, gaze through television at the vulgar, declamatory vaudeville of an Ed Sullivan show. Thanks to radio, our air today, like that of Prospero's island, "is full of voices," most of them, especially from the private stations, ninety-nine per cent Caliban and one per cent Ariel. On the other hand, my Hi-Fi genie can spread me, on demand, a banquet of Mozart, Beethoven, Sibelius, Khatchaturian, and Orff beyond the reach of musical epicures a generation ago. Our age may have given us the complete textural disintegration of the twelve-tone lunatics and the infantile droolings of the popular jazz bands, but we still have composers with something noble and significant to say.

Public architecture, with its new uses for glass, steel, and concrete, has produced municipal and industrial structures that are simple in line, honest in structure, and not without grandeur in rhythm, scale, and contrast. The city hall in Oslo and the Lever Building in New York come to my memory as examples. I wish that I could be as happy over current fashions in dwelling-houses. Modern domestic architecture may have become "functional" and "organic," but this brings in question the function that the structural organism is supposed to fulfil. If that function is to force the home's occupants into inescapable company with one another in an "open planned" merging of living-spaces, not to mention putting the victims on exhibition to their neighbours through a twenty-foot picture window, then the incorrigible, back-slapping extrovert has indeed won the day in home-building as fully as in our pedagogy. The ideal of the recent interior decorators seems to be an interminable life of cocktails and vapid conversation, shared in by everybody. To a family of introverts, each of whom craves a book-lined retreat of his own in which to read and think, this full-time compulsory companionship would become pure torment.

A contrast of symbols in our time is easy to come by. When I revisited Port Hope recently, I wondered if sixty years had brought a finer civilization to the little old town. On a shoulder of Monkey Mountain, where my boyhood had found the fringed gentian and the grass of Parnassus blooming in quiet beauty, a high wire fence now hedged off a rusty-brown abomination of desolation. A notice at the gate warned the wayfaring man that here the worthless but still dangerous residue from the lake-side radium plant was being dumped. Nuclear chemistry has turned a green Ontario hillside into a plague spot where men approach at their peril—and no bird sings. On the other hand, the sandy deserts on the upper reaches of the Ganaraska, from which the spring run-off used to send an annual torrent through the streets of the town, are now being planted with millions of little pine trees in an attempt to recapture the primeval balance of nature. It remains to be seen which area is the more valid symbol of the age into which we are moving.

At the moment, the forces of exploitation and "development," as represented by the radium dump, overshadow the work of the conservationists. Across the far continents, billions of *homines sapientes*—hungry, sex-driven, pugnacious, imperfectly tamed—press ever harder against the eroded earth's limits of yield and sink ever deeper into starvation, *les damnés de la terre, les forçats de la faim*. The West has taught them how to conquer disease but not how to control their own biology. The Grand Inquisitor waits cunningly to exploit them.

And what of my own brief record in such a world? Looking back over the experience of a lifetime, I can realize wistfully that my performance has not been really first class in any of the things to which I have turned my hand—music, sport, linguistics, translation, original prose and verse, teaching, administration, research, nature study, soldiering, politics, church work, or social service. If I had not galloped off wildly in all directions, I might perhaps have ridden down one of the foxes. In such matters, it is doubtless futile to speculate. Sometimes I think that what I prize most is my experience of happy marriage, with its fruit in two King's Scouts and three Girl Guides, all grown up to useful maturity. Yet I realize that I have been driven by other compulsions as well. Most of all, my passion for research and productive scholarship compelled the omission of many things. Our home did so little entertaining that we were almost unsocial. For fifteen of my first twenty-six years as a professor, we had no car. Neither I nor my family ever saw a professional game in any sport. My salary was diminutive, but so important did my studies seem that only three times in all my career did I teach summer school in order to help balance a slender budget. My college had no pension plan and in the bleak 1930's I sacrificed two of my three small insurance policies to help feed the family. Amassing a scholar's library of several thousand volumes in many languages was another factor in the budget. Yet I still refused to lay my pen aside and seek gainful supplementary employment. For forty-five years, my average annual output in publication has been one book, three brochures, and fifteen articles. In helping me to meet this objective, my wife and children long missed some of the amenities available to the families of stockbrokers and steelworkers. Yet they never suffered real privation. Perhaps the chief loss to us all has been in the lack of abundant playtime together as a family. "Daddy" might emerge from his study long enough to build a sandbox, a swing, or a toboggan-slide, but he would then disappear again into his silent lair among the bookcases and leave the little folks to make their own fun. Yet we were, I think, a happy family.

Canadians are this year celebrating the centenary of their country's establishment as a federal state. My own lifetime covers nearly three-quarters of that centennial span. In my slice of experience as a Canadian, special weight might well be given today to the issues of higher education and to those of national life.

In my youth, Canada's universities were frequented by a small élite from a population of seven millions. Today the college enrolment consists of about fourteen per cent, or one youth in seven, in the relevant age group in twenty millions. This was the ratio of college enrolment to population in the United States in 1939, but the development of mass affluence and of a more scientific society has extended today's higher education in the United States to nearly one-half of the country's young people, or almost all those who might conceivably have mental capacity beyond a secondary school level. There are as many Negro students in colleges and universities in the United States today as there are students of every sort in higher education in England. There seems no doubt that a similar trend is under way in Canada and will be greatly accelerated in the next two or three decades. A quadrupling of Canadian enrolment is conceivable by 1984, and the growing pains will be acute. Only crash programmes for the training of instructional cadres and very massive financial help from government towards buildings and salaries will enable us to pass through the ordeal without the risk of disaster.

The building of higher education on a new mass base will encounter special demands from the youth of the new mass society. Here we may watch with profit the challenges now being encountered by the more heavily massed institutions of the United States. The "student protests" at Berkeley's multiversity in 1964 have already had echoes on almost all Canadian campuses, partly through mere anthropoid mimicry of American television and radio broadcasts, partly through subterranean political machinery that can produce simultaneous push-button demonstrations for leftist causes at most colleges in the world, and partly through a growing concern for genuine academic problems. While some of the campus agitators are identifiably Marxist activists, others seem closer to turn-of-the-century long-haired anarchists, allergic to any form of student discipline whatever. Some condemn so-called student government as "sandbox government" and demand more radically that the university budget be taken out of the hands of the administration and turned over to joint student–faculty control. Others denounce any system of grading students, regardless of the need for ensuring that physicians and engineers are competent to practise. Still others demand that the students grade their professors, yet betray a tendency to equate pedagogical effectiveness with mere popularity. Overlooked, or concealed, in all this agitation is the fact that higher education in the Soviet Union, intent on efficiency, rigidly screens all students both for academic fitness and for political orthodoxy and then rules them with a rod of iron. Perhaps, in spite of the effervescence of our tiny minority of student agitators, the chief danger facing Canadian universities will be a fatal uniformity in which all institutions will be as identical as turnpike restaurants. Standards we must have, in a world where human knowledge doubles every decade and advanced skills will presently be necessary in every walk of life, but we shall also need variety in the values and goals set before higher education.

Vaster but vaguer than Canada's university problem is its existence as a nation. Confederation was a political solution forced on our comparatively incompatible little colonies a century ago by the frustrations of internal dissension and by the external threat of invasion. Like many of the new principalities in Central Africa today, it was the shell of a state with no mature egg of community inside. The future depended on the success of the federalism, for a federation that succeeds becomes a nation, while one that fails will tend to fall apart, especially when the outside forces that called it into being are relaxed.

The nation-state of the past two hundred years has been one of the most dynamic and revolutionary forces in human history. It is a form of emotional self-assertion on the part of whole populations with the sense of a common tradition and a common mission. It has torn old dynastic structures to pieces (as in the Austro-Hungarian Empire) and it has merged people of a common language into one state (as briefly in Grossdeutschland). Many had thought that western Europe might be able, after World War II, to federate several wrecked states into a single co-operative commonwealth, the European Economic Community, but with a nuclear stalemate holding the two great hegemonies of the Soviet Union and the United States in uneasy equilibrium, the ancient ambitions and dreams of French nationalism have been revived by Charles de Gaulle, who seems bent on grandeur for the French regardless of the welfare of the rest of Europe. As for the UN, only the nuclear umbrella of the Soviet-American balance of terror makes possible the posturing of dozens of little would-be nation-states, each a welter of tribalisms, administratively jerry-built, economically absurd, militarily negligible, but wielding the same UN vote as the greatest superstate in the world. If half a dozen of the most advanced and authentic nation-states in Europe cannot surmount their ancient prejudices and dreams in a higher unity, how can we expect to achieve a regional or universal federation of half-born states that are chiefly concerned with stoking the fires of a factitious nationalism? Meanwhile, on the other side of the European curtain stands a superstate that has suppressed nationalism by force, except for the Great Russians, and looks forward to a time when all of the captive nationalities will have been cheerfully digested into one Russian-speaking Soviet consciousness. The World Federalists are apparently blind to the nation as it is in the world as it is.

It is in such a world that Canadians are celebrating their nationhood in 1967. The Fenian thrust that called Confederation into being in 1867 has faded entirely away. The American fact today is rather a friendly and largely unconscious process of absorption—by newspaper columnists and comic strips, by radio and television, by the entire moving picture industry, by the dictates of New York in styles, music, and amusements, by the domination of Canadian labour by American unions and the domination of our industries by American capital and American corporations, by the domination of Canadian advertising and political campaigns by Madison Avenue techniques, by the domination of Canadian schools by American pedagogy, by the assumption by the United States of most of our tasks of self-defence. One reason for the resurgence of a regional nationalism among the French in Quebec is their consciousness that they are a "nation" of six million French-speaking citizens on a continent where 214,000,000 neighbours, American and Canadian, speak English and share in an almost identical American culture. The threat of an outside force is no longer military but includes just about every other form of sociological pressure, and it is a thrust of which most Americans and Anglo-Canadians are innocently unaware.

A native Canadian, however, whether he speaks English or French, covets some sort of Canadian identity for his people. In the past century we have endured great hardships together and have made great achievements together. We have a common regional consciousness, parliamentary and judicial systems distinct from those of the United States, and transalantic sentiments based not on an eighteenth century act of repudiation but on eighteenth century ties of loyalty. While the ingredients in the Canadian and American amalgams are very similar, the proportions are very diffeernt. A search for Macdonalds and Lauriers in the New York telephone directory will make this clear. The Scots and the French in particular have added a special tinge to the Canadian tincture. We can approach our Centennial in a state of modest certainty as to our own identity and modest pride in the Canadian achievement.

APPENDIXES

APPENDIX I

Curriculum Vitae

(A) Major Dates

1895. May 16, born in Port Hope, Ontario, third child of headmaster of the local high school.
1908. Father became headmaster, Collegiate Institute, Lindsay, Ontario.
1913. Entered Queen's University, Kingston, Ontario.
1916. Received Master of Arts degree, Honours Classics.
1916–19. Military service (rank of captain); Musketry officer, Barriefield camp; Adjutant, Fort Henry; Paymaster, Kapuskasing Internment Camp; Transport Officer, Quebec–Rotterdam.
1919–20. Music student (voice), Toronto Conservatory of Music.
1921–22. Graduate student (economics), Oxford University.
1922–40. Professor in Wesley (United) College, University of Manitoba: eleven years in English and seven in Latin.
1924. Married Isabel Peel (died 1925), of Lindsay, Ontario.
1925. Twin sons (James and Thomas) born.
1930. Married Hope Kitchener, of Lindsay, Ontario. Three daughters born: Helen (1934), Janet (1936), and Susan (1945).
1938. Summer lecturer at University of Debrecen, Hungary.
1940–48. Head of the department of English, McMaster University.
1942–44. Chairman, Writers' War Committee of Canada.
1943–47. Chairman and joint founder, Humanities Research Council.
1948. Appointed president, Acadia University, Wolfville, Nova Scotia.
1963. Lectured, July, University of Iceland.
1964. Retired. Home in Wolfville.
1966. Head of department of English, Acadia University.
1921–66. Author of 170 books and brochures and of over 600 articles, chiefly in the field of comparative literature.

(B) Decorations, Medals, and Awards

Knight Commander, Order of the Icelandic Falcon, 1963.
Knight Officer, Order of Polonia Restituta, 1936.
Lorne Pierce Gold Medal in Literature, Royal Society of Canada, 1942.
Gold Medal of Freedom, Hungarian Freedom Fighters, 1964.
Silver Laurel, Polish Academy of Literature, 1935.
Great Silver Medal, French Historical Institute, 1935.

Czechoslovak Gold Medal, 1940.
Coronation Medal, Elizabeth II, 1953.
Humanities Research Council Medal, 1964.
George Washington Medal, American Hungarian Studies Foundation, 1967.
Hungarian Community Medal, 1963.
Shevchenko Medal, Ukrainian Canadian Committee, 1962.
Great Shevchenko Plaque, Ukrainian Canadian Committee, 1964.
Copernican Award, Koscinszko Foundation, 1952.
Medal of Honour, P.E.N. Club of Hungary, 1938.
Nova Scotia Drama Trophy, 1956.
University Medal in Greek, Queen's University, 1916.
University Medal in Latin, Queen's University, 1916.
Fourteen university scholarships and prizes (honour matriculation, undergraduate and postgraduate, including I.O.D.E. Overseas Scholarship), 1913–21.

(C) Honorary Degrees

Honorary Doctor of Letters, University of Manitoba.
Honorary Doctor of Letters, University of Windsor.
Honorary Doctor of Letters, Laval University.
Honorary Doctor of Letters, McMaster University.
Honorary Doctor of Letters, Acadia University.
Honorary Doctor of Letters, St. Francis Xavier University.
Honorary Doctor of Humane Letters, Alliance College.
Honorary Doctor of Philosophy, University of Debrecen, Hungary.
Honorary Doctor of Political Economy, Ukrainian Free University, Munich, Germany.
Honorary Doctor of Laws, University of Ottawa.
Honorary Doctor of Laws, University of New Brunswick.
Honorary Doctor of Civil Laws, St. Mary's University.

(D) Membership in Learned Societies

Fellow of the Royal Society of Canada.
Fellow of the Royal Anthropological Institute.
Fellow of the Royal Economic Society.
Fellow of the Royal Geographical Society.
Fellow of the Royal Historical Society.
Fellow of the Royal Institute of International Affairs.
Fellow of the Philological Society, London.
Member, London School of Slavonic Studies.
Member, London Institute of World Affairs.
Honorary Member, Icelandic Society of Letters, Reykjavik.
Honorary Member, French Historical Institute, Paris.
Honorary Member, Polish Institute of Arts and Science, Brussels.
Member, International Institute of Political and Social Science, Brussels.
Fellow, International Institute of Arts and Letters, Switzerland.
Foreign Member, Petőfi Society, Budapest.

Corresponding Member, Kisfaludy Society, Budapest.
Honorary Member, Paderewski Foundation, New York.
Associate, Institute of Ethnic Studies, Washington, D.C.
Member, International Comparative Literature Association.
Member, American Association for the Advancement of Science.
Member, American Academy of Political and Social Science.
Member, Polish Institute of Arts and Science in the U.S.A.
Member, American Philological Association.
Member, Linguistic Society of America.
Member, Modern Language Association.
Honorary Member, Polish Institute of Arts and Science, Canadian Branch.
Member, Canadian Historical Association.
Member, Humanities Research Council of Canada.
Member, Canadian Social Science Research Council.
Member, Canadian Institute of International Affairs.
Member, Canadian Association of Slavists.
Member, Canadian Classical Association.
Member, Ukrainian Free Academy of Sciences.
Member, Shevchenko Society of Sciences.
Member, Canadian-Scandinavian Foundation.
Member, American Name Society.

APPENDIX II

Partial List of Publications by Watson Kirkconnell

(Selected from approximately one thousand items and arranged according to relevant chapters in *A Slice of Canada*)

CHAPTER 1. *Roots of the Family Tree*

A Canadian Headmaster. Toronto: Clarke, Irwin, 1935, pp. 156.
A Tale of Seven Cities. Hamilton. Women's Civic Club, 1948, pp. 32.
The Kirkconnell Pedigree. Wolfville, privately printed, 1953, pp. 54.

CHAPTER 2. *Student Days*

"One Hundred Years of School" (*Watchman-Warder*, Oct. 13, 1954).

CHAPTER 3. *In the Margins of Science*

Botanical Survey of South Victoria. Lindsay: Warder Press, 1926, pp. 16.
"The Flora of Kapuskasing and Vicinity" (*Canadian Field Naturalist*, May 1919).
"The Record of the Rocks" (*Watchman-Warder*, 1920).
"Annals of the Red Man" (*Watchman-Warder*, 1920).
"The Trenton Cuesta" (*Canadian Mining Journal*, Mar 18, 1921).
"Bryophyta of Boskung" (*Canadian Field Naturalist*, Nov. 1921).
"The Palaeogeography of Ontario" (*The School*, Oct. 1925).
"Mendelism and Cephalic Index" (*American Journal of Physical Anthropology*, Oct.-Dec. 1925).
"Three Acres of Vacation" (*The School*, June 1945).

CHAPTER 4. *The Sinews of Speech*

"Physiology and Phonetic Change" (*Manitoban*, Oct. 7, 1926).
"Linguistic Laconicism" (*American Journal of Philology*, Jan.-Mar. 1927).
"Unesmi impresiones de novial" (*Novialiste*, Stockholm, March, 1935).
"Progresivi tempes in novial" *Novialiste*, Sept. 1935).
A Primer of Hungarian. Winnipeg: serially in the *Young Magyar-American*, 1936–39.

"The Languages of Britain" (*Winnipeg Free Press*, Oct. 15, 1936).
"Loan-Words in Latin" (*Manitoba Arts Review*, Fall 1938).
"Norse Names in Scotland" (*United Scottish Association Annual*, 1936).
"Greek History in Greek Vocabulary" (*Trans. Roy. Soc. Can.* 1947, also offprint as pamphlet).
Icelandic History in Icelandic Vocabulary. Winnipeg: Columbia Press, 1948, pp .12.
Common English Loan-Words in East European Languages. Winnipeg: Ukrainian Free Academy of Sciences, 1952, pp. 20.
Canadian Toponymy and the Cultural Stratification of Canada. Winnipeg: Ukrainian Free Academy of Sciences, 1954, pp. 16.

CHAPTER 5. *Original Verse*

The Tide of Life, and Other Poems. Ottawa: Ariston, 1930, pp. 80.
Canada to Iceland. Lindsay: Warder Press, 1930, pp. 8.
"Manitoba Limericks" (*Winnipeg Free Press*, one hundred issues, Nov. 1932–Jan. 1933).
"Saskatchewan Limericks" (*Regina Leader-Post*, fifty issues, Jan.–March 1933).
"Christmas in Flanders" (*National Home Monthly*, Dec. 1933).
The Eternal Quest. Winnipeg: Columbia Press, 1934, pp. 136.
"The Lay of Elijah" (*Canadian Forum*, August 1934).
"The Ayrshire Muse" (*Canadian Forum*, Feb. 1935).
"Georgius V, Rex et Imperator, 1935" (*National Home Monthly*, May 1935).
To Horace. Winnipeg, privately printed, 1935, pp. 4.
"Pilsudski's Heart" (*Warsaw Weekly*, July 17, 1936).
"Manitoba Symphony", contributed, pp. 1–9, to *Manitoba Essays* (Toronto, Macmillan, 1937).
The Bridge-builders. Winnipeg, privately printed, 1938, pp. 4.
Lyra Sacra. Winnipeg, privately printed, 1939, pp. 8.
A Western Idyll. Hamilton, privately printed, 1940, pp. 8.
The Flying Bull, and Other Tales. Toronto: Oxford University Press, 1940, pp. 189.
"Easter" (*National Home Monthly*, April 1941).
"Aesop for Canadians" (*Evening Telegram*, Aug. 4, 1942).
The Crow and the Nighthawk. Hamilton, privately printed, 1943, pp. 8 (also in *Saturday Night*, May 29, 1943).
"The Agony of Israel" (*Canadian Jewish Review* and *Jewish Standard*, June 1943).
Christ and Herod, and Other Poems. Hamilton, privately printed, 1947, pp. 8.
"Holy Joe" (*Eastern Chronicle*, New Glasgow, Feb. 17, 1949).
"Nova Scotia Suite" (*Saturday Night*, Feb. 22, 1949).
"A Rime of Glooscap" (*Dalhousie Review*, Oct. 1950).
"A Ballad of Saint Andrew" (*Halifax Chronicle-Herald*, Nov. 30, 1950).
"Foreword on Request" (*Canadian Poetry Magazine*, Autumn, 1956).
The Primordial Church of Horton. Wolfville, privately printed, 1963, pp. 8.
Centennial Tales and Other Selected Poems. Toronto, University of Toronto Press, 1965, pp. 550.

CHAPTER 6. *Verse Translation*

GENERAL

"The Greek Epigram" (*Queen's Quarterly*, Jan.–Mar. 1925).

An Outline of European Poetry. Winnipeg, serially in six issues of the *Western Home Monthly*, 1927.

European Elegies. Ottawa: Graphic Press, 1928, pp. 166.

Ten poems in *An Anthology of Czechoslovak Verse*. New York: Columbia University Press, 1929, pp. 72.

"The Genius of Slavonic Poetry" (*Dalhousie Review*, Jan. 1930).

"The Rhaetoromanic Tradition" (*Trans. Roy. Soc. Can.*, 1937). Also as an offprint.

"John MacLean's 'Gloomy Forest' " from the Gaelic (*Dalhousie Review*, July 1948).

ICELANDIC

North American Book of Icelandic Verse. New York: Carrier & Isles, 1930, pp. 228.

"Icelandic Poetry Today" (*Life and Letters Today*, London, Winter 1936).

"Four Decades of Icelandic Poetry in Canada, 1922–62." Winnipeg, *Icelandic-Canadian*, Winter 1963.

MAGYAR

A Magyar Miscellany. Serially in the *Slavonic and East European Review*, 1931, 1938, 1943, 1945.

The Magyar Muse. Winnipeg: Kanadai Magyar Ujsag Press, 1933, pp. 228.

"Hungary's Linguistic Isolation" (*Hungarian Quarterly*, Spring 1936.

The Death of King Buda (With Lulu Putnik Payerle). Cleveland: Benjamin Franklin Bibliophile Society, 1936, pp. 159.

Some 155 translations and articles in the *Young Magyar-American*, 1936–39.

"The Poetry of Ady" (*Hungarian Quarterly*, Autumn 1937).

Budapest University Chorus Program. New York, Jan. 1937, pp. 20 (29 verse translations).

"Quintessence of Hungary" (*Hungarian Quarterly*, Autumn 1938).

A Little Treasury of Hungarian Verse. Washington: American Hungarian Federation, 1947, pp. 55.

Some 28 translations in *Hungarian Poetry*, Sydney, Australia, 1955.

"The Tapestry of Hungarian Literature" in *World Literatures* (University of Pittsburgh Press, 1956).

The Slaves Sing: Selected Poems of László Mécs. DePere, Abbey Press, 1964, pp. vi, 55.

POLISH

"A Polish Miscellany" (*Slavonic Review*, July 1935).

A Golden Treasury of Polish Lyrics. Winnipeg: Polish Press, 1936, pp. 109.

"Recent Polish Poetry" (*Life and Letters Today*, London, Winter 1937).

Major contributor to *Poems by Adam Mickiewicz*, New York, Polish Institute of Arts and Sciences, 1944, pp. 486.

"The Epic Poetry of Mickiewicz" (*Transactions, Roy. Soc. Can.* 1955), also as an offprint.

Pan Tadeusz, English verse translation from the Polish of Adam Mickiewicz. New York, Polish Institute of Arts and Science, and Toronto, Canadian Polish Congress, 1962, pp. xix, 388.

UKRAINIAN

"Ukrainian Poetry in Canada" (*Slavonic Review*, July 1934).

"Ukrainian Canadiana" (*Canadian Forum*, Jan. 1934).

"Ukrainian Poetry" (*The New Magazine*, Oct. 1935).

Prince Ihor's Raid Against the Polovsti (with Paul Crath(. Saskatoon: P. Mohyla Institute, 1947, pp. iv, 14.

Contribution, "Ukrainian Literature", to the *Columbia Dictionary of Modern European Literature*, Columbia University Press, 1947, pp. 899.

"Ukrainian-Canadian Literature" (*Opinion*, Sept.–Oct. 1947).

"Les Ukrainiens au Canada" (*Relations*, Nov. 1947).

Contribution, "Ukrainians in Canada", to *Encyclopedia Slavonica*, New York, 1950.

(With C. H. Andrusyshen) *The Ukrainian Poets, 1189–1962*. Toronto, University of Toronto Press, 1963, pp. xxx, 500.

(With C. H. Andrusyshen) *The Poetical Works of Taras Shevchenko*. Toronto, University of Toronto Press, 1964, pp. li, 563.

CHAPTER 7. *Canada's Unseen Literatures*

See Chapter 20, below.

CHAPTER 9. *Concerning Things Military*

"Fort Henry, 1812–1914" (*Queen's Quarterly*, July–Sept. 1920).

"The First Authentic Story of Our Internment Camps" (*Maclean's Magazine*, Sept. 1, 1920).

Kapuskasing, An Historical Sketch. Kingston: Queen's University Press, 1921, pp. 15 (also in *Queen's Quarterly*, Jan.–Mar. 1921).

"War and Peace in the History Class" (*Western School Journal*, June 1935).

Canada, Europe and Hitler, Part I. Toronto: Oxford University Press, 1939, pp. 213.

The Ukrainian Canadians and the War. Toronto: Oxford Pamphlets on World Affairs, No. C-3, 1940, pp. 30.

Twilight of Liberty. Toronto: Oxford University Press, 1941, pp. xv, 193.

Policy Post-Mortem. Pamphlet offprint, 12 pp., from *Public Affairs*, Autumn 1951.

"Canada: Second World War", contributed to the *Encyclopedia Americana*.

CHAPTER 10. *In the Cause of Peace*

"The International Labour Bureau" (*Saturday Night*, July 7, 1923).

"A French League Plan" (*Interdependence*, June 1929).

"Disarmament" (*Journal des Poètes*, Brussels, March 1932).

"Canada and European Peace" (*Country Guide*, Feb. 1940).

"The Future of European Freedom" (*Ukrainian Quarterly*, Sept. 1946).

CHAPTER 11. *Social Service*

"Mechanism and Meliorism" (*Challenge*, London, Sept. 28, 1923).
"Research into Canadian Rural Decay" (*Eugenics Review*, July 1926).
"Western Immigration" (*Canadian Forum*, July 1928).
Canada and Immigration. Toronto: Empire Club, 1944, pp. 24.
Towards a Christian Social Order. Toronto: Baptist Convention of Ontario and Quebec, 1945, pp. 11.
"A Threat to Civil Liberties" (*Maritime Baptist*, Nov. 28, 1945).
"Red Threat to Labour" (*Evening Telegram*, March 16, 1946).
"UNRRA Accomplice of Greatest Slave State (*Evening Telegram*, Jan. 2, 1947).
"Primrose Path of Liquor Legislation" (*Canadian Baptist*, Jan. 17, 1947).
"Property Rights in Russia Doom of Human Rights" (*Saturday Night*, Oct. 18, 1947).
"Our Moral Problems as a Nation" (*Maritime Baptist*, Feb. 18, 1948).
"Galloping Consumption of Alcohol" (*Canadian Baptist*, May 15, 1948).
"Two Soviet Labour Documents" (*Revue de l'Université d'Ottawa*, Oct.–Dec. 1950).

CHAPTER 12. *The Teaching Tradition*

"Maintaining Our Educational Highways" (*Western School Journal*, March 1935).
Golden Jubilee of Wesley College. Winnipeg: Columbia Press, 1938, pp. 60.
"Education in Canada" (*Culture*, Dec. 1945). Also as an offprint.
Liberal Education in the Canadian Democracy. Hamilton: McMaster University, 1948, pp. 20.
The Crisis in Education. Toronto: Canadian Club, 1948, pp. 32.
"The Universities of Canada" (*Universities Review*, May 1948).
"Church and University" (*Acadia Bulletin*, May 1949).
"Academic Guidance" (*Acadia Bulletin*, Sept. 1949).
"Religion in Higher Education" (*Acadia Bulletin*, Nov. 1949).
"The Contents of the Arts Curriculum" (*Acadia Bulletin*, March 1950).
"Higher Education and the Church College" (*Maritime Baptist*, 1950).
"Education", chap. xix in *Canada*, United Nations Series: University of California Press, 1950.
"Faith and Education" (*Maritime Baptist*, Oct. 3, 1951).
"Canada's Language Policy in Education" (Paris: UNESCO data-paper for Ceylon Conference, 1953).
The Acadia Record, 1838–1953. Wolfville: Associated Alumni, 1954, pp. 563.
"Canadian Scholars" (*Acadia Bulletin*, April 1955).
"Some Thoughts on Education," Chapter IV in *Challenge and Response*, ed. R. C. Chalmers and J. Irving. Toronto, Ryerson Press, 1959.

CHAPTER 13. *The President's Desk*

"The Universities of Canada." In *Commonwealth Universities Yearbook*, London, 1958.

CHAPTER 14. *The Political Pendulum*

Victoria County Centennial History. Lindsay: Warder Press, 1921, pp. 261; Second (revised) edition, 1967, pp. 324.
International Aspects of Unemployment. London: Allen & Unwin, 1923, pp. 214. Also New York: Henry Holt.
The European Heritage. London: Dent, 1930, pp. 184. Also New York: Coward McCann.
"The New Roman Empire" (*Dalhousie Review*, April 1937).
"The Four Freedoms" (*Canadian Messenger*, July 1943).
"The Blanket of the Dark" (*Baltic Review*, 1947).
"Pattern for Extermination" (*University of Ottawa Review*, Jan.–Mar. 1947).

CHAPTER 15. *Religio Grammatici*

"The Bunyan Tercentenary" (*Dalhousie Review*, July 1928).
"The Mystery of Life" (*Western Baptist*, Jan. 1930).
"The Dykes of Civilization" (*Acadia Bulletin*, Nov. 1948).
"At the Feet of Gamaliel" (*Maritime Baptist*, Oct. 11, 1950).
"The Spirit of Lazarus" (*Maritime Baptist*, May 1951).
"The Preëminent Name" (*Maritime Baptist*, Oct. 17, 1951).
"Metaphysics and Human Freedom" (*Acadia Bulletin*, Nov. 1951).
"Einstein's Influence on Philosophy" (*Einstein Memorial Symposium*, Dalhousie University, 1955).
"After Twenty-five Centuries" (*Maritime Baptist*, Oct. 11, 1956).
"The Place of Understanding" (*Maritime Baptist*, Oct. 23, 1957).
"A Text from Numbers (*Maritime Baptist*, Mar. 5, 1958).

CHAPTER 16. *Towards Baptist Unity*

"With the Baptists of Budapest" (*Western Baptist*, Feb. 1939; *Canadian Baptist*, Feb. 16, 1939).
"Our Western Work" (*Canadian Baptist*, July 1, 1941).
"The Twilight of Canadian Protestantism" (*Canadian Baptist*, Nov. 1, 1942).
"Baptists from Sea to Sea" (*Canadian Baptist*, Dec. 1, 1946).
"Tide of Anti-Catholic Propaganda Rising" (*Saturday Night*, Jan. 4, Feb. 8, 1947).
"Canadian Baptists and the World Council of Churches" (*Maritime Baptist*, Feb. 18, 1948).
"Seven Years of Federation" (*Maritime Baptist*, Dec. 5, 1951).
"Some Tasks of a Federation" (*Canadian Baptist*, Nov. 15, 1954).
The Baptists of Canada: A Pocket-book History. Toronto, Baptist Federation of Canada, 1958, pp. 16.
"Baptist Highlights of the Past Hundred Years." (*Canadian Baptist*, July 1958).
"The Baptist Federation of Canada," being pp. 131–5 in *Baptist Advance*. Nashville, Tenn., Broadman Press, pp. 512. 1964.

CHAPTER 17. *The Milton Project*

Some Latin Analogues of Milton. Offprint from *Trans. Roy. Soc. Can.* 1946, pp. 173–189.

Avitus' Epic on the Fall. Offprint from *Laval Théologique et Philosophique,* 1947, pp. 222–242.

Six Seventeenth Century Forerunners of Milton's 'Samson Agonistes'. Offprint from *Trans. Roy. Soc. Can.,* 1949, pp. 73–85.

"Salandra and Milton" in *Festschrift, Ukrainian Free University,* Munich, 1951.

The Celestial Cycle: The Theme of "Paradise Lost" in World Literature With Translations of the Major Analogues. Toronto: University of Toronto Press, 1952, pp. xxvii, 701.

That Invincible Samson: The Analogues of "Samson Agonistes" in World Literature. Toronto, University of Toronto Press, 1964, pp. xi, 218.

CHAPTER 18. *Organizing the Humanities*

The Humanities in Canada (with A. S. P. Woodhouse). Ottawa: Humanities Research Council of Canada, 1947, pp. 287.

"Les humanités à notre époque" (*Le Canada Français,* Sept. & Oct. 1945).

"The Humanities" in *Canadian Education Today* (Toronto: McGraw-Hill, 1956, pp. 243.

CHAPTER 19. *The Masonic Brotherhood*

The Antiquity of Masonry. Halifax: Grand Lodge of Nova Scotia, 1953, pp. 4.

Comments on the Antiquity of Masonry. Minneapolis: Bulletin No. 28 of Educational Lodge No. 1002, Dec. 1, 1956.

The Unconquerable Hope. Halifax, Keith Sovereign Chapter, Rose Croix, 1960, pp. 9.

CHAPTER 20. *The New Canadians*

Canadian Overtones. Winnipeg, Columbia Press, 1935, pp. 104.

"Canada's Leading Poet, Stephan G. Stephansson, 1853–1927" (*University of Toronto Quarterly,* Jan. 1936).

"Survey of Letters in Canada: New-Canadian Literature" (*University of Toronto Quarterly,* annual survey, critique and booklist, 1935 to 1965). Also issued as offprint pamphlets.

"A Skald in Canada" (*Trans. Roy. Soc. Can.,* 1939).

Canada, Europe and Hitler, Part II. Toronto, Oxford University Press, 1939, pp. 213.

"The European-Canadians in their Press" (*Proceedings of the Canadian Historical Association,* 1940).

European Elements in Canadian Life. Toronto: Canadian Club, 1940, pp. 20.
Canadians All: A Primer of Canadian National Unity. Ottawa: Director of Public Information, 1941, pp. 48.
Our Communists and the New Canadians. Toronto: Canadian Club, 1943, pp. 24.
Brief Canadian Biographies. Syndicated serially in several languages through the Citizenship Branch, Ottawa, 1943–44.
Homesickness in Several Minor Keys. Offprint from *Transactions of the Royal Society of Canada*, 1961.
The Place of Slavic Studies in Canada. Winnipeg, Ukrainian Free Academy of Sciences, 1958, pp. 16.
"A Scotch-Canadian Discovers Poland." Being pp. 57–70 in *The Polish Past in Canada*, ed. Wiktor Turek, Toronto 1959.
"The Shevchenko Monument." (*Svoboda*, May 29, 1965).

CHAPTER 21. *Les Canadiens*

The Quebec Tradition (with Séraphin Marion). Montreal: Collection Humanitas, University of Montreal, 1946, pp. 245.
"Religion and Philosophy: An English-Canadian Point of View." Chapter in symposium, *Canadian Dualism: Studies in French-English Relations*, ed. Mason Wade. Toronto, University of Toronto Press, 1960, pp. 427.
"Le Témoinage des Oies Sauvages." (*Revue de l'Université Laval*, Sept. 1963).

CHAPTER 22. *The Embattled Authors*

Editor, *The Authors' Bulletin*, vols. III and IV (1925–27).
"Towards a National Literature" (*Authors' Bulletin*, May 1932).
"Writing on the Prairie" (*Authors' Bulletin*, Sept. 1932).
Editor, *Manitoba Poetry Chapbook*. Winnipeg, Israelite Press, 1933, pp. 32.
"Poésie Canadienne" (*Courrier des Poètes*, Brussels, March 15, 1937).
Editor, *Canadian Poetry Magazine*, Toronto, 1944–46.
"Some Thirty Years Ago with the C.A.A." (*Can. Author and Bookman*, Winter 1955–56).
"Thirty-six Years of Constitutions" (*Can. Author and Bookman*, Winter 1956).
"The Canadian Arts Council" (*Can. Author and Bookman*, Summer 1958).
"Royal Commission on Copyright" (*Can. Author and Bookman*, Autumn 1958).

CHAPTER 24. *Confronting Communism*

"Russia's Foreign Policy" (*Western Home Monthly*, May 1929).
"Proletarian Poetry" (*Canadian Spectator*, Nov. 22, 29, 1934).
Our Communists and the New Canadians. Toronto: Canadian Club, 1943, pp. 24.

Our Ukrainian Loyalists. Winnipeg: Ukrainian Canadian Committee, 1943, pp. 28.

Seven Pillars of Freedom. Toronto: Oxford University Press, 1944, pp. xiv, 226. Also 2nd edition, Burns & MacEachern, 1952, pp. xi, 189.

"Independence of Soviet Republics is a Myth" (*Saturday Night*, Mar. 25, 1944).

"Preface to San Francisco" (*Evening Telegram*, Toronto, Apr. 14, 1945).

"On Soviet Imperialism" (*Evening Telegram*, May 12, 1945).

"Jewish Tribulation under the Soviet Régime (*Evening Telegram*, May 17, 1945).

"Communism and Christianity" (*Evening Telegram*, May 26, 1945).

"Eclipse of Baltic Freedom" (*Evening Telegram*, Feb. 16, 1946).

"The Crucifixion of Poland" (*Evening Telegram*, Feb. 23, 1946).

"Tito's Red Terror" (*Evening Telegram*, Mar. 2, 1946).

The Ukrainian Agony. Winnipeg: Ukrainian Canadian Committee, 1946, pp. 8.

The Red Foe of Faith. Toronto: Presbyterian Publications, 1946, pp. 8.

National Minorities in the U.S.S.R. Winnipeg: Ukrainian Canadian Committee, 1946, pp. 12.

"Spawn of a Conspiracy" (*Canadian Messenger*, May 1946).

"Nothing to Celebrate in U.S.S.R.'s Laws" (*Saturday Night*, Nov. 15, 1947).

"The Kremlin Organizes Canadian Women" (*Echoes*, Autumn 1947).

"Social and Economic Security in the USSR" (*American Economic Security*, Washington, D.C., 1947).

"Communism in Canada and the U.S.A." (*Trans. Can. Cath. Hist. Ass'n.*, 1948).

"Canadian Communists and the Comintern" (*Trans. Roy. Soc. Can.*, 1948). Also as an offprint.

"Canada in the Moscow Press" (*Financial Post*, Sept. 10, 1949).

"Canada's Communist Party" (*New Leader*, Oct. 29, 1949).

"Some Aspects of Soviet Legislation" (*Trans. Roy. Soc. Can.*, 1950). Also as an offprint.

Stalin's Red Empire. Winnipeg: Free Press Pamphlet No. 38, 1951, pp. 26.

"Soviet Law" (*New Leader*, June 2, 1958).

UNCLASSIFIED

"The Clue of the Twisted Letter" (murder mystery, *National Home Monthly*, Nov. 1936).

Titus the Toad (juvenile). Toronto: Oxford University Press, 1939, pp. 60.

Contributor to *Encyclopaedia Britannica, Encyclopedia Americana, The Book of Knowledge, Americana Annual, Grolier Encyclopedia, All Nations Song Book, Manitoba's Diamond Jubilee*, etc., etc.

Index of Persons

www.ingramcontent.com/pod-product-compliance
Lightning Source LLC
LaVergne TN
LVHW090800070826
844660LV00022B/1040

* 9 7 8 1 4 8 7 5 9 2 7 0 7 *